Orwell Award
Winner – 2016

The Invention of Russia

THE INVENTION OF RUSSIA

The Journey from Gorbachev's Freedom to Putin's War

Arkady Ostrovsky

ATLANTIC BOOKS
LONDON

First published in hardback in Great Britain in 2015 by Atlantic Books, an imprint of Atlantic Books Ltd.

1 2 3 4 5 6 7 8 9

A CIP catalogue record for this book is available from the British Library.

Hardback ISBN: 978-0-85789-158-7
Trade paperback ISBN: 978-0-85789-159-4
E-book ISBN: 978-1-78239-741-0
Paperback ISBN: 978-0-85789-160-0

Text design by Richard Marston
Printed in Great Britain by Bell and Bain Ltd, Glasgow

This book contains extracts from articles by the author that were previously published in the *Financial Times* and *The Economist* and are reprinted here with permission.

Atlantic Books
An Imprint of Atlantic Books Ltd
Ormond House
26–27 Boswell Street
London
WC1N 3JZ

www.atlantic-books.co.uk

To Becky

Contents

	Acknowledgements	ix
	Dramatis Personæ	xiv
	Prologue: A Silent Procession	1
Part I	FIRST WAS THE WORD	
1	The Soviet Princes	11
2	New Beginning or Dead End	58
3	'We Suffered a Victory'	98
4	Fathers and Sons	129
Part II	'IMAGE IS EVERYTHING'	
5	Normal Television in Abnormal Circumstances	179
6	Lights, Camera, Putin	245
7	Remote Control	283
	Epilogue: Aerial Combat	327
	Notes	349
	Select Bibliography	363
	Index	368

Acknowledgements

In 1991, when still a student at the Moscow Institute of Theatre Arts in the Soviet Union, I met a man to whom I owe my journalistic career and who inspired me to write this book. John Lloyd was the Moscow Bureau Chief at the *Financial Times*. He did not just report on Russia – he lived it – and made that story part of his own life. Twelve years later, I was a Moscow correspondent for the FT and John asked me to write about Russian television and its impact on politics for the *FT Weekend Magazine*, which he edited. This book grew out of that seed. I could never have attempted or completed it without his support and friendship.

Toby Mundy, the former publisher of Atlantic Books, commissioned the book and put his faith in it on the basis of a single conversation. His enthusiasm, encouragement and interest in the subject allowed me to broaden its scope and explore different avenues even as one deadline passed after another. When Toby departed from Atlantic, he left me in the most capable hands of James Nightingale, whose calm professionalism, intellectual curiosity and patience steered this book into publication. He made the editing a creative and enjoyable process. I am grateful to Jane Robertson, who proofread the book and Jenny Overton who copy-edited it. I thank my agent Zoë Waldie for her advice and professionalism.

I have been blessed with my colleagues and friends at *The Economist* who made writing this book possible. John Micklethwait, hired me for the job of Moscow correspondent and gave me generous book leave. The late Peter David, my foreign editor, gave me the freedom to venture outside politics and the economy; Ann Wroe indulged my interest in Russian intelligentsia, while Fiammetta Rocco and Edward Lucas offered valuable tips. Andrea Burgess helped with sources and references. Edward Carr, the deputy editor, who has turned editing into an art form, has been immensely kind, supportive and encouraging and gave me time to complete the book. The unwavering support and comradeship of John Peet, my Europe editor, who put up with my absences and late filings, has been a source of strength and sanity. Anne Foley, *The Economist*'s managing editor, looked after me and my family at times of need during our years in Russia.

In writing this book, as in every other endeavour, I relied on my teacher, friend and mentor who has guided me in life and in work – Inna Solovyova. She directed me in my thinking and supported me at times of desperation. She read every draft and gave invaluable feedback both on content and structure. I owe her far more than this book. Her ideas, willpower, ethics and judgements have had by far the most formative influence on me over the years. I thank Andrew Miller for reading, correcting and commenting on the manuscript, but even more so for his and Emma Bell's unfailing counsel, loyal friendship, forbearance and encouragement that has sustained me and my family ever since we had the good fortune to meet them in Moscow ten years ago.

Maria Lipman gave enormously generously of her time, undertaking to review the entire manuscript. She saved me from many errors and made me re-examine some of my contentions. I could not have done without the assistance of Ksenia Barakovskaya who stoically checked endnotes and missing references. Her help in preparing the book for publication has been invaluable.

I benefited from the unassuming advice of Andrei Zorin whose research in the development of the Soviet intelligentsia laid the base for the chapters about the end of the Soviet Union. He and Irina Zorina also kindly lent us their house in Oxford in the summer of 2012. Kirill Rogov helped cut through the noise and fog of Putin's era, formulating the key events and turning points that led Russia to its current state. Sam Amiel came up with the title for one of the chapters. Mikhail Iampolski, a scholar and essayist, kindly commented on the early chapters of the book and challenged its conventional wisdom.

Many people gave freely of their time, granted interviews and provided documents. Igor Malashenko has been an indispensable guide through Russia's modern history. Hours of conversations with him in Kiev and Moscow provided the carcass of the story of the 1990s and helped to conceptualize the book. Evgeny Kiselev meticulously recollected the story of NTV, the original motives and sequence of events. Irina Yakovleva enlivened the portrait of her late husband Yegor Yakovlev who burst his way in, and remained one of the main characters of the book. I am grateful to Sir Rodric Braithwaite for letting me read his unpublished Moscow diaries. I also benefited from the help of Valentina Sidorova of the Russian State Archive who allowed me to work with Yegor Yakovlev's papers before they were even catalogued. Natalia Kurakina helped with television archives at NTV.

I thank for their time and thoughts: Yevgenia Albats, Nina Andreeva, Viktor Anpilov, Peter Aven, A. Craig Copetas, Anatoly Chubais, Marietta Chudakova, Sergei Dorenko, Mikhail Dmitriev, Boris Dubin, Konstantin Ernst, Maria Gaidar, Mikhail Fishman, Mikhail Fridman, Natalia Gevorkyan, Mikhail Gorbachev, Lev Gudkov, Vladimir Gusinsky, Natalia Ivanova, Mikhail Khodorkovsky, Veronika Kutsyllo, Yulia Latynina, Alexei Levinson, Viktor Loshak, Dmitry Muratov, Alexei Navlalny, Boris Nemtsov, Alexander Nevzorov, Elena Nusinova, Alexander Olson, Leonid Parfenov, Sergei Parkhomenko, Gleb Pavlovsky, Irina Petrovskaya, Irina Prokhorova,

Grigory Revzin, Yuri Saprykin, Masha Slonim, Anatoly Smeliansky, Maxim Sokolov, Svetlana Sorokina, Alexander Timofeevsky, Alexei Venediktov, Alexander Voloshin, Anatoly Yakovlev, Vladimir Yakovlev and all others who shared their stories with me.

In telling the story, I relied both on primary and secondary material. Leon Aron's excellent biography of Boris Yeltsin was an invaluable guide through the 1980s and 1990s. Bruce Clark's prophetic *An Empire's New Clothes*, the diaries of Veronika Kutsyllo and reporting by Sergei Parkhomenko helped build the picture of the nationalist and communist mutiny of October 1993. David Hoffman's thorough and exhaustive *The Oligarchs* and Chrystia Freeland's vivid *Sale of the Century* shone light on the workings of the oligarchy. Peter Baker's and Susan Glasser's *Kremlin Rising* helped with the early 2000s, while Fiona Hill's and Clifford Gaddy's authoritative *Operative in the Kremlin* remains the best overall portrait of Putin and his background. My own reporting for the *Financial Times* and *The Economist* form the basis of the chapters about the 2000s.

I enjoyed the company and the inspirational working space provided by St Antony's College and the Reuters Institute for Journalism in Oxford, and the Institute for Human Sciences in Vienna.

I also benefited from the help, advice and friendship of Maria Alexandrova, Elena Amelina, Anne Applebaum, Edward and Charlotte Baring, Catherine Belton, Kakha Bendukidze, Inna Berezkina, Tony and Catherine Brumwell, Neil and Emma Buckley, Larisa Burakova, Guy Chazan, James Coomarasamy and Nanette Van der Laan, Katharina Coudenhove-Kalergi, Bjorn Fagerberg, Peter Favorov, Olga Fedianina, Ralph Fiennes, Floriana Fossato, Dina Goder, Maria Gordon, Varya Gornostaeva, Lilia and Sergei Grachev, Igor Gurovich, Andrew Higgins, Fiona Hill, Nato Kancheli, Lidia Kolpachkova, Ivan Krastev, Andrei Kurilkin, Sophie Lambroschini, Maya Lavrinovich, Dominic Lieven, Michael McFaul, Elena Nemirovskaya, Konstantin Oganesyan, Anna Panikhina, Quentin and Mary Peel,

Illaria Poggiolini, Marc and Rachel Polonsky, Peter Pomerantsev, Pavel Ponizovsky and Richard Wallis, Irina Reznik, Carolyn Sands, Simon Sebag-Montefiore, Yuri Senokosov, Robert Service, Lyuba Shats, Richard Shillito, Adele and Sebastian Smith, Tatyana Smolyarova, Noah Sneider, Ekaterina Sokiryanskaya, Alexander Sorin and Katya Bermant, Angela Stent, Olga Stepanova, Tiffany Stern and Dan Grimley, Sir Tom Stoppard, John Tefft, John and Carol Thornhill, Marcus and Sally Vergette, Tom de Waal and Georgina Wilson, Alex, Rupert and Joss Wilbraham, Andrew Wilson, Janice Winter, Joshua Yaffa and Natalya Zorkaya.

My family has been the rock that made everything possible. I thank my brother Sergei and my parents Misha and Raya for all their unconditional love, support and care. I am indebted to Diana Hewitt for looking after me in the Welsh mountains. My biggest debt, however, is to my wife Becky, who carried the burden of this book. She unfailingly read and edited various drafts and kept the family on an even keel. I thank her for her forbearance. My children Petya, Liza and Polina gave me the strength and reason to write this book in the hope that they would one day read it. I dedicate it to Becky with love and in friendship.

Moscow, June 2015

Dramatis Personæ

Princes and patricians

Alexander Yakovlev, a Soviet statesman, member of the Soviet Politburo, close ally of Gorbachev and the ideologist of Perestroika and Glasnost.

Yegor Yakovlev, referred to as Yegor, journalist and editor of *Moskovskie novosti*, the mouthpiece of Perestroika, and briefly the head of post-Soviet television.

Alexander Bovin, the *bon vivant* of Russian journalism, a speechwriter for Leonid Brezhnev and an expert on foreign relations.

Otto Latsis, economist and author, a columnist for *Izvestia* newspaper and editor of the *Kommunist* journal.

Sons and Daughters

PRINT

Vladimir Yakovlev, the son of Yegor Yakovlev and the founder and editor of *Kommersant*, Russia's first capitalist newspaper.

Maxim Sokolov, the erudite and sceptical chief political columnist at *Kommersant*.

Alexander Timofeevsky, an essayist and *Kommersant*'s in-house reviewer.

Sergei Parkhomenko, a liberal journalist and editor of *Itogi* magazine.

Natalia Gevorkyan, the daughter of a KGB resident, a journalist at *Moskovskie novosti* and Putin's interviewer.

Veronika Kutsyllo, a young intrepid reporter at *Kommersant* who kept a diary about the siege of the White House.

TELEVISION

Oleg Dobrodeev, the son of a documentary film-maker, the head of news and current affairs at NTV and later the general director of the state television corporation Rossiya.

Konstantin Ernst, one of the country's top television and film producers, the head of Channel One.

Evgeny Kiselev, TV anchor, the face of NTV Russia's first large private television channel.

Leonid Parfenov, a style-conscious television journalist and presenter of the *Namedni* programme that turned him into a celebrity.

Alexander Nevzorov, a stuntman and maverick television journalist.

Sergei Dorenko, a popular television presenter and a mercenary known as the 'TV hit man'.

Reformers

Yegor Gaidar, a child of the Soviet intelligentsia, a prime minister and the author of Russian economic reforms.

Anatoly Chubais, the economist in charge of privatization and later Yeltsin's chief of staff.

Boris Nemtsov, a governor from Nizhny Novgorod, Yeltsin's groomed successor and deputy prime minister.

Nationalist and Communists

Viktor Anpilov, an archetypal Soviet proletarian, agitator and leader of the Working Russia movement.

Alexander Borodai, the son of an orthodox nationalist philosopher, a PR man helping the Kremlin with the annexation of Crimea and the war in Ukraine.

Oligarchs

Vladimir Gusinsky, the founder and owner of the Media Most holding, including the NTV television channel.

Boris Berezovsky, the wheeler-dealer and manipulator of Russian politics, in charge of Channel One.

The individualist

Igor Malashenko, ideologue, creator and first president of the NTV television channel.

Prologue: A Silent Procession

It was after midnight on 27 February 2015. I was making final changes to this book when I learned that Boris Nemtsov, a liberal politician once groomed to be president of Russia, had been shot four times in the back on a bridge just metres away from the Kremlin.

It was the most resonant political assassination in Russia's post-Soviet history and it did not seem real. I knew Nemtsov well – he was more than a journalistic contact. Of all the Russian politicians I kept in touch with, he was the only one I considered a friend. He was charismatic, determined, honest, unpretentious and very full of life. Now his large body lay on the wet asphalt, covered by black rubbish bags, with the cupolas of St Basil's behind him: his was a postcard murder – continue past the cover image of this book and you would hit the spot.

Those who killed Nemtsov acted with impudence and did not expect to be arrested. When one of them was detained, he turned out to be an officer linked to the service of Ramzan Kadyrov, Chechnya's strongman and former rebel installed by Russian president Vladimir Putin to keep the territory under his thumb. Kadyrov had sworn his personal loyalty to Putin, helped annex Crimea and promptly defended the alleged killer as a 'true patriot'.

Nemtsov's murder marked the first anniversary of Russia's annexation of Crimea and its 'hybrid' war against Ukraine. Now the violence ignited by Russia over the border returned to the homeland. The war in Ukraine, stoked and fanned by the Kremlin, has not just devastated a former Soviet republic that has dared to break free from its grip. It has devastated Russia itself – its sense of decency and moral fibre. It turned hatred, xenophobia and aggression into a norm and civility into an offence.

The murder of Nemtsov was first and foremost a murder of a good man, who tried to stop the war. In the state media this has earned him the title of a national traitor and an American stooge. In the weeks before his death he was demonized by television. Hate banners carrying his image were hung on building façades with the words 'Fifth column – aliens amongst us'.

Six days before Nemtsov's death, I watched thousands of people – some paid, others not – marching through the heart of Moscow, bearing slogans denouncing Ukraine, the West and Russian liberals. Muscle-bound toughs representing Kadyrov bore signs proclaiming 'Putin and Kadyrov prevent Maidan in Russia', alongside photographs of Nemtsov identifying him as 'the organizer of Maidan' ('Maidan' had become shorthand for Maidan Nezalezhnosti, or Independence Square, in Kiev, the epicentre of Ukraine's revolution).

I was born and bred in the Soviet Union and have worked for many years in Russia, but never have I seen such levels of hysteria. This was something out of a photograph or a documentary of 1930s Germany. As Nemtsov said in an interview recorded hours before his death, 'Russia is quickly turning into a fascist state. We already have propaganda modelled on Nazi Germany's. We also have a nucleus of assault brigades, like the [Nazi] SA.'[1]

Andrei Sakharov, Russia's great humanist and nuclear physicist, once argued that a country which violates human rights at home poses a threat to international security. In fact, it was partly Sakharov's knowledge of the potential impact of his thermonuclear device that turned him into a human rights activist. Russia today has no Sakharov. It has propagandists who talk about the use of nuclear arms with a flippancy unimaginable in the Soviet period.

'Russia can reduce America to nuclear ash,' boasted Dmitry Kiselev – the anchor on the main television channel Rossiya. After Stalin's death, the personal power of Soviet leaders was checked by the collective Politburo. Now, Kiselev said a decision to use nuclear arms 'will be taken personally by Putin, who has the undoubted support of the Russian people'. In a documentary about the 'return of Crimea', Putin admitted he was ready to make such a decision if NATO forces tried to interfere in the peninsula.

The situation is more dangerous than the Cold War. The Soviet Union and America both emerged as winners from the Second World War and did not suffer from an inferiority complex. Russia's current rulers, on the other hand, were shaped by what they consider to be a loss in the Cold War and by feeling rejected by the West despite all their fabulous wealth.

A mixture of hostility and jealousy has triumphed in Russia thirty years after Mikhail Gorbachev ended the Cold War, opened up the country and proclaimed the supremacy of human values over the interests of the state. The withdrawal of Soviet forces from Eastern Europe, which is today deemed a fatal mistake in official textbooks, was greeted with approval not just by the West, but by Russia's own people. The end of communism gave hope that Russia would become a normal country and join the civilized world. As a drama student in Moscow at the time I remember that feeling of hope.

The attempted communist coup in August 1991 seemed like a last spasm of the regime and its defeat was a celebration of freedom. On Christmas Day 1991 I watched the Soviet flag go down over the Kremlin towers and listened to Gorbachev bid farewell to the Soviet Union:

> Destiny so ruled that when I found myself at the helm of this state it already was clear that something was wrong in this country... We had a lot of everything – land, oil and gas, other natural resources – and there was intellect and talent in abundance. However, we were living much worse than people in the industrialized countries... suffocating in the shackles of the bureaucratic command system. All the half-hearted reforms... fell through, one after another. This country was going nowhere and we couldn't possibly live the way we did. We had to change everything radically...

Gorbachev could not save the country, but he paid tribute to what had been achieved:

> Free elections have become a reality. Free press, freedom of worship, representative legislatures and a multi-party system have all become a reality. Human rights are being treated as the supreme principle and top priority... We're now living in a new world. An end has been put to the Cold War and to the arms race... We have opened ourselves up to the rest of the world, abandoned the practices of interfering in others' internal affairs and using troops outside this country, and we have been reciprocated with trust, solidarity, and respect. We have paid with all our history and tragic experience for these democratic achievements, and they are not to be abandoned, whatever the circumstances, and whatever the pretexts.[2]

In 1992, a year after the Soviet Union ceased to exist, I left to do my PhD in English Literature at Cambridge, grateful to Gorbachev for giving me the freedom to travel, study and write. A decade later, I returned to Moscow as a journalist, first with the *Financial Times*, then with *The Economist* – a foreign correspondent in my native land. By that time Russia had a former KGB man for a president who marked his first anniversary in the Kremlin by restoring the Soviet anthem and began to revise the Cold War order. In the process of 'restoration', Russia has not returned to the

Soviet past; but it has arrived at a new junction. An old-fashioned nationalism – in neo-Stalinist costume – has become the most powerful force in Russian society, which threatens its own citizens and its neighbours.

How did Russia get from 1991 to 2015? Has a counter-revolution taken place in Russia? When did it happen and how did I miss it? Over the past quarter-century Russian thinkers have often been obsessed with trying to find a particular point in time at which the country went wrong: they viewed history as a tape that could be wound back and forth in order to identify that crucial junction, so that a different route could then be tried. Yet while the history was not reversible, it was not pre-determined either. There was no one event after the collapse of the Soviet Union that made Russia's state today inevitable, and while it may be tempting to blame the state of Russia on Putin that would be missing the point. While he bears enormous responsibility for it, he is as much a consequence as he is a cause of Russia's ills.

In this book I have sought an answer to the question of how Russia got here by following its story, narrative and dominant ideas over the past quarter-century, hoping to illuminate the turning points in its history. The main characters are not politicians or economists, but those who generated the 'meaning' of the country, who composed the storyline, who produced and broadcast it and in the process led the country from freedom to war. They are ideologists, journalists, editors, television executives: people in charge of the message and the media.

From the time of Gorbachev's Perestroika onwards, journalists have been more than transmitters of ideas and designs conceived elsewhere. They became a source of these designs and ideas and, as such, they are responsible both for Russia's emergence from authoritarianism and its descent back into it. This book is not the history of Russian media, however; rather, it is the story of the country they have invented.

Russia is an idea-centric country and the media play a disproportionately important role in it. As Ivan Pavlov, Russia's Nobel Prize-winning physiologist famous for his work on conditional reflexes, observed in a lecture he gave in the cold and hungry Petrograd of 1918, the task of every mind is to comprehend reality accurately. But in Russia, he remarked, 'we are mostly interested in words and have little concern for reality'.[3] He blamed the mind of the intelligentsia – 'the brain of the country' – for leading Russia into the Bolshevik Revolution.

As with any utopia, communism disregarded reality and as a pseudo-religion it operated through words and images. It is not for nothing that Vladimir Lenin, the Bolshevik leader who sacrificed the country to the communist idea, described himself as a 'journalist'.

The Bolsheviks began by taking over the printing presses and guarding their monopoly over printed words. Words were used to conceal facts and construct an alternative reality. Lies and repressions were the two main pillars that upheld the Soviet system. Words justified repression. Repression enforced the words. It worked like an arch. The mind dealt with the disconnection between signals and real life by developing double-think – a condition described by George Orwell in *Nineteen Eighty-Four*. But the system which emerged 'by the word' also vanished by the word. The Soviet Union expired not because it ran out of money – after all, it could have turned into a North Korea – but because it ran out of words.

Alexander Solzhenitsyn, who wrestled with the Soviet system, knew there was only one way to defeat it: 'Live not by lies', as he wrote on the day of his arrest. The paradox was that the opening-up of the media could be achieved only by engaging in half-truths. But when reality burst through that opening in the form of live television broadcasts and uncensored publications, the Soviet Union crumbled.

Whoever controlled the media also controlled the country. 'To take the Kremlin you must take television,' Alexander Yakovlev, a good man and the main ideologist of Perestroika, once said.[4] This was no metaphor, for the fiercest and often deadliest battles that unfolded in the lead-up to and the aftermath of the Soviet disintegration were for the television tower. In the 1990s television and main newspapers were in the hand of pro-Western liberals who set out to project a new reality by the means of the media. But in the end they used the media to enrich themselves and to consolidate their power.

Television turned Putin, an unknown KGB operative, into Russia's president within months of his eruption into the national consciousness. His first step as he settled in the Kremlin was to take control over television, only then could he seize the commanding heights of the economy. It has been the main tool of his power, his magic wand that substituted a TV picture for reality. As Putin's friend Silvio Berlusconi once said: 'What is not on TV does not exist.' Putin took it further: things that did not exist could be turned into reality by the power of television. This alchemical power was displayed vividly both in the annexation of Crimea and the war in Ukraine.

I was in Crimea when 'polite green men', as Russian soldiers with no markings would soon be known, turned up under the pretence of protecting the local Russian population from Ukrainian 'fascists'. In Sebastopol, a large crowd of people waved flags and danced along to old Soviet songs in celebration of their liberation. Yet the 'enemy' was nowhere to be seen. 'We saw them on television,' one man explained. Signals and reality swapped their places: words and images no longer signalled reality, rather reality was constructed to validate signals or, to put it simply, provide the right picture. 'You furnish the pictures, I will furnish the war,' William Randolph Hearst famously told his correspondent in Cuba in 1897. As is often the way in its history, Russia pushed this concept to its extreme.

Television has been the primary weapon in Putin's 'hybrid war' against Ukraine. It has created a narrative that is enacted on the ground at the cost of thousands of lives. Television news has turned into a war serial. Yet those who conduct Russia's aerial battles are not some crazy nationalists bent on the idea of world domination. Nor are they the helpless pawns in the hands of a despot. They are sophisticated and erudite men who started their careers during Gorbachev's Perestroika and prospered in Yeltsin's 1990s, but who now act as demiurges – the creators of reality. The purpose of the show they have staged is to perpetuate the power and wealth of Putin and his elite, of which they are a part. In doing so they have stirred the lowest instincts and intoxicated the country with the aggression, hatred and chauvinism that made Boris Nemtsov's murder possible.

Shortly before Nemtsov was shot dead, he was handing out leaflets for an anti-war rally he had organized. But the rally turned into his funeral march. Two days after his murder, I walked with my wife and nine-year-old son among tens of thousands of Muscovites to the place where he was killed. It was a silent procession.

PART I

FIRST WAS THE WORD

ONE

The Soviet Princes

The Last Supper

Five minutes before 7 p.m. on 25 December 1991 Mikhail Gorbachev walked briskly along a Kremlin corridor into a wood-panelled room teeming with photographers, technicians and cameramen to record his last speech as president of the USSR. Gorbachev sat at the desk, put down his papers and looked at his watch. 'Oh, we still have plenty of time,' he told the cameramen who were too overwhelmed with the historic significance of the moment to appreciate the irony. The Soviet Union was about to expire and Mr Gorbachev's presidency with it.

Waiting for the clock to strike the hour, a large, grey-haired man energetically approached the desk and leaned over Gorbachev. 'Don't sign it now,' he told him. 'First you will [say] "I want to sign a decree relinquishing my duties". The camera will show a close-up [of you signing it] and will then move back. Then you will start your speech.'[1] The man was Yegor Yakovlev, the head of Soviet television and a former editor of *Moskovskie novosti* (*The Moscow News*) – the mouthpiece of Gorbachev's Perestroika. Yakovlev had persuaded Gorbachev that his final days in office should be recorded by Soviet and American television crews and turned into a documentary, *Ukhod* (*Departure*).

Yakovlev and Gorbachev had spent the past hour in Gorbachev's office reminiscing about their mutual Soviet past. Now Gorbachev looked up at Yakovlev as if he was seeing him for the first time. Gorbachev leafed through the papers. 'I'll simply sign it now and we will move on,' he said, turning abruptly to his press secretary for a pen and trying it on an empty sheet of paper. 'A softer one would be better,' Gorbachev said.[2] The president of CNN, who had flown to Moscow to interview Gorbachev on his last day in office, held out his pen. Gorbachev accepted it and, with a journalist's pen, signed his abdication from power. Nobody in the room noticed the moment. The clock struck 7 p.m. and Gorbachev began to speak. At first his voice sounded soft and forced, almost trembling, but gradually it became more controlled.

As one of the people present in the room recalled, once Gorbachev had finished speaking, Yegor Yakovlev rushed up to him. He was unhappy with Gorbachev's intonation and suggested that the speech should be re-recorded. Gorbachev looked at Yakovlev in astonishment. It did not just seem tactless – it was absurd. A historic event was not a staged performance. It could not be repeated, just as the empire could not be restored or the clock turned back. The Soviet flag was lowered over the Kremlin for the last time, to be replaced with the Russian tricolour.

The country that had come into being after the Bolshevik revolution in 1917 had ceased to exist. Minutes later, Gorbachev passed the nuclear briefcase to Yeltsin. Most of the television journalists who followed Gorbachev around in his last days were foreign – the Russian ones had lost interest. Bizarrely, the film about Gorbachev's departure was shot by an ABC crew, with some assistance from Soviet television, and narrated by an American journalist, Richard Kaplan. This was partly the result of a difference in attitude between Russian and Western journalists towards Gorbachev, but also towards 'historic' media events. Soviet training did not leave space for the proclaiming of a historic event of this kind since historic events were defined by the party and the state. The Western media, which prioritized the personal over the ideological and had already elevated Gorbachev to a world figure, of course treated his resignation as a huge moment, even a tragedy. The Russian public did not see it in those terms.

A few hours later, in an empty and largely dark Kremlin, Gorbachev and five others gathered around a table in the Walnut Reception Room for a simple meal that resembled a wake or a last supper. Among them was Alexander Yakovlev, the chief ideologist of Gorbachev's Perestroika.

The role played by Alexander Yakovlev in the dismantling of the Soviet Union was second only to Gorbachev's. He was the spiritual leader of Gorbachev's Perestroika. One of the most senior figures in the Soviet Politburo, Yakovlev was formally in charge of propaganda and ideology and in effect responsible for smashing both. He was also the author of Glasnost – the most successful part of Gorbachev's reforms – which opened up the media by removing ideological constraints, knocking out one of the key elements of the Soviet construction.

Alexander Yakovlev's relationship with Gorbachev was complex and often fractious. When Yakovlev died, Gorbachev did not attend his funeral, although Yakovlev had been by his side at one of the most difficult moments in Gorbachev's life. Shortly before Gorbachev's television announcement, Yakovlev had mediated an eight-hour long meeting between Gorbachev and Yeltsin at which power was transferred from the last president of the USSR to the first president of Russia. Yakovlev recalled the resolute step of Boris Yeltsin as he walked down the long Kremlin corridor 'as if on a parade ground' ('It was the walk of a victor') and the weakness of Gorbachev. When Yakovlev walked into Gorbachev's office, he found him lying down on a sofa.

'There were tears in his eyes. "You see, Sasha, that is how it is." Thus spoke a man, perhaps in the hardest minutes of his life. I tried to console him. But I myself was choking... A feeling that something unfair had happened was suffocating me. A man, who had brought drastic change to the world, who only yesterday ruled the fates of billions of people on earth, today was a helpless victim of the cruelty and capriciousness of history.'[3] The irony was that it was Gorbachev and Yakovlev who had set this history in motion.

Next to Alexander Yakovlev at Gorbachev's dinner table sat his namesake, Yegor Yakovlev. Despite their common last name, the two Yakovlevs rarely got confused with one another. The elder Yakovlev was always referred to as Alexander Nikolaevich; the younger one was always Yegor, rarely with his patronymic and often without adding his surname. When he died, obituaries referred to him as Yegor. This was partly a reflection of his mythological status. He was not just the editor-in-chief of *Moskovskie novosti*, he was simply 'the chief editor'. Legends were, and still are, told in Russia about Yegor's talent for nurturing authors, his oozing of irresistible charm which affected men and women alike, his habit of falling in and out of love, his despotic and dictatorial manner, his sparkle.

The two Yakovlevs were not related but the bond between them was no less real for that. Yegor saw Alexander, 'Uncle Sasha', as a patron saint and a father figure who enabled him to stretch the limits of Perestroika and protected him when he crossed them. Although the difference between them in age was only six years, they belonged to different generations, separated by the experience of the Second World War. (Alexander was born in 1923 and fought in the war.) Yet the two Yakovlevs were to die within one month of each other: Yegor on 18 September 2005 and Alexander on 18 October 2005. Gorbachev spoke at Yegor's funeral with a sincerity unusual for a politician: 'I counted him among my closest people and friends. One could always rely on him. He was close to me in spirit, in his attitude to life and to people... We remember the role his newspaper, *Moskovskie novosti* has played... Yegor and everything that he did was a yardstick by which people measured themselves...' *Moskovskie novosti* was a newspaper that tested Soviet ideology to destruction.

The Soviet system rested on violence and ideology. The death of Stalin in 1953 put an end to mass terror and repression. Violence, administered by the security services on behalf of the Communist Party, became more sporadic, and was now used mainly against dissidents. Nikita Khrushchev, who seized power after Stalin's death, shifted the weight of the system from repression to ideology, promising to build communism by 1980. Writers and ideologists were to play a more important role in this than the security services. As Khrushchev told Soviet writers in 1957: 'Just like a soldier cannot fight without ammunition, the party cannot conduct a war without print. Print is our main ideological weapon and we cannot pass it into unreliable hands. It must be kept in the most reliable, most trustworthy hands which would use this weapon to destroy the enemies of the working class.'[4]

By 1980 the ideology was completely rigid and lifeless. The economy was barely functioning and the grand utopia of building communism was dead. As Alexander Bovin, a speech writer for Leonid Brezhnev who replaced Khrushchev in 1964, and one of the leading Perestroika-era journalists, wrote: 'Only the lies – the end product of ideologists – provided the effectiveness of the violence (real or potential) which the system had rested upon.'[5] Once the ideology and propaganda started crumbling, the system came down, crushing those who had aimed to reform it. The Soviet collapse was determined not so much by the economic meltdown, a revolutionary uprising in the capital, or a struggle for independence on the periphery of the empire (at least, not directly), but by the dismantling of lies. Without lies, the Soviet Union would have had no legitimacy. The ruling elite no longer saw any reason to defend the system which constrained their personal enrichment and comforts. The paradox was that the dismantling of propaganda was not the result of some spontaneous and accidental process. As Otto Latsis, a prominent economics journalist of the time, a friend of Yegor Yakovlev's and one of *Moskovskie novosti*'s regular authors, wrote in his memoirs, it was 'a meticulously planned suicide'.[6]

The decisive blow was struck not by the dissidents – although their writing certainly undermined the system – but by the people who were in charge of this ideology and who had access to mass media. While Gorbachev carried the banners of Perestroika, it was Alexander Yakovlev and his team of like-minded journalists and editors, including Yegor and Latsis, who wrote the messages on those banners.

As Yegor himself put it, 'This was a completely unique period in the history of the Russian, and possibly world, press. What we wrote was aimed at liquidating this state. At the same time all the newspapers were fully subsidized by the state.'[7] The question is why did the men who had the most comfortable lives in the Soviet Union, commit this 'suicide'? Alexander Yakovlev wrote in his memoirs:

> I often asked myself: why did you need to do all this? You were a member of the Politburo, a secretary of the Central Committee – you had more power than you knew what to do with. Your portraits were displayed everywhere – people even carried them along the streets and squares during official holidays. What the hell else did you need? But what was eating away at me was something else. For years, I was betraying myself. I had doubts, looking for all sorts of excuses to what was happening around me only to quieten down the grumbling conscience. All of us, and particularly the nomenclatura [the class of Soviet administrators], lived a double, or even a triple, life. Step by step, such amorality became a way of life and was deemed 'moral', while hypocrisy became a way of thinking.[8]

These men were not heretics, rather many of them were faithful followers of the communist religion: they studied its sacred texts, paid tributes to its gods and participated in its rituals. Their Perestroika zeal stemmed not from a lack of faith, but from their desire to purify and cleanse communism of the orthodox bureaucracy. Alexander Yakovlev called Perestroika a reformation. This was not only its literal translation but also its historic meaning. Like the sixteenth-century Protestants in

Europe, they rose up against the priests who inserted themselves between God and the people and who, they believed, had corrupted his teaching.

They fought against the corrupt nomenclatura under the slogan 'more socialism', holding Lenin's teaching in their hands. They believed in the ideals of justice and equality and hoped to make the system more humane and moral. Had they wished to do anything other than that they would have most definitely shared the fate of many of the Soviet dissidents who were sidelined, exiled, jailed, or incarcerated in psychiatric wards. Stylistically, the reformers operated within the strict boundaries of Soviet language. Stepping outside the canon, breaking into a different style of writing, was a crime greater than criticizing the system within the Soviet mantra. A literary critic and writer Andrei Sinyavsky, who was tried and sentenced for anti-Soviet propaganda, said that his differences with the Soviet rule were mainly of stylistic nature. For the generation of the communist reformers, their objections to the Soviet system were ethical rather than stylistic.

'We, the reformers of 1985, tried to destroy the Bolshevik church in the name of a true religion and a true Jesus not realizing yet that our religion was false and our Jesus was an imposter,'[9] wrote Alexander Yakovlev. Yakovlev himself went further than anyone else of that tribe. His evolution from a Soviet apparatchik to liberal freethinker was perhaps the most deliberate of any high-ranking Soviet official, Gorbachev included. 'I came to hate Lenin and Stalin – these monsters who had cruelly deceived me and crushed my romantic world of hopes.'[10] In a country that had never fully repented for its crimes against its own people, Yakovlev embarked on – and completed – his own journey of repentance and atonement.

The fact that the reformation began with print also attested to its almost religious nature. The communists destroyed and defaced churches but borrowed from religion its attitude to the written word. Texts by Lenin and Marx were studied in every high school and university: they defined the approach to history and the view of the world. The battles on the pages of Soviet newspapers were conducted with the aid of citations from their sacred texts.

From the very beginning of the Bolshevik rule in 1917, words were nationalized and guarded by the party. Nothing could be printed without its permission. The first 'black' lists of banned books were compiled by Nadezhda Krupskaya, Lenin's wife, and included the Bible as well as many children's books. In the 1930s a librarian was tried and exiled for issuing philosophical works that were not even banned, but which simply did not fit into the Marxist view of the world. Libraries had 'closed' sections and special permission was required for reading books there. Some books were marked with a stamp: 'not to be issued'. Subscriptions to literary magazines and newspapers were strictly regulated by the state. A death sentence during Stalin's Terror was euphemistically called 'ten years without the right to correspondence'. The fear of the written word penetrated deep into the system. The secret police that carried out arrests and executions were specifically banned from issuing written statements to the relatives of those who were murdered. The relatives could only be told verbally (lied to) that a father, a wife, a son, a sister, had been sentenced to 'ten years without the right to correspondence' when he or she was in fact dead.

By the mid- and late 1940s – when the ten-year sentences were supposed to have expired – the families began to ask what had happened to their dear ones, and they were told (again verbally) that the relative had died while serving their sentence. The practice remained in place after Stalin's death. Only in 1989 – three years into Perestroika – did the KGB (the initials stood for 'Committee of State Security') allow the true dates of and information about executions to be printed in formal documents and death certificates.[11] The letters of those who were not executed and who were sent to the Gulag were censored. Words equalled life. The denial of words equalled death.

Words, like people, were kept behind the Iron Curtain. Publishing a book in the West without the permission of the state was considered no less a crime than illegally crossing the frontier without a special 'exit' visa. In 1958 Boris Pasternak was expelled from the Writers' Union and viciously vilified for the publication of *Doctor Zhivago* in the West. The poet Joseph Brodsky, who was expelled from the Soviet Union in 1972, acknowledged the magic ability of words to transcend closed borders: being effectively barred from seeing his parents before their death, he wrote about them in English – a language they did not understand – as 'their only chance to see me and America' and 'the only way for me to see them and our room'.[12]

In the 1980s the main ideological battles unfolded in print – rather than on television or the radio waves. All the men who led this new reformation were men of letters. Yegor was a student of history and archives; he was Lenin's biographer which gave him strength in 'theological debates' about the purity of the teaching. Otto Latsis worked as an editor of a magazine called *Kommunist*. Alexander Bovin was a speech writer for Brezhnev. The list goes on. These men were members of one generation known as *shestidesiatniki* – the men of the 1960s, when they became most active. They were almost exact contemporaries of Gorbachev, born within a few months of each other in 1930 or 1931. They shaped the narrative of Perestroika and articulated the values of their generation. In the West, Gorbachev is often seen as a visionary historic figure solely responsible for the liberalization of the Soviet Union. In fact, he was a man of his generation, which determined his sensibilities and choices.

These men shared childhood memories of Stalin's repressions, but their teenage years were overwhelmingly shaped by the Second World War and the Soviet victory which gave legitimacy to Soviet rule. They graduated from universities in 1953, the year of Stalin's death, which had profoundly changed the country, and began their professional careers at the time of Nikita Khrushchev's historic speech at the 20th Congress of the Communist Party in 1956, where he denounced Stalin's repressions and his cult of personality. Khrushchev's Thaw gave them encouragement and a chance to pursue political careers without becoming either murderers or victims. To belong to the *shestidesiatniki* was not just a matter of age, but of background and values. Most of the members of this club were well-educated, like-minded liberal intelligentsia, largely pro-Western, certainly anti-Stalinist. They moved together as a group, seeking out and helping each other along the way. Some of the most active members and ideologists of that generation were born into the families of Old Bolshevik revolutionaries, many of whom were purged by Stalin. Their *raison d'être* was to restore socialist justice and clear the names of their fathers.

In the early years of Perestroika, young journalists keen to find their own roots turned to these men for their experience. A few years later, as is often the case with fathers and sons, they were to reject and ridicule them.

Fireglow

> Every person bears the reflection of history. On some it glows with a hot and fearsome light, on others it is barely visible, barely warm, but it is there on everyone. History blazes like a huge bonfire, and each of us throws into it our own brushwood.
>
> (Yuri Trifonov, *Fireglow*, 1965)[13]

A cardboard folder with Yegor Yakovlev's personal file; a snapshot for a Soviet-passport-sized photograph; a serious-looking Soviet man in a dark suit and thick-framed glasses. 'Yakovlev, Yegor Vladimirovich, born 1930, member of the Communist Party from 1953. In 1954, graduated from the Moscow State Historical Archival Institute, writes articles on the subject of party propaganda, Soviet development and Communist ethics; pays particular attention to the subject of Lenin.' A standard sign that stated: 'politically literate, morally stable and ideologically sound'.[14]

Yegor was neither the most talented nor the cleverest of his generation. But he was one of the most colourful and active. He encapsulated its traits and its defining features with a clarity that is not obscured by genius. He remained an active player in Russian political life longer than many others. As such he makes an ideal subject for the study of the generation that attempted to reform the Soviet Union but instead contributed to its demise.

How and why did this 'ideologically sound' journalist, a fervent member of the Communist Party, come to undermine the system? If the Soviet Union was a monolith totalitarian system, how did he manage to break through it? And what gave him and his circle the strength and determination to rise to the top? Some of the answers can be gleaned from their '*anketa*' or official forms which had to be filled in with every move – a change of a job, a trip abroad, a promotion, a demotion. The first question was always about 'fathers'.

Yegor's first 'autobiography' is dated July 1949, when Yegor was about to go to the Historical Archival Institute. Blue, faint ink on aged, poor-quality yellow paper. 'Father: Yakovlev Vladimir Ivanovich, participated in the revolutionary movement since 1911, a member of the Communist Party since 1 January, 1919. The first years after the revolution worked in Ch.K in Ukraine...'[15]

Ch.K (pronounced Cheka) was an abbreviation for the All Russian Extraordinary Commission for the Struggle against Counter-Revolution, Sabotage and Speculation. It was set up to stop looting, but quickly developed into a secret police force designed to prevent counter-revolutionary actions and execute 'class enemies'. Yegor's father was the head of Ch.K in Odessa, which was taken by the Bolsheviks in April 1919. Ivan Bunin, one of Russia's finest writers and its first winner of the Nobel Prize for Literature, an ardent anti-Bolshevik, who fled St Petersburg after the revolution, described Odessa in 1919 as 'a dead and empty port; a dead burned-out city...'. The office of the Ch.K, where Yakovlev's father served, was 'decked with red flags which, extremely filthy and droopy from the rain, cast thin and bloody reflections on the wet asphalt'.[16] 'Day and night we live in an orgy of death. They keep talking in the name of some "bright future" and will supposedly issue forth from this satanic gloom. There have already appeared on this earth an entire legion of specialists and contractors who seek to fashion human well-being,'[17] Bunin wrote.

Yet in his own imagination Yegor placed his father, whom he barely remembered, in a context created by Isaak Babel, an Odessa writer who embraced the revolution and painted colourful portraits of local gangsters 'squeezed into crimson waistcoats, their steel shoulders enveloped in red-brown jackets'. Yegor believed it was his father who had nailed the most notorious bandit Mishka 'the Jap', who had served as a prototype for Babel's Benya Krik – the 'King' of Odessa gangsters. Whether Yegor's father actually caught Mishka 'the Jap' is unknown. What is known, though, is that according to Grigory Besedovsky, a former Soviet diplomat who defected to Paris in 1928, he was a 'strange and sinister' figure of extreme cruelty who, in three months as the head of the Ch.K, ordered the execution of 5,000 people – among them his own father, who was an active member of the ultra-nationalist, monarchist and anti-Semitic organization called the Union of Russian People. Yegor described his grandfather as a drunken and abusive man who occasionally threatened his wife – Yegor's grandmother – with a knife. When he was detained for counter-revolutionary activities, Yegor's father decided he should be dealt with according to the law of the revolution and so he sanctioned his own father's execution. Afterwards, Yegor's paternal grandmother apparently committed suicide in her son's flat.

Was this inhuman? Perhaps. But so, Yegor argued, was the death of his father's sister, who was beaten to death with metal rods by the Cossacks when they found revolutionary literature on her. The harshness of the revolutionary years was dictated not by cruelty but by 'the purity of the revolution and its ideals' and by '*neterpenie* [intolerance or impatience] – the most wonderful quality of a revolutionary',[18] Yegor concluded in a short book published in 1965.

The book was written in the form of an imaginary conversation with his father. Yegor called it *Ia idu s toboi* (*I Am Walking Alongside You*). It was preceded and probably inspired by a novel by Yuri Trifonov, one of the most prominent and talented post-Second World War Soviet writers, called *Otblesk kostra* (*Fireglow*) – a semi-documentary book about the life of his father, an Old Bolshevik who participated in the revolution and the civil war. People of Yegor Yakovlev's generation and background lived in the glow of the fire that their fathers had started in order to burn the old Russia, which eventually consumed them too. Soviet history was their family history and they perceived it as such.

Yegor's father died in 1935, two years before Stalin's purges of his own elite reached their peak. Yegor was five years old. Though his father apparently died of cancer, there were rumours that he had been poisoned. 'Within a few years most of Yegor's father's colleagues vanished. Yegor remembered a family friend coming to see his mother in 1937 and telling her stories of people being taken away in the middle of the night. Her response was placid and common: "When you chop down trees chips fly."'[19]

'Chopping trees' was something that Yegor's father himself oversaw. Metaphors in the Soviet Union had a physical dimension. In the late 1920s to early 1930s Yegor's father was responsible for timber harvesting which was almost entirely carried out by the slave labour of the Gulag. When Yegor was born, his father was in Vologda and Archangel – overseeing the logging of trees by the inmates. Some of this Gulag timber was exported to England. British timber yards received logs which had markings and inscriptions made by the Gulag prisoners as it was the only way of communication with the outside world that was still available to them. 'With suffering you get this timber', read one such inscription.

Yegor's father had travelled to England on business, which probably included the export of that timber. That is where Yegor's parents actually met. In 1929 – the year of Stalin's 'Great Break' – his mother, who had worked at the Soviet Trade Representation, moved back to the Soviet Union pregnant with Yegor. As Yegor's father was a senior member of the Soviet nomenclatura, the family was given an old merchant's house in a quiet part of Moscow across the river from the Kremlin. Yegor's mother chose it in preference to a flat on the embankment, in a luxury apartment block where many of the Bolshevik elite lived – and where most of them would be arrested (Trifonov wrote a novel about this place called *The House on the Embankment*). Such was the scale of the purges that nobody living in the Moscow of the 1930s could claim ignorance. The show trials of the enemies of the people were public; the stories of those who returned from the labour camps were plentiful. But seeing the arrests, or hearing about them, was not the same as comprehending them as evil. That required a remarkable independence of thought and few people possessed it. Yegor was not one of them. He grew up with the cult of his father in his head and a portrait of Stalin on the wall – just like any nomenclatura family.

When, in 1949, Yegor's school friend cursed Stalin and accused those who worshipped him of hypocrisy, Yegor kicked him out of the house. 'I never heard anyone talk about Him [Stalin] like this. He called hypocrites those who spoke of their love for Stalin, he chose the worst epithets for him. It was unbelievable. But he spoke calmly and firmly – just like he talked about astronomy in school. First, I argued with him. Then I said: "Go away! Go away! You are a bastard." He was walking down the stairs and I was shouting something offensive at his back.'[20]

The next time Yegor heard something like this said about Stalin was in 1956, three years after Stalin's death, and this time the words were spoken by Nikita Khrushchev in the Grand Kremlin Palace.

—

Stalin's death in 1953 was a watershed as great as his coming to power: it marked the end of one country and the beginning of another. But the realization of this did not come overnight. In the first days after Stalin's death the country seemed numb, as if holding its breath. His death was greeted with a mixture of disbelief, fear and grief. Gods cannot die the way mortals do. His cult had hypnotized the brightest minds. Andrei Sakharov, one of the world's greatest physicists and humanists, wrote to his first wife at the time: 'I am under a spell from the death of a great man. Thinking about his humanity.'[21] Sakharov cited this letter in his memoirs, struggling to explain his own reaction.

Nikita Khrushchev, who succeeded Stalin, was a man who started to lift this spell. His own appearance – short, round, bald, with sticking-out ears – evoked laughter rather than terror. His national Ukrainian collarless shirt was an antithesis to Stalin's buttoned-up, high-necked, military-style tunic. Khrushchev loosened the suffocating collar. 'I like him ever so much,' enthused Sakharov.[22] 'After all he differs so much from Stalin.' A wild, uneducated, capricious man, complicit in Stalin's Terror, with blood on his hands, Khrushchev nonetheless displayed some human features. Like a folk-tale hero who slays the dragon and opens up the castle, one of Khrushchev's first acts was to open up the Kremlin to the public. The paralysing fear which enveloped the country during the years of Stalinist rule began to lift. 'People were still scared to make any sharp move, but the nooses around their necks suddenly got looser.'[23]

Yegor Yakovlev, who joined the Communist Party just before Stalin's death, was working as a low-level party official. A few months after Stalin's death, he organized street patrols in central Moscow to help the police to catch drunks and prostitutes. Yegor remembered the sensation of walking back at night along Moscow's main streets. 'For the first time, we walked the Moscow streets like masters, aware of our strength.'[24] Only a few months earlier, the nocturnal streets of Moscow had been ruled by the NKVD (People's Commissariat for Internal Affairs – the secret police) who whisked people away from their homes. Trade returned to Red Square. Three weeks after Stalin's death, the nineteenth-century trading galleries facing the Kremlin, which had been occupied by state offices in the 1930s, became the main department store in the country – GUM. Yegor's first journalistic job was in a small-circulation newspaper called *Za obraztsovuiu torgovliu* (*For the Exemplary Trade*), published by GUM.

The main marker of Yegor's generation was Khrushchev's secret speech at the 20th Congress of the Communist Party in 1956 in which he denounced Stalin's cult of personality and revealed the scale of purges within the party. It had the impact of an exploded bomb. 'Everything seemed unreal, even the fact that I was in the Kremlin... Everything [I lived by] was blown up into small pieces – like shrapnel in war,' Alexander Yakovlev recalled.[25] The speech was delivered at an unscheduled secret session held on the last day of the Congress and lasted nearly four hours. It was not printed in newspapers or broadcast by television and radio. The most important events in the Kremlin that defined the fate of millions of people occurred with the media outlets being 'switched off'.

Just like newspapers that were glued over windows during the war as protection against flying shards, the role of newspapers in the Soviet political system was to block out information and protect the façade of the state. (A few hundred copies of Khrushchev's speech were printed for internal use and marked 'strictly secret'. The first public text appeared in English a few weeks later in the *New York Times* but did not make it into the Russian press until 1989.) Instead of using the media, the party resorted to the most arcane and direct way of delivering information – through messengers by word of mouth. Perhaps one reason was that the spoken word was meant to have a greater impression on the listener than the printed one. (After all, people go to church to hear the Bible, not to read it.)

Yegor was one of the messengers charged with reading out the text of Khrushchev's speech to the rank and file of the party. He did not like what he read. He remembered his feeling of protest at and rejection of the speech. When he came home that day and saw that his wife had taken Stalin's portrait down, he touched the nail in disbelief. Yegor got angry and demanded that the portrait should be put back. Soon, he took it down himself – this time for good. The portrait of Dzerzhinsky, which the founder of Ch.K had given to his father, remained on the wall. Yegor was not alone in his initial reaction: many of the party activists felt the same way. As Gorbachev recalled, while those who directly encountered Stalin's repressions welcomed Khrushchev's speech, many either refused tobelieve it or rejected the need to bring it up, even if the facts cited by Khrushchev were true. 'Whom will that benefit?' Vyacheslav Molotov, one of Stalin's senior henchmen, asked. 'What will that give us? Why stir up the past?'[26] After all, the Soviet Union could have developed the same way as China after Mao. Swearing their allegiance to Stalin, his followers could have moved the country's economy into a different direction. Lavrentiy Beria, the most feared boss of the NKVD, who primed himself as Stalin's successor, could have played the role that Deng Xiaoping played in China. So why did Khrushchev do it?

Partly, it was an instinct of self-preservation. Khrushchev, like most of the high-ranking party nomenclatura, was exhausted by the constant fear and expectation of another super-purge which Stalin had probably been planning. The main reason, however, was not rational but emotional: he denounced Stalin because he could and because he wanted to. As William Taubman, Khrushchev's biographer, wrote, it was partly 'a way of reclaiming his identity as a decent man by telling the truth. On the night he gave the speech, he later recalled he could "hear the voices of comrades who perished".'[27]

Khrushchev's speech had several vital implications. One was that it removed the fear of being murdered, particularly among the elite. After the execution of Beria in true Stalinist fashion in 1953 (Beria was accused of being a British spy and promptly shot), Khrushchev effectively called a halt to the use of violence against political rivals. The first test of the new rule came a year after the speech, in 1957, when a group of hard-line Stalinists, including Molotov, Kaganovich and Malenkov, fearing that Khrushchev was undermining the foundation of the regime, attempted to overthrow him. The media once again were silent.* The conspirators were labelled as an 'anti-party' group – a charge which a few years earlier had carried a death sentence. This time none of the plotters was executed or even jailed. The same rule saved Khrushchev's own life when he was finally toppled in 1964, and it was observed by his successors. In 1991 Mikhail Gorbachev spared those who led a coup against him and in 1993, although Boris Yeltsin jailed those who took up arms against him, he quickly let them out again.

In fact, the main reason the plotters lost in 1957 was a significant mood shift within the elite. As Alexander Yakovlev wrote, the new generation, which supported Khrushchev in 1957 and then turned against him in 1964, did not want a return to the hyper-tension of Stalinist times. It was striving for a measured, safe and comfortable life. Its main goal was to stay in lifelong power without the fear of being purged. This pact applied not only to the top political ranks but to the Soviet elite more generally. Members of the ruling class who fell out of favour could be pushed aside, 'exiled' into far-flung embassies or put under house arrest, but they were not physically eliminated.

In the 1960s this pact allowed the growth and survival of a new party elite which could pursue its own goals. Its members were happy – not with Stalin's death as such, but with their own youth, their hopes and their strength and, above all, just with being alive. Khrushchev opened up the Kremlin – both physically and figuratively – to a new generation which had been too young to serve under Stalin.

* The crucial role in thwarting the coup was played by the minister of defence, Marshal Georgy Zhukov, who lent Khrushchev a hand (and military planes that briskly delivered members of the Central Committee to Moscow).

As Alexander Bovin, one of the young communist reformers in the Kremlin, wrote in his memoirs: 'A critical mass started to form, a mass which a quarter of a century later blew away the mightiest totalitarian regime of the twentieth century.'[28] An invisible shift of the generations – the engine of all big social changes in Russia – was taking place.

Members of the generation empowered by the 20th Congress of the Communist Party did not seek to destroy the system, they tried to work their way into it in order to seize its tools and aim them against the old Stalinists. The denunciation of Stalin did not undermine the *shestidesiat-niki's* faith in socialism. On the contrary, it reinforced their belief in its self-cleansing quality. Stalinism was seen not as the ultimate manifestation of the Soviet regime but as a distortion. The goal, as Yakovlev's generation understood it, was to improve the system of proofs rather than to throw out the theory. As Yegor reflected:

> We would disrespect the memory of those who innocently suffered [from Stalin's repressions] if we were to equate Stalin's cult of personality with the regime... No, the cult of personality was never part of our socialist order, but emerged despite it... The greatness of the revolution is not just in the fact that the workers took power into their hands, but in the creation of an order which would inevitably reject everything that is alien to it.[29]

It is usual for the sons to reject the experience of the fathers. But the untimely deaths of the old Bolsheviks at Stalin's hands meant that their children saw their duty in clearing and redeeming the names of their fathers and carrying on their socialist cause. Yegor's generation lived with Hamlet's complex: his urge to redeem and carry out his father's commandments while reconciling his actions with morals. *Hamlet*, a play that was effectively banned under Stalin, returned to the Soviet stage after his death when these men graduated from universities and entered active life. In 1954, the first post-Stalin *Hamlet* was full of vitality, strength and determination: as he delivered 'To be or not to be', Hamlet viciously shook the iron bars of what looked like a prison gate.

By the right of their revolutionary fathers, who had started the socialist experiment, the children were the Soviet princes, or patricians empowered by a sense of entitlement and personal responsibility for their country. They were the Soviet aristocracy. They did not try to escape the Soviet reality either physically or mentally, and never considered emigrating. It was their country – they were entitled to it – and they wanted to change it according to their own needs and views of what was right and wrong. 'If only I was at the top' was the thought that Yegor and his generation lived with. They were born for active life, had the strength for it and were constantly looking for a cause to which they could apply their energy.

Private Thoughts

The removal of terror also opened up space for individual thought and action and Russian artists, writers and journalists were quick to take advantage of it. Their work formed the consciousness of those who, thirty years later, would launch Perestroika. The word 'thaw' – which the writer Ilya Erenburg used as the title of his novel published in 1954 – gave a name to an entire period in Russian culture, and captured the sensation of new life breaking through the ice. One of the main discoveries and joys of the post-Stalinist years was that the nation, exhausted by collectivization, shattered by the war, tortured by the Gulag, managed to preserve some healthy instincts and lively qualities.

While the Soviet system still barred private ownership of land and property, it allowed space for privacy, for intimate feelings and thoughts. Khrushchev's main urban projects of building five-storey-high apartment blocks throughout the country transformed the living space of millions of people who moved out of communal flats with one kitchen and one bathroom for up to ten families into small, individual apartments each equipped with its own kitchen and bathroom. These apartments were cramped and inconveniently designed but they were separate from one another. The impact of the transformation from communal into private living can hardly be overestimated. Individual tape-recorders and individual television sets now populated individual flats. With them came artists, poets and bards who filled up the intellectual space of that era. Their works were designed for an intimate audience rather for the echoing public halls.

Normal human feelings were cultivated by theatres and literature, but nowhere more so than in a journal called *Novy Mir* (*New World*). 'All of us in those years – I mean the people of my circle – worshipped *Novy Mir*, we lived according to *Novy Mir*,' Yegor recalled.[30] Whereas *Pravda* (*Truth*) appealed to the mass consciousness, *Novy Mir* appealed to private minds.

The Bolsheviks did not just nationalize private land and assets, they also nationalized humankind and individual consciousness. And while physical assets were expropriated by means of physical violence, minds were claimed through ideology and the media. The paternalistic state was supposed to take care not only of the livelihoods of its citizens but also of their morals. The aim of the media had been to standardize the minds of their readers by treating them as one collective body, feeding it the same (mis)information so that it would also think collectively. In the 1960s *Novy Mir*, which had a circulation of 130,000 copies, countered the very principle of a collective mind, restoring the individual as an entity. After the 20th Congress, the yearning for such an individual approach became a mass one.

At the head of *Novy Mir* stood Alexander Tvardovsky, a Russian poet from a solid peasant family whose father, brother and sisters had been 'collectivized' and exiled as kulaks (well-off peasants with their own land). His own consciousness was formed by his peasant background. His father was the son of a soldier who bought a patch of land with the earnings he had made as a blacksmith. 'From a very tender age our father impressed on us the love for this sour land, mean and unkind, but our own – our "estate" as he called his farm jokingly.'[31] C. P. Snow, an English author and essayist who met Tvardovsky in London, described him as 'an honest and rooted man. He stood like a rock, exceptionally subtle in his emotional nature, strong and simple in his intellect.'[32]

Tvardovsky, who was appointed the editor of *Novy Mir* by the Central Committee, gained his national fame as the author of a connected cycle of poems in which the central character is Vasily Tyorkin – a folk-style Russian private soldier, life-loving, instinctively patriotic, with an acute sense of duty and camaraderie, who never loses heart and defies death with his wit and courage. The rhyming poem, made up of scenes from Tyorkin's own life, reads like a comic book. It was easy to remember and easy to tell to others. There was a folkloric sound to it – as though it was specially written to recite during short breaks in the trenches.

Alexander Solzhenitsyn, who read *Vasily Tyorkin* during the war, wrote:

> Amid the fume and crackle of gibbering propaganda which always accompanied our bombardments, Tvardovsky had succeeded in writing something timeless, courageous and unsullied, helped by a rare sense of proportion, all his own, or perhaps by a sensitive tact not uncommon among peasants... Though he was not free to tell the whole truth about the war, Tvardovsky nevertheless always stopped just one millimetre short of falsehood, and nowhere did he ever overstep the one millimetre mark. The result was a miracle.[33]

Tvardovsky first heard of Solzhenitsyn in December 1961 when the reclusive schoolteacher from the provincial city of Riazan submitted to *Novy Mir* his story *Щ-854*, better known as *One Day in the Life of Ivan Denisovich*. To get it printed, Tvardovsky went straight to Khrushchev, who was moved by the story of a hard-working peasant in Stalin's Gulag and saw it as a validation of his own attack on Stalin. He allowed it to be printed – 'a fact', Tvardovsky recorded in his diary, 'remarkable not only for my daily life and which, I think, will have a pivotal importance in it, but one that will have serious consequences in the flow of literary (which means not only literary) affairs'.[34]

Tvardovsky saw *One Day…* not as a subversive story – as did Solzhenitsyn – but as deeply therapeutic prose which would help to heal a society traumatized by Stalin's excesses. It was printed in November 1962 and had an impact similar to Khrushchev's own speech at the 20th Congress. Its novelty and power was not in the description of the Gulag system, but in the choice of the protagonist. Ivan Denisovich was not an inventor, an artist, or a communist. He was a Russian peasant: hard-working, conscientious and self-reliant – a close relative of Tvardovsky's Tyorkin.

One Day… and *Vasily Tyorkin* had a common theme: the survival and continuation of life, and its resilience in any circumstances. Be it in the Gulag or the wartime trenches, life – physical and artistic – had its own rights that could not be squeezed out by politics. Both Tyorkin and Ivan Denisovich were survivors and they kept alive the best traits and qualities of the Russian peasantry however hard the system tried to erase them. Solzhenitsyn was invited to attend a reception at the Kremlin and was toasted by Khrushchev as Ivan Denisovich.

But having let thousands of such Ivan Denisovichs out of the Gulag, Khrushchev was not prepared to give them economic power. He allowed individual thinking, but not individual action, private land, or economic freedom. As Alexander Yakovlev wrote, having achieved a spiritual breakthrough, Khrushchev did not dare to touch the economic foundation of socialism.

Otto Latsis, a Latvian by birth and one of the most respected economic journalists and proponents of Gorbachev's Perestroika, recalled the draconian rules on private ownership in the late 1950s and early 1960s when his father, an Old Bolshevik, was expelled from the Communist Party on the pretext that he had built with his own hands and his own money a country house that did not fit in with the strict limits imposed by the party. The law banned the ownership of a private house that exceeded 60 square metres (51 square yards) of living space, regardless of the number of people living in it. It specified the height of ceilings in cellars and banned fireplaces in country dachas. 'People were forced to physically bend down to the authorities: a cellar where a person could stand up to his full height was prohibited.'[35]

The young party elite, which included Yegor Yakovlev, Bovin and Latsis, longed for economic and political reforms and was frustrated by Khrushchev's failure to deliver either. His ousting in 1964 did not, at the time, spell disaster or the end of an era – at least not straight away. Bovin summed up the mood of the liberally minded part of the elite: 'In less than ten years Khrushchev had exhausted his positive resources... He started turning into a monument to himself or rather did not stop others from turning him into a monument. The trouble was that Khrushchev was ousted by people of smaller calibre. Khrushchev would not let them have a quiet life. He destabilized them. Not the system, but each one of them. And he paid for it.'[36]

A coup against Khrushchev was the work of two rival camps in the party: on the one hand, neo-Stalinists and nationalists led by Alexander Shelepin and his protégé and KGB chief Vladimir Semichastny, and on the other hand, the mediocre but less militant regional clan led by Leonid Brezhnev. Brezhnev, who came out on top, oversaw nearly two decades of stagnation. He did not seem like a master of evil. He had been through the war, though not as a soldier, but as a political commissar. He was no reformer, but nor was he a bloodthirsty Stalinist or nationalist like Shelepin. His motto was 'live and let live'. An obsessive hunter, he preferred shooting game at his country residence to dealing with international affairs in his Kremlin office. A man of little education, he was generally good-natured and not afraid to admit his own ignorance even to his own speech writer, Alexander Bovin.

'Listen, do you know what "upland game" is?' Brezhnev asked him after listening to one of the speeches Bovin had drafted for him.

'Vaguely', said Bovin.

'Let's do it this way,' Brezhnev suggested. 'I will tell you about upland game, and you will explain to me what the word *konfrontatsiya* [confrontation] means. Agreed?'

Bovin, who held a doctorate in philosophy, agreed.[37]

Unlike Yegor Yakovlev and Otto Latsis, each of whom was born into a family of Old Bolsheviks, Bovin came from a less revolutionary background. His grandfather was a priest, his father a military officer in the Far East. Bovin trained as a lawyer, held two graduate degrees and worked as a judge. His enormous size, hussar-style moustache and side-whiskers, his sense of humour and *joie de vivre*, made an immediate comic impression on his interlocutors. But behind this appearance was a man of great brain and decency.

In the early 1960s, having spent a few years at the influential journal *Kommunist*, Bovin became a staffer at the Central Committee, which was a fairly large and diverse body that de facto governed the country. Bovin joined the department that dealt with communist parties in the Soviet bloc and was led by Yuri Andropov. 'They needed people who on the one hand would give no grounds for doubting their allegiance to the political regime and ruling ideology and, on the other hand, who could look at the world openly and be able to understand and explain the changes that were coming.'[38]

The biggest change of all was that that the country could no longer be held together by terror, nor could it be completely isolated from the rest of the world. Although the Iron Curtain was still very much in place, it worked more like one-way tinted glass than a brick wall. The Soviet people could not be seen by the West but they could see out to the West.

The system could bar its people and their ideas from travelling abroad, but it could not stop the fashion for mini-skirts, long hair worn loose, songs by the Beatles and films by Fellini from moving in the opposite direction (Fellini's *8½* received a Grand Prix at the Moscow Film Festival in 1963). Unable to travel abroad, Soviet youths started roving around the country with rucksacks on their backs and guitars in their hands, spurring along the way an entire sub-culture of tourism. Journalism transcended the domain of the official party ideology and became romantic and fashionable.

Yegor Yakovlev set the fashion in a new magazine called *Zhurnalist* (*Journalist*). Its cutting-edge design, its illustrations and photographs by Henri Cartier-Bresson and the Magnum photographer Dennis Stock caught the attention of the urban intelligentsia that lived by the idea of the West, dreamt of the West, idealized it and longed for it, and tried to steal any glimpse of Western life from films and journals. A lucky few who travelled to the West on business brought back stories and pictures: friends and family were invited for an annotated show of slides. *Zhurnalist* aimed to satisfy that longing.

Before Yegor's time, *Zhurnalist* had been called *Sovetskaia pechat'* (*Soviet Press*). Yegor borrowed the title *Zhurnalist* from a magazine that had existed in the 1920s. He wished *Zhurnalist* to express what people of his own circle 'talked about in their Moscow kitchens'. This suggested a new way of organizing the mind: not vertically, where the party through print dictated what its readers were to think, but horizontally, where a network of like-minded individuals shared views put forward in print.

Zhurnalist reflected all the strengths and weakness of the *shestidesiatniki*. Idle conversations around a kitchen table among the liberal intelligentsia all too often were a substitute for real action or work; it gave them relief, but yielded few results. It created a comfortable cocoon, but also increased the intelligentsia's isolation from the rest of the country. The 'cocoon' itself, however, was growing larger in size. By the time Yegor was fired less than two years later, its circulation exceeded a quarter of a million copies.

Zhurnalist tried to break down geographical and intellectual barriers, moving freely between the village and the city, between Russia and the West. One of its authors was Yury Chernichenko, an agricultural economist and essayist who grew up in a Russian village that was devastated by Stalin's collectivization and subjected to famine and cannibalism (his parents would not leave him at home alone, fearing that he would be stolen and eaten). Soviet bureaucracy not only spoilt the land by draining the rivers and destroying forests, it also drained the human and moral resources of the nation. Chernichenko, who turned to the Russia village in search of a positive, hard-working, entrepreneurial national type, was one of its finest examples.

Chernichenko's essays about rural Russia happily coexisted on the pages of the *Zhurnalist* with themes and articles that constituted the world of Russian Westernizers. In one of the issues, Yegor published his interview with a prototype of Hemingway's *For Whom the Bell Tolls* – a Soviet spy who had taken part in the Spanish Civil War in 1936. (The novel itself was only available in samizdat – the clandestine copying and distribution of material banned by the state.) Hemingway was an icon of the *shestidesiatniki*: his photograph in a black-and-white roll-neck was displayed on glass-fronted bookshelves as a sign of belonging.

In the same issue, only a few pages apart, in a section called 'If You Happen to Be in…', Yegor published an illustrated essay about the ancient Russian town of Suzdal', written and drawn by the artist Tatyana Mavrina. Ornamented wooden houses and white churches were accompanied by similarly ornate texts that conjured up the world of the Russian fairy tale with its fire-birds, magic horses, lively fairs and its pagan gods. The onion domes of Suzdal' and the smoky bars of Valencia were equally exotic.

While the official Soviet press was cultivating the image of the Soviet

Union as a besieged fortress, *Zhurnalist* took its readers to an American television studio and around Fleet Street, inside *The Economist* tower in St James's and the Chicago mansion of Hugh Hefner, the publisher of *Playboy*, with a revolving round bed and pictures of Marilyn Monroe as the first 'Girl of the Month'. These articles were not the usual rife propaganda about the bourgeois press, but surprisingly accurate and respectful descriptions of how the Western media operated. To be sure, the article about *Playboy* was written by a French journalist and accompanied by a commentary by a Soviet media guru who lamented the 'depravity and degradation' of Western readers. Positioned on the side of the main text in white letters on black ink, the commentary was quite literally marginal.

Inevitably, such articles prompted comparisons and planted ideas in the heads of those who were supposed to 'propagate, agitate and organize'. Yegor's generation tried to square the circle: how did one reconcile socialism, which rejected private ownership, with individual initiative, and the idea of a 'party-minded' media with the free flow of information? This was not a philosophical question, but a highly practical one. These people had an allegiance to the Bolshevik ideas of social justice and equality, but they wanted a good life for themselves and for their children, a life no worse than the lives of their counterparts in the 'decaying' West.

For a moment, it seemed that the answer was found in the Prague Spring of 1967–8 when the government of Alexander Dubček tried to reform the Czech economy by freeing it from state control and introducing competition. 'There is no thick wall between economy and ethics: under socialism the rouble rewards honest and pure creative work,' *Zhurnalist* enthused, displaying as evidence the experience of the socialist Czechoslovakia and backing it with a quote from the Czech ministry of the interior: 'Our first problem is how to teach a cobbler, a vendor or a barber not to be afraid to earn a lot of money.' It was a hymn to private initiative and to common sense.[39]

Dubček's idea of socialism with 'a human face' was a Eureka moment for the reformists in Moscow. The Czech reforms that offered more democracy, economic liberalization and constraints on the all-powerful security agencies filled Russian liberals with hope and enthusiasm.

The events in Prague inspired Andrei Sakharov to write an article which he titled 'Reflections on Progress, Peaceful Coexistence and Intellectual Freedom'. The article warned of the threat of a thermonuclear Armageddon and called for an economic, social and ideological convergence with the West. It was circulated in samizdat and 18 million copies of it were printed around the world, more than any Agatha Christie novel. Yet, as far as Brezhnev's Kremlin was concerned, the danger posed to the survival of the Soviet system by Sakharov's proposed 'convergence' was greater than the threat of a nuclear war. The link between the Prague Spring and the advances of liberal thought in Russia was apparent.

In June 1967 *Zhurnalist* reprinted the new Czech media law which guaranteed freedom of speech, without giving up state ownership of the media. A group of intellectuals, including Sakharov, proposed a similar law at home. 'It proclaims, in effect, the right of any citizen, to print any material, to stage any performance and to show any films,' the KGB reported to the Central Committee in horror. The KGB added that 'it was undertaking measures to prevent the further activity of those who have organized this document'.[40]

In April 1968 Yegor was fired ostensibly for publishing a poetic and subtly erotic black-and-white photograph and a reproduction of a Soviet painting depicting a female nude in a bath-house. Yet the deeper reasons had to do with the publication of the Czech media law. There was talk in the Kremlin that if *Zhurnalist* was not closed down, the Soviet leadership would soon face the same situation as the one in Czechoslovakia.

As transcripts of telephone conversations and meetings between Brezhnev and Dubček testify, the Soviet leaders were much more worried about the media than by any other aspects of the Czech reform. Remarkably, newspapers were the main subject of the Soviet attack on Dubček. 'We have not got much time,' Brezhnev told him on 13 August 1968. 'I once again turn to you with my concern about the media which not only distort our agreements, but spread anti-Soviet and anti-Socialist ideas... We had agreed that all media – print, radio and television – would be brought under the control of the Central Committee of the Czech Communist Party and all anti-Soviet and anti-socialist publications would stop...'[41] Brezhnev accused Dubček of breaking the agreements and used examples supplied to him by the KGB.

The Czech reformers insisted they never intended to break away from the Soviet allegiance and argued that they imposed a threat not to socialism but 'to bureaucracy which has been slowly and steadily burying socialism on an international scale.' The Soviet bureaucracy perceived this threat as a serious one and prepared for a military invasion. A few rational heads in the Central Committee, such as Bovin, tried to talk Brezhnev out of it. On 14 August, a day after Brezhnev's conversation with Dubček, Bovin submitted a memo to Andropov which argued that military action could be justified only if Czechoslovakia tried to move over to the West, which was not the case. A use of force, Bovin wrote, would irreparably damage the Soviet reputation among socialist countries. It would also isolate the Soviet Union from the rest of Europe, pushing Western Europe to form a tighter allegiance with the United States, at Russia's expense. (The situation would repeat itself more than half a century later in Russia's actions against Ukraine.)

Bovin even got to present his views to Brezhnev, who told him: 'The Politburo has already made its decision. We disagree with you. You can disagree [with us] and leave the party, or you can fall in line with the decision. You decide.'[42] A few days later, Soviet tanks rolled into Prague. On 19 August 1968 Bovin recorded in his diary: 'Another session of the politburo. The situation is approaching the dénouement. Those who made the decision about sending in the troops have signed their own sentence. When it will be carried out is a matter of time.'[43] The 'sentence' was deferred but was carried out twenty years later when Gorbachev – with the help of people like Yakovlev, Latsis and Bovin – launched his Perestroika.

In Moscow, among the intelligentsia, the invasion created a sense of mourning, for the Soviet tanks in Prague crushed not only Dubček, they crushed the hopes of the Russian intelligentsia for reforming socialism into something humane and just. It showed that the Soviet system could be held together only by force. It was a breaking point. The Soviet leadership had alienated the smartest and the most creative part of the intelligentsia and lost control over the intellectual life of the country, Alexander Yakovlev reflected. For those who signed up to the idea of 'socialism with a human face', as Yakovlev, Bovin and Latsis had done, this was a personal defeat.

Dare You Come to the Square?

Just the same, no simpler
Are the tests of our times:
Can you come to the square?
Dare you come to the square?
Can you come to the square?
Dare you come to the square?
When that hour strikes?

Alexander Galich, 'St. Petersburg Romance'[44]

The crushing of the Prague Spring had divided the intelligentsia into two groups – those who joined a dissident movement trying to apply pressure on the system from the outside and those who condemned the invasion but stayed inside the system, hoping to push its boundaries from within. The two circles overlapped and complemented each other.

On 25 August – the first Sunday after the invasion – seven dissidents came out onto Red Square. As the clock on the Kremlin tower struck midday, they unveiled the banners they had brought with them. Some were in Czech: 'Long Live a Free and Independent Czechoslovakia', others in Russian: 'Free Dubček' and 'Hands off Czechoslovakia'. One slogan read: 'For Your Freedom and Ours'. They lasted a few minutes before the KGB pounced on the demonstration, beat up the dissidents, banged them into a car and drove them off. (Two of the demonstrators were put in a punitive psychiatric clinic. The rest were exiled or sent to a labour camp.) It was an act of extraordinary individual responsibility and willpower.

Bovin, Yegor Yakovlev and Latsis did not come out on Red Square. They did not leave the party or even resign their jobs in protest. It was not merely a question of self-preservation, although it played a big part. They also believed that they could do more by staying inside than by moving out. They compromised and pretended, they did not speak the truth and took comfort when they managed not to lie. In the end their role in bringing down the system was probably greater than that of the dissidents. 'It is easy to condemn us. We had to go against our beliefs... but we are not ashamed of what we did. We saw our task in preventing the destruction of the shoots which came through after the 20th Congress. And our generation managed to achieve this. Otherwise Perestroika would not have been possible.'[45]

The generation of the children of the 20th Party Congress carried the curse of Oedipus: they came to vindicate their fathers' ideas and avoid the destruction of socialism, but they were the ones who ended up unknowingly slaying it with words rather than tanks.

'Words are Also Deeds' was the title of an essay drafted by one of Yegor's closest friends, Len Karpinsky, whose father had been Lenin's friend and copy editor, and who was named after Lenin.[46] It was read out by its author at a secret meeting held at Yegor's flat. Karpinsky suggested starting an underground political group and his essay was its manifesto. 'Our tanks in Prague were, if you will, an anachronism, an "inadequate" weapon,' he wrote. 'They "fired" at ideas. With no hope of hitting the target.'[47] Conversely, the only weapon which the educated class of Soviet intelligentsia should use against this bureaucracy that monopolized power under the slogans of socialism, Karpinsky argued, was words and ideas. A bureaucratic system would not withstand the spread of facts and ideas, he concluded. Ironically, the ideologues of the Soviet bureaucracy had arrived at precisely the same conclusion, recognizing the risks of opening up the media during the Prague Spring.

As Mikhail Suslov, the shrewd and feared ideologue and guardian of the regime, said in August 1968, 'It is known that the time gap between the abolition of censorship in Czechoslovakia and the sending of the Soviet tanks [there] was only a few months. I want to know: if we passed [a similar] law, who will send the tanks to us?'[48] Instead of abolishing censorship, they introduced jail sentences for spreading thoughts that blackened the Soviet regime. Yet, as Karpinsky wrote, this could barely stop a process that had already begun within the party itself. 'The new times are percolating into the apparatus and forming a layer of party intellectuals within it. To be sure, this layer is thin and disconnected; it is constantly eroded by co-optation and is thickly interlaced with careerists, flatterers, loudmouths... But this layer could move toward an alliance with the entire social body of the intelligentsia if favourable conditions arose.'[49] One day, Karpinsky predicted, 'our words can become their deeds'. In 1968 nobody knew how long the wait would be.

After 1968, time seemed to stop. While officially nobody revoked the decisions made by the 20th Congress, in practice they were frozen along with the very subject of Stalin's repressions. As Alexander Yakovlev wrote, the policies of those years amounted to a 'creeping rehabilitation of Stalin'.[50] The main political battles for the future of the country shifted from the corridors of the Kremlin to the pages of literary magazines. Tvardovsky's *Novy Mir*, which refused to endorse the invasion of Czechoslovakia and continued to defend the line of the 20th Congress, came under fierce attack from nationalists and Stalinists who gathered around two literary journals *Oktiabr* (*October*) and *Molodaya Gvardiya* (*Young Guards*). They lashed out at a devious intelligentsia corrupted by Western influence that posed a threat to the 'unique' Russian spirit and way of life. 'There is no greater threat to Russian people than the lure of a bourgeois welfare,' wrote *Molodaya Gvardiya*, advising the Kremlin to rely on a simple Russia peasant.[51]

The liberals close to *Novy Mir* deployed the language of Marxist internationalism and the equality of nations to fight back. But the attack on Tvardovsky was sanctioned by the KGB that had rightly sensed a connection between *Novy Mir* and the 'bourgeois' ideas of personal freedom both in thinking and in the economy. The illustrated weekly *Ogonyok* (*Little Flame*) – the bastion of collective party-mindedness – which was edited by Anatoly Sofronov, a cheerleader of a late 1940s hate campaign against 'rootless cosmopolitans' (a euphemism for Jews) and a master of conflictless comedies, joined in the attack on Tvardovsky by publishing a 'collective' letter by anti-Semitic hack writers dubbed as 'gunmen'.

Unable to quietly fire Tvardovsky, who was protected both by his fame and by his status as a candidate member of the Central Committee, the Kremlin forced him to resign by firing his key deputies. On 12 February 1970, the same day that Tvardovsky signed his resignation, he received a telephone call from the Central Committee informing him that he would continue to receive a generous salary, would remain attached to the 'special' Kremlin clinic and would be provided with 'special' Kremlin food supplies. In addition, his selected poems would be printed in a 'special' expensive-looking edition. 'So, instead of a journal which "reigned over the mind" – a Kremlin feeding, a 500 rouble sinecure and the perspective of a jubilee,'[52] Tvardovsky wrote in his diary.

The articles in the foreign press about his resignation reminded Tvardovsky of 'funeral bells'. Tvardovsky himself did not survive the violation of his magazine. The conflict between Tvardovsky, a decorated Soviet poet and candidate member of the Central Committee, and Tvardovsky, a national Russian poet, had become irreconcilable. National poets could not live on a Kremlin diet. The dissonance between the ideal of personal freedom and Communist ideology caused tremendous stress. Soon after losing *Novy Mir*, he was diagnosed with cancer and died less than a year later.

Dukhobor

The fight over *Novy Mir* pushed the conflict between Stalinists and liberals within the party into the open. One of the main protagonists in this fight was Alexander Yakovlev, a short, round-faced balding man with a limp, a potato nose and clever, smiling eyes under bushy eyebrows. He was formally in charge of the press and wrote both the parting *Pravda* leader about Khrushchev and the first greeting speech for Brezhnev, but did not participate in the most odious attacks on the dissidents. Yakovlev, who began his political career under Khrushchev, was the main opponent (and target) of the nationalists and Stalinists in the Central Committee.

When Tvardovsky fell, Yakovlev struck back. In internal memos for the Central Committee, he identified Russian nationalism and chauvinism as the greatest threats faced by the country. He used all his weight and bureaucratic dexterity to get the editor of *Molodaya Gvardiya* fired. In 1972 he published an article in *Literaturnaya gazeta* with the headline 'AGAINST ANTI-HISTORICISM'. Splashed across two full pages it was a head-on attack on the Russian nationalists, anti-Westerners and anti-Semites who constituted an informal group within the higher echelons of the Communist Party.[53]

Yakovlev's article was couched in Soviet phraseology and accused the nationalists of deviating from the Marxist-Leninist principle that states the superiority of class over ethnicity. The old patriarchal ways of life, which the nationalists eulogized, stood in the way of socialist progress and split the unity of Soviet society, Yakovlev wrote.

None of this coaching could conceal the seriousness of the target which Yakovlev had chosen. 'You know that they will probably fire you for this article,' the editor of *Literaturnaya gazeta* told Yakovlev. 'I don't, but I can't rule it out,' Yakovlev replied.[54] The stakes were high. Yakovlev recognized the dangers of Russia's own home-grown fascism emerging from the alliance between nationalists and Stalinists. Stalin, who had swapped the ideas of internationalism, proclaimed by the Bolsheviks, for the resurrection of the empire, exploited nationalism and the Orthodox Church during the Second World War, invoking the spirit of its warrior saints, such as Alexander Nevsky. At a Kremlin victory reception held for the generals in 1945, Stalin had raised a toast to the Russians as the 'elder brother' of all Soviet nations. 'I should like to propose a toast to the health of our Soviet people... and above all the Russian people... the most outstanding nation of all the nations comprising the Soviet Union.' Soon Stalin launched his campaign against all things foreign and against 'rootless Cosmopolitans'.

Anti-Semitism, which was rife among the White Army emigrants, was reimported into the Soviet Union from Germany after the Second World War and served as a common ground between Stalinists and nationalists: both saw Jews as agents of Western influence and enemies of the traditional Russian faith and the Russian state. Although nationalists rejected communist ideology, they considered the Soviet regime and its Iron Curtain as some protection against the spread of liberalism into Russia which they saw as an even greater threat.

As a German SS officer explains to an Old Bolshevik in Vasily Grossman's *Life and Fate* – a novel which openly drew parallels between Stalinism and fascism:

> When we look one another in the face, we're neither of us just looking at a face we hate – no, we are gazing into a mirror. That's the tragedy of our age... Today you're appalled by our hatred of the Jews. Tomorrow you may make use of our experience yourselves... You know, as well as we do, that nationalism is the greatest force of our century. Nationalism is the soul of the epoch. Nationalism is the soul of the era.[55]

Yakovlev was almost certainly familiar with *Life and Fate*. Grossman finished the novel in 1959 and submitted it to one of the literary magazines. The KGB instantly raided his apartment, seizing all copies, notebooks and even the ribbon from his typewriter. The book, however, was read by members of the Politburo and in Suslov's department for ideology where Yakovlev served. But Yakovlev's resentment of Stalinism and fascism was not acquired from books; instead it was engendered by his own life and fate.

He was born in 1924 into a peasant family in a village near the ancient city of Yaroslavl'. In his appearance and in the broad vowels of his Volga-region accent, he retained the features of the Russian peasantry – its wiliness, dignity and respect for toil. Six years older than Gorbachev, he belonged to a different generation; he was already six when Stalin's collectivization began. He remembered the arrest of a village groom for harming socialist property (he had tied up horses too tightly at night) and of his school teacher for displaying a disrespectful attitude to the party leaders (in fact, it was the opposite: the teacher had torn a photograph of Stalin out of a newspaper that was to be used for toilet paper and out of respect pinned it to the wall in an outhouse).

Yakovlev's own father nearly disappeared into Stalin's grinder but was saved by a man called Novikov, with whom he had served in the Red Army and who by chance was appointed the village's district military commissar.

Yakovlev finished school in the spring of 1941, a few weeks before Nazi Germany attacked the Soviet Union, and was conscripted on 6 August. An eighteen-year-old lieutenant in the Baltic Marines 6th Brigade, he led an attack on a battlefield outside Leningrad. He remembered the bodies of young soldiers left in the frozen snow-covered swamps and resurfacing in the thaw. 'They were dead but did not know this.'[56] He nearly ended up as one such body himself with three bullets in the leg and one near the heart. Four of his comrades carried him from the field – three of them were shot dead. Yakovlev was taken by horse-drawn cart – the broken bones of his legs rubbing against each other and rendering him unconscious – into a field hospital, then by plane to another one. A doctor from Armenia saved his leg, though Yakovlev had a limp to the end of his life.

After the war, Yakovlev studied history and steadily climbed the career ladder as a party official. He spent a year at Columbia University in 1959 as one of the first Fulbright scholars sent by the Soviet Union to America to study American propaganda. He was supervised by David Truman, Columbia's political science professor, and attended lectures by George Kennan, the master of Cold War diplomacy. One impression Yakovlev brought back was the gap between propaganda and real life – be it Russian or American. His personal experience and his own mind proved stronger than the Soviet ideology that he was put in charge of; he never lost his peasant sensibility, just as he never lost his vowel-singing accent.

The fact that Yakovlev's first serious political battle was over Tvardovsky and *Novy Mir* was not accidental. In many ways, Yakovlev was Tvardovsky's character. A positive variant of a national type if ever there was one, a man who had nearly lost his life in the war, he hated nationalism and anti-Semitism with every fibre of his soul. The Stalinists recognized Yakovlev's article in 1972 for what it was – a declaration of war. Sofronov, the editor of *Ogonyok*, got Mikhail Sholokhov, a celebrated Soviet writer and the winner of the Nobel Prize for Literature, to write a letter to the Central Committee attacking Yakovlev.

Brezhnev did not like the article either – not because he shared the ideas of the opposite camp, but because he resented confrontation within the party. He was neither a nationalist nor a liberal and so he decided to rid himself of both groups in order to rule in peace. Shelepin's henchmen, who constituted the informal 'Russian Party' and attacked Tvardovsky, lost their administrative positions, but so did Yakovlev who was dispatched overseas, as ambassador to Canada.

Yakovlev picked Canada himself and this choice was not, perhaps, completely accidental, even if it was not fully conscious either. Canada was where Russian Dukhobors or 'Spirit Wrestlers' – a religious pacifist sect – had settled at the turn of the twentieth century with Tolstoy's help. While in Canada, Yakovlev went to stay in one of their settlements. 'Incredible people – hardworking, open, caring,' Yakovlev recalled.[57] He was struck by the fact that Russian people who had settled on the other side of the globe at the end of the previous century had kept the language and traditions of the country they had left behind. It would be fanciful to suggest that Yakovlev was impregnated with their ideas, but he could hardly help drawing parallels between them and his own plight as someone who had split off from the main church.

In his concise memoirs, several pages are dedicated to the Dukhobors' ethics, their dignity, their aspiration towards perfection, their belief in the superiority of human beings, their humility. This passage in his memoirs is immediately followed by one in which Yakovlev describes the sense of deep, burning shame he felt for Soviet policy which he had to represent and defend. 'Almost every year I had to explain about those who had been thrown out of the country for "anti-Soviet" propaganda. And lowering my eyes I had to lie or change the subject. It was shameful to explain the reasons for our invasion of Afghanistan and to read and distribute the material sent from Moscow about Solzhenitsyn, Shcharansky, Rostropovich...'[58]

The same year as Alexander Yakovlev was 'exiled' to Canada, Yegor Yakovlev and Latsis were packed off to Prague to a journal called *Problemy mira i sotsializma* (*Problems of Peace and Socialism*) – an heir to the Third International, also known as Comintern, which was an international communist organization that existed from 1919 until 1943. The most important result of the years spent in comfortable exile was that it offered time for thinking.

Time for Reflection

'Dear compatriots, dear comrades, friends! The last minutes of 1970 are passing by. The Soviet people see it off with a feeling of completed duty and in good mood... It was an unforgettable year of new victories and achievement... Everywhere on Soviet land – from the Baltic to the Pacific Ocean, from the Northern Sea to the Caucasus Mountains, the passing year has left a kind mark.' With this speech, Leonid Brezhnev, the general secretary of the Communist Party, the Soviet commander-in-chief, greeted the country on New Year's Eve 1970.

His speech ushered in a decade of 'developed socialism', otherwise known as *zastoi* (stagnation), a period in which the volume of empty words and slogans about economic achievements was matched only by the number of jokes about them. As one of the jokes went, it was a period when 'the difficulty of growth turned into the growth of difficulties'. Every New Year's Eve from 1970 until 1982, when Brezhnev died, Soviet citizens would hear him address the nation, hailing its achievements and victories. Void of meaning, these addresses were merely a prompt for popping the corks from bottles of oxymoronic 'Soviet Champagne'. With time, the words got more slurred and the meat in Russian salads got more sparse.

Political seasons moved against the laws of nature. Khrushchev's Thaw was followed not by spring but by winter. News and current affairs were replaced by the celebration of historic jubilees. The frosts were not nearly as severe as they had been, but they were substantial enough to grip the surface. The people and words which had populated the pages of *Novy Mir* were forced underground, into samizdat.

The regime, guarded by Mikhail Suslov, the ideology secretary, preserved a bleakly cynical system of reward and punishment: reward, often in the form of foreign trips; punishment in the form of the withdrawal of publication or performance rights. For those who strayed far – often defined as trafficking with the West in the form of interviews with foreign journalists or publication there – there was exile or, in the worst cases, a psychiatric ward or jail. The strayers included Alexander Solzhenitsyn, Andrei Sinyavsky, Joseph Brodsky and Vladimir Bukovsky. The stayers, including Yegor Yakovlev, Latsis and Bovin, worked the system – stretching it here, being cramped by it there.

In 1974, after *Gulag Archipelago* was published in France, Solzhenitsyn was stripped of Soviet citizenship and expelled from the country. As a parting shot, Solzhenitsyn wrote a letter to the Soviet intelligentsia which he called 'Live Not by Lies'. It was a mixture of a scathing reprimand and a sermon. It ended with a commandment in capital letters: 'DON'T LIE! DON'T PARTICIPATE IN LIES, DON'T SUPPORT A LIE!' 'In our country', he wrote, 'the daily lie is not the whim of corrupt nature, but a mode of existence, a condition of the daily welfare of every man. In our country, the lie has been incorporated into the state system as the vital link holding everything together, with billions of tiny fasteners, several dozens to each man.'[59]

Solzhenitsyn appealed to the personal dignity and individual consciousness of the intelligentsia – not to the Soviet social class that implied higher education and loyalty to the regime which he despised. 'The intelligentsia as a vast social stratum has ended its days in a steaming swamp and can no longer become airborne again,' he wrote. Solzhenitsyn described them by an ugly and derogative term: *obrazovanshchina* or 'educatedness'.

His main charge was that the intelligentsia had failed in its most vital task – to speak on behalf of the people suppressed by an authoritarian state. Members of the intelligentsia had become part of the system, allowing themselves to get comfortable in its folds, nooks and crannies. 'A hundred years ago,' he wrote in 1974, 'the Russian intelligentsia considered a death sentence to be a sacrifice. Today an administrative reprimand is considered a sacrifice.' The educatedness had little in common with the nineteenth-century thinkers who had been wiped out by the revolution and Stalinist repressions.[60]

At the core of the Soviet intelligentsia, as Stalin conceived it, were the scientists, physicists particularly, who were bred and cultivated by the system with the particular military purpose of producing the nuclear bomb and strengthening the country's military and industrial complex. The conditions created for the scientists were close to ideal: they had status, money, equipment and no distractions. Beria, who oversaw the nuclear project, realized that apart from physical conditions, they also needed a degree of freedom to stimulate their creativity.

Russian nuclear physicists were settled in closed or semi-closed scientific towns, and were often provided with dachas, or country cottages, amid forests. The scientific colonies were well supplied not only with food but also with culture. The political clout that scientists possessed allowed them to invite artists who were barred from giving official concerts. As Andrei Zorin, a Russian cultural historian, argued, Soviet military needs led to an overproduction of all kinds of scientists, matched by a hyper-production of culture. The consumers of this culture were the millions of engineers and scientists who worked in research institutes and construction offices with a postbox number for an address. Throughout the 1970s the size and the economic weight of the intelligentsia increased manifold. The number of people with a higher education doubled from the early 1960s to the mid-1980s to 20 million people. The share of specialists employed in the economy had more than tripled from 9 million to 33 million people.

Solzhenitsyn's essay was partly a response to Andrei Amalrik, a historian by background and a dissident by conviction, whose essay *Will the Soviet Union Survive Until 1984?* had been published a few years earlier. Like Solzhenitsyn, Amalrik refused to define the intelligentsia in spiritual or ethical terms and described it as a social stratum, a Soviet version of 'the middle class':

> Its members have gained for themselves and their families a standard of living that is relatively high by Soviet standards – regular good food, attractive clothes, nicely furnished co-operative apartments, sometimes even a car and, of course, available entertainment. They pursue professions that assure them a position of respect in society... This group includes people in liberal professions, such as writers or actors, those occupied in academic or academic-administrative work, the managerial group in the economic field and so on.[61]

In the 1970s this urban social stratum became conscious of its own unity; it began to acquire both the physical and the cultural attributes of a European middle class. People started to holiday in the Baltic republics – the Soviet equivalent of the West. In 1970 the Soviet Union bought an old Fiat factory to produce the first middle-class car – the Lada. Over the following two decades car ownership in the Soviet Union went up tenfold. Thanks to the rising oil price, in the 1970s the Soviet people were getting better off. The ownership of flats and houses also increased. Like the middle class anywhere it required certain freedoms, but like any other middle class, it was also risk-averse. In reality, the Soviet economy could not accommodate them all: as the Soviet joke had it, they 'pretended to work and the state pretended to pay'. The large number of educated, intelligent and underemployed people in their thirties and forties with little prospect of moving up the career ladder provided a perfect milieu for brewing liberal ideas. With time, they formed a political class. They were not dissidents and they relied on the state for provisions, but they were fed up with the restrictions imposed by Soviet ideology and they were critical of the system. As Zorin has noted, it was a familiar pattern: the state first creates an educated class, which then gets emancipated and starts undermining the state, which finally collapses and it gets buried under its rubble.

For all its political nastiness, the 1970s was also a golden era for the Soviet intelligentsia – a period of accumulation of knowledge and cultural experience. It produced a cultural layer that sustained the nation for years to come. Real life was happening on stage, on the screen, in libraries, while pretence, boredom and falsehood dominated reality. For those who dealt in reality – as journalists were supposed to – the 1970s were the least productive years.

Unable to write about current life, they turned to history. Latsis used the time in Prague to write a book, preparing for a new opening by accumulating knowledge and ideas. He sought to answer the question that possessed his generation: how had the revolution, which promised universal happiness, turned into universal misery? When and how had it gone wrong? Were there alternatives?

He went back to 1929 – a year which Stalin had called a 'great break' (wrongly translated in English as a Great Leap Forward) which marked the end of Lenin's New Economic Policy and the start of the forced collectivization (or elimination, to be precise) of peasantry. He saw a holy grail in the ideas of Nikolai Bukharin. A charismatic Bolshevik leader executed by Stalin, Bukharin in the late 1920s called on peasants 'to enrich' themselves, defended competition between private and state enterprises, and argued that the market was a necessary step towards socialism.

Bukharin provided a point in history which beckoned liberal communists like Latsis with the unexplored, and therefore highly tempting, prospect of correcting the socialist course. Thirty-five years after his execution, Bukharin's name was still anathema to Soviet ideologists and Latsis's secret manuscript, seized by the KGB, landed him in trouble. But while Latsis, more academic by nature, found some satisfaction in his intellectual work, Yegor, more energetic and less reflective, felt bored and restless. Work in Prague gave him little satisfaction. 'He would come home, have supper and go to bed at 9 p.m. He just wanted each day to go quicker,' his wife recalled.[62]

Upon his return from Prague, Yegor went back to *Izvestia* but was advised to 'write less'. Instead he turned to a subject that was hard to ban: Lenin. By the 1970s the official Soviet iconography had produced a Lenin who was completely devoid of any human or even historic features. He had turned into a vehicle, a device for carrying almost any political message. Citations from Lenin could be used to prove diametrically opposite points of view. In the 1930s, Lenin justified Stalinism, in the 1950s and early 1960s he justified anti-Stalinism. In the 1970s he was adopted by the liberal thinkers to show the inadequacies of the Soviet economic and political system.

To make the device workable and convincing, their Lenin had to be distinctly different from the official mummified version. Yegor was among those who used his talent to 'enliven' Lenin's image, or as Solzhenitsyn put it more crudely, 'sucked surreptitiously on one solace that "the ideas of revolution were good, but were perverted"'. As Yegor said himself: 'I only needed Lenin for one thing: to show that the system in which we live has nothing to do with Lenin.'[63] In fact, these intellectual games were dangerous and costly – not only to those who played them, but to the country's future. They created a mythology about Lenin that lasted almost to the end of Soviet rule and held the country captive to an idea that had long been dead.

—

In the early 1980s few people thought that change would come any time soon. Time moved at a sticky pace, unaffected by the physical deaths of the country's leaders. When Brezhnev died in 1982, he was succeeded by Yuri Andropov who lived for only eighteen months longer, and then by Konstantin Chernenko who, as the joke went, 'gained office without gaining consciousness'. Soon he too was dead, on 10 March 1985. The rapid succession of general secretaries became known as 'the hearse race'. It seemed it would never end.

The biggest frustration for people like Latsis, Bovin and Yakovlev during those years was not the food shortages or discomforts – their personal lives were perfectly comfortable – but the futility of their own work. By the time Brezhnev died they were in their early fifties. Born for an active life, they felt their energy seeping into the sand. They engaged in meaningless imitations of intellectual activity. This was both exhausting and humiliating, causing anguish and pain similar to that of Chekhov's characters.

Latsis described this anguish in his memoirs. He was working on some useless document in one of the government sanatoria which offered the dubious comforts and petty luxury of Soviet bureaucratic life – better food, a large room with a television set, and a supply of fruit in a crystal bowl – when his thoughts started to wander. He gazed at important-looking people faking intellectual process, and his thoughts turned to his fourteen-year-old daughter who was ill. He was locked in the sanatorium, while she had been in intensive care; Latsis had no time to visit. 'Suddenly came a thought which I had been trying to drive away for several years. There, at home, unfolds real life and a real drama: a person who is dear to me is suffering and fighting for her life. And I am sitting in the company of apparatchiks, who are engaged in useless talking, imitating their concern about important state affairs. Here nothing is real…' Unable to bear it any longer, he snapped: 'Nobody needs our work and I don't want to take part in it any more.'[64] His outburst resembled that of Chekhov's Uncle Vanya who rebels against the professor, whose meaningless articles he had been copying out for years: 'I am clever and brave and strong. If I had lived a normal life, I might have become another Schopenhauer or Dostoevsky. I am losing my head! I am going crazy!'

Uncle Vanya was the play at the Moscow Art Theatre that the still little-known Mikhail Gorbachev went to see on 30 April 1985, the eve of May Day, a month after his appointment as general secretary of the Communist Party. A few days later he telephoned Oleg Yefremov, the director, to share his impressions. He liked Astrov, the doctor, but it was Vanya's part that he found 'simply heart-rending'. He also told Yefremov that it was time to 'get our flywheel moving again'. In 1998, seven years after Gorbachev had ceased to be the president of the USSR and the country itself was gone, he described why that performance of *Uncle Vanya* had made such an impression on him: 'I understood a lot while watching it. I realized that we, the whole of society, were seriously ill and that we needed immediate surgery.'[65]

TWO

New Beginning or Dead End

March is the hardest month in Russia. The snow which has been on the ground since November turns grey and slushy. The temperatures stay sub-zero, the winds pick up, making the country's landscape look particularly desolate and hostile. The cold air, the lack of sunlight and the stubborn snowfall drain the body and the soul. The lack of fresh fruit and vegetables in Soviet days meant that people were starved of vitamins. The knowledge that somewhere – a flight away – birds are singing and spring flowers are blossoming makes the early Russian spring particularly depressing. This is how the country felt when Konstantin Chernenko died on 10 March 1985. Only that winter had lasted for nearly eighteen years. The next day Gorbachev was appointed the general secretary of the Communist Party.

Two months later, the country got a chance to have a good look at its new leader with his birthmark across his forehead. Gorbachev's first trip to Leningrad – the cradle of the Bolshevik Revolution – occupied almost all of the state television news programme *Vremya*. It started in the usual staged and stale way: Soviet bureaucrats in grey suits meeting the general secretary off the plane, brightly dressed young pioneers saluting him on the tarmac, Gorbachev laying wreaths of flowers by a war memorial. But suddenly something changed in the picture: the new party boss walked briskly up to a crowd of onlookers and started talking to them. He smiled and told people about his plans to revive the economy and improve standards of living. Stunned by this impromptu engagement with the crowd, one woman uttered a Soviet cliché: 'Stay close to the people and the people won't let you down.' Gorbachev, barely able to stretch his arms in the crowd, quipped: 'Can't get any closer.' The crowd broke into laughter – not staged, but genuine.

After watching the 'hearse race' of gerontocratic general secretaries over the previous three years, such a display of human emotions by a relatively young, energetic, smiling leader won over the country. 'We will all have to change,' Gorbachev said in Leningrad. Long speeches about Perestroika came later, but it started there and then – in front of the television cameras. The first signs of freedom came not in the form of laws and manifestos, but in the form of sensations and impressions. It felt like a new start, the country slowly opening up, letting in fresh air from the West in the form of films, exhibitions, theatre productions. It was a period of 'new thinking' as Gorbachev defined it. Yet the thinking behind it was not very new.

In fact, one of the sensations of that period was that of déjà vu; one of the joys, the joy of recognition. Summing up his impressions of the theatrical season of 1985–6, Anatoly Smeliansky, the literary director of the Moscow Art Theatre and a theatre critic, wrote what many felt: 'Something has changed in the literary climate. You open another issue of a thick literary journal, which you did not even feel like leafing through for the past few years, and you get glued. It is as if time has rewound its tape by some twenty years and has taken us back to the epoch of Alexander Tvardovsky's *Novy Mir*.'[1]

The energy of the mid-1980s and the sense of renewal were sustained by the release of a vast body of art and literature which had been created over the previous seventy years and kept under lock and key. It was an archival revolution: the previously banned works of Boris Pasternak, Vasily Grossman and Anna Akhmatova were published over a period of some four or five years in literary journals whose circulation soared to the levels of Western tabloid newspapers. By the late 1980s, the sales of *Novy Mir*, which published *Doctor Zhivago* and *Gulag Archipelago* for the first time in the Soviet Union, reached nearly 3 million copies.

The ideas and ideals of Tvardovsky filled the air of the 1980s. In 1987 two literary journals published an anti-Stalinist poem which he had written in the late 1960s entitled 'By Right of Memory'. In a tribute to the poem and to link the two eras, Yuri Burtin, a literary critic and a former *Novy Mir* editor, wrote an essay which he called 'To You, from Another Generation', tracing the spiritual roots of Perestroika to Tvardovsky's journal.

As Burtin wrote, Tvardovsky and his circle had formed a socialist opposition that derived its legitimacy from the presumption that socialism was open to democracy and did not have to resort to violence. 'The idea was so strong that even today we live by it in our hopes for Perestroika. There is no other idea.'[2] In the 1980s that 'opposition' came to power – not through an election but through a generational shift. Their lifelong dream – 'if only I was in charge' – became a reality. It was only natural that this 'opposition' tapped into the pool of ideas that had formed them in the first place.

They started from the point at which they considered the country to have gone wrong – August 1968. Perestroika was carried out under the slogans of the Prague Spring: socialism with a human face. Its declared goal was a revival of Lenin's principles distorted first by Stalinism and then by eighteen years of Brezhnev's stagnation. It was an aspiration which Gorbachev's generation had harboured since Khrushchev's Thaw and which was quashed by Soviet tanks in Prague. Gorbachev was picking up from the point where Alexander Dubček had left off in 1968.

The violent abortion of the Prague reforms had a crucial and unforeseen consequence which became clear only twenty years later: it created a powerful myth that had it not been for the Soviet intervention, the Prague reforms would have succeeded, that 'socialism with a human face' was compatible with democracy and could be achieved. In fact, this was a utopia, a no-place. Had the reforms in the Czechoslovakia been allowed to proceed, there is every likelihood that they would have ended with Czechoslovakia's becoming a normal Western-style capitalist country. By prematurely ending the experiment, the Soviet government turned the Czech reforms into an alluring and evasive goal which Perestroika reformers tried to pursue twenty years later.

Gorbachev had had a personal experience of the Prague Spring. One of his closest friends at university in Moscow was Zdeněk Mlynář, Dubček's right-hand man. In 1967 Mlynář had visited Gorbachev in his native Stavropol region where he worked as party secretary and the two discussed the reforms in Czechoslovakia. When the Soviet tanks invaded Prague in 1968, Mlynář was brought to Moscow in handcuffs, along with Dubček himself, for a meeting with Brezhnev.

A year after the Soviet invasion, Gorbachev went to Prague as part of the Komsomol (the Young Communist Party League) to build bridges with Czech youth. He did not see Mlynář, who by then had retreated and worked in a museum – that would have been political suicide. But he saw anti-Soviet slogans and hostile workers who refused to talk to the Russian visitors. It was an uncomfortable trip. 'I understood that there was something in our country that was not right,' Gorbachev told Mlynář during one of their later conversations.[3] Now he had a chance to put it right. The spring air of 1985 was filled with enormous optimism and hope. It seemed so simple: shift the heavy tombstone of Soviet bureaucracy and the nation would spring back to life with force and vitality. In the minds of Gorbachev's reformers, socialism was the best system for releasing the creative potential of the people.

Perestroika reformers were obsessed with the idea of history as a tape that could be rewound to the point where the country took a wrong turn. In 1986, they called the country back to 1968 and even further back to Lenin's New Economic Policy. In search of healthy economic forces, they turned to farmers and small-time entrepreneurs. Writer Anatoly Strelyany made a documentary about a smart, hard-working Russian man called Nikolai Sivkov who lived in a remote part of Archangel Region, on the northern edge of Russia, 'in a Kingdom far, far away...'. Strelyany unhurriedly narrated the story of a model Russian farmer who survived the collectivization of land and spirit. His common sense, quick brain and able hands retained the muscle memory of hard work. He was a modern-day Ivan Denisovich who still carried the gene of the Russian peasantry. 'There must be [other] Sivkovs. It can't be that there are not any. There are, there are Sivkovs,' Strelyany almost chanted at the end of the film.

But the miracle of revival did not happen. History could not be wound back. Sivkov was a rare sample of a nearly extinct breed eliminated through collectivization and subsequent negative selection. The likes of Sivkov may still have existed in the late 1950s but his type was almost gone by the mid-1980s. As Gorbachev himself admitted a couple of years after the launch of reforms, 'There is something that prevents us from moving forward... We have passed more than 60 decrees on agriculture since April 1985. But people don't believe in these decrees.' The problem was not the decrees but the shortage of people who could respond to them. The roots suppressed by the tombstone of the socialist economy atrophied. In their obsessive striving to rewind the tape of history, the reformers followed the logic of the Sleeping Beauty. It was as though the country, which went into a slumber in the 1960s, could wake up fresh and strong twenty years later. There is a second part to Charles Perrault's fairy tale, which is rarely included in children's books. In it the Prince's mother turns out to be a cannibal and orders that the children of the Prince and Sleeping Beauty be cooked for her dinner. (Luckily, they are spared by the cook and saved by the Prince.)

Gorbachev formally launched Perestroika in February 1986, at the 27th Congress of the Communist Party – thirty years to the day after Khrushchev's secret speech at the 20th Congress in 1956. In the years that had passed since Khrushchev's Thaw, the country had not become cannibalistic, but it was in bad shape: exhausted, demoralized, economically crippled and, most important of all, drained of its human resources.

Perhaps one person who understood that the system had to be carefully defused and dismantled before it blew up itself and the world was Alexander Yakovlev, whom Gorbachev had appointed in charge of ideology and propaganda. Unlike Gorbachev, Yakovlev had few illusions about the critical state of the system and its ability to transform into something humane without drastically changing its foundation.

Gorbachev first met Yakovlev in 1983, two years before taking office, during his visit to Canada where Yakovlev was still ambassador. They had instantly struck a chord and spent hours talking about the state of the country. A common understanding which underlined their conversation was that the country simply could not go on in the same way any more. Things had to change. The question was how.

This was the eleventh year of Yakovlev's honorary 'exile' in Canada and he had had ample time to dwell on this subject. Unlike the *shestidesiatniki*, who tried to find support in the ideas of Lenin and Bukharin, Alexander Yakovlev began to review the very foundation on which the system rested: Marxism and Leninism. In particular he questioned one of the key postulates of Marx's materialism – that being determines consciousness. Does it mean, Yakovlev asked himself, that the way people live and relate to each other is simply the result of their material conditions rather than their will?

The essence of a man cannot be derived from his profession or way of life (what difference did it make that Jesus was a carpenter?) but only from his consciousness. The same was true of nations. 'Consciousness determines being to a much greater extent than the other way around,' Yakovlev concluded. 'From my point of view, the source of everything, including progress, is information... Information is primary, the matter and spirit are secondary... Without a human brain – this perfect synthesizer of information – neither an atomic nor a hydrogen bomb could go off...'[4]

The only way to change the Soviet way of life was through opening up the flow of information and altering people's consciousness. The 'means of mass information' – as the media were and still are called in Russia – were far more important in altering the country than the means of production. Glasnost – the opening-up of the media – was in large part the practical result of that idea.

In December 1985, a few months after his appointment, Yakovlev drafted a memo that was more radical in its views than anything that was to follow over the next few years. 'The dogmatic interpretation of Marxism and Leninism is so unhygienic that it kills any creative and even classical thoughts. Lucifer remains a Lucifer: his satanic hoof stamps out any fresh intellectual shoots... Marxism is nothing but a neo-religion, subjected to the interests and whims of the absolute power... Political conclusions of Marxism are unacceptable for civilization.'[5] Thus wrote the man in charge of Soviet ideology.

Yakovlev also believed that the country needed a free market and private ownership to overcome its economic sclerosis. 'Socialism without a market is a utopia and a bloody one at that...' Society needed a normal exchange of information, which was possible only in a democracy. Yakovlev defined the ingredients of Perestroika as a market economy, private ownership, democracy and openness:

> Civil life is poisoned by lies. Presumption of guilt is a guiding principle. Two hundred thousand different instructions tell a person that he is a potential villain. One has to prove integrity with references and certificates. Conformism is seen as a sign of trustworthiness. Socialism has cut itself off from a way forward and started moving backwards towards feudalism and in some places... descended into slavery... For thousands of years we have been ruled by people and not by laws... What we are talking about is not the dismantling of Stalinism, but a replacement of a thousand-year old model of statehood.[6]

Yakovlev did not show this memo to Gorbachev fearing that it would be too radical for his tastes. True to the principle of 'divide and rule', Gorbachev had split in two the job once held by Suslov, the Stalinist guardian of Soviet ideology, and Yakovlev's position was complicated by the fact that he had only half of it and the other half was held by Yegor Ligachev, his ideological opponent. Although formally the two halves were equal, with Yakovlev controlling the workings of the media and propaganda, Ligachev was a secretary of the Central Committee and oversaw ideology. Moreover, Ligachev was a watchdog, one of the most senior people in the party, and he physically occupied Suslov's office, which, in the Byzantine topography of the Kremlin, signalled superiority.

Wary of spooking Gorbachev and raising alarm within the party nomenclatura, Yakovlev had to tread carefully. As Yakovlev himself wrote, he often had to act like a 'secret agent', resorting to tricks and covert operations to advance his ideas. Here was a paradox: in pursuit of truth, people still had to resort to lies.

One of the 'covert' operations performed by Yakovlev was the release of the most powerful and honest film about the Stalinist legacy – *Pokaianie* (*Repentance*). It was a work by a Georgian director, Tengiz Abuladze, and was made a year before Perestroika, in 1984, under the patronage of Eduard Shevardnadze, one of Gorbachev's closest allies, who headed Georgia at the time. Made like a philosophical fable and set in a small Georgian town, the film starts with a scene of a woman making cakes. A man in a rocking chair reads from a newspaper that the town's mayor Varlam Aravidze has died.

The day after Aravidze's funeral, his corpse turns up in the garden of his relatives' house. The body is reburied, but next day springs up again in the same place, propped up in a garden chair. Aravidze's grandson hounds and shoots 'the corpse digger', who turns out to be Keti, the cake-maker. Put on trial, she tells the court that Aravidze has no right to be buried and, through cinematic flashbacks, narrates the story of his repressions, including the murder of her parents. (One such flashback shows Keti, as a young girl, searching for her father's name in a log pile of timber produced by Gulag prisoners. While she looks, the logs are being ground into sawdust which she sieves through her fingers.)

Aravidze's son, Abel, defends his father and tries to get Keti declared insane. At the end, his own son commits suicide and Abel himself digs up Aravidze's body and throws it off a cliff. The film ends as it begins – with Keti preparing a cake. An old woman, played by a legendary Georgian actress, the eighty-six-year-old Veriko Andzhaparidze, asks Keti at the window whether this is the road that leads to the temple. The woman replies that the road is Varlam Aravidze's street and will not lead to the temple. The old woman replies: 'What good is a road if it doesn't lead to a temple?'

In the highly politicized atmosphere of the mid-1980s, with little time for reflection, Abuladze's philosophical film was too often used for a quick political commentary; pulled into quotes and soundbites. It was like using a telescope as a sledgehammer. *Pokaianie* was not about a distortion of the system, but about the universal nature of evil which can take any shape. The name Aravidze in Georgian means 'nobody' and 'everybody' and the mayor, dressed in a Stalin-like military tunic, had Hitler's moustache, Beria's rimless glasses and Mussolini's operatic manner.

Yakovlev, who watched the tape at home, felt overwhelmed by the film. 'It was merciless and convincing. It smashed the system of lies, hypocrisy and violence like a sledgehammer... I had to do everything in my power to get the film out.'[7] (He argued to the Central Committee that the film was too complex to be understood by a broad audience, so there would be no harm in showing it 'once or twice', while ordering the official Committee for Cinema to produce hundreds of copies to be shown throughout the country.) The release of the film was scheduled for April 1986, but had to be put off because of the disaster that struck the country.

—

In the early hours of 26 April 1986, nuclear reactor no. 4 at the Chernobyl nuclear station suffered a massive power surge, resulting in a fire and the release of 400 times more radioactive material than the atomic bomb dropped on Hiroshima. The reactor had been built in the 1970s with severe safety breaches. The only reason it passed an examination by foreign experts was that, prior to inspection, its engineers had temporarily replaced Soviet electronics with Swedish and American ones. As Filipp Bobkov, first deputy chief of the KGB, told members of the Politburo a couple of months later, it embodied the carelessness, arrogance and window-dressing that were the essence of the Soviet planned system which commanded people to fulfil a plan at all costs, including the safety of people. As often was the case with such disasters, the cover-up was even more deplorable than the initial errors that led to the explosion. Despite the Politburo's call to 'provide honest and measured information', the officials acted on their inbred instincts.

The main goal of the official media has traditionally been not to reveal, but to conceal the facts. When, in 1962, an uprising by workers in Novocherkassk, an industrial town in the south of Russia, was brutally put down by government forces, the media's role was *not* to report it. The bloodstained streets were repaved and amateur radio reports were jammed. Discerning readers deduced facts from what newspapers did not say rather than from what they did: omissions were more informative than inclusions. If the media said something did not happen, people understood it to mean the opposite. In later years television played the role of a universal plug that kept the facts from leaking out into the open.

The public was informed about the Chernobyl catastrophe only two days later with an announcement merely twenty seconds long in the evening news on the state television channel. 'There has been an accident at the Chernobyl Nuclear Power Plant. One of the nuclear reactors was damaged. The effects of the accident are being remedied. Assistance has been provided for any affected people. An investigative commission has been set up.' People in Moscow saw the announcement as a signal to tune to foreign radio stations which reported that a huge explosion had taken place and a radioactive cloud was moving westwards. But in the nearby town of Pripyat, children were playing football on the streets and sixteen weddings were held outdoors in the epicentre of the accident. Evacuation did not start until thirty-six hours after the catastrophe. On 1 May, while the communist bosses were evacuating their own families, hundreds of thousands of ordinary people attended a May Day parade in Kiev, where radiation levels were eighty times higher than normal. Many came with children in short-sleeved shirts. The lies were all the more pointless since the whole world was aware of what was going on.

Moskovskie novosti, a propaganda sheet, printed in a dozen languages, published an article headlined 'A POISONED CLOUD OF ANTI-SOVIETISM'. It listed foreign nuclear incidents and harangued the West for stirring anti-Soviet hysteria. 'Yes, we are talking about a premeditated and well-orchestrated campaign, the aim of which is to soil the political atmosphere in the East–West relationship and to use this poisoned cloud to cover up criminal acts of militarism by the USA and NATO against peace and security.'[8]

Politically, the cover-up had a more devastating effect on Gorbachev's reputation than the disaster itself. In the eyes of his two most important constituencies – the Soviet intelligentsia and the West – his pledge to openness and the supremacy of human values failed its first important test. As a transcript of an emergency Politburo meeting shows, Gorbachev himself had limited access to information, which made him furious: 'We had no information about what was going on. Everything was kept secret from the Central Committee. The whole system was penetrated by the spirit of boot-licking, persecution of dissidents, clannishness, window-dressing and nepotism. We will put an end to all this.'[9]

It was a catalyst for Glasnost – the opening-up of the media. 'Don't be afraid of your own people,' he told his comrades. 'Glasnost is the true socialism.'[10] Gorbachev neither planned nor imagined where the opening-up of the media would lead the country to five years later. He came to give the Soviet Union a new lease of life. But Chernobyl was a bad omen – and the 'new life' would turn out to be a short one.

The opening of the media was not as quick and sudden as many retrospectively remember it. Glasnost did not mean a removal of censorship and a sudden burst of the freedom of speech. Nor was it meant to be all-embracing. Glasnost was a limited licence issued to a select few who could target the social groups that were most perceptive to Perestroika – students, young professionals and the urban intelligentsia. The purpose of Glasnost, as Gorbachev understood it, was to inject vitality in socialism. The consequence of Glasnost as Yakovlev saw it was to change the country.

The main medium of Perestroika was print. Two publications were selected for this task of mobilizing the intelligentsia and promoting Perestroika to the world. One was *Ogonyok*, the odious colour weekly still edited by the old Stalinist playwright Anatoly Sofronov who had led the attack on Tvardovsky and Yakovlev. *Ogonyok*, which had a circulation of 1.5 million, had one obvious advantage: it was so reactionary and anti-Western that any shift to a more liberal and pro-Western position was immediately noticeable. Yakovlev offered the job of the editorship to Vitaly Korotich, a secondary poet from Kiev who had spoken out about the deliberate attempt by the head of the Chernobyl nuclear station to conceal any information from the outside world.

At the same time as Korotich's appointment to *Ogonyok*, Yegor Yakovlev was offered the editorship of *Moskovskie novosti* (*The Moscow News*), the propaganda tabloid meant for foreign consumption. It was the oldest

English-language newspaper in the Soviet Union and had been started in 1930 by an American socialist to spread the Soviet message to the world. By the 1980s it was published in all the main foreign languages and circulated mostly outside the Soviet Union. As part of the vast News Press Agency (APN) – a propaganda outfit closely linked to the KGB – it was mostly staffed with failed spooks, rogue mercenaries from Arab countries and KGB minders. Its Russian edition, which Yegor was asked to edit, was launched only in 1980 for the Moscow summer Olympics, to advertise Soviet achievements.

Now its task was to advertise and rally support for Perestroika in the West. Yegor was well aware of this task. A year after being appointed as the editor, during which the circulation soared, Yegor told the newspaper's local party committee: 'Jointly we have managed to create a newspaper which is read, cited and trusted. [Now] we have a publication which can be used for very important actions/projects in regard to international public opinion.'[11] Yegor did not mind being used, for it gave him a chance to use Perestroika and Gorbachev for his own ends. It was the moment for which Yegor and his peers had been waiting for eighteen years.

Moskovskie novosti did not adhere to a Western idea of a newspaper. Fact-based material was still forbidden. The news was not gathered by the newspaper but distributed through the Soviet telegraphic agency TASS. For example, one of the biggest news items of the first Perestroika years – the release of Andrei Sakharov from exile that was splashed across front pages of the international press – in *Moskovskie novosti* was given forty words at the bottom of page three – a space usually reserved for corrections.

The early Perestroika press was not about reporting, it was about opinion and essay-writing and each one of those pieces was a milestone by which people measured the changes in the country. The most popular page in the newspaper was called 'The Opinion of Three Authors', where three public figures – writers, academics, essayists – shared their views on some current topic.

Within a couple of years of Yegor becoming the editor, *Moskovskie novosti* was the most sought-after newspaper in the Soviet Union. It came out weekly and every Wednesday a long queue of people would start forming outside newspaper kiosks at about 5 a.m. to buy a fresh issue. The print run was still strictly regulated by the Communist Party and limited by the censors, so by 9 a.m. all copies were gone. Those lucky enough to have one in their possession passed the read issue to friends. The unlucky ones read it on billboards outside the newspaper's offices by the central Pushkin Square. The spot quickly turned into Moscow's equivalent of London's 'Speakers' Corner'. People did not come to *Moskovskie novosti* for news in the strictest sense of the word, but to get a sense of the direction in which the country was heading.

Reading through the thick tomes of bound issues of *Moskovskie novosti* twenty years later, it is hard to see what the fuss was about. Why would anyone want to get up at dawn on a cold December morning to queue for a newspaper that did not tell you much in the way of news but wrote about Anna Akhmatova? But at the time every issue of *Moskovskie novosti* was a political event. What *Moskovskie novosti* wrote about was not new – it had long been the subject of private discussions around kitchen tables. 'New' was the fact that the same things could now be printed in a newspaper under someone's byline, that some of the things that had been banished into the world of samizdat were now published material. The very existence of such a paper was the biggest news of all.

A joke started circulating in Moscow:

One friend telephones another:

'Have you read the latest issue of *Moskovskie novosti*?'

'No, what's in there?'

'It is not something we can talk about on the phone.'

In the early Perestroika years Alexander Yakovlev warned television and radio bosses that the jamming of foreign radio stations was to be stopped and that they would have to compete for the young audience which normally shunned drab Soviet news programmes and instead tuned in to the Russian service of the BBC or the Voice of America. One of the first 'competing' projects was a television programme called *Vzglyad* (*Viewpoint*) which was broadcast on Friday nights to coincide with a popular music show on the Russian service of the BBC.

To make it appealing, its presenters had to look and sound like the audience they were trying to capture. They had to be slightly cynical, well-informed, knowledgeable about Western popular culture. Yet they also had to be trustworthy. There was only one place within the Soviet television-and-radio empire that could provide such cadres: the foreign-language service of Radio Moscow – which broadcast Soviet views in dozens of languages around the world and was staffed by young linguists who wasted their time anonymously broadcasting Soviet propaganda.

It was effectively one of the branches of the KGB and many of the journalists who worked there were affiliated with it. One of *Vzglyad*'s main presenters was Alexander Lyubimov, the son of a legendary KGB spy in London, who had worked with Kim Philby and was expelled from the UK in the 1960s. Lyubimov Jr was born in London and had studied at the Moscow Institute of International Relations, a prestigious school for future diplomats and intelligence officers. He was the ultimate golden youth, one of the elite.

Unlike Soviet dissidents who listened to 'enemy' radio stations in the privacy of their homes and in secret, with the risk of being informed on, people like Lyubimov did so openly as part of their duty. They knew more about – and lusted more for – the openness of the West than those who worked in Soviet television. They had access to the Western media, they knew foreign languages, read foreign newspapers. As part of the Soviet counter-propaganda, they had to know what they were supposed to counter; they were supposed to misinform others, but they were very well informed themselves.

'We had Solzhenitsyn's writings at home. I knew well who Sakharov was. They do say that a gendarme is the freest man in Russia,' Lyubimov said.[12] When Perestroika started in earnest, he and his peers were best equipped to shape the new Soviet television. They also stood to gain most from it. *Vzglyad* became the incubator for some of the most influential TV figures in the following two decades. They knew how to use the system to maximum effect.

The first *Vzglyad* progammes were anything but controversial: a young man from an orphanage reading his own poetry, one of the presenters instructing the audience how to distinguish real Levis from fakes, advice on how to open a small private business – a total novelty in a country where making a profit was a crime. The subjects were divided from each other by musical numbers. But every programme tested and pushed the limits, discussing things that allegedly did not exist in the USSR: homosexuality, drugs, AIDS, corruption.

Vzglyad talked about removing Lenin from the Mausoleum and carried an interview with a captain whose submarine had sunk in the Arctic Sea and said that Soviet submarines were death traps. It was the first programme to interview Sakharov when he was released from his exile at the end of 1987. Its dimly lit studio was set up like a Moscow kitchen where friends sat around the table talking about youth culture, music and politics, listening to the latest rock bands, watching video clips. In the late Soviet days the accumulation of wealth meant that people owned more than one television set, and in the 1980s one of these often lived in a kitchen. So kitchens became the settings for television programmes, albeit their format was more akin to a magazine than a TV show.

Past Present

The opening-up of the Russian media began not with a discussion about the country's present condition, but with the past.

Three quarters of all publications in the years of Perestroika were dedicated to the past. As Boris Dubin and Lev Gudkov, two Russian sociologists, wrote, Soviet society resembled a man who was walking backwards into the future, fixated on his past. History dominated the discourse of Perestroika, one of the most transformative periods of Soviet history. It was not just a small group of intellectuals – the whole country seemed obsessed with history. In 1988, when the Soviet economy was in its death throes and bloody conflicts began to erupt on the periphery, street demonstrations were held in Moscow for unlimited subscriptions to the multi-volume edition of *A History of Russia* by Vasily Klyuchevsky, and an even more academic historic *magnum opus* by Sergei Solovyov. (Like everything else in the Soviet Union, the amount of paper and number of copies of each publication were regulated by the state.)

As historian Andrei Zorin has said, behind this was the notion that the state constantly concealed the truth about the past; once a true knowledge of history was obtained, the country could break out of the vicious circle of repeating past mistakes. Yet the actual study of history was often the last thing on the minds of participants in the historic debates of the 1980s. What communist reformers took from the past was the dominance of ideology over all other spheres of life, including the economy and history itself.

Thus the main ideological battles of the 1980s unfolded over history. Latsis wrote:

> Facts from the lives of our grandparents, episodes which took place fifty or seventy years ago, were discussed with such fervour as though the

> question of whether Bukharin should be executed or acquitted was being decided now and not half a century ago... Had it not been for the stupidity of the Soviet bureaucracy [over the previous twenty years], debates about Stalinism would have been concluded in the late 1950s and would not have become a fact of current politics thirty years later.[13]

The liberals and their hard-line opponents fought over the past with the same ferocity as though they were fighting for natural resources. In many ways they were, for whoever controlled the past also controlled the present. The very word 'memory' became the reason for a fight. One of the country's first openly anti-Semitic and right-wing organizations, patronized by the KGB, was called *Pamyat* (Memory) – a name it 'stole' from dissident historians who published a samizdat journal under that title. A human rights group launched by former dissidents with the support of Andrei Sakharov, which originally focused on rehabilitating the victims of Stalinist repressions, was called Memorial.

De-Stalinization, aborted with the ousting of Khrushchev in 1964, started with new vigour. Articles about Stalin poured from the pages of *Moskovskie novosti*. But the real repentance – a way of coming to terms with the past – never took place. That would have required the re-examination not just of Stalin, but of the entire system that led him to power. It would also have meant 'digging out' the bodies of millions of people who supported the regime. And this was something that the 1960s generation was still not ready to do. Faithful to the memory of their fathers, they continued to perpetuate the myth that Stalinism was a distortion rather than a consequence of the Soviet system based on 'a thousand-year-old model of statehood', as Alexander Yakovlev put it. Publications about the crimes of Stalinism appeared next to those about the virtues of Lenin. Perestroika was carried out under the slogan of 'more socialism'.

In January 1987 – the year of the seventieth anniversary of the October Revolution – *Moskovskie novosti* launched a new rubric: 'Byloe' (the Past).

The first article in 'Byloe' was written in the form of a Q&A with Lenin: the newspaper posed questions to Lenin and provided answers from his works. On the same pages, Mikhail Shatrov, the playwright who specialized in plays about Lenin, and Stephen Cohen, a biographer of Bukharin and a left-wing historian at Princeton University, discussed the relevance of Lenin's ideas under the headline: 'TO RETURN IN ORDER TO MOVE FORWARD'. 'Of course we must again and again go back to Lenin, to the full volume of his ideas, particularly to the ideas of the last years of his life. We must understand and make use of them to move forward,' Shatrov said.[14] The notion that the ideas of Bukharin and Lenin were still relevant in the late 1980s was validated by Cohen.

The Stalinists were not about to surrender history to the liberals, however: they hit back. In March 1988 *Sovetskaya Rossiya*, a mouthpiece of the hardliners in the party, printed a reader's letter headed 'I Cannot Forsake Principles', signed by one Nina Andreeva, a chemistry teacher from the Leningrad Polytechnic. A nearly full-page Stalinist attack on Glasnost and Perestroika, it was a manifesto of conservatives in the country. 'The subject of repressions has been blown out of all proportions and overshadows an objective interpretation of the past,' she wrote. 'They try to make us believe that the country's past was nothing but mistakes and crimes.'[15]

In particular, Andreeva singled out Shatrov for attack – not only as an ideological opponent but as competition for control over historic discourse. The letter also contained more than a grain of anti-Semitism. The Soviet national interests had been betrayed by the Jewish followers of Trotsky, she wrote, while ethnic Slavs had heroically stood up to fascism.

As David Remnick, who met Andreeva at the time, wrote, she was a woman of letters. She used to write false anonymous denunciations about her colleagues' ideological faults and was even thrown out of her institute's party cell, though she was restored at the request of the KGB. The letter was expanded and printed by *Sovetskaya Rossiya* on the instructions of Yegor Ligachev – Yakovlev's opposite number on the conservative flank of the party.

After the publication of Andreeva's letter, Ligachev gathered media chiefs in his office to tell them that everyone must read this 'wonderful' article and instructed provincial papers to reprint it, giving it the prominence due to a party line. Many obediently followed the instruction.

Both Gorbachev and Yakovlev were out of the country when the letter came out and took it as being 'nothing less than a call to arms, an attempted coup'. 'It was meant to overturn everything that had been conceived in 1985... It had a firm, sort of Stalinist accusatory form as in the style on the front pages of our old newspapers... This was a harsh bellow of a command: "Stop! Everything is over!"' Yakovlev said later.[16] He interrupted his visit to Mongolia and urgently flew back to Moscow.

Andreeva's letter was meant and, more importantly, perceived as a signal of a shift in the party line. There was a history of such 'impromptu' letters in the Soviet press. In 1952 there was a letter from a woman called Lidia Timashuk that prompted an ugly prosecution of Jewish doctors who were accused of deliberately harming senior Soviet figures, the so-called Doctors' Plot.

In the same week as Andreeva's letter was published, *Vzglyad*, the liberal television show, was taken off air. But the fact that the anti-Perestroika manifesto was printed in a newspaper rather than broadcast on television or radio gave it weight, permanence and most importantly historic context. The article put the intelligentsia into a state of stupor. The liberal press fell silent for nearly three weeks. Almost nobody dared to respond. 'It was a terrifying time,' Yegor Yakovlev said. 'Absolutely everything we had ever hoped for and dreamed of was on the line.'[17] *Moskovskie novosti* was the first to break the silence. Gorbachev also took the article as a frontal attack on his policies and convened a special Politburo meeting which lasted two days.

Alexander Yakovlev was charged to draft an editorial in *Pravda* that would spell out the party line. Liberal editors and journalists breathed a sigh of relief. *Vzglyad* was put back on air. The Andreeva affair was the last test of the 'signalling' system which had operated throughout Soviet history. The whole point of the printed word was its permanence. But when two opposing signals went through two party newspapers within two weeks, the system went into convulsions. It was clear that there was no single party line. As Korotich, the editor of *Ogonyok*, told Yegor at the time: 'We used to keep trying to find out what's going on. We overlooked the fact that we ourselves were creating the situation.'[18]

The clash over Andreeva's letter was part of a wider conflict between two opposite ideologies. Behind Andreeva and her backers stood a centuries-old ideology of the absolute and sacred power of the state, which had been exemplified by Stalinist rule. A human being in that system was only a small cog. Closely related to the ideas of National Socialism or fascism, which Yakovlev had risen against back in the early 1970s, it was a noxious compound of anti-Semitism and chauvinism. The opposite ideology was one of 'socialism with a human face' that extolled individual human values such as dignity and privacy as supreme. It rejected Stalinism in all its forms and looked back to Bukharin and the New Economic Policy as a way towards a Western lifestyle.

The Communist hardliners, who resorted to Stalin, and the liberals, who extolled Bukharin, were both using history merely as a proxy for current political battles. In the process, both sides distorted history either by demonizing it or by idealizing it. Bukharin's actual rehabilitation was an act of historic justice (in the same way Beria should have been rehabilitated from the false charges of spying for Britain). But there was a big difference between rehabilitation – a legal act of clearing a person of false charges – and turning him into a myth.

History did not like being mythologized and used as device and it took its revenge on both camps. The biggest problem was that by casting Perestroika in terms of the 1920s New Economic Policy and

Bukharin's idea of socialism, the reformers were not only distorting the picture of the past, they were also distorting the picture of the present. Perestroika was described as a new beginning, not as the ending that it actually was. But an ending, misconceived as a beginning, is nothing but a dead end.

Jumping off the Train

One person who did not care much about ideology and who recognized Perestroika for what it was – an ending of the Soviet command system rather than its second incarnation – was the secretary of the Moscow Party Committee and Russia's future president, Boris Yeltsin. Like everyone else, Yeltsin made ritualistic speeches about the revolution and Lenin, but he also understood, earlier than most, that the party was heading towards self-destruction.

In the summer of 1987 Yeltsin wrote a letter to Gorbachev, who was on vacation, complaining that Perestroika was turning into empty words and asking him to relieve him from his duties as the secretary of the party organization and a candidate member of the Politburo. There were many cases when people were pushed out of the Politburo but nobody in the party's history had ever asked to be removed from it voluntarily. When Gorbachev returned from vacation, he called Yeltsin, suggesting they should find time to talk. But a week passed, then another. Gorbachev was too busy working on a speech marking the seventieth anniversary of the October Revolution, in which he would mention Bukharin, to meet Yeltsin.

For several generations of Soviet leaders, Bukharin represented something they feared most: political opposition. Yet, too preoccupied with history, few paid attention to the fact that political opposition to Gorbachev was emerging in present time.

On 15 October a draft of Gorbachev's speech was discussed by members of the Politburo. Andrei Gromyko, the chairman of the Supreme Soviet, the party's elder statesman, enthused: 'What an act is being born! Such acts are not your regular anniversary stuff. They make history. What does [the speech] say? From start to finish it conveys the following idea: there is capitalism and there is socialism, which was born seventy years ago... And in 1,000 years socialism will still be bringing good to the nation and to the world.'[19] The time to the end of the Soviet Union was four years and counting.

With hindsight, the discussion among members of the Politburo was almost insane – as if train drivers were to discuss how to make an engine work faster, while their train, having lost its brakes, was heading towards a dead end. Yeltsin decided to jump off that train before it reached its destination.

Six days later, at a plenum of the Central Committee, Yeltsin publicly attacked hardliners in the Kremlin, warned that Perestroika was losing popular support (unsurprising given the empty shops) and, in conclusion, offered his resignation as a candidate member to the Politburo.

Most of the liberal reformers close to Gorbachev saw Yeltsin's speech as a reckless acceleration of events which could only harm Gorbachev in his fight with the hardliners. In fact, Yeltsin's speech was useful to him in two ways: first, it attacked the hardliners; and second, it allowed Gorbachev to slap down Yeltsin himself. As soon as Yeltsin sat down, Gorbachev launched a vicious and humiliating attack on him. He then invited members of the Politburo to speak.

When it came to Alexander Yakovlev's turn, he said that Yeltsin was 'immoral' and 'put his personal ambitions, personal interests, above the interest of the party'. Strictly speaking, Yakovlev, who shared Yeltsin's frustration with the pace of Perestroika, was right: Yeltsin did have his own game. It was simpler and more strategic than that of Gorbachev. A politician of great animal-like instinct, what Yeltsin cared about was power – something that he understood better than anyone in the audience. Being held responsible for the worsening of the economic situation in the country without being able to implement reforms was politically dangerous. What may have seemed like political suicide from the outside, was, in fact, an act of self-rescue and survival. This did not, however, minimize the drama of his actions: jumping off an accelerating train was a risky business.

A few days later he was subjected to another savage attack – this time by the Moscow Party Organization which he headed. Stylistically, the language of many of their speeches resembled that of the 1930s show trials. But only stylistically. Yeltsin was no Bukharin and Gorbachev was certainly no Stalin. The dogs barked, but their teeth had been spoilt by all the sweets they had been handing out to each other over the past decades. In the 1930s, party renegades were shot. In the late 1950s, they were forced into retirement or placed under house arrest. In the more 'vegetarian' 1970s, they were parked in far-flung embassies. In the 1980s, they were propelled to the top. Gorbachev appointed Yeltsin as minister for construction and pledged 'never to let Yeltsin into politics again'. He did not realize it was far too late for that and that he had just helped to create a new hero.

Once again, the role of the media was *not* to report Yeltsin's speech. The protocol of the October Plenum, which contained Gorbachev's speech, was kept secret and newspaper editors were strictly prohibited from mentioning Yeltsin's name in print. This only boosted his popularity and his status as a martyr who suffered for the truth. Yeltsin's speech struck a chord with the grievances of ordinary Russians, who, after two years' talk about reforms, wanted to see and feel results. Instead they saw empty shelves and rising black market prices. By giving up his position within the Politburo and lashing out at the privileges enjoyed by the apparatchiks, Yeltsin gained far greater power – deriving its legitimacy from popular support.

Unable to read Yeltsin's speech, people started to make up their own apocryphal versions of it. At least eight such 'speeches' circulated in Moscow. The most popular one read: 'It is hard for me to explain to the factory worker why, in the seventieth year of his political power, he is obliged to stand in line for sausages in which there is more starch than meat, while on our table there is sturgeon, caviar and all sorts of delicacies easily acquired from a place which he cannot even approach... How can I look them in the eye?'[20] Yeltsin himself could not have put it better.

Yeltsin was focused on the present and the present gave little ground for optimism and illusions. 'Where is Perestroika?' a worker from the Urals asked a party conference convened by Gorbachev. 'The stores are just as badly supplied with food as before. There was no meat before and there is no meat now. Popular consumption goods have vanished.'[21] In the first issue of 1988, *Moskovskie novosti* ran a page-long *vox populi* conducted over a ten-day train journey from Moscow to Vladivostok on the Pacific. Like any long-distance train conversation in Russia, it started over the traditional fare of boiled chicken and hard-boiled eggs, which passengers pulled out of plastic bags minutes after the train's departure from Moscow, and continued over a bottle of vodka in the dining car. But as the train left Moscow further behind, the comments became more outspoken and the fare on compartment tables more primitive. In the old days, passengers were able to buy steaming boiled potatoes with dill, fried and salted fish, pickles and berries from an army of local men and women who ambushed the train at every station. Now, locals ambushed the train not to sell but to buy produce from the passengers: meat, butter and anything else.

The local shops were empty and so was the dining car which sold its own supplies to entrepreneurial re-sellers along the way. Amid the train conversations, *Moskovskie novosti* distributed a questionnaire among the passengers. In response to the question, 'Do you believe in Perestroika's results?' 64 per cent answered negatively. More generally, only 16 per cent enthusiastically supported Perestroika and 13 per cent rejected it. This was hardly a scientific poll, but it amply bore out Yeltsin's point. It was this train that Yeltsin was jumping off.

The first wave of street protests swept the country from Omsk in Siberia to the centre of Moscow. They were carried out under slogans that could have been written in the editorial offices of *Moskovskie novosti*: 'No democracy without socialism; No socialism without democracy'. Yegor's heart and the hearts of the Soviet intelligentsia swelled with pride and hope. 'I am certain that Soviet workers value democracy over goods... It is true that there still are terrible shortages, but you would not believe how Glasnost has changed the way workers think,' Yegor told Stephen Cohen a year later.[22]

Yet under the slogans of democracy and Glasnost, people all too often meant 'clothes' and 'sausages'. In fact, democracy and sausages were seen as part of one package: once the country had freedom of speech, sausages and clothes would follow and Russia would miraculously turn into a nice-smelling Western-style country. Unlike China, which kept the ideology and reformed the economy, Russia changed the ideology but did not reform the economy.

Food shortages had an important moral dimension. An article about queues in *Moskovskie novosti*, by the writer Alexander Kabakov, had the headline 'HUMILIATION' set in large, bold type. 'Queuing for everything – from sausages to razor blades – has become a necessary part of Soviet life. For the citizens of a country which built atomic power stations and space shuttles, queuing for a bar of soap is humiliating,' he wrote.[23] It was not just about the inability to sate one's needs, it was also about wasting one's precious life in queues.

The need to move to a free market and to liberalize state-controlled prices was obvious to almost everyone in the Soviet government. But Gorbachev dithered. Raising or deregulating prices would mean breaking the social contract that implied that food was affordable even if it was not available.

The memory of the riots in Novocherkassk in 1962, which were provoked by a sharp rise in meat prices and a reduction in real pay, outweighed any arguments about the current situation. 'I know only one thing,' Gorbachev told one of the free market proponents, 'that after two weeks, this "market" would bring people out on the streets and sweep away any government.' As it happened, a few months later, people were out on the streets anyway, but the economy was in a much worse state. Instead of deregulating the prices, Gorbachev effectively liberalized politics and loosened control over state property.

The ideologues of Perestroika, those who concentrated around *Moskovskie novosti*, had not thought through, any more than had Gorbachev, the nature of the Soviet failure and had assumed that Leninism was a pure doctrine morally, as well as one that could be the spine of a governing class. Consumed with inner party struggles, they missed the point that the system was unravelling and the governing class itself was fast abandoning the ship. By the late 1980s the ghost of Stalinism was just that – a ghost; nobody had an appetite for repressions. The likes of Nina Andreeva were sidelined, if not marginalized.

In May 1988 the government passed a law allowing the setting-up of private co-operatives. The word and the idea of a co-operative were, once again, borrowed from the 1920s New Economic Policy. The hope was that the spirit of private entrepreneurship and small-time trade would help revive the Soviet economy as quickly as it had done in the mid-1920s. The difference was that in 1925 only eight years had passed since the Bolshevik Revolution; in 1988 the distance was measured in generations.

In everything but name, the co-operatives of the late 1980s were private firms which were allowed to set their own prices for anything they produced. The only problem was that most of them did not produce anything. Instead they bought goods from state enterprises at subsidized prices and sold the same goods at market prices, keeping the profit or splitting it with a state manager.

'The co-operator's job was to legitimize the black market which the corrupt bureaucracy did not want to see legitimized, and to destroy the prejudices which the communist power structure did not want to see destroyed.'[24] Thus spoke a chronicler of the co-operation movement and himself a successful 'co-operator', Vladimir Yakovlev – Yegor's son. At the same time, by loosening control over state enterprises – all strictly in the spirit of the 1960s reforms – the government allowed state managers to participate in these schemes. The vast majority of these co-operatives were attached to state plants and enterprises and affiliated with their management.

If that was not enough, a number of state Soviet oil refineries were given special licences to export their oil products and keep the revenues, bypassing the state export monopoly. This gave rise to people like Gennady Timchenko who worked for the ministry of foreign trade and who, along with his partners, lobbied a state-owned refinery near Leningrad to set up an in-house trading arm that hired them to export some of its products. A few years later, this 'trading desk' was sold, turning Timchenko and his partners into private oil traders. Fifteen years on, under Vladimir Putin, Timchenko emerged as one the biggest private traders of Russia's state-owned oil, and, critics say, a symbol of crony capitalism and the corporatist state. In 2014 he was designated as a member of Putin's inner circle by the US government and was subjected to sanctions. According to the *Wall Street Journal*, he was also investigated for money laundering, which he denied, by the US prosecutors. Yet he started his career at the same time, and in the same city, as that in which Andreeva wrote her letter. 'My luck started there,' he said.[25]

Many of Russia's first businessmen, including Mikhail Khodorkovsky, the future oil tycoon turned political prisoner, emerged from the ranks of the Young Communist Party League. Komsomol activists were young, cynical and ruthless. They had none of the idealism or the baggage of their fathers and all the frustrations of a hungry elite constrained by the doldrums of Soviet ideology. They could not care less for Bukharin or the New Economic Policy and they embraced with a vengeance the opportunity offered by Perestroika. None of the names, which a few years later would make up a *Forbes Magazine* list of billionaires, those who would shape Russia's economy and politics over the next decade, featured on the pages of *Moskovskie novosti*, even though some placed advertisements in the paper.

The reason for this was not censorship, fear, or lack of professionalism. These events and these people simply did not fit into the picture of the world that *Moskovskie novosti* had created for its readers. They did not even enter its field of vision. The paper carried on arguing about socialism, the benefits and disadvantages of the market and the legacy of Lenin and Bukharin when a large part of the party corps was already making its millions.

In 1990, Nikolai Ryzhkov, the head of Gorbachev's cabinet, posed a question: 'Are we building socialism or capitalism?' By that time, the question had long been answered, not only by the co-operators but also by a large number of the red directors who had begun the transfer of state property into their own hands well before the official privatization of the 1990s. The signs of this major shift of economic power from the central government to the Soviet managerial corps were out there, but few, including Ryzhkov, understood the consequences.

In May 1989 Viktor Chernomyrdin, a fifty-one-year-old archetypal corpulent minister for the Soviet gas industry, with bushy eyebrows, an instinctive sense of humour and a mastery of unprintable Russian expressions, came to Ryzhkov with a proposal to transform his ministry of gas into a state corporation called Gazprom, swapping his ministerial position for the job of the company's chairman. Ryzhkov struggled to grasp the logic. After one long conversation he asked Chernomyrdin:

> 'So, as I understand it, you don't want to be a minister any more?'
>
> 'No, I don't,' Chernomyrdin replied.
>
> 'And so you won't be a member of the government? And you understand

that you will lose everything – the dacha and the privileges?' Ryzhkov quizzed him.

'I do understand,' Chernomyrdin said.

'And you are doing this yourself?' Ryzhkov asked in disbelief.

'Myself. You see, Nikolai Ivanovich, it is not the time to be a minister. We will create a firm.'[26]

Ryzhkov assumed that Chernomyrdin had gone mad. No Soviet minister had ever voluntarily given up his perks, which included a chauffeur-driven car, a large apartment in Moscow and a dacha in the country, free holidays in a Crimean sanatorium and jars of black caviar from a special shop. A smart Soviet industry boss, Chernomyrdin had sensed that the centrally planned command economy administered through ministries like his own was crumbling. No longer backed by the threat of coercion or economic benefit, ministerial orders had no power and were getting ignored.

A few months later, Ryzhkov was gone, the Soviet Union had collapsed and within another two years, Chernomyrdin became prime minister in capitalist Russia, reaping the benefits of his creation. Gazprom became the largest and most powerful firm, worth billions of dollars, offering privileges no Communist Party could match. This story of Gazprom's creation goes a long way to explain why the disintegration of the Soviet regime was relatively peaceful, but also why its transformation was so incomplete. The economic foundation of the Soviet system was destroyed not by an external enemy or the dissidents, but by the proprietor's instinct of the Soviet red directors who gladly exchanged their petty privileges for something far bigger – a piece of socialist property. It was this nomenclatura that undermined the core principle of socialism.

The elimination of private property and of individual thinking was the Bolsheviks' *idée fixe*. The artists of the 1920s dreamt up a utopia of collective living devoid of any individualistic habits. Stalin got rid of Lenin's

New Economic Policy that allowed small-time private enterprise, not because he doubted its economic results, but because he had correctly judged that any such enterprise was a threat to the totalitarian regime. Stalin bestowed upon his courtiers royal privileges, grand state apartments, cars and dachas, but the ownership of all these assets stayed with the Kremlin. The fact that nothing could be sold or bequeathed bred a sense of dependency and impermanence.

The ideologists of the regime watched vigilantly for any expression of the proprietor's instinct. After Stalin's death the threat of execution was lifted but the taboo on ownership remained. But by the late 1980s the deal by which the nomenclatura had to satisfy itself with perks and delicacies doled out from special shops had started to break down. Worse still, the food packages themselves started to shrink thanks to the worsening of the economic situation. A populist campaign against privileges, led by Yeltsin, added to the discomfort.

For years their proprietorial instinct had been constrained by the ideology of state ownership and the threat of violence on the part of the state. However, when ideological constraints were loosened and private enterprises legalized those who were charged with managing state assets gave in to their ownership instinct. They realized that instead of being rewarded for looking after the assets, they could actually own the assets.

The Soviet Party elite and the 'red directors' embraced and handsomely benefited from Perestroika. As Yegor Gaidar, who would come to reform the Russian economy a few years later, wrote: 'The nomenclatura moved forward, testing its way through, step by step – not according to some thought-through plan, but by submitting to its deep instinct. It followed the scent of property, like a predator follows its prey.'[27] Everything was done by trial and error and the benefits of the trials went into the pockets of the bureaucracy. The costs of the errors stayed with the state.

In the late 1980s, Gaidar, a bright young economist, was working for the *Kommunist* journal that was supposed to set the ideological tenets of the party, but instead worked to destroy them. Gaidar was brought to *Kommunist* by Latsis, its deputy editor and a close friend of his father Timur. Yegor Gaidar was the grandson of two writers, Arkady Gaidar, the universally famous author of children's stories who had fought on the Bolshevik side in the civil war of 1918–22, and Pavel Bazhov, an author and collector of folk tales. Born in March 1956, during the 20th Congress of the party, Gaidar was barely thirty-three years old in 1989 and belonged to a generation that harboured no illusions about a socialist utopia. As a student at the Moscow State University, Gaidar read his way through the works of the Western economists, including J. M. Keynes and Milton Friedman. One book that perhaps influenced him more than any other was the *Economics of Shortage* by the Hungarian economist János Kornai.

Kornai's book was published in 1980 when the oil price was still high, but shortages were widespread throughout the Soviet bloc. Unlike the communist reformers, Kornai argued that those shortages were the consequences not of planners' errors or of the wrong prices, but of a systemic flaw in socialism, its integral part. Gaidar met Kornai in 1981 at a conference in Moscow. They strolled along grey Moscow streets arguing about whether the system could be reformed. In August 1986 Gaidar and a group of bright young economists gathered in Zmeinaya Gorka, a sanatorium outside Leningrad, to discuss their countries' economic prospects – much as Timur Gaidar and Otto Latsis had done in August 1968. But, unlike their fathers, the young economists did not look for fifty-year-old historic models but examined the subject that was before them.

By night, they made bonfires, grilled *shashlyk* and sang songs from their fathers' repertoire. By day, they spoke a different language – one free of euphemisms and nostalgia for the revolutionary ideals. Their diagnosis was clear: socialism cannot and will not work. The only way forward was to move the Soviet economy towards the market and private property. At the concluding seminar, Gaidar offered two possible scenarios: in the optimistic one, this club of economic boffins would soon run the country, steering it towards capitalism; in the pessimistic one, they would all be sent to the Gulag.

Yet, the biggest difference between 1968 and 1986 was in the balance of probabilities. In 1986, the prospect of repression already seemed increasingly outlandish. The general atmosphere was one of excitement and hope spiced up with disbelief and apprehension. It was this feeling and these ideas that Gaidar brought to *Kommunist* when he joined the journal in 1987. The taboos were falling too fast for any official to follow the line. Occasionally Gaidar would receive a telephone call from the Central Committee. 'Are you sure this problem can be discussed in the open?' a caller would ask. 'Have you not heard?' Gaidar would reply, implying he knew something that the caller did not.

With figures at hand, he showed that the Soviet economy was heading towards an abyss. In 1988 he wrote an article which he headed 'The Foundation Pit',[28] borrowing the title from the novel by Andrei Platonov in which socialist workers dig out a giant foundation pit for building a house for the entire proletariat: the deeper they dig, the more futile their work becomes, sucking out their energy and their lives. The novel had been written in 1930 but was not published until 1987.

The figures cited by Gaidar were devastating. In the period from 1976 to 1985, when the Soviet Union invested $150 billion into its agriculture, the increase in agricultural product was... zero. Soviet workers mined seven times the amount of iron ore extracted in America, cast three times as much iron and yet they smelted the same amount of steel. The waste was enormous. The Soviet Union made twelve times as many combine harvesters as America did, but harvested less wheat. The point of the article, however, was not to lament past losses but to warn of the dangers ahead. By continuing to pour money into an inefficient economy the country was digging itself a grave.

Gaidar introduced a new language and a way of thinking about the economy which moved beyond the communist ideology and which operated in concepts that were alien to Soviet party bosses: budget deficit, inflation, unemployment. His voice sounded calm and cold. The question, he wrote in a column for *Moskovskie novosti*, was not whether capitalism was preferable to socialism, but how to avoid another social explosion.

> History left us no chance to repeat an English model of social evolution. The idea that we could simply erase seventy years of history from memory and try and replay the game which had been already played, that we could consolidate the country by transferring the means of production into the hands of the new rich, operating in the shadow economy, the most agile [communist] bosses, or international corporations, demonstrates the power of utopian traditions in our country.[29]

As far as Gaidar was concerned there was no point in trying to retrace one's steps back to Lenin, just as there was no point in fantasizing about a painless transformation of a socialist economy into a capitalist one by taking Lenin's body out of the Mausoleum. The situation in which the Soviet Union – a superpower with nuclear arms – found itself in the late 1980s simply had no historical precedents.

End of Mystery

In the summer of 1989 a group of American Sovietologists asked the young, bright analyst and academic Igor Malashenko what Gorbachev was doing with the country. 'I told them: he is dismantling the whole system of the communist regime, the Soviet Union. Then they asked me what he was planning to do next and suddenly I was stuck for an answer.'[30] A Moscow University graduate with a degree in philosophy, Malashenko had joined the international department at the Central Committee of the

Communist Party. A few years earlier this would have seemed like a smart decision, but in 1989 the omnipotent Central Committee was suddenly no longer seen as a good career move; indeed, many staffers were heading for the exit. But Malashenko was curious. 'I thought that there must be a plan and that I was simply not getting it because I did not have access to information. It was only when I got into the Central Committee that I realized that not only was there no plan, but that Gorbachev did not even understand the consequences of his own actions. Unlike Alice in Wonderland, he did not remember that "if you cut your finger very deeply with a knife, it usually bleeds".'[31] In fact, had Gorbachev foreseen the consequences of his actions, he was unlikely to have started.

In the absence of coherent economic reforms and policy towards the Soviet republics, Gorbachev proceeded to loosen political control as the communist reformers had urged him to do, transferring power to the Soviets – government bodies, or councils, which were in theory electable even though in practice they were simply enacting the policies of the Communist Party.

It was the opposite of China where economic reforms were happening under authoritarian rule. But in June 1989, the Chinese way led to Tiananmen Square. The Soviet way led to the first democratically elected Congress of People's Deputies which proclaimed 'all power to the Soviets'. What had long been an empty slogan suddenly became reality. It was the strongest signal that Moscow was letting go of the centralized system and dissolving power.

The Congress started with a minute of silence: a few weeks earlier, in the small hours of 9 April, Russian troops and armour had moved in against 10,000 people who had come out onto the streets of the Georgian capital, Tbilisi, to demand cessation from the Soviet Union. The soldiers used a paralytic gas of unknown origin and spades to crack skulls open. Twenty people were killed, sixteen of them women, including one seventy-year-old and two sixteen-year-olds.

Gorbachev was in London and apparently only learned the facts when he returned to Moscow on the evening of 9 April. Everyone tried to distance themselves from the massacre. It was not clear who had ordered it. What was clear was that the country's leadership was not prepared to take responsibility for cracking down on a protest and had run away at the first sight of blood. Yegor Yakovlev, along with several other deputies of the Supreme Soviet, went to Tbilisi to investigate and concluded that the use of force was completely unjustified. At the opening of the Congress, a deputy from Lithuania demanded that everyone should stand up to pay their respects to those killed in Tbilisi, effectively implying that the leadership had committed a crime of murder – in the presence of the party hacks who occupied most seats in the audience.

This was just a start. Independent deputies from the ranks of the liberal intelligentsia insisted that the Congress, in the spirit of Glasnost, should be broadcast live on the central television channels. In the past, important decisions were always made behind closed doors. The amount of information the public received about official meetings was usually in reverse proportion to their importance. Congresses of the Communist Party that decided nothing were broadcast almost in full. Central Committee meetings and Politburo sessions were never made public. This was the first time a genuinely important convention was not only reported but televised.

As the Grand Inquisitor explains in Dostoevsky's *Brothers Karamazov*, 'There are three powers, three powers alone, able to conquer and to hold captive for ever the conscience of these impotent rebels for their happiness. Those powers are miracle, mystery and authority.' Soviet rulers, and Stalin in particular, learned the lessons of the Grand Inquisitor well. But the three powers that had been guarded by Soviet ideologists for decades were destroyed in a two-week-long televised drama.

The country was glued to the television screen, listening to speeches and debates which were considered too radical for newspapers to print or for television news programmes to repeat. People watched Andrei Sakharov, whose name was taboo in the media only a few years before, propose radical political reform and challenge Gorbachev; they heard a former Olympic weightlifter attack the KGB – 'a veritable underground empire' – and a Dostoevskian scholar demand the removal of Lenin from the Mausoleum; they heard that their 'country was bankrupt', that the war in Afghanistan was a criminal mistake; that the rate of child mortality in the Soviet Union was higher than in many African countries and that life expectancy was up to eight years shorter than in the developed world; that half of all processed baby milk contained a dangerously high concentration of chemicals. But the most shocking part was not what was said but that it was being said on a state television channel. As Alexander Yakovlev said at the outset of Perestroika, 'the television image is everything'.[32]

With this cloak of mystery torn into pieces, authority was irreversibly seeping from the Kremlin. As Sakharov wrote at the time: 'The Congress has cut off all the roads back. Now it is clear to everyone that there is only the road forward or ruin.'[33] As it happened, it was both: the road forward led to the ruin of the empire.

The Congress produced an astonishing sense of exhilaration and euphoria. But it also revealed an unbridgeable divide between the minority of the liberal intelligentsia and what one of its members called an 'aggressively obedient majority' – the grey and menacing mass of Soviet-bred men and women who applauded the military commander who had led the crackdown in Tbilisi and who tried to boo Sakharov off the stage. They belonged to the same breed as Nina Andreeva, usually known as '*Homo soveticus*', which had little in common with Soviet people such as Alexander Yakovlev. These were two different species.

The fact that *Homo soveticus* made up the majority was not merely the result of the election rules of the Congress. It was a fair reflection of a negative selection process which first eliminated the best and the brightest physically and then nurtured double-think, suspicion, isolationism, dependence, and discouraged independence of thought and action. As the fairy-tale dragon from a play by Evgeny Shvarts, the 1940s Soviet playwright, tells the hero who slaughters him before he dies: 'I leave you burnt souls, hollow souls, dead souls.'

In the same year, 1989, a group of Russian sociologists led by Yuri Levada launched a research project about *Homo soveticus*. Its aim was to describe a vanishing social type created by several decades of oppressive regimes, but one that could no longer reproduce in the new circumstances. But as the sociologists realized over the next decades, the breed of *Homo soveticus* was immensely resilient. The type did not vanish: it mutated and reproduced, acquiring new characteristics along the way. Conversely, the social genes of Alexander Yakovlev and Andrei Sakharov would over the years become weaker.

But for a short period in the late 1980s this liberal minority had the upper hand – not least because of its broad and even unlimited, at some point, access to the media. Despite all the hushing and stamping, their voices were more audible and their speeches far more powerful than those of the 'aggressively obedient majority'. Members of the Politburo were exiting through a guarded back door to escape the journalists – both foreign and Russian – who were harassing them with microphones and notepads. As Sakharov wrote in his memoirs, drafted a few months after the 1st Congress, 'That evening we felt triumphant. But, of course, this feeling was mixed with a sense of tragedy and complexity of the situation in general. If our feeling can be described as optimism, it was tragic optimism.'[34]

The Congress ended – just as it had begun – with a speech by Sakharov. He called for a repeal of the Communist Party's rule, transfer of power to the Soviets, privatization of land and reorganization of the country along federal lines. During this speech Gorbachev grew increasingly impatient, telling Sakharov that his time was over, trying to send him back to his seat. Then Gorbachev simply switched off the microphone. But Sakharov continued to speak. Remarkably, while the audience was no longer able and willing to listen to Sakharov, his speech continued to be broadcast on television. At the end of his speech Sakharov demanded that the Soviet Union recall its ambassador to China in protest against the bloody massacre in Beijing.

Sakharov did not have long to live. He died on 14 December 1989. With his death, the country lost the moral authority that no politician could replace. Coming from the depths of the Stalinist system, he was the closest thing to a saint that Russia could produce. He was the elite in a way that neither the intelligentsia nor the nomenclatura ever were. On the day of his funeral, attended by long lines of mourners in a terrible frost, *Moskovskie novosti* printed a special issue dedicated to 'Andrei Sakharov – Our Bitter Conscience', carrying tributes from Russian intellectuals, writers and politicians. The most poignant was written by Sergei Averintsev, the scholar of early Christianity and one of Russia's finest thinkers. Averintsev overturned the popular perception of Sakharov as an other-worldly, unpragmatic and inept politician. A truth searcher and a good speaker are not the same thing, Averintsev wrote.

> A prophet does not see the audience in front of himself, he sees what he talks about. Andrei Dmitrievich often did not see what was next to him. His eyes were fixated on the distance; he saw the whole. The way in which he thought about modernity brought him closer to the great thinkers and theoreticians of natural laws and social contracts: his thought moved top down, from great abstractions to specifics, always orientated towards immovable stars. Sakharov was a man of principles, not in Nina Andreeva's sense of the word, but in its original classical sense: a foundation, a basis, an essence.[35]

In many ways, Sakharov was the moral foundation of Perestroika. With his death, the ground turned into shifting sands.

A few hours before he died, Sakharov spoke to a group of liberal deputies. His short speech was printed in *Moskovskie novosti*: 'We cannot take responsibility for the actions of the country's leadership. It is leading the country towards a catastrophe, prolonging the process of Perestroika for years. It leaves the country in a state of intense decay. All the plans of moving towards an intensified, market economy will turn out to be unattainable and the disappointment is already rising.'[36]

By May 1989 the parliaments of all three Baltic republics now dominated by non-communists, declared their sovereignty. To give their demand historic legitimacy, the deputies from the Baltic states requested that a special commission should be set up for a historic assessment of the Molotov–Ribbentrop pact and its secret protocol that carved up Europe, something that the Kremlin continued to insist had not existed. The commission was headed by Alexander Yakovlev. At the same time *Novy Mir* started printing chapters from Solzhenitsyn's *The Gulag Archipelago* – 'the most powerful single indictment of a political regime ever to be levied in modern times,'[37] as George Kennan, the dean of American diplomats, put it. The Soviet Union had little to offer its people in way of economic benefits. Now it was also deprived of its historic legitimacy.

THREE

'We Suffered a Victory'

By the end of 1989 the excitement and euphoria inspired by Perestroika and sustained by *Moskovskie novosti* were evaporating. Hopes of reviving socialism and rewinding the tape of history to the point where socialism had gone astray clashed with the economic reality. By 1990, the queues had subsided: there was simply nothing to queue for anymore. Shortages of tobacco in Leningrad risked sparking off riots. Ration cards became a reality. Newspapers did not have to write about shortages – they were literally visible in the poor quality of their paper and in the fading colour of the print. The foreign firms that provided the Soviet Union with ink and paper were not getting paid and halted their supplies. As economists warned Gorbachev, from 1 January the state would not be able to pay salaries to the army and the police.

The last year of the 1980s was also the end of an historic era. As a policy, Perestroika would continue for another two years, but its spirit had left the country. The future seemed bleak and utterly unpredictable. Millions headed to the West. Gorbachev's traditional New Year's greeting for 1990 conveyed a sense of gloom. As Marietta Chudakova, a literary historian, recorded in her diary: 'Gorbachev started his greetings with a serious, almost tragic face. A momentary glimpse of fear, if not horror, touched his face. What does he see in front? What does he feel?'[1]

Popular culture was swept by a wave of *noir*. One of the most gifted and popular producers of the genre was the television journalist Alexander Nevzorov, Russia's first TV star, who over the years had tried himself out as a church choirboy, a professional stuntman, an investigative reporter, a crusader, an ultra-nationalist, a parliamentarian, an imperialist, a romantic individualist, a mercantile cynic, a con man and in the end even a liberal. Nevzorov was the product of television and its embodiment, a man who constructed reality and his own image.

He made his first television appearance at the end of 1987 in the daily news show *600 Seconds*. The handsome Nevzorov, clad in a black leather jacket and sporting fashionable stubble, sat under a blinking clock that was counting down 600 seconds during which he was uncovering dirt and corruption, shaming bureaucrats, showing murderers and their victims, talking to prostitutes and alcoholics. Watching his show broadcast live was a sport. Some people made bets: will he make it in 600 seconds or not? His stunts were flawless. Although *600 sekund* (*600 Seconds*) was initially produced and broadcast by a regional Leningrad channel, it was watched by 50 million people across Russia.

Nevzorov was both the presenter and a reporter. He and his crew burst into offices and hospitals, broke into prisons and abattoirs. He showed the underworld in all its gory details. His journalistic stunts and his chutzpah mesmerized the audience. He pushed his microphone into the faces of city council officials and prisoners. While *Vzglyad* was made and watched by the Westernized urban elite, *600 Seconds* had a much wider appeal and peddled anything that sold: gratuitous violence, nationalism and death pornography. The more corpses the merrier.

'I was a conquistador who was conquering virgin information territory and crushing savages along the way. I did not give a damn about morality or public interest. I was simply dealing in the most profitable information. And the most profitable information at the time was crime... I had impudence, courage and an exceptional lack of principles,' Nevzorov explained.[2] Some of Nevzorov's 'revelations' were simply staged. His nightly prime-time programmes created the sensation that the country consisted entirely of criminals, drunkards and the homeless. How much of what Nevzorov showed was actually true was a very different matter. In his programmes, he called Leningrad 'Petrograd', as the city was known at the time of the Bolshevik Revolution and civil war.

In 1990 Nevzorov played himself in a full-length documentary film called *You Can't Live Like That*, directed and narrated by Stanislav Govorukhin, a film-maker best known for his thrillers. Nevzorov appeared in the film in the part of a lone crusader against crime, a heroic reporter-investigator fighting for the truth. *You Can't Live Like That* was a classic *film noir* which people queued to see as though it was a thriller, not a documentary, deriving odd pleasure from self-deprecation. The film presented a Bosch-like picture of the country's physical and moral degradation. Rapists, serial killers, thieves, drunkards and prostitutes populated the film which showed the lowest depths of Russian society. 'This is what seventy years [of Soviet rule] have done to us,' Govorukhin lamented.

In 1989 most people in the Soviet Union favoured 'socialism with a human face'. Between 1989 and 1991 the number of those who felt that socialism brought nothing but queues and repressions and that 'we are the worst country in the world', destined to teach others how not to live, grew from 7 per cent to 56 per cent. People started to refer to the Soviet Union as 'this country' rather than 'our country'. The word 'Soviet' morphed into '*Sovok*' (dustpan) and was used as an antonym to 'normal' or 'civilized'. This self-deprecation had nothing to do with repentance. It was the reverse side of the imperial superiority complex that had been hammered into people for decades and which was to resurface a decade and a half later when Russia got richer. The narrative of revenging the humiliation of the 1990s, 'imposed on Russia by the West', would become the centrepiece of the restoration ideology under Vladimir Putin. In fact, this 'humiliation' was imposed not by the West but by those who cultivated the idea of *Sovok* and by Putin himself.

The pessimism that engulfed the country in 1990 was as exaggerated as the euphoria had been four years earlier. It partly reflected the worsening economic situation in the country, uncertainty about the future, the rise in criminality and the weakness of the government. But as Alexander Yakovlev remarked at the beginning of 1990, 'It seems to me that there is a lot of theatricality and exaggeration in this confusion of minds, this whirlwind of events, outbursts of emotions and ambitions'. The paradox was that for all the difficulties and pessimism, Russian society was more friendly and receptive to the outside world than it was a decade later when life had become more comfortable and people started to holiday abroad, while lamenting the loss of the empire and its influence. At the time, the majority of people felt the most significant achievements of the Perestroika years were the withdrawal of Soviet troops from Eastern Europe and freedom of speech. Russian society seemed more agitated than depressed. And however apprehensive people felt about the future in 1990, few wished to go back to Brezhnev's era of 'developed socialism'.

This spirit of the last years of the Soviet regime revealed itself in a raft of anti-Utopian novels which appeared in the late 1980s. The most interesting one was a short novella by Alexander Kabakov, an author and staff writer for *Moskovskie novosti*. It was called *Nevozvrashchenets* (*The Man Who Doesn't Return*) and painted an apocalyptic picture of the future. A scientist, transported into the future at the instructions of his KGB minders, finds Moscow in 1993 run by quasi-military juntas who arbitrarily execute people in the name of Great Reconstruction. Tanks roam around the ruined city. Orthodox 'knights' spear Jews gathered by the stands of a liberal newspaper, while bearded members of the Revolutionary Committee of Northern Persia hunt people wearing Orthodox crosses. The scientist – an ultimate intelligentsia type – moves around the dark and cold streets with a Kalashnikov, dexterously dodging death like a Hollywood movie hero.

The novella ends on an unexpectedly optimistic note: offered the chance to go back to the good old times where people 'drank milky tea and read family novels', the scientist decides to stay in 'catastrophic' 1993. Walking up a desolate Tverskaya Street, he spots a car containing his KGB minders who are pointing a gun at him. 'I fell to the ground, having already undone a gun holster under my coat – at the ready. Here [in 1993] I was not afraid of them…'[3] The dissipation of fear was one of the most important results of the Perestroika years.

Looking for Cover

If anyone had a reason to feel fearful in 1990, it was the party and the KGB that were fast losing control over the situation in the country. Faced with mass rallies outside the Kremlin, the Communist Party was forced to abolish the sixth article of the constitution that guaranteed its monopoly on power. The KGB – the 'combat division' of the Communist Party – was also under pressure. By 1990 the liberal media, with *Moskovskie novosti* in the vanguard, turned its cannons on the KGB. Watching the party surrender its political monopoly, many KGB officers felt disoriented and exposed.

Yegor assigned the job of assailing the most formidable bastion of Soviet power to two young female reporters – Yevgenia Albats and Natalia Gevorkyan. Albats tracked down Stalinist investigators who were still alive and grilled them about themselves and their victims.* Gevorkyan mainly dealt with the KGB's present. 'Yegor called me in and told me: "I want you to write about these bastards – the security services, the KGB, you know…" I told him that I had never even read a law book in my life. "Never mind: you will go to these KGB guys, cross one leg over another and look at them with your silly eyes – you will see they will tell you stuff that they would never tell any man." It worked.'[4]

The reason for choosing Gevorkyan for the job was not just her good

* Albats also wrote one of the best political profiles of the KGB: *KGB: State Within a State* (New York: Farrar Straws Giroux, 1994)

looks and journalistic talents: she was someone Yegor had an affinity with and could trust. The granddaughter of an old Bolshevik, she was the next generation of the Soviet aristocracy – with roots not dissimilar to his own. Her father was at the heart of the Soviet intelligence service – first at the United Nations in New York where he befriended Andrei Gromyko, the Soviet foreign minister, then in Ethiopia. At the time when she walked into Yegor's office, in 1989, her father had just retired as the chief of the American department at News Press Agency (APN) to which *Moskovskie novosti* was subordinated. Like Yegor, she had spent time in Prague (as a journalism student she specialized in Czechoslovakia) but instead of returning to the Soviet Union at the end of her year out, she had married a foreigner and stayed in Czechoslovakia – a move which turned her into a renegade in the eyes of the Soviet authorities, closing most career paths.

One of Gevorkyan's first articles about the KGB was based on an open letter, which a former KGB staffer sent to *Moskovskie novosti*. The man was neither a senior KGB officer nor even a member of the party. He was an English-language interpreter mistakenly sent to work in Dresden. After he quit the service the KGB barred him from travelling to West Germany to see a friend, so he wrote to *Moskovskie novosti* to complain. All he did in Dresden, he wrote, was take the wives of KGB officers shopping and deliver matches and soap to his boss.

The years when the unfortunate interpreter served in Dresden – 1985 to 1988 – coincided with the service of another young KGB operative there: Vladimir Putin. (Gevorkyan's next-door neighbour in Moscow was Putin's boss in Germany.) Fast forward to 2000 and Gevorkyan, by that time a star reporter, was chosen, along with two other people, to interview Putin for a book to be called *First Person*. He told her how in 1989, in Dresden, he burnt documents fearing that an angry crowd could storm the KGB headquarters at any moment. When the crowd appeared outside the building where Putin worked, he came out to talk to them. 'These people were in an aggressive mood. I called our group of forces and explained the situation. And I was told: "We cannot do anything without orders from Moscow. And Moscow is silent."'[5]

Eventually, Putin said, military personnel did come and the crowd dispersed, but Moscow's silence stayed with him: 'At that moment I had a feeling that the Soviet Union had disappeared.' That feeling of betrayal experienced by many KGB officers around the Soviet bloc was exploited – with significant damage to the country – when former KGB men seized power in Russia a decade later. But in 1990 many of them felt uncertain and were desperately looking for political cover. Vladimir Putin ended up working for Anatoly Sobchak, the liberal mayor of St Petersburg. Then a far more senior man – Major-General Oleg Kalugin who was in charge of Soviet counter-intelligence – came to knock on the door of *Moskovskie novosti*.

Kalugin had spent thirty years as one of the most senior Soviet intelligence officers; his code name was Petrov. In the late 1980s clouds started gathering over Kalugin's head and he was put under surveillance personally authorized by the KGB chief as a suspected double agent (Kalugin always denied this). The day when Kalugin was forced into retirement, he 'handed' himself over to the 'democratic camp'.

A few months later he gave an interview to Gevorkyan. He did not disclose any secrets, but he made a political statement: 'The KGB remains untouchable. Its structure remains unchanged and so does its mighty potential which for years was the main power base of Soviet dictators. Even after five years of Perestroika, it is a state within a state, an organ endorsed with enormous power, able to trample down any government.' At the end, Gevorkyan asked Kalugin why he was undermining the system which he had loyally served for thirty years. In reply, Kalugin quoted Donald Maclean, a British diplomat who had spied for the KGB. 'Maclean said: "People who read *Pravda* every day are invincible". People who are well-informed and get their information from different sources inevitably start thinking,' Kalugin explained.[6]

Within days of *Moskovskie novosti* running the interview, Kalugin was stripped of his military rank and his medals. But this only boosted his 'martyrdom' status. *Moskovskie novosti* rushed to his defence, demanding explanations from the government. A few months later, Kalugin was elected as a parliament deputy and began his political career.* There was a certain irony in Kalugin's relationship with the media: a man who had used a journalistic cover when he served as a Soviet spy in America, went to a newspaper for political cover when the power moved away from the KGB. Going to a foreign embassy would have meant treason. Going to *Moskovskie novosti* meant insurance. Kalugin even deposited his medals in its safe.

A month after Kalugin's interview, *Moskovskie novosti* ran another interview – also by Gevorkyan – this time with Jan Ruml, the new Czech minister of the interior, a former dissident and a friend of the Czech president, Václev Havel. He told Gevorkyan how the new government had compiled a list of 140,000 people who collaborated with the State Security Service (STB). 'We wish the reformers in Czechoslovakia good luck, particularly since many of their problems are inseparable from ours. We hope that their ideals will never again be countered with Soviet tanks,' Gevorkyan concluded her article.[7] In 1990, the Soviet KGB was still immensely powerful, but the prospect of sharing the fate of their Czechoslovakian counterparts was alarming and real. The liberal media were a power to be reckoned or sided with.

The KGB was particularly demoralized by Gorbachev's resolution not to resort to force. At a Politburo meeting on 3 January 1990, Gorbachev explained his reasons.

* 'I have a feeling that he was really eyeing the job as the head of the [pro-Yeltsin] KGB,' Gevorkyan said later.[8]

> I was nine years old when my grandfather was arrested. He spent fourteen months in jail, they [the investigators] beat him up, tortured him, blinded him with a lamp. He was the head of a collective farm... After they had arrested him, we became untouchable in the village; nobody would come and see us, people would not say 'hello' to us – of course, [we were the family of] the enemy of the people! Grandfather came back a different person. He told us what they had done to him, cried.

Then without the slightest pause, Gorbachev switched back to the present. 'I think my greatest task is to take the country through Perestroika without a civil war. Some casualties are inevitable. Here and there someone gets killed – you can't get away from this. But to use force, weapons – that is a different matter. I will not do it.'[9]

Emboldened by Gorbachev's aversion to violence and repression, regional elites started to pull away from Moscow, declaring 'sovereignty' in their own affairs. Lithuania, which had been occupied by the Soviet forces since the Second World War, was among the first to use this window of opportunity. Its Communist Party quit the all-Soviet structure. 'Do you really want to leave?' Gorbachev questioned the Lithuanian intelligentsia as he tried to persuade them to stay with the flock. 'Yes' came a resolute answer.

In May 1990 Yeltsin was elected president of Russia – the largest and most important of the Soviet republics – and a month later, on 12 June 1990, Russia's Supreme Soviet followed the example of Lithuania and voted for Russia's sovereignty. On the same day the Soviet government abolished censorship and passed a new media law that turned freedom of speech from a privilege granted from above into a legal right. The coincidence of dates was symbolic.

Gorbachev desperately tried to stop Yeltsin's being elected as Russia's leader. The KGB planted stories about him in *Pravda* and showed embarrassing videotapes of Yeltsin's visit to America where he appeared to be drunk. But with the media no longer under central control, this did not have much impact: few people in 1990 read *Pravda* or paid attention to the party line. Yeltsin enjoyed mass popular support and was unstoppable.

The attitude of Perestroika reformers towards Yeltsin was more ambivalent. On the one hand Yegor and his circle of journalists refused to participate in a campaign against Yeltsin. On the other hand, they considered Yeltsin as a dangerous populist force who was calling for the break-up of the Soviet Union under the guise of Russian sovereignty. At the end of May 1990, Rodric Braithwaite, the British ambassador in Moscow, who dropped in on Yegor, found him unusually depressed. 'He says that the new government structures are simply not working, and there is a real risk of chaos... He is as gloomy as I've ever seen him: not the volatile gloom to which the Moscow intelligentsia has always been subject, but a settled depression which is much more worrying.'[10] Yegor was not alone in this. Braithwaite himself was apprehensive.

Foreign governments felt far more comfortable with an enlightened party man like Gorbachev, in whom they had heavily invested, than with a popular leader like Yeltsin. When, in September 1990, Douglas Hurd, the British foreign secretary, and Braithwaite went to see Yeltsin, they were almost hostile in their predisposition.

> Yeltsin receives us in a small room on the fourth floor – part no doubt of his pose of simplicity... But he still exudes raw power – though, as far as I am concerned, very little of the charm he is also said to possess... In general, I conclude that Yeltsin has very little interest in policy matters. He is interested in power, and his current tactic is to ... emasculate and discredit the Union government, and so isolate Gorbachev – as a step towards eliminating Gorbachev as well. He hopes to achieve this, not by intellectual ability or imagination, but simply by the force of this will.

> Many of his proclaimed policy objectives look hopelessly unattainable. But like Hitler, he evidently believes in the Triumph of the Will, in its ability to achieve what more ordinary people say is impossible.[11]

Few people realized at the time that Yeltsin, while seeking to eschew Soviet power structures, was the only consolidating figure in the country, who offered the best hope for preserving Russia itself from disintegration and a collapse into civil war. There was no reason why some of the regions of Russia, particularly the ethnically based ones, should not demand their own sovereignty. In fact, many of them did. Yeltsin's offer to the regional elites 'to take as much sovereignty as they could swallow' but stay within the Russian Federation was the only way of keeping Russia together.

The party, which in the eyes of Gorbachev's supporters – at home and abroad – was 'the only force capable of holding the fractured society together', in Yeltsin's eyes was a superfluous burden which had to be cast off altogether. This was precisely what Yeltsin did, formally quitting the party at the 28th Congress which also turned out to be its last.

Alexander Yakovlev, who had as few illusions about the party as did Yeltsin, faced the choice of abandoning the ship or staying with Gorbachev to the end. He stayed with Gorbachev. So did Yegor. As he wrote in *Moskovskie novosti*, 'I am far from blaming people who have acted according to their convictions [and quit the party]. I will be honest: there were moments at the Congress when I also had an inexpungible desire to return my mandate along with my party membership card.'[12]

His reasoning for not succumbing to this desire had nothing to do with ideology. 'There is no power equal to that of the party. And this party boasts a politicized army and the KGB, a combination of Soviet and party posts, ownership of a vast amount of property and monopoly over the media... And if that is so, how can one distance oneself from this colossus and transfer it into the sole possession of the conservatives?'[13]

The status of a patrician entailed a sense of personal responsibility. At the same time, Yegor faced the dilemma of what to do next with the paper.

On 1 October, *Moskovskie novosti* was published with the new strapline 'an independent newspaper'. The question of its future was openly debated on its pages. Alexander Yakovlev suggested that the task of *Moskovskie novosti* should be to appeal to and form the middle class – not the intelligentsia, dependent on the state, but a class of professionals who could support themselves and not rely on the state for handouts. These were the people who could move Russia forward. Nikolai Shmelev, a popular economics writer, backed Yakovlev: people were fed up with any party-mindedness or ideology. 'Let the newspaper follow in the footsteps of the 18th-century enlighteners. Let it try to appeal to the intellectual and humane features of the bourgeoisie, to those shoots of goodness which are not yet completely destroyed in people. Let its slogan be: "Long live common sense and decency."'[14] Decency and common sense were in very short supply. The benign instincts of the European bourgeoisie were virtually extinct. The Party and the KGB still had a few surprises in store.

Denouement

Faced with mounting pressures – both economic and political – Gorbachev dithered. His attempts to reconcile Yeltsin's programme of economic liberalization with retaining state control predictably yielded nothing but more frustration. Yeltsin, fed up with Gorbachev's unwillingness to face reality and agree to urgent reforms, threatened a complete secession of Russia from the Soviet Union – effectively a liquidation of the USSR.

Yeltsin's speech was an ultimatum and Gorbachev perceived it as such. 'What does Yeltsin's speech mean?' Gorbachev questioned his presidential council. 'It is a declaration of war to the Kremlin. If we don't take retaliatory measures, we will be defeated,' replied Kryuchkov, the head of the KGB. Nikolai Ryzhkov, Gorbachev's prime minister, painted a gloomy picture: 'The country is becoming ungovernable. It is on the verge of disintegration. Our power may not extend beyond the Kremlin walls or the Garden Ring [Road]. And that is all. The system of government is destroyed and we are responsible for it. We have to show that we are in power!'[15]

Like every Soviet government before it, Gorbachev's Politburo reached out for the two main levers of power – the police and the media – only to discover that neither of them was available. The police was headed by Vadim Bakatin, an intelligent, decent and pragmatic man of liberal views who refused to ban mass demonstrations or to use force against them. This was not a matter of softness, but of common sense. Dispersing a crowd of 400,000 people was physically impossible. When Kryuchkov demanded that Bakatin should 'demonstrate power', Bakatin told him: 'You show it. Let those who wish to ban those protests put these bans into practice. The police are not going to do this.'[16]

The media were even less compliant. As Ryzhkov told the presidential council: 'It is sickening to watch a TV presenter pronouncing Yeltsin's name with aspiration! [We should] remove half of the people from television! And kick out all these... from newspapers!' Gorbachev agreed: '[It is time] to restore some order in the media.' In fact the time for doing this had long passed. On 14 November, Yegor printed an appeal from the country's most highly regarded artists, writers and thinkers who were now also the founders of the new independent *Moskovskie novosti*. The letter was headed 'The Country is Tired of Waiting' and was addressed to Gorbachev. It drew a line under the period which had started in the spring of 1985. 'The peaceful changes are over. Blood has been spilled in many republics and could now be spilled in the centre. The country is sliding towards an abyss and a civil war.' It ended with an ultimatum: 'You cannot escape responsibility for today's state of affairs by swearing an allegiance to the socialist choice and communist perspective. Either you confirm your ability for decisive actions, or resign.'[17]

Gorbachev felt he had been hit in the solar plexus. 'Gorbachev is more upset by this than by anything else these days. He saw in it a personal betrayal,' Gorbachev's aide Anatoly Chernyaev recorded in his diary on 15 October 1990. 'The country is in a state of collapse and panic. Every newspaper predicts revolts, civil war and a coup. Every critical statement ends with the demand on the president: if you cannot even use the powers which you have been granted – "Go!"'[18]

The liberal reformers were not the only ones who presented Gorbachev with an ultimatum. So did the hardliners. The same day as the article in *Moskovskie novosti* printed its open appeal to Gorbachev, Viktor Alksnis, a Latvian army colonel – a reactionary figure dubbed the 'black colonel' by liberals – demanded that Gorbachev either restored order in the country and brought the republics to heel, or resigned.

Two days later Gorbachev addressed the Supreme Soviet with a short and dramatic speech, marking his sharp swing towards the hardliners. In his twenty-minute-long speech – one of the shortest in his political career – Gorbachev put the government under his direct control, dismissed the Presidential Council that included Alexander Yakovlev and a few other liberals and replaced it with a hawkish Security Council. The liberals were appalled. The conservatives were delighted. 'We will have to become more right-wing,' Gorbachev told his aides. The country, he argued to himself, could not cope with the pace of reforms and the liberals were irresponsible in their criticism.

Kryuchkov smeared Yakovlev, telling Gorbachev that he had been plotting against him. Having emasculated Yakovlev, the KGB took over the key appointments in the media and the police. The liberal-minded Bakatin was replaced as the head of the police with one of the KGB's own men, Boris Pugo. Leonid Kravchenko, a conservative party hack, was put in charge of television and promptly removed liberal TV presenters from the air.

All the signs pointed to a counter-revolution. Yet its creeping nature meant that nobody called it that. But, on 20 December, Eduard Shevardnadze, Gorbachev's foreign minister who had helped to end the Cold War, 'detonated' the situation by announcing his resignation. He said dictatorship was coming and a 'junta' was preparing to take over. Shevardnadze knew what he was talking about: half of the foreign ministry staff was seconded from the KGB and many of them had told Shevardnadze about its plans.

Vzglyad, which refused to go on the air without interviewing Shevardnadze, was shut down. Interfax, the first independent news agency in the country, was kicked out from its offices. 'It begins to look more and more like a crackdown on the organs of Glasnost. Glasnost is the central principle of Perestroika: a real crackdown would be very serious, close to the beginning of the end,' Braithwaite recorded in his diary.[19]

At the same Congress of People's Deputies that Shevardnadze used to make his resignation, Ales Adamovich, writer, war veteran and one of the founders, along with Sakharov, of Memorial, gave a prophetic warning. 'Gorbachev is the only leader in Soviet history who has not stained his hands with blood, and we would all like to remember him as such... But the moment will come when the military will instigate a bloodbath, and later they will wipe their bloodstained hands against your suit,' he told Gorbachev.[20]

The moment Adamovich warned about came on 12 January 1991 when interior ministry troops and the KGB tried to overthrow the government of Lithuania which had declared independence. There was shooting on the streets of Lithuania's capital, Vilnius. Tanks went in. It all seemed like a repeat of 1968. Events seemed to follow a familiar script: a call for 'normalization' in Lithuania, clearing the ground at home and cracking down on the media. There was one big difference, however. Those who had lived through 1968 were not about to give in. They still controlled print and print was still powerful. Most important of all, there was an alternative source of political power in the country – Yeltsin – who overtly supported the Baltic states.

That evening, Yeltsin was among the reformers, artists, journalists and foreign diplomats who gathered to mark the sixtieth anniversary of *Moskovskie novosti*. Yegor considered cancelling the party, given the events in Vilnius, but his journalists persuaded him otherwise: it was decided they should use the occasion to rally the country's elite and tell Gorbachev what they thought about Vilnius – while they still could. Yegor was on the stage at the Moscow Film-Makers Club when the news came in about tanks surrounding the television and radio centre and the main print-works in Vilnius. Yegor looked at his journalists who were in the audience and dispatched them to the three Baltic republics. They left before the evening was over – still dressed in their party wear. Boris Yeltsin also left early and went to Tallinn for an emergency meeting with the heads of the Baltic republics.

Shortly after midnight, Soviet special troops burst into the Lithuanian television and radio centre. The Lithuanian news presenter reported the attack live until she could do so no longer. The screens went blank. The main fighting, however, unfolded outside the television transmitting tower. Fourteen Lithuanians were killed and 140 wounded by Soviet soldiers who opened fire at the unarmed crowd that tried to defend the television tower. None of this was shown on Soviet television, which presented the crackdown as an attack by Lithuanian nationalists. Apart from one young newsreader, Tatyana Mitkova, who refused to read out the official statement on the late-night news programme *Televezionnaia Sluzhba Novostei* (*Television News Service*), most television programmes, including *Vremya*, fell into line. The main source of information in Moscow was a private radio station called Echo Moskvy (Moscow Echo).

The fact that the main fighting occurred over a television tower was a tribute to the power and importance of television as a way of controlling the minds of the people. To prevent the bug from spreading to Russia, the KGB had reinforced its forces with its own information offensive led by the television paratrooper, Alexander Nevzorov.

He raced to Vilnius to shoot a ten-minute 'documentary'. With a Kalashnikov slung over his shoulder and with Wagner's *Das Rheingold* as the soundtrack, he strode into the television tower, talking to the stern-looking Russian 'heroes', the 'defenders of the empire' and the Russian-speaking population against the 'fascist threat' posed by the 'nationalist Lithuanian traitors'. As for those Lithuanians who had had their skulls smashed by the riot police, or been run over by the tanks, they had died of 'heart attacks' or in 'car accidents', according to Nevzorov.

Nevzorov's ten-minute 'reportage' from Vilnius grew into a two-part documentary which he called *Nashi* – 'Ours', or 'Our Guys' – as opposed to Lithuanians or any non-Russians who were not 'ours'. '*Nashi*' is how Petr Verkhovensky, the scoundrel and agent provocateur in Dostoevsky's *The Devils*, describes his circle of pseudo-socialists. (A decade later Nevzorov said he was infatuated with Dostoevsky, and in particular with *The Devils*. He was particularly fascinated by Nikolai Stavrogin, a charismatic prince of darkness and nihilist who confesses to seducing a fourteen-year-old girl and driving her to suicide.)

Nevzorov said that behind him stood Kryuchkov, the bald and bespectacled head of the KGB: 'I always had connections with the KGB and it never ceased.'[21] According to Nevzorov, he was brought up by his grandfather – a KGB general who, between 1946 and 1953, fought against Lithuanian partisans who organized an armed resistance to the Soviet occupation. 'I grew up in the KGB family.' Kryuchkov, Nevzorov boasted, was a friend who often asked him for favours. 'To me, he was a romantic figure – the keeper of a great deal of explosive secrets, living under their spell.'[22] How much of what Nevzorov says is actually true and how much is 'romantic' fiction is impossible to say.

As Nevzorov himself later admitted, it was not about what happened in Vilnius, it was about whose side he was on. The anonymous Lithuanians were 'fascists', who were shooting at '*Nashi*'. Standing by the window of the television tower and staring into the darkness outside, Nevzorov was told by one of the Russian officers how Lithuanian snipers were aiming at his soldiers. The fact that the room was lit by camera flashes and would therefore be an obvious target for any sniper persuaded Nevzorov's critics that the whole thing was staged. 'They did not understand that I turned on the lights in the hope that they would shoot at us. I needed an action shot, windows being shattered – that is why I did it,' Nevzorov countered the criticism.[23]

Not a single Lithuanian was interviewed in the film. For Nevzorov's purposes, the enemy had to be collective and anonymous. 'I was very sincere then. I defended our soldiers not from the position of a Soviet man, but from the position of a Russian patriot. To support savages who rise against your country is not in the tradition of a Russian patriot.'[24] The film was praised by *Pravda* and was subsequently shown fourteen times on national television. Whereas Soviet television propaganda was drab and dull, Nevzorov's version was thrilling. Nevzorov set the precedent of an information offensive which was to be repeated many times over subsequent years, including during Russia's conflict with Georgia in 2008 and then again –with tenfold vigour – against Ukraine in 2014.

Yet while the main purpose of Putin-era propaganda has been to consolidate the power of Vladimir Putin, in 1991 neither Nevzorov nor those who were outraged by his film looked favourably at the Soviet president. Nevzorov blamed Gorbachev for not acting more decisively and for abandoning Soviet soldiers in the Baltic republics without reinforcements. The intelligentsia blamed him for moving in on the troops in the first place. There was no decision that would have satisfied both sides. Gorbachev said he was asleep when the attack took place and blamed it on the local authorities.

For the generation of Yegor Yakovlev and *Moskovskie novosti*, the events in Vilnius were a breaking point that annulled everything they believed in and had worked towards since the beginning of Perestroika. It turned out that socialism with a human face was an illusion after all, that the only things that could hold the regime together were the violence and lies which poured out from state television screens.

The morning after the bloodshed in Lithuania, *Moskovskie novosti* was printed with a black mourning border and eight full pages of stories about events in Vilnius. The journalists and editors also hung a flag with black ribbon on the side of the building and put up a sign on the door: 'The bloodshed in Lithuania is our blood.' The front-page editorial, printed under a photograph of a young man holding a national Lithuanian flag against a Soviet tank, was headlined: 'THE CRIME OF THE REGIME THAT DOES NOT WANT TO LEAVE THE STAGE'. 'After the bloody Sunday in Vilnius, what is left of our president's favourite topics of "humane socialism", "new thinking" and a "common European home"? Virtually nothing,' it said. (To be fair, it was not just Gorbachev's favourite topic – it was theirs too.) The editorial concluded with an appeal that echoed Solzhenitsyn's 'Live Not by Lies': 'We particularly appeal to journalists: If you don't have the strength or ability to tell the truth, at least do not participate in lies! This lie will become evident not tomorrow, not in the future. It is already obvious today.'[25] In the bottom right-hand corner of its last page *Moskovskie novosti* printed the names of its own journalists who had decided to leave the party. In alphabetical order, the last name was that of Yegor Yakovlev. After thirty-six years as a member of the Communist Party, Yegor had finally called it quits.

Soon after the Lithuanian events, a few of Yegor's closest friends came to mark his sixtieth birthday. His son Vladimir was also there. 'It was a meeting of people who did not know what to say to one another,' he told

David Remnick afterwards. 'The energy they used to have was gone, and the world around them was no longer their world. And, most important, they did not know how to relate to this world. It was the feeling you see at the traditional gatherings in Russia forty days after someone dies. No one is crying any more, but no one knows quite what to say. These birthday gatherings had always been such celebrations. Now it was just silence, a complete breakdown.'[26]

The turn-around by *Moskovskie novosti* and its readers made such an impression on Gorbachev that he proposed suspending the media law and putting the print and television media under the direct control of the Supreme Soviet – to 'ensure its objectivity'. In anger, he referred to the newspaper by its English name, *The Moscow News*, to stress its foreignness and alienation. But the genie could not be put back in the bottle. The days of Glasnost, when Gorbachev had handed out to a select few a licence to speak up, were over.

When one of the newspaper's journalists publicly and in his face challenged Gorbachev's proposals about suspending the media law, Gorbachev backed off from the idea as easily as he had put it forward a few minutes earlier. Gorbachev's swing to the right was easy to defy because it did not seem convincing. But the hardliners also sensed Gorbachev's weakness and volatility and found his refusal to endorse their actions in Vilnius deeply worrying.

A month after the failed coup in Vilnius, Gorbachev received an analytical report from the head of the KGB which urged him to impose control over the media in the interests of protecting the Soviet constitutional order. 'It is clear that the weakening of ideological work as a means of defending socialist ideals cannot be replaced by any other political force,' Kryuchkov wrote.[27] Just like in 1968 in Prague – the media were the biggest threat to the regime. And just like in 1968, the only tools available to the Soviet regime to save itself were tanks – with or without Gorbachev at the top.

In April 1991, Alexander Yakovlev wrote to Gorbachev:

> My information and analysis suggest that a coup d'état is being prepared from the right. Something like a neo-fascist regime will be established. The ideas of 1985 will be trampled. You and your allies will be declared an anathema. The only way out (politically) is to unite all healthy democratic forces to form a party or movement for public reform... Of course, all this should stay between us, just as it did in 1985. I understand the seriousness of this action both for you and for me. It would be easier for me to retire and turn to scholarship and memoirs, which is what I have decided to do. For you, of course, there is a possibility of leading such a movement, since you won't be able to play someone else's 'part' and 'game' for long... P.S. You know, Mikhail Sergeevich, that it is too late for me personally to strive for power. Here everything is clear.[28]

Gorbachev dismissed Yakovlev's prophetic and sincere note. He believed there was still a way out. On 23 July, Gorbachev, Yeltsin and the leaders of Ukraine and Kazakhstan met at Gorbachev's dacha to thrash out the final details of a treaty that would govern the relationship between the Soviet Union and its republics. Yeltsin, backed by the leaders of Ukraine and Kazakhstan, demanded that the three men responsible for the bloodshed in Vilnius – Kryuchkov, Pugo and Yazov, the heads of the KGB, the police and the army – should be dismissed. Gorbachev agreed, unaware that the whole conversation was secretly being recorded by Kryuchkov.

The same day *Sovetskaya Rossiya* published a manifesto entitled 'A Message to the People': 'Our Motherland... this great state which history, nature and our predecessors willed us to save, is dying, breaking apart and plunging into darkness and nothingness.' Yeltsin and other 'scheming, eloquent leaders, cunning dissidents and greedy rich exploiters... who hate this country and are now slavishly seeking advice and blessings from overseas' had to be stopped. 'Let us all rise up in unity and challenge the destroyers of the Fatherland... Russia, unique among nations, is calling for our help.'[29] The letter, Nevzorov said, was drafted by him. This time, it was signed not by the unknown Leningrad teacher, but by men who, as Braithwaite put it in his diary, 'could do something about it if they wished'. Among them was General Varennikov, the head of the Soviet ground forces. The liberals and the hardliners were racing each other.

On 16 August Alexander Yakovlev, whose letter to Gorbachev was left without reply, quit the Communist Party and published an open letter about the possibility of a coup: 'I'd like to warn society that a powerful Stalinist group has been formed in the leadership of the party, which opposes the course chosen in 1985... [It is] leading the country toward a revanche and a state coup.' Two days later, at 4.50 p.m., a group of coup leaders arrived in Foros in the Crimea, where Gorbachev was vacationing, to tell him he had a choice – either to resign or to support the self-appointed Committee for Emergency. 'Yeltsin's been arrested. He'll be arrested... Mikhail Sergeevich, we demand nothing from you. You'll be here. We'll do all the dirty work for you,' one of the group told Gorbachev. Gorbachev told them to get out.[30] Soon his lines of communications, including those by satellite, went dead.

In the small hours of 19 August 1991, special interior forces surrounded the Moscow television centre and TASS, the Soviet telegraphic agency. Leonid Kravchenko, the head of Soviet TV, was summoned to the Central Committee and instructed about an upcoming state of emergency. Once it was in place, 'television should work to the same regime as during the funerals of the leaders of the Communist Party and the country'. At 5 a.m. he was handed the decrees of the Emergency Committee abbreviated into the all-consonant GKChP. An hour later, a Soviet television announcer read out a statement: 'In view of Mikhail Sergeevich Gorbachev's inability, for health reasons, to perform the duties of the USSR president and of the transfer of [his] powers to Vice-President Gennady Ivanovich Yanayev, we resolve: to declare a state of emergency in some parts of the Soviet Union for six months from 04:00 Moscow time on 19 August 1991.'

The coup leaders stated: 'The policy of reforms, launched at Mikhail Gorbachev's initiative... have led to a dead end... Using the granted freedom... new extremist forces have emerged aimed at liquidating the Soviet Union...' The statement was repeated on the hour throughout the day with no commentary. In between, television channels played classical music and showed the ballet *Swan Lake* – just like during the funerals of the Communist Party leaders. The bells were tolling for the USSR. The television centre was put under the control of the KGB. Gorbachev was under house arrest in Foros.

Yeltsin was at his dacha when the coup broke out and like everyone else in the country learned about it from state television. Remarkably, though, he was not arrested. Having ensured that some of the military were on his side, he went to the White House – the seat of Russia's parliament 'that would become the main bridgehead of the events that were to come', Yeltsin recalled.[31]

First of all, Yeltsin held a press conference in which he defined the actions by the GKChP as a coup, demanded an immediate reinstatement of Gorbachev as the Soviet president and appealed to Muscovites to resist the junta. In the midst of the press conference, Yeltsin received information that another fifty tanks were moving towards the White House. Following his political instincts, he walked out of the building and climbed onto a tank, shaking hands with its crew. In scenes resembling Lenin reading out his first decrees, Yeltsin took a piece of paper from his pocket and read his appeal to the 'citizens of Russia'. In the days of the disintegrating empire, imagery and symbols had far greater power than any legal papers or even guns. And none was more important than that of Yeltsin on a tank reading out his appeal. It gave political focus and meaning to everything that unfolded in Moscow over the next three days. Thousands of people – young and old – flocked to the White House to defy the coup – not in the name of Gorbachev but in the name of Russia and Yeltsin.

And just like seventy years earlier, this battle unfolded over the printing press and telegraphic agencies. The first decree of the GKChP, after announcing the state of emergency was a ban on the publication of all independent newspapers. *Moskovskie novosti* was the first on the list. Its offices were heaving with people – not just journalists and editors, but everyone who considered it a key venue on the political map of the country. Yegor came back from the White House at about 2 p.m. on 19 August. He was collected and calm. He told his staff that, since they could not print the paper, they would print and photocopy leaflets and distribute them around Moscow by hand. He also told his journalists they were free to decide whether to stay or leave since *Moskovskie novostis* could be stormed at any moment. Everyone smiled but nobody left.

Yegor got an anonymous call on his *vertushka* – a special frequency 'Kremlin' line. The caller did not introduce himself: 'You tried to do me in, now listen to the radio, you son-of-a-bitch…'[32] The radio broadcast the decrees of the GKChP. Yegor was in his element. He relished it. This was his finest and most heroic hour – something that he had waited and longed for all his life. It was his answer to the revolutionary life of his father's generation. It was the moment that allowed him – and everyone who defied the coup – to show their best side. With tanks in the centre of Moscow, there was the beautiful simplicity of moral choice.

A few weeks later, life would return to its complexity, but in August 1991 most people lived for the moment. Alexander Kabakov, who reported the news from a window sill of the *Moskovskie novosti* building via a makeshift radio, wrote a few days later that these were the happiest days of his life. Journalists stuck their leaflets on the side of the tanks. 'A tank is the best advertising vehicle' someone joked. It was their war: words against tanks. Fear was lifted by the sense of the absurdity of the situation. For every KGB officer who wished to hang journalists on lamp-posts, there was one who supplied them with information.

Yeltsin appointed himself the commander-in-chief of all the armed forces on the territory of the Russian republic and at the same time Yegor effectively appointed himself the editor-in-chief of all liberal media. He gathered the editors of all closed newspapers in his office and suggested they unite their forces and publish one newspaper – *Obshchaya gazeta* – literally a 'common newspaper'. To print it, they used the offices of *Kommersant*, the first private newspaper that was edited by Yegor's son, Vladimir, which was equipped with photocopiers and old rotary printers. The four-page broadsheet *Obshchaya gazeta* carried descriptions of the distribution of troops around Moscow.

Nobody, however, inflicted as much damage to the coup leaders as they did to themselves when, inspired by Yeltsin's press conference, they decided to call one of their own. The very proposition was absurd: a militant junta which had brought tanks onto the streets of Moscow was paying heed to Glasnost. Remarkably, the press conference was broadcast on television.

The entire country saw five grey, middle-aged Soviet apparatchiks sitting behind a long table on the stage of the foreign ministry's press centre, preparing to answer questions from Russian and foreign journalists. Yanayev, the man who had assumed power in the country, tried his best to look composed, but his hands gave him away: they were shaking – either from fear or drinking and most probably from both. Constantly sniffing, as though searching for a drink, he and those next to him looked pathetic rather than scary.

Then it got worse. Halfway through the press conference, Tatyana Malkina, an open-faced and good-looking, twenty-four-year-old journalist in a light chequered summer dress, stood up and, fixing her eyes on the men in grey suits, said with a smile: 'Tell me, please, do you realize that you carried out a state coup last night? And which comparison do you find more appropriate – 1917 [the Bolshevik Revolution] or 1964 [the overthrow of Khrushchev]?'

Instead of suppressing this obvious revolt, by having Malkina arrested on the spot, Yanayev proceeded to answer her question: 'As for your assertion that we have committed an anti-constitutional coup, allow me to disagree with you, because our actions were based on the constitution... Historic comparison is not adequate here and is, in fact, dangerous.' If this was a thinly veiled threat, it did not scare the journalists.

Vremya, the main news programme, followed the broadcast of the official statements by the GKChP with the footage of Yeltsin on top of the tank, and protesters gathering in the centre of Moscow. A smooth, bespectacled reporter, Sergei Medvedev (soon to become Yeltin's press secretary), was allowed to gather news material under the innocent-sounding rubric 'Moscow today'. With a microphone in his hands, he stood under the bridge next to the White House, talking to men who were setting up the barricades and saying they had learned the lessons of Vilnius. With the acquiescence of Kravchenko's deputy, the report was put on air. Yeltsin, who also watched the programme, could not believe his eyes.

The report demonstrated that the coup leaders were not in full control of television and, therefore, of the country. Individual editors and reporters exercised their own will and judgement as far as they could. Elena Pozdniak, a long-serving news director at *Vremya*, who was entrusted with video-editing Brezhnev's speeches and 'correcting' mispronounced words, was asked to edit out Yanayev's shaking hands. She did not.

In the absence of any enticing idea or any overt violence, the orders issued by the coup leaders were worthless. Not a single person in Moscow came out in support of the coup. But thousands came out against it despite reports that the KGB's special forces were preparing to storm the White House.

From a military point of view, storming the White House presented no difficulties. But with tens of thousands of civilians defending the building, bloodshed was inevitable and someone had to take responsibility for giving an order. Finding such a person in Moscow in August 1991 proved impossible.

As Yegor Gaidar later wrote, the military commanders marked time, waiting for the KGB to act, the KGB waited for the army and the police waited for both of them. Nobody wanted to make the first move and shoot at people shouting '*Rossiya*' and '*Yeltsin*' in front of the building. Yet those who spent that night defending the White House could not be confident that the KGB would not use force. In fact, the experience in Vilnius and Tbilisi suggested the opposite. However ridiculous the coup might look in retrospect, the heroism of the 40,000 people who stood by the White House in the rain that night was real. As were the deaths of the three young men who were dragged under the tanks' treads in a tunnel under the Garden Ring Road across from the American Embassy.

In the morning of 21 August, tanks started to pull out of Moscow. Less than twelve hours later the coup leaders were arrested and Gorbachev returned to Moscow. For the first time in Soviet history, the state apparatus – armed with tanks, nuclear rockets and the largest military in the world – capitulated before its unarmed citizens. Vasily Rozanov, a nineteenth-century philosopher, wrote after the revolution of 1917 that 'Russia faded away in two days – three at the most'.[33] So did the Soviet Union.

With the coup over, emotions ran high. A vast crowd of up to 200,000 people moved to the building of the party's Central Committee and the KGB headquarters, threatening to smash up both. Inside the Central Committee building, the shredding machines were overheating, as party apparatchiks rushed to destroy whatever papers they could. Behind the darkened windows of the KGB headquarters, its few remaining officers were preparing to defend themselves with machine guns and hand-held grenades.

Ironically, the man who prevented the crowd from attacking the building was Alexander Yakovlev, the man most hated by the KGB. Standing on a makeshift podium and cheered by a jubilant crowd, Yakovlev sensed that 'a critical moment was approaching. One comment about "why people in the building behind my back are not applauding", or the question "What are they doing in there?" would have been sufficient for the irreparable to happen. People were wound up and ready for any action and had to be led away.' He quickly came down from the stage and walked towards Manezh Square, away from the KGB headquarters. People in the crowd picked him up, lifted him in the air and carried him all the way down to the turn of Tverskaya Street. 'Probably only my mother and the nurses in hospitals during the war had held me in their arms before then,' he recalled.[34]

Meantime, a crane appeared on the square and the anger of the crowd was diverted to the statue of Felix Dzerzhinsky, the KGB's founding father. A couple of men climbed up and slipped a rope around his neck. Then he was yanked up by the crane. Watching 'Iron Felix' sway in mid-air, many KGB officers felt betrayed 'by Gorbachev, by Yeltsin, by the impotent coup leaders'.[35] The death of the regime was accompanied by a series of suicides. Marshal Akhromeyev, Gorbachev's military adviser, was found dead with a rope around his neck and a stack of suicide notes on his desk. Pugo, the head of the interior ministry, shot himself and his wife minutes before investigators came to arrest him. A man who oversaw the finances of the Central Committee jumped out of the window. There were a dozen other suicides in the first post-coup days.

With hindsight, most of these suicides were needless. After about eighteen months in jail, the coup leaders were granted amnesty. Both Gorbachev and Yeltsin respected the rule made by Stalin's heirs after his death not to use violence against members of the ruling elite. Kryuchkov, who orchestrated the coup, lived long enough to regain wealth and status. So did many other conspirators. A decade later, Russia would be ruled by a KGB officer and his former colleagues who would project their sense of defeat and humiliation in August 1991 onto the rest of the country.

Mikhail Gorbachev and his circle of Perestroika lieutenants were both the winners and the biggest casualties of the coup. Gorbachev was physically alive but politically dead and so were most of the Perestroika reformers. As Latsis wrote in his book, 'we suffered a victory'.[36] If any hope of saving the union existed before the coup, it was certainly dead afterwards. 'After the events of 19–21 August, the death of the empire became not just inevitable, it happened,' pronounced Yegor Gaidar.[37]

That day *Moskovskie novosti* was published – the first time since the coup – with the headline: 'WE WILL LIVE!' Soon, however, the sense of victory and joy gave way to anxiety and reflection. The question was not 'Will we live?' but 'How will we live?' Humiliating Gorbachev may have given Yeltsin satisfaction, but it did not resolve any of the big questions, the main one being 'What next?' After the excitement and heroism of those three days, a downturn in the mood was perhaps inevitable. But this was a symptom of something far deeper than just a temporary anti-climax. The defeat of the coup did not become an ideological watershed; for all its revolutionary imagery, including Yeltsin on a tank, it was not celebrated as the birth of a new country, only as the collapse of the old one.

There was an expectation that, once the communist system was gone, Russia would become a 'normal' country, part of the civilized world. It was as if the main problem was ideology rather than a ruined economy, a demoralized workforce, a corrupt and greedy bureaucracy and a lack of institutions. Nobody had warned the hundreds of thousands of people who had demonstrated on the streets for sovereignty and democracy in the late 1980s that a collapse of the Soviet empire would be accompanied by continued hardship – otherwise why would people come out for it? Neither Gorbachev nor even Yeltsin as Russia's first president had any coherent plan or idea of what kind of a country would succeed the Soviet Union.

The Soviet intelligentsia, as a class, was the engine of the 1991 revolution, but it was caught unprepared by it. Used to raising toasts to 'the success of our hopeless cause', it did not know what to do when its cause succeeded. The intelligentsia and the state had been joined at the hip. It was a product of the Soviet system and could not exist without it. Having lost its main opponent (as well as its feeding hand), the intelligentsia lost a sense of its meaning and purpose; it felt depressed and disoriented. Many Russian intellectuals left the country. Others lamented their own fate. There was a vacuum of power, but there was also a vacuum of ideas.

A week after the coup, Alexander Kabakov wrote in *Moskovskie novosti*: 'Fairy tales end with weddings and revolutions; life only begins with them. Communism is over in our country. "What joy," one would have thought: I could have only dreamt to live to such a day. But there is no joy. Instead there is growing anxiety. How can one be glad of an ending if there is no beginning to follow or if the beginning is too hazy? For now, it is still a funeral.' Kabakov called his article 'A Ghost at the Feast'.[38]

The motif of the ghost was persistent in the months after the coup. Around the same time, the scholar and philosopher Sergei Averintsev wrote the essay published by the *Literaturnaya gazeta* (*Literary Gazette*) – a newspaper of Soviet intelligentsia – entitled 'God Keep Us from Ghosts'. It resembled a sermon illuminating the risks and opportunities of the coming era. 'It seems that we are entering an era of politics when any amateurism – however noble, sincere and morally invincible – is inadequate and therefore dangerous,' he wrote.[39] 'This does not mean that moral problems, moral examples become irrelevant – God forbid – but the period which is starting is more prosaic, where political weight is determined not by emotional and ideological criteria, but by the ability to offer particular solutions to particular problems.' The new era required Aristotle, not Plato, Averintsev argued. The problem was that Aristotles were few and far between.

Averintsev's sermon also contained a warning to the generation that was to follow the Soviet intelligentsia and which felt confident that it knew 'particular solutions to particular problems'. 'Beware of the difference between feeling right and displaying one's righteousness and superiority,' he wrote, citing the example of Pharisees.

According to Averintsev, 'the younger ones are always more guilty, because the older ones are feeble. It is never easy for the young, but it is nevertheless harder for the old. I would not want the righteous anger against totalitarianism to be exploited by those who are entering the stage as an excuse not to follow God's commandment "Honour your father and your mother so that you can live long on this land..."'[40] Above all, he argued, do not distort reality. Facing the past was one thing, reinventing it was quite another. 'Christ tells people to return from the imagined world to reality and from the imagined self to one's actual self. A return to God is possible from any real place – however shameful and disgusting, but not from an imagined one – because we are not there. An imagined self in an imagined world cannot start a journey toward God. Let us try to choose reality and God saves us from any ghosts,' Averintsev concluded.[41] Inevitably, his words of wisdom fell on deaf ears.

FOUR

Fathers and Sons

Look Who Is Here

The coup induced or coincided with a generational shift in Russian public life. Rarely had the transition been so clear-cut. The *shestidesiatniki*, or the generation of the 1960s, were succeeded by their children. Naturally mistrustful of Gorbachev's circle of reformers, Yeltsin surrounded himself by people who were twenty or thirty years younger. But the generational shift was even more pronounced and meaningful among those who came to control the media and the narrative of the country.

Unlike Yegor's generation of reformers who grew up in the 'fireglow' cast by the revolution, their children had no reverence for their fathers' generation. They did not suffer from Hamlet's urge to redeem their fathers or to carry on their deeds. First, their fathers were still alive; second, they were bankrupt, both intellectually and financially.

The idea of 'socialism with a human face' was as dead as the Soviet economy. While Yegor's generation wished to carry on their fathers' deeds, their children presented the *shestidesiatniki* with a hefty bill for their failures: 'How could they justify the Bolshevik Revolution even when its consequences were so obvious?' Settling scores with the *shestidesiatniki* became one of the popular intellectual pursuits of the first post-Soviet years. The young 'liberals' were too quick to blame their fathers (and the

Soviet intelligentsia as a whole) for getting too close to state power, for playing cat-and-mouse games with the authorities, for their slogans of 'more socialism', but above all for their civic pathos.

Public rejection of the *shestidesitaniki*'s 'pathos' and 'idealism' became the main *raison d'être* of their children's generation. In 1992, in a television programme called *Moment istiny* (*Moment of Truth*), Andrei Karaulov, a journalist at *Nezavisimaya gazeta* (*Independent Newspaper*), talked to two intellectuals of his generation – Alexander Timofeevsky and Andrei Malgin. 'What they [*shestidesiatniki*] cried over – we laugh at,' Malgin summed up the motto of his generation. 'You have to take life lighter and more ironically,' he explained. Karaulov questioned his interlocutors: Did they support Yeltsin? 'We would support him if he took the country down the same path as South Korea.' What Russia needed, they argued, was an Augusto Pinochet who could reform the country and establish order while building capitalism.

Karaulov, who was also the son-in-law of Mikhail Shatrov, author of plays about Lenin, reprimanded his interlocutors for taking too radical a position. To him, the *shestidesiatniki* were neither right nor wrong – they were irrelevant. People like him, Karaulov said, were the real winners of August 1991. It was a disturbing thought.

The divisions between people and generations at the time of the Soviet collapse occurred not just along political lines – those were simply the most visible. Most people with a brain joined the 'democratic' camp whether they believed in it or not. Far less visible, and in the long term far more important, were the rifts that were opening up along moral and ethical lines.

The irony is that Karaulov, who appeared to be claiming the high moral ground, was arguably one of the most cynical Russian journalists. In *Lenin's Tomb*, David Remnick describes Karaulov as a 'journalist-hustler the likes of whom I never had seen before or have since – at least not in Moscow'.[1] One day Karaulov took Remnick to see the editor-in-chief of

Nezavisimaya gazeta, Vitaly Tretyakov. As they passed the KGB buildings on Lubyanka Square, Karaulov tried to sell Remnick – literally, and for dollars – 'some crackpot spy-story documents involving the Bolshoi Theatre... When I refused Karaulov's "tip" on the Bolshoi and explained the rules about not paying for information, he seemed alternately bemused and hurt. "Besides, you'd never find the place without me. You owe me for that at least."' In the following decade Karaulov would become one of the most despised figures in television journalism, whose *Moment of Truth*, even by the relative standards of Russian journalism, became a byword for cynicism and slander.

After the television programme, Malgin had a debate with Yegor Yakovlev, which he printed in his magazine *Stolitsa* (*Capital City*) under the headline 'LOOK WHO IS GONE'.[2] Yegor had just been fired as the head of Central Television – the job he had taken immediately after the August 1991 coup – and decided to start his last newspaper *Obshchaya gazeta*. Malgin attacked Yegor and his circle. 'You served the power. You persuaded our poor, brainwashed generation that revolution is good, that socialism is even better and we should all march towards communism.' Yegor tried to defend his generation. 'You don't understand the tragedy of our generation: we tried to improve the political system, not to bring it down... Was it possible? I don't know. The problem was that whenever you try to improve the system, it begins to self-destruct.' But, as Yegor argued, there was nothing wrong with the ideas of social justice and equality in themselves.

Malgin cut him short: 'After everything the country had been through, to say anything good about socialism is indecent.' A year after the collapse of the Soviet Union, Yegor was in no position to defend socialism as a political system, but he told Malgin that extolling capitalism and boasting about the bourgeoisie were equally improper. 'Yet, in Russia everyone is now dreaming of capitalism in its most primitive and inhuman sense.' At the end of the conversation Malgin told Yegor: 'For young people – those who are not even thirty-four, but half that age – you are hopeless [as a generation].' Yegor did not argue: 'It is sad, of course, but I have to say that my generation has gone from the stage. One could, perhaps, publish a newspaper of a "gone generation" but every obituary in such a paper would mean that the paper had lost a reader.'

Yegor sensed the generational shift personally and acutely because it occurred within his own family. His son Vladimir Yakovlev was the founding editor of *Kommersant*, the first and most formative newspaper of the nascent capitalist era that became the manifesto of the 'sons'' generation. A true journalist, fond of an effective ending, Yegor marked the signing-off of his last issue of *Moskovskie novosti* in 1991 by interviewing his own son.

The conversation between the father and son was tense. Undercurrents ran through every question and answer and much was left between the lines. Politics did not interest Vladimir. When Yegor asked his son to come to Gorbachev's leaving party hosted for journalists, Vladimir did not turn up. To him, Gorbachev and his father were history. He was far more excited by the opportunities that were opened up by the Soviet collapse to deliberate on the reasons for that collapse. He saw the Soviet system as a hindrance, an aberration that prevented people making money without falling foul of Soviet bureaucracy.

For Yegor, who was a Soviet man with a state salary, the idea of his son becoming an entrepreneur was incomprehensible. 'I could never understand you, nor agree with you. Even in the smallest thing: in your readiness to receive money not from a state exchequer, but elsewhere...' Yegor concluded the two-page spread with a reminiscence that had neatly encircled the conversation. 'A quarter of a century ago, I published my first book. In it, I dwelled on the problem of fathers and sons. It was called *I Walk Along With You*, confirming that I was ready to carry on along my father's path. I thought it was possible at the time. I dedicated it to my son, "Vovka [diminutive of Vladimir], a participant in future debates". I could hardly imagine what kind of conversation I would have with him quarter of a century later.'[3]

Vladimir Yakovlev, named after his Ch.K grandfather, certainly did not plan to walk alongside his father. In fact, he directed his energy towards shaking off his father's grip over him. Yet he shared some of his father's traits, including his energy, ambition and belief in the transformative power of information and the printed word. *Kommersant* (its name comes from 'commerce') did not just reflect but defined and directed Russia's transition to capitalism, in the same way as *Moskovskie novosti* defined Perestroika.

Like the capitalist era itself, *Kommersant* was born out of a co-operative that Vladimir Yakovlev had started in the late 1980s while working as a journalist at *Ogonyok*, the Perestroika weekly. The co-operative dealt in information and was a by-product of a journalistic assignment: an editor had asked Vladimir to write an article about how to open a co-operative and, in the interest of the story, to open one himself. Vladimir soon realized that while there was no shortage of people wanting to start a business, few of them had any idea of how to do so.

For all the openness of the Soviet print media, factual information was the privilege of the powerful. Telephone directories were classified. To get a telephone number for a government office, an embassy, or a co-operative, one had to have connections in the right places. Vladimir realized this was a golden opportunity. He advertised his services in finding people work in private co-operatives and helping with starting a business. 'The next day we had 235 responses. We sat down that morning, looking at each other in panic, and asked "Well, now, how the hell are we going to help these people get work?" We had no idea.'[4] Thus was born a co-operative called Fakt. Getting hold of information about co-operatives was not as difficult as it seemed. As Vladimir soon discovered, it was not just he who needed that information – most co-operatives looking for clients and for staff wanted to have it. All he had to do was to make his own presence known. Fakt operated like the Yellow Pages.

People flocked to his office which had been set up in an accordion store, and paid him 1 rouble for getting information on anything from a co-operative restaurant to plumbing, or ten times that much for offering their own services to co-operatives that were on Fakt's database. Fakt also sold manuals, along with a set of documents, for starting a business – at 30 roubles apiece – and published a bulletin about co-operatives and black market prices, a prototype of a future newspaper.

The idea to start a newspaper, Vladimir Yakovlev said, was forged in a conversation with Artem Tarasov, the first Soviet legal millionaire whose business was to import computers and repair second-hand Japanese electronics. Tarasov, who headed the co-operative movement, argued that it needed its own print organ and urged Vladimir to create one. Vladimir saw the co-operatives for what they were – not some marginal experiment in private business, but a way of legitimizing one of people's basic instincts: making money. His talent was to recognize the future Russian businessmen as a social force.

Vladimir's plans were more ambitious than anything that Tarasov had suggested. He wanted to create the first truly Western-style newspaper like the *New York Times* which he saw at home. It would come out both in Russian and in English and the information would be supplied by its own news agency which he called Postfaktum.

Vladimir had an unlikely partner – Gleb Pavlovsky, a former dissident from Odessa who was first picked up by the KGB in the mid-1970s for possession and distribution of anti-Soviet literature. In exchange for naming his contacts, he was let go. A few years later he was arrested again – this time for publication of a samizdat magazine. He agreed to co-operate with the investigation and was sent into exile instead of to a labour camp. He had a dubious reputation among Moscow dissidents as someone who was said to have closely collaborated with the KGB and testified against fellow dissidents. Pavlovsky was put in charge of the Postfaktum news agency. Vladimir became the editor of *Kommersant*.

In 1989, censorship was still formally in place. To circumvent it, Vladimir presented *Kommersant* as the organ of the Association of the United Co-operatives of the USSR and persuaded Glavlit, the main censorship body, that it was not a newspaper but an advertisement, which was exempt from censorship under a new Perestroika law. 'Why does your advertisement look like a newspaper?' a suspicious censor queried. 'It is an advertisement for a newspaper,' Vladimir explained. Vladimir's explanation was not entirely misleading. In many ways, *Kommersant* was an advertisement. It advertised a new capitalist life as Vladimir envisaged it at the time. Its title sounded provocative. Officially, there were no *kommersanty* in the Soviet Union and commerce itself was an offence punishable by prison.

Kommersant was the antithesis of *Moskovskie novosti* and a reaction to it. It rejected its civic pathos, its elevated language, its speaking of the Truth, capitalized and accentuated with exclamation marks, its sense of calling and duty, its political stand. 'What we did was anti-journalism, from the point of view of my father's circle. Theirs was journalism of opinion. Ours was journalism of facts,' Vladimir said.[5] Only a few of *Kommersant*'s reporters were Soviet-trained journalists. Most were intelligent young men and women who had never written a newspaper article in their life.

As a bourgeois paper, it was not supposed to be read on a newsstand, like *Moskovskie novosti*, by politically minded intelligentsia. It was a newspaper for serious people involved in the serious business of making money and it was supposed to be read in the comfort of one's home, at breakfast, with a glass of orange juice (non-existent at the time) and a cup of coffee on the table. The irony was that having established itself as a paper of the new times, *Kommersant* was as concerned with the question of the past as the print media run by Yegor's generation, which it rejected. Searching for the key historic junctions at which Russia took a 'wrong' turn, Yegor had rewound the tape to 1968 and then further back to the times of Lenin's New Economic Policy. The only difference was that while

Yegor was trying to reach back to the origins of the Bolshevik Revolution, his son was rewinding the tape even further back – to the notional (and much idealized) era before the First World War, when Russia had a fast-growing entrepreneurial class. While Yegor had borrowed the title of *Zhurnalist* from the 1920s, Vladimir borrowed the title of *Kommersant* from the early 1900s.

The paper started with a manifesto printed in its test issue:

> Today's Soviet businessmen are people without a past. They are people without the weightiest argument in their favour – historical experience. Isn't this the root cause of many present troubles? A rootless tree is so tempting for a lumberjack... *Kommersant* was published in Moscow between 1909 and 1917. It was a newspaper for business people, and many of its stories are still fit to print today, after a little editing. So we decided against launching a completely new newspaper... We also decided to stick to the old title and even kept the pre-revolutionary 'hard' accent at the end [КоммерсантЪ].[6] Since the use of this letter is a matter of principle for the Editorial Board, we will keep it... We do have a past after all.[7]

The pre-revolutionary *Kommersant* had hardly been a newspaper of note. Started as a trade sheet, it quickly ran out of money and was bought by a paper manufacturer and publisher of pornographic pamphlets. Having predicted, on the eve of the revolution, that the Bolsheviks would never succeed, *Kommersant*, along with other newspapers, had been promptly shut down when the Bolsheviks came to power.

But the fact that a newspaper with that title and a pre-revolutionary hard sign Ъ on the end had existed in the past was more important than what kind of paper it really was at the time. Vladimir Yakovlev was not reviving an old newspaper, he was reinventing the past and historical experience – supplying Russian capitalism with the biography it lacked.

The masthead of the newspaper carried an important message: 'The newspaper was established in 1909. It did not come out from 1917 until 1990 for reasons outside editorial control.' *Kommersant* was defining a period – 1917–1990 – and simply extracting it from its own experience. The entire Soviet era was being disposed of as irrelevant to the readers and writers of *Kommersant*. If *Kommersant* had not come out in those years, then why should they be of any interest?

'We did not know the history of the country well. We saw the whole of the Soviet period as one muddy stretch and we wanted to reconnect, to establish a connection with an era of common sense and normality,' said Vladimir Yakovlev.[8]

Kommersant fought against Soviet ideology but its own rejection of Soviet culture – dissident or official – was deeply ideological. Anything that was touched by the Soviet aesthetics was out – regardless of its content or artistic merit. The 'sons' were not only disposing of wooden Soviet language, newspaper headlines and party-minded literature, they were throwing out an entire layer of culture that contained, among other things, strong antidotes to nationalism and totalitarianism. By doing so, they severely damaged the country's immunity to these viruses, making it easier, a decade later, to restore the symbols of the Soviet imperial statehood.

Kommersant readers and authors treated the Soviet civilization not as an object of study or reflection but as a playing area for postmodernist games and mockery, a source of puns and caricatures. The written Soviet language, which had long lost its connection with literature, had become so petrified that it easily lent itself to this exercise. The post-communist Russia lacked its own serious language to describe the biggest transformation of the century. Words such as 'truth', 'duty' and 'heroism' were completely devalued. In 1990, the year when *Kommersant* started to publish, literary historian Marietta Chudakova noted in her diary: 'Do our people expect any "new word" from themselves? No. Nobody expects anything. What could come out from such a total absence of pathos?'[9]

What came out was *styob* – jeering, imitation and denigration of anything remotely serious. *Styob* became a house-style for *Kommersant* headlines loaded with wordplay and double-meanings: 'THE CITY COUNCIL ORDERS MEAT TO GET CHEAPER. MEAT REFUSES'; 'HOMOSEXUALS ARE MAKING ENDS MEET'; 'SOCIALISM WITH A HUMAN END'. *Styob* was infectious and spread through the Russian media like a rash. It pricked and deflated the fake pathos of the Perestroika era, but it contributed nothing in terms of new ideas and meanings. The smirk and imitation concealed emptiness.

In the early 1990s, however, *Kommersant* emerged as a new type of newspaper that not only described reality differently, but also aimed to shape it. To do so, it needed a new language. A man who was largely responsible for creating this new language, not just in *Kommersant* but in much of the post-Soviet media, was Maxim Sokolov, its chief political columnist. 'At the time when I started writing for *Kommersant*, there was either the canon of the Soviet Communist Party print, or the revolutionary "auf Barrikaden, auf Barrikaden" which called to the struggle against the forces of darkness.'[10] Sokolov introduced a third one: detached, ironic, drawing on the tradition of nineteenth-century popular prose.

Maxim Sokolov was not a journalist. He was an intellectual and a liberal conservative. Both in his writing and his appearance Sokolov cultivated the image of an erudite individualist and sceptic who belonged in a pre-Soviet era, who had been asleep for the last seventy years of Soviet history and who had been catapulted by a time machine into the present day and was now trying to make sense of a contemporary Russia through a nineteenth-century monocle. Each issue opened with his column called 'The Logic of the Week' (later becoming 'What Happened This Week'). Unlike the columnists of *Moskovskie novosti*, who always took a stand and expressed their position, Sokolov sounded nonchalant and detached from the subject: the only stand he took was that of an impartial observer, looking at current affairs and their main actors from the height of historic wisdom. He placed political events into a traditional church calendar and applied words that did not suit them, making them sound comical and absurd. His columns were laced with nineteenth-century phraseology and peppered with Latin words, quotes from literature and hidden allusions.

The fact that his articles were for the most part impenetrable for those who were supposed to be *Kommersant*'s main audience – the nascent class of businessmen more versed in prison slang than in Sokolov's Latinisms – was part of his selling point. It created a sense of exclusivity and belonging among the new rich. Although it would be hard to imagine Sokolov's column in any Western or Soviet newspaper, it was a perfect match to *Kommersant*. His literary 'monocle' was as much an imitation as *Kommersant*'s 'long tradition'.

Kommersant exemplified the contradiction of the 1991 transition. As a product of a revolutionary era, it rejected the immediate past. At the same time *Kommersant* shunned revolutionary aesthetics, mainly because, as Sokolov himself wrote ten years later, 'Revolution is a time when people say and write an unbelievable amount of banalities.'[11] Its coverage of the August 1991 coup was completely devoid of any revolutionary pathos. Whereas *Moskovskie novosti* came out under the banner 'We Will Live!', *Kommersant* came out under the headline 'THANK GOD, PERESTROIKA IS OVER'.

Sokolov's lead article was preceded by a silly ditty: 'I woke up at 6 a.m. and felt a wave of joy / The elastic in my pants was gone and so was Soviet rule.' 'The past two days in Moscow have been a funeral: the idiotic regime died in an idiotic way. The coup turned out to be foolish, because people stopped being fools,' Sokolov summed up his impressions.[12] A week later, in the Markets & Exchanges section, *Kommersant* wrote: 'An attempt to stage a coup by a group of people on 19 August was so short-lived that it has not had an impact on the prices of goods which were defined by orders placed beforehand.'[13]

The end of the Soviet Union produced none of the cultural vitality which accompanied its birth in 1917. The energy of the 1920s was sustained by the emergence of a vision of a great utopia, even if it turned out, like all utopias, to be a deception. In contrast, August 1991 was the end of utopia and the end of ideology. As Sokolov wrote phlegmatically, all he wanted to do after three days in the White House was to 'have a bath and sleep'. In Chudakova's words, what could come out from such a total absence of pathos?

Lacking a new project, or even a vision of a future country, Russia searched for a mythical past. Those who came to power after the Soviet collapse, both in the Kremlin and in the media, portrayed themselves not as revolutionaries but as keepers and followers of the tradition that had preceded the Soviet era. (The inauguration of Yeltsin as Russia's first-ever president was announced, absurdly, as being carried out in the style of long historic tradition.)

Alexander Timofeevsky, a young belletrist who articulated the ideas of the thirty-something generation, enthused about *Kommersant*'s conservatism, its deliberate and measured tone, its sense of solidity which 'like in a thick, British paper implies a centuries-long stability of life, which has been set and planned for centuries'. In reading articles with enigmatic foreign words such as 'leasing' and 'banking clearing' and 'exchanges', 'one gets an illusion not just of common tone, but of something infinitely bigger – an illusion of a different life which has been watered and mowed for 200 years'.[14]

The fact that this life was a pure invention did not bother him. *Kommersant*, he wrote, 'unfolds a different life on its pages – charming and desirable. The common reproach that *Kommersant* lies a lot, is irrelevant. It does not matter. What matters is that it lies confidently and beautifully.' After that article was published, in December 1991, Vladimir Yakovlev invited Timofeevsky to be his personal, in-house critic. Timofeevsky's article was headed 'Bubbles of the Earth' and was pre-empted with an epigraph from *Macbeth*: 'The earth hath bubbles, as the water has / And these are of them…' The line in the play refers to the witches whose lures are as deceptive as their appearances. It applied both to *Kommersant* and to Timofeevsky himself.

'Moscow in December 1991 is one of my most painful memories. Grim food lines, even without their usual squabble and scenes. Pristinely empty shops. Women rushing about in search of any food to buy. Dollar prices in a deserted Tishinsky market. An average salary of seven dollars a month. Expectations of disaster were in the air.'[15] This is how Yegor Gaidar, who took charge of and responsibility for the Russian economy, remembered the month when the Soviet Union came to an end. There was talk of hunger, complete paralysis of transportation, collapse of the heating system. Russia was bankrupt.

On 2 January 1992 Gaidar removed the state regulation of prices for most products, which led to a threefold increase in the price of food, revealing an inflation which had been previously hidden by shortages and which now wiped out people's nominal savings. Destroying worthless rouble savings was the only way of making money work again. A few weeks later, Gaidar lifted restrictions on trade, allowing people to sell anything anywhere, and removed import barriers.

Almost overnight central Moscow filled up with makeshift trading stalls. People – young and old – came to sell anything they had – a pair of socks, a bottle of vodka, a packet of butter, pornographic magazines, Bibles, apples, anything. It was an unseemly sight, but in the winter of 1991 nobody was thinking about aesthetics apart from *Kommersant*, of course. The younger and more energetic travelled to Turkey and China, filling up cheap plastic holdalls with jackets, coats and underwear, and brought them back for sale. These shuttle traders clothed the country. This was not a sign of poverty. It was a liberation of forces and instincts that had been fermenting under the surface of official Soviet propaganda for years and were constrained by the state. The people who sold bread and butter on the street did so not because they themselves could not afford it, but because they were allowed to trade.

In the early 1990s Russian capitalists bubbled up from underground. They were black-marketeers, opportunists, adventurists, hustlers and so on. Most of them had cut their teeth in co-operatives. They were colourful and they marked themselves out by dressing brightly, extravagantly and mostly tastelessly. They favoured purple and fluorescent yellow jackets. But bright did not mean beautiful or nutritious. Poisonous flowers or plants often mark themselves out in bright colours – a form of defence or a warning to birds and animals: eat me and you will die.

These bright bubbles were *Kommersant*'s people, whom it wished to fashion and educate, but above all to whom it wanted to give a veneer of respectability and self-awareness as a class – or to use Lenin's term, 'class consciousness'. 'The most important quality in a newspaper is not its information or emotions, but a sense of social belonging. You pick up a newspaper and you feel part of a certain class,' Vladimir Yakovlev explained.[16] The paper appeared first; the class came later.

Kommersant organized life that lacked structure into rubrics and subjects. 'We have always argued at our editorial meetings which page this or that character should go on. Is he on page two – which was about economic policy and those who made it – or should he be on the business pages, or should he be moved to page nine which was about crime,' recalled Elena Nusinova, an editor who started along with Yakovlev at *Kommersant*. 'The usual progression was from an official, to a businessman, to a criminal. Although sometimes it worked the other way around. The conversation went like this: "Should he be on your page or on mine? OK, let him stay on your page (business) one more time, and then he will move to mine (crime) unless they kill him first in which case he moves to obituaries."'[17]

The early 1990s was a wild and entrepreneurial time, when anything seemed possible. The state was weak and private initiative and individualism were strong. It was, perhaps, the freest time in Russian history. As Vladimir Yakovlev said, 'We were like kids in a kindergarten with real machine guns.'[18]

Kommersant was the flesh and blood of Russian capitalism and and bore some of its unattractive birthmarks. It was partly funded by an American grain trader Thomas Dittmer, whom Vladimir Yakovlev had courted in the late 1980s.* Dittmer, who hosted Vladimir Yakovlev at his forty-two-acre (16.2-hectare) Chicago estate, was so impressed with his chutzpah and ambition that he agreed to finance $400,000's worth of equipment for *Kommersant* in return for exclusive rights to *Kommersant* or Postfaktum information in the West.† (Vladimir was planning to have an English-language edition of *Kommersant*.) This did not stop Pavlovsky trying to peddle the content of Postfaktum to Dow-Jones and Reuters directly.

Within a few months of launching a short-lived English-language edition of *Kommersant*, Yakovlev started to lose interest in Dittmer and his Refco trading business and decided to ditch the arrangement. After a series of rows, Vladimir, in order to free himself from any obligations, secretly renamed Co-operative Fakt – with which Dittmer had signed a contract – as Joint Stock Company Fakt. 'There is no Co-operative Fakt any more. And if there is no more Co-operative Fakt, there is no more *Kommersant*,' Vladimir explained to Copetas. This was a very Russian way of doing business. At the same time Vladimir Yakovlev was negotiating a new deal with a French media group, La Tribune de l'Expansion, which agreed to pay $3.5 million for a 40 per cent stake in *Kommersant*.

* Yakovlev was introduced to Dittmer by an American journalist and one of *Kommersant*'s co-founders, A. Craig Copetas. In his racy and captivating book about the venture, *Bear Hunting with the Politburo*, Dittmer, the CEO of Refco, is disguised as 'Tom Billington'.

† Copetas said that the total investment by Refco in *Kommersant* was nearly $1 million.

Yakovlev argued that from a legal point of view the deal with the French holding did not contradict his arrangement with Dittmer. 'Refco had the right to all our content outside Russia. The French formed a joint venture with us. But from the point of view of human relationships, it was questionable.'[20] In the early 1990s, though, nobody asked questions about the ethics of doing business. 'There were no rules. A businessman was driven or stopped only by what was inside him. Some people thought it was OK to steal, but not OK to kill. Some people thought it was OK to kill, but not to touch family members,' said Nusinova.

The new class of businessmen that emerged from the rubble of the Soviet economy thought of themselves as the champions of capitalism as they understood the word. In some ways they were victims of a Soviet propaganda and ideology that portrayed capitalism not as a set of rules and ethics based on the ideas of honest competition and fair play, but as a cut-throat cynical system where craftiness and ruthlessness were more important than integrity, where everyone screws each other and where money is the only arbiter of success.

Russian capitalism had nothing to do with Weber's Protestant ethics. It was not built on a centuries-long tradition of private property and feudal honour and dignity. In fact it hardly had any foundation at all, other than the teaching of Marxism-Leninism that described private property as theft. Since they favoured property, they did not mind theft. The words 'conscience', 'morality' and 'integrity' were tainted by ideology and belonged in a different vocabulary – one that was used by their fathers' generation. 'For us these were swear-words which the Soviet system professed in its slogans while killing and depraving people,' Vladimir Yakovlev said.[21]

The tenets of Soviet 'morality' and socialism were removed only to reveal a vacuum of morals – in itself the result of the Soviet experiment of breeding a new being. The transition from the Soviet to the post-Soviet society was accompanied by a change in perception of what makes one succeed in life. In 1988, 45 per cent of the country felt it was 'diligence and hard work'. In 1992 only 31 per cent felt these would get you anywhere. The factors that gained importance, on the other hand, were 'good connections', 'dexterity' and 'being a good wheeler-dealer'. The first Russian businessmen had all those qualities and boasted about them.[22]

In June 1992 Mikhail Khodorkovsky, the head of Menatep Bank, published a book that could be considered a manifesto of a new capitalist man. He called it *Chelovek s rublem (Man with a Rouble)* – an ironic take on a famous Soviet play about the Bolshevik Revolution, *Chelovek s ruzhiem (Man with a Gun)*. Imitating the combative style of 1930s agitprop, Khodorkovsky wrote:

> MENATEP is the realization of the right to riches... Our goals are clear, our tasks are defined – we aspire to be billionaires... Membership of the Communist Party was a good school for us... The Party took away a lot, but it also gave us a lot: experience, connections, life status. Not to use all these would have been a mistake... Enough of living according to [Vladimir] Ilyich [Lenin]! Our compass is Profit, gained in strict accordance to the law. Our hero – His Financial Majesty, the Capital, since only he can lead to riches as a norm of life. Enough of utopia, the future is Business! A man who can turn a dollar into a billion is a genius.[23]

The laws did not really apply, but profit was certainly the compass. One 'genius' who turned a dollar bill into millions through an alchemy of Russia's banking system was Alexander Smolensky, the owner of Stolichny Bank, who lent money to *Kommersant*.

A man with no higher education who began as a typesetter in a state printing house made his first money in the 1970s by printing Bibles for the black market. After a two-year jail sentence for the theft of state property (ink and paper), he worked in construction and decoration firms, selling building materials on the side. In the early 1990s Stolichny Bank handled co-operators' accounts. He used the rouble to speculate on the foreign currency exchange rate. With the rouble depreciating nearly 100 per cent between 1991 and 1994, this was easy money made quickly. 'You give money in the morning and collect your earnings in the evening. It was like a machine that was printing money,' Smolensky explained.[24]

Vladimir Yakovlev borrowed money from Smolensky partly to pay for the paper's new editorial offices. As part of the 'debt service', Yakovlev blocked any negative news about Smolensky and allowed an occasional puff story to appear in print. *Kommersant* journalists got their own measure of Smolensky's bank, though. Their salaries were paid into Stolichny accounts and when, in 1998, Russia defaulted on its domestic debt, Smolensky declared his bank insolvent and froze deposits while reshuffling assets into a new banking empire. *Kommersant* journalists later managed to get their money back. But foreign investors, who had put more than $1 billion into it, never did. All they deserved, Smolensky said in an interview to the *Wall Street Journal*, was 'dead donkey ears'.[25] Such was the newspaper, such was the capitalism.

The 1991 turmoil brought to the surface not the hardest working, but the most impertinent. 'Men with a Rouble' were the biggest winners of the Soviet transition to capitalism and the main beneficiaries of the mass privatization. Gaidar entrusted privatization to his friend Anatoly Chubais, another participant of the economic seminars in the 1980s. Both men saw its aim as breaking the communists' grip on the commanding heights of the Russian economy and creating a class of proprietors who would have a vested interest in liberal reforms. 'We were perfectly aware that we were creating a new class of owners and we did not have a choice between an "honest" privatization and a "dishonest" one. Our choice was between "bandit communism" or "bandit capitalism",' Chubais explained.[26]

To create a veneer of inclusion and justice, the reformers decided to sell state firms for special vouchers issued to all 148 million people in the country. Yeltsin unveiled the 'privatization cheque' on 19 August 1992 – the first anniversary of the August 1991 coup – as a reward for people's defiance. In fact the cheques were just a marketing gimmick since their value was determined not by the nominal figure of 10,000 roubles printed on them but by the amount of property on sale. But when Chubais went on television and told people, most of whom had no idea what 'shares' meant, that each voucher was worth two Volga cars, metaphorically speaking, everyone took it literally, only to realize that they had been duped.

Instead of symbolizing reward, the vouchers came to symbolize deceit. Not knowing what to do with these 'vouchers', most people either sold them straight away or entrusted them to mutual funds that sprang up overnight, promising to invest them in gold and diamonds and disappearing without a trace. Yet, in the course of two years, 70 per cent of the state economy, including natural resources, was sold.* A new class of private owners was created and the free market experiment began.

Confident that its audience had increased and that it needed information to manage its new wealth, the weekly *Kommersant* turned into a daily. If Russia was to have a proper market, it had to have a proper business newspaper first. 'For those who don't know what A2 [format] is – it looks like the *Wall Street Journal*,' *Kommersant* addressed its readers. 'For those who don't know what *Wall Street Journal* is, it looks like *Pravda* – in terms of the page size... A daily newspaper of such a size – at least a relatively NORMAL newspaper – has not been published since 1917... We've decided to try.'[27]

Nobody really knew what 'normal' was, but, like the title of КоммерсантЪ-*Daily*, it consisted of two parts – Russia's pre-revolutionary past and its Western 'daily' future. This 'normal' life was supposed to be organized by a 'normal' daily newspaper. The mention of *Pravda* in *Kommersant*'s jokey editorial was not entirely accidental. A 'collective organizer and propagandist', as Lenin called newspapers, *Pravda* in the

* The majority of Russians supported market reforms and the privatization of land plots and small businesses, but not of large factories and natural resources. Still, most saw entrepreneurs as a positive force that could pull the country out of its economic trough.

1930s tried to model a New Soviet man – an exemplary worker and citizen – and set the tenets of the state-dominated, collective life. Seventy years later, *Kommersant* assumed a similar role in setting the tenets of the new capitalist orders dominated by the individual. It tried to model a new type of man and called him a 'New Russian' (spelled in English): 'Clever, calm, positive, and rich – these are the people who are forming a new elite and who are setting a new style and new standards of living.'[28]

Kommersant hailed private values and initiative and above all success – something that the vast majority of the country, brought up on the ideas of paternalism and equality, had little affinity with. Almost 90 per cent of New Russians, according to *Kommersant*, considered themselves self-made people who had had a lucky break. To visualize a new Russian, *Kommersant* made a short advertisement with a young, suave actor who had all the attributes of an 'ideal' reader: a dark suit, a tie with a pin, a shirt with cuff-links, talking on a massive satellite phone, sitting in the back of a limousine, an office in some Stalin-era factory club and a copy of *Kommersant-Daily* in hand. 'Your newspaper, boss,' an invisible voice intoned.

The 'Old Russian' was represented in *Kommersant* by the caricature 'Petrovich' – a humorous Soviet character trying to adapt to modern reality with a mixture of naivety, cunning and the dumb insolence of the good soldier Svejk. The New Russians almost immediately turned from a model into a caricature – the subject of popular jokes and stories. (One New Russian shows off his tie to another New Russian: 'I paid a hundred bucks for it.' The second New Russian replies with contempt: 'You've been done. I bought exactly the same one for a thousand.') One reason was the actual behaviour of the New Russians. Another was that the image did not fit into a national tradition where the commercial and entrepreneurial spirit was never seen as a virtue and the rich were mostly hated. The most entrepreneurial men in Russian literature were Chichikov who traded in dead souls in Gogol's poem, or Lopakhin in *The Cherry Orchard* who chopped the old trees down to make way for dachas. *Kommersant* was clearly trying to challenge that perception.

Kommersant conveyed and projected the energy and optimism of this new class. It published a regular column under the bold rubric 'What is Good'. 'NOTHING BAD HAS HAPPENED. AND COULD NOT HAVE HAPPENED' read one headline. 'EVERYTHING IS NORMAL', read another. Vladimir Yakovlev's wife, a *Kommersant* editor, wrote: 'We think that everything that is happening around us is logical and therefore right. If this is called looking at the world through rose-tinted glasses, so be it. They are better than dark glasses... A free man is responsible for his own actions. This is why such life is considered natural, or, in other words, normal, or, in other words, happy.'[29] The optimism was supposed to extend not just to New Russians, but also to the old ones. The benefits of the market economy seemed so obvious compared to the planned one, that it was hard to imagine that anyone would disagree.

In the early 1990s a new character burst onto the Russian screen and conquered the minds of millions of Russians. His name was Lenya Golubkov and he was a tractor driver who beamed with optimism over his capitalist future. He had greasy black hair, closely set eyes, a large flat nose and a metal tooth. He wore a baggy suit and was unburdened with intellect or education. But he had done well. He had fixed a pair of leather boots and a fur coat for his wife and was aiming to buy a car in a few months' time with the money he had got from MMM, an investment company that offered 1,000 per cent profits.

The only trouble was that none of this was real. MMM was a pyramid scheme and Golubkov merely a fictional character who advertised it. It was probably the most successful television project of the 1990s and beat Latin American soap operas. The Russian Ponzi was Sergei Mavrodi, a bespectacled mathematician turned con artist who devised a scheme that financed itself by issuing shares in an empty shell company and repaying earlier investors with new ones. The price of MMM shares which became ubiquitous in the early 1990s was set by Mavrodi himself. By the time it collapsed, the scheme had attracted some 15 million people.

It was the commercial created by Kazakh film director Bakhyt Kilibaev that kept the scheme going. MMM's ads consisted of short skits set to a jolly foxtrot tune and featuring the same characters. Apart from Golubkov, these included Rita, Golubkov's chocolate-crazy, plump wife with a beehive hairdo, his older brother Ivan, a tattooed coal miner from Vorkuta, the lonely spinster Marina Sergeevna and a newly wed couple.

The middle-aged Golubkov was a Soviet joke character: a lazy simpleton and free-loader, a product of the Soviet paternalistic system who embraced the easy reaches offered by Russia's dysfunctional capitalism with an enthusiasm that horrified Russian market reformers. With the use of a pointer, he showed his wife a chart that marked the stages of family happiness: new furniture, a car and a house. 'A house in Paris?' asked Rita as she gobbled up another chocolate. 'Why not, Lenya?!' intoned the voice of an announcer. Another episode showed Lenya and his brother Ivan sitting at a kitchen table over a bottle of vodka and a large jar of pickled cucumbers: 'You are a *khaliavshchik* [free-loader], Lenya. You forgot what our mother and father taught us: to work honestly. And you are running around buying shares. *Khaliavshchik!*' said Ivan. 'You are wrong, brother. I am not a *khaliavshchik*, brother... I am a partner,' said Lenya. 'That is right, Lenya, we are partners,' said the MMM voice.

In the Soviet era, Lenya would have been a character of a Soviet satire condemning infantilism and the petty bourgeois lifestyle. In the early 1990s he became a household name whose popularity exceeded that of any Russian politician, including Yeltsin, who grumbled that Lenya was getting on his nerves: 'We have too many touts of every ilk who promise fantastic dividends in the future or homes in Paris. But very often there is no basis for this. They are just conning the people.'

Very few people shared Lenya's enthusiasm in the early 1990s. Opinion polls in 1992 showed that only 5 per cent of the country felt optimistic, some 40 per cent felt stable and half of the country experienced anxiety, frustration and tension.[30] The dominant sentiment, however, was one of defiance: while life is going to be difficult, we can manage.

The Battle for the Nuclear Button

In 1992 Maxim Sokolov wrote an essay called 'So Which War Did We Lose?' 'The paradox is that while the most vulnerable [people] more or less agreed with Gaidar's "draconian reforms", the least vulnerable turned into a state of fury.'[31] To understand this 'paradox', Sokolov argued, one has to look at the spiritual and aesthetic side of reforms and here the loss of the Russian nationalist-communists and chauvinists who extolled the imperial state and its geopolitical status as the ultimate good that trumps universal human values was far greater than that of ordinary people who mostly got on with their lives.

Sokolov drew parallels between contemporary Russia and Germany after the wars. The key question was whether Russia resembled Germany after the Second World War, when it was forced to rebuild its economy and move towards democracy? Or was it more similar to the 1918 Weimar Germany that had led to fascism? There was certainly no shortage of populists and demagogues after 1991 willing to exploit the frustration of ordinary Russians under the nationalist, communist and imperial flags for the sake of their own revanchism.

The nationalists and communists openly embraced each other to form a red–brown coalition. Whatever differences they had had in the past, they were united in their struggle against a common enemy: the West, with its liberal democracy, and those who tried to impose it on Russia – Yeltsin and his Zionist government. As often in Russian history, liberals were synonymous with Jews.

The leader of the Russian communists was Gennady Zyuganov, a second-tier communist functionary who worked in the ideology department of the party and was one of Alexander Yakovlev's main adversaries. He was a patron of the *Sovetskaya Rossiya* newspaper which had published Andreeva's Stalinist letter and formulated the new Russian communist ideology as anti-Western, anti-liberal, nationalist and traditionalist, allied with the Orthodox Church. Central to this ideology was the idea of the sacrosanct state.

As Natalia Narochitskaya, one of the ideologists of state nationalism, wrote in *Nash sovremennik* (*Our Contemporary*), a right-wing literary journal, 'Russia was a unique, giant Eurasian power "with an Orthodox nucleus and the cosmic spirit of its stately idea"'. 'The future of Russia is in the creation of an organic state where an individual is not opposed to society but is a manifestation and carrier of the state idea,' she wrote.[32] Stripped of the rhetoric about equality and internationalism, communist ideology seamlessly morphed into fascism. The first full Russian-language edition of Hitler's *Mein Kampf* was printed and started to sell openly on the Moscow streets in 1992.

The consolidation of imperialist, nationalist and communist forces was taking place against the background of Russia's withdrawal to its current borders and a series of conflicts that flared up between Russia and its former vassals, including Georgia and Moldova. The nerve point for the imperialists was the loss of Crimea which had been transferred to the Ukrainian Soviet Republic in 1954 by Nikita Khrushchev – a symbolic act that commemorated the 300 years of union between Russia and Ukraine.

Since the times of Catherine the Great, Crimea had been at the heart of Russia's imperial project. When the Soviet Union fell apart, Crimea stayed within Ukraine. No other territory, including the Baltic states or even Georgia, touched the nerve of imperial nostalgia as much as Crimea. The nationalists exploited the dispute between Moscow and Kiev over the fate of Russia's Black Sea Fleet to lay claim to Crimea. This was one of the main subjects of the nationalist press, including *Den'* (*Day*), 'a newspaper of spiritual opposition' as it was called by its editor Alexander Prokhanov, a writer devoted to the idea of Russian imperialism who reconciled nationalists and communists in the struggle against Yeltsin and his Westernizers.

One of Prokhanov's regular authors was Igor Shafarevich, a distinguished mathematician, an ideologue of Russian nationalism and anti-Semitism, and a friend of Solzhenitsyn. Shafarevich wrote in early 1993:

> Sebastopol is a key to the resurgence of the country... First of all – it is one of the historic shrines of Russia. Khersones is where Saint Vladimir was baptized, where admirals Kornilov and Nakhimov were buried... Secondly, Sebastopol is key to the Black Sea Fleet. Thirdly, Sebastopol is a key to Crimea, which has been torn from the body of Russia by the unconstitutional and voluntaristic decision of Nikita Khrushchev. People in Crimea have an acute sense of belonging to Russia and have the will to fight for this belonging. Fourthly, Crimea has great influence on what is happening in all of the southern lands – in Novorossiya [Russian imperial territory north of the Black Sea]. The plan for the unification of Sebastopol, Crimea, Novorossiya and Russia is not some treacherous plan of Russian imperialism. It is an attempt to define a natural and organic form of Russia's existence after the current catastrophe.[33]

The disintegration of the Soviet Empire was blamed on the West and its agents of influence in Russia. An émigré Russian philosopher, Alexander Zinoviev, wrote in *Nash sovremennik*: 'The West wished to destroy Russia by the hands of [Nazi] Germany. It failed. Now it is trying to do the same under the guise of a fight for democracy, human rights etc. This is a war of two civilizations.'[34] The only reason the American and Western economies were still afloat was because of cheap natural resources supplied by Russia. 'Without our resources, the well-being of the West will immediately collapse,' asserted *Den'*. America was not just parasitic, it was suffering from an innate sin that started with the elimination of its indigenous people and which had led to the bombing of Hiroshima and the killing of 150,000 Iraqis, wrote Shafarevich.

Few people at the time, including the nationalists themselves, could have predicted that twenty years later this narrative would move from the pages of the extremists' *Den'* newspaper onto the main television channels, that Russia would annex Crimea, try to annihilate Ukraine and carve out Novorossiya, and wage a war on the West.

In parallel with the ideological conflict between the red–brown coalition and the liberals, a power struggle unfolded between Yeltsin and his government of reformers, on the one hand, and the parliament, on the other. Formed before the Soviet collapse and still known as the Congress of People's Deputies, the parliament was dominated by Soviet factory bosses, who had been pushed out of the way during the privatizations, and representatives of the military and industrial complex and the powerful agricultural lobby, none of whom fitted into Gaidar's market reforms. Out of more than a thousand deputies, only 200 were Yeltsin loyalists. The rest opposed him either openly or covertly. The parliament was chaired by its Speaker, Ruslan Khasbulatov, a clever and manipulative deputy from Chechnya who played the deputies like a fiddle.

Khasbulatov's ally in his stand-off with Yeltsin was Alexander Rutskoi, a former air force pilot and a hero of the Afghan war – a man of limited intelligence and imposing looks. In 1991 Yeltsin chose Rutskoi as his vice-president to capture the 'patriotic' votes and melt the hearts of Russian women and Khasbulatov as his deputy to appeal to ethnic minorities. A former economist, Khasbulatov had his eye on the job of prime minister and felt snubbed by Gaidar. He played on Rutskoi's vanity, luring him to his side. They publicly attacked Gaidar and his government, whom Rutskoi called 'boys in pink pants', for moving too fast in building capitalism and Americanizing the Russian economy.

The red–brown coalition used the parliament as a way of legitimizing itself. In the meantime, Khasbulatov was using the communists and nationalists as a force that could bring people out on the streets and help him come to power.

As Alexander Yanov, a historian of Russian nationalism, argued, an outburst of imperial nationalism under Yeltsin was inevitable. 'The collapse of a 400-year old empire and, even more importantly for Russia, the loss of a utopian, but great national goal, could not but produce "patriotic hysteria".'[35] The whole question was whether this 'hysteria' could turn into regime change. By the end of 1992, the nationalists' opposition was laying out plans for the overt throwing-over of Yeltsin's government. What it needed was a powerful amplifier in the form of mass media.

Being a truly conservative force, the nationalists consolidated not around television but around old literary magazines such as *Nash sovremennik* and Prokhanov's newspaper *Den'*. Television was in the hands of the liberals. At the helm of post-Soviet television was Yegor Yakovlev who was appointed to the job by Gorbachev (with Yeltsin's approval) almost immediately after the August 1991 coup. His first step was to clear the television centre of the KGB staff who worked both openly and under cover. His second step was to dispose of *Vremya* – the main nine o'clock evening news programme – replacing it with the plain-sounding *Novosti* [News]. The change of title, theme tune and format was as symbolic as the lowering of the red flag over the Kremlin or the change of the Soviet anthem.

Vremya had a sacred status in the Soviet Union. Its two serious-looking, buttoned-up presenters were the oracles of the Kremlin. It did not actually report the news, but told the country what the Kremlin wanted its audience to think the news was. It was a nightly ritual in which nothing 'new' or unpredictable could ever happen. *Vremya*, a name that in Russian means 'time', was as regular as the chimes of the Kremlin clock that preceded the programme. Like time, *Vremya* seemed infinite. By changing the format, Yegor was removing the sacred function of television and desacralizing the state itself.

Yegor saw the role of television in helping people adjust to the disappearance of the country that they were born in. He tried to save a common information space – a union in the ether – when the actual union had fallen apart and conflicts erupted on the periphery. As Igor Malashenko, who worked as Yegor's deputy, explained:

> The army was falling apart, flights were getting cancelled, trains were grinding to a halt, the rouble zone was shrinking, former Soviet republics were fencing themselves off with borders and customs... but television in Moscow continued to broadcast across the entire former Soviet Union... The very knowledge that people in Russia, Georgia, the Baltic States and Central Asia were watching the same programmes helped many people feel part of one historic entity – even though it had lost its name.[36]

As a print journalist, Yegor neither understood nor particularly liked television and tried to turn it into a version of *Moskovskie novosti*, appealing to the same audience of liberal intelligentsia, said Malashenko. But above all Yegor was hoping to turn television from a means of propaganda and mobilization into a private activity. As he told his staff: 'My generation lived by the hope of bringing politics and morality together. All the lessons I learned from 1956 persuaded me that this is impossible... Television must help an individual to go back to his own world, to find values other than politics. Our task is to make politics occupy as little space in our lives as possible.'[37] The politics kept bursting in, though, and television soon turned into a battleground.

On 12 June 1992 – the first anniversary of Russia's independence –

a hysterical and xenophobic mob of diehard communists beseiged the television centre situated in Ostankino, in the north of Moscow. They were led by Viktor Anpilov, the hot-tempered, foaming-at-the-mouth leader of the radical left-wing Working Moscow and Communist Workers' Party. Anpilov, who started as a journalist, understood the importance of television well. 'I was an ideal Soviet journalist – from the working class,' he said.[38] He was trained to broadcast Soviet propaganda in Spanish to Latin America. Unusually for the time when he graduated – the early 1970s – he was an orthodox Leninist. After university he went to Cuba to work as an interpreter. In a book of memoirs, poignantly called *Our Struggle*, he described how Fidel Castro addressed a vast crowd with the words: 'A revolution is worth something only if it knows how to defend itself.'[39] A decade later, reportedly recruited by the KGB, he was posted to Nicaragua during the war between the Soviet-backed Sandinista and the American-backed Contras. He informed on his cameraman for his 'anti-Soviet' views.

In August 1991, he was on the side of the coup leaders. As a true communist and a tireless speaker he never shunned the basic forms of propaganda. He agitated workers at factories and could always rally a few thousand hard-core supporters to come onto the streets.

In June 1992, Anpilov's thugs blocked entrances and exits to the television centre for seven days, demanding access to the air waves. Anpilov called it 'A Siege of the Empire of Lies'. 'Television has become a tank which is killing the fragile soul of the Russian people,' he shouted. His followers spat and hurled abuse at journalists – 'Zionists' and 'agents of American influence' – demanding 'Russian television for Russian people'. Anpilov tried to storm Ostankino and clashed with the police who showed little resistance. 'It was a dark and ugly mob: the twisted, hateful faces, saliva in the corner of a mouth, the openly fascist slogans,' the liberal *Izvestia* wrote. 'A movement that makes pogroms their main goal cannot have any future,' it added hopefully.[40]

Trying to deflate the situation, Yegor invited Anpilov and a few others inside the television centre to negotiate and even offered Anpilov a chance to come on air and comment on the siege. Anpilov demanded a daily prime-time slot on television and Yegor's resignation, and threatened a sit-in hunger strike if his conditions were not met. After a five-hour-long discussion, Yegor gave his own ultimatum, both to Anpilov and to the government: if the situation around Ostankino was not restored to normal, the centre would stop broadcasting. 'And I will be the first to make an appeal to all staff to go on strike,' said Yegor. With that, he left his 'guests' in the company of government officials and the police. 'I don't know why Anpilov and his people have not taken over the television centre yet. I can't imagine a more impotent executive power,' Yegor told *Moskovskie novosti*, his former paper, a few days later.[41]

Anpilov's siege and Yegor's response made a strong impression on Yeltsin. 'I realized,' Yeltsin wrote in his memoirs, 'that "Ostankino" is almost like a nuclear button... and that in charge of this button should not be a reflective intellectual, but a different kind of person.'[42] Not only did Yeltsin see Yegor as Gorbachev's man, but he also saw him as being too independent. In early December 1992 Yeltsin fired Yegor, replacing him two months later with Vyacheslav Bragin, a former party apparatchik from Tver. A mediocre and slavishly obedient man with no experience in television, Bragin saw his job as simply providing free air time to the Kremlin whenever it needed it, even if this meant interrupting scheduled programming and cancelling the Latin American soap operas. Yeltsin's unceremonious and unjustified firing of Yegor looked ugly and outraged the liberals. Yeltsin knew the dismissal was unfair, but his main concern was not the quality of programming, but the use of television as a weapon.

With parliament paralysing the governance of the country, a direct televised appeal to the people was the only way of conducting power and he needed an obedient loyalist in charge of the television button.

Most institutions in the country were malfunctioning, the economy was in free fall and television had turned from a fourth estate into the first one.

In December 1992 Khasbulatov out-manoeuvred Yeltsin, forcing him to surrender Gaidar as his prime minister in exchange for holding a referendum on the constitution the following year. Gaidar was replaced with Viktor Chernomyrdin – the former minister for the gas industry who was (mistakenly) seen by the communists as their man. In fact, giving up Gaidar made things worse for Yeltsin, not just economically, but politically. The parliament took Gaidar's removal as a sign of Yeltsin's weakness rather than as a compromise, and within a few months reneged on the agreement to hold a constitutional referendum and stripped Yeltsin of his powers to rule by decree.

The nationalists smelled blood. At the beginning of February Prokhanov's *Den'* declared: 'A new clash is fast approaching. It will peak in March–April when the regrouping of political forces will be completed, when the economy will be ruined, food reserves exhausted… The opposition will have to carry the burden of power in a ruined, disintegrating country engulfed by chaos.'[43] Yeltsin, too, was ready for a fight. On 20 March 1993 he went on television to announce that he had signed a decree introducing a period of 'special rule' in the lead-up to a nationwide referendum to be held on 25 April. In fact, when the decree was published four days later, it was couched in much more careful terms with no mention of the 'special rule'. The real event, however, was not the decree – that never came into force – but its announcement on television.

Khasbulatov declared Yeltsin's decree 'unconstitutional' and called an emergency session of the parliament to impeach Yeltsin. On the day of the vote, tens of thousands of Muscovites came out on Red Square under Russian flags in support of Yeltsin. Gaidar and his father were at the forefront of the demonstration. On the other side of Red Square a much smaller, but more aggressive, crowd gathered under Soviet red flags. A few hours later, Yeltsin came out to his supporters to announce that the impeachment had failed.

Yeltsin's popularity was confirmed a month later in a referendum that posed four questions. 1. Do you trust President Yeltsin? 2. Do you approve of his economic policies? 3. Do you consider it necessary to carry out early presidential elections? 4. Do you consider it necessary to hold early parliamentary elections? Television played a crucial role in mobilizing people to support Yeltsin. It ran a relentless advertising campaign in which ordinary people, pop stars and famous actors repeated the answers to the four questions like a chant: *da, da, net, da* (yes, yes, no, yes).

Just before the vote, the seventy-minutes-long *Odin den' iz zhizni prezidenta* (*A Day in the Life of the President*) was aired – directed and presented by one of the country's most popular film directors, Eldar Ryazanov – which showed Yeltsin in his intimate family circle. This was a sharp contrast to the image of Yeltsin on a tank in August 1991. Then he was a symbol of a revolution. Now he was a symbol of the peaceful, domesticated, normal life that people longed for and which was being jeopardized by the opposition.

The result of the referendum was better than anyone could have expected. Not only did 58.7 per cent say 'yes' to Yeltsin, but 53 per cent also said 'yes' to Gaidar's reforms, despite the loss of savings and rising prices. However hard things were economically, nobody wished to go back to the past. Remarkably, however, Yeltsin failed to capitalize on his victory in the referendum to disband the parliament and to fire his mutinous vice-president. The struggle grew more vicious and personal.

The media resources of the opposition were more limited but not insignificant. Khasbulatov managed to get the state Russia Channel, which was formally under Russia's Supreme Soviet, to put out the *Parlamentskii chas* (*Parliamentary Hour*) – a lengthy anti-Western and anti-Yeltsin diatribe which was broadcast at first weekly and then daily in a prime-time slot. Far more important, though, the nationalists had one of the most charismatic and popular TV showmen on their side: Alexander Nevzorov, who saw the unfolding drama as a continuation of his old battle with the liberals in Vilnius in 1991. By his own admission, Nevzorov experimented with ideas of fascism in Russia and turned his 600 *Seconds* into the mouthpiece of the red–brown coalition. Attempts to shut it down inevitably led to mass street protests by his fans.

Yeltsin also began to line up his weapons. At the beginning of August he gathered television executives and managers in his office. 'We have to get ready for the decisive battle which will come in September. August has to be used for artillery preparations, including in the mass media,' Yeltsin told them.[44] He stopped short of revealing any concrete plans, other than to say, 'We are studying the situation very carefully and are preparing different variants of action, but the action will come.' A month later, Yeltsin told his aides to draft a decree to disband parliament. He visited an elite military unit, the Dzerzhinsky Division, where he combatively announced the return of Gaidar to the government. Military and television powers were equally important and were intertwined in the upcoming battle.

On 21 September Yeltsin again appeared on television. Collected, clear and charismatic, he made one of the most forceful speeches of his career: 'Parliament has been seized by a group of persons who [are] pushing Russia towards the abyss. The security of Russia and its peoples is more important than formal obedience to contradictory norms created by the legislature. I must break this disastrous vicious circle... to defend Russia and the world from the catastrophic collapse of Russian statehood and of anarchy with the vast potential of nuclear arms.' With this, Yeltsin said, he had signed decree number 1,400 dissolving the parliament and calling for early parliamentary elections and a referendum on the constitution.

'It is a tragic and almost irreparable stupidity,' Nevzorov dramatically stated in his programme that night, as the blinking clock in the corner counted down the seconds. 'The usual way of life has been upset for months. Life will become even harder and even more anxious. People are already gathering to defend the White House [the seat of the parliament] and those who have come to realize that the past two years, since August 1991, were shameful and catastrophic... The opposition will not surrender it without a fight.' The outlawed parliament 'impeached' Yeltsin and pronounced Alexander Rutskoi Russia's president.

Within the next forty-eight hours, a motley crowd of Anpilov's communists, nationalists and Cossacks started to gather at the White House. Rutskoi distributed firearms, kept inside the White House, among the 'defenders', many of whom had fought as mercenaries and regular soldiers on the periphery of the empire. They had started off in the Baltic republics, then moved to a bloody conflict in Moldova and most recently had taken part in a vicious war against Georgia on the side of separatist Abkhazia. They were attracted by the promise of armed action in the heart of Moscow. Among them was Nevzorov who was issued with every possible bit of paper by Rutskoi and Vladislav Achalov, a high-ranking Soviet military commander who had led the anti-Gorbachev coup in 1991 and was now appointed as defence minister by Rutskoi. The picture inside the White House did not inspire Nevzorov with confidence.

Whether Achalov or Rutskoi actually controlled any of the armed men inside the White House was very much in question. In the words of Sergei Parkhomenko, a young liberal journalist for *Segodnya* (*Today*) newspaper, the White House looked like a 'partisan republic', lacking discipline and cut off from communications. Achalov presided in a vast ministerial office, barricaded by old furniture and surrounded by a dozen telephones, none of which worked, so he had to borrow mobile phones from reporters. Rutskoi paraded a motley crew of 200 volunteers, including a short plump man in a rusty Second World War helmet, a thin unshaved one with a skiing pole for a rifle and an 'intelligentsia type' in a hat with a shopping bag in his hands. 'It was clear that we were not going to get very far with these commanders,' Nevzorov reflected.[45]

The only person who looked the part and impressed Nevzorov was Alexander Barkashov, the Hitler-praising leader of the neo-Nazi Russian National Unity who was called to the defence of the White House by Achalov. Barkashov refused to be lumped together with Anpilov's communists, commanded a small but well-disciplined group of young men and women in black shirts with swastika-like signs who threw their arms up in a Nazi-style salute shouting 'Hail Russia'. They did not think much of the porous police cordon that surrounded the White House. The cordon was supposed to stop the leakage of weapons in and out of the White House, but journalists like Parkhomenko, who wandered in and out of the place, were miffed by the seeming lack of coordination in its sealing-off.

'The only logic that can be deduced from the actions of the police and security chiefs is that their goal is to pique, provoke and madden the armed rebels. If so, they've done a fine job,' Parkhomenko wrote.[46] Veronika Kutsyllo, a young reporter for *Kommersant*, who spent two weeks inside parliament, put in a call to Yeltsin's chief of staff, Sergei Filatov. 'You said you were not going to let people through, so don't! You have put guards around the building but people are wandering to and fro! And anyway, how long are you going to wait? This crowd, in front of the White House – can't you clear it? The crowd is growing bigger by the day – it is not going to dissipate. There are people with weapons in the crowd – and also inside...'[47]

While Nevzorov took the side of the opposition, the liberal journalists obviously took the side of the Kremlin. Those who were inside the White House, like Kutsyllo and Parkhomenko, acted almost like undercover agents on enemy territory. 'There was no distance or etiquette between the Kremlin and the liberal journalists at the time. We got too close to each other,' Sergei Parkhomenko recalled a decade later.[48] At some point Parkhomenko got so close to the Kremlin that he was able to impersonate its chief of staff.

As Parkhomenko walked into the Kremlin, he was struck by the atmosphere of utter confusion that reigned there. 'Kremlin officials seemed to have lost control over the situation in the country: aides were arguing with one another but nobody had any information or idea of what to do next,' he recalled. Parkhomenko asked one of the aides about the strength of the Kremlin's defences. The aide had no idea and irritatingly told him to find out for himself. Parkhomenko walked into Filatov's empty office and called the Kremlin's chief of security, asking him how many people were guarding the Kremlin in case of an attack by the rebels. 'Where are you calling from?' the security chief asked. 'Filatov's office,' Parkhomenko replied. 'Two battalions… do you think I should ask for reinforcements?' 'Go ahead,' Parkhomenko replied.[49]

'I don't know and may never know what played a greater part in the events of 3–4 October: confusion of the authorities or cynical calculations,' Kutsyllo wrote in the introduction to her published diary. 'Both sides needed blood: the parliament side – because it hoped that after the blood of at least some peaceful civilians, the people and part of the army would come to the defence of the constitution; the president – because only the blood of the same peaceful citizens could justify the storming of the White House.'[50]

Few people in Moscow during those days cared about the lawfulness of Yeltsin's decision to disband the parliament. (In fact, most events that occurred at the time of the Soviet collapse were dictated by the logic of a revolution rather than legal procedure.) As Maxim Sokolov wrote in *Kommersant*, what mattered to the ordinary man was which side posed the biggest threat to his own safety and the security of his family. In October 1993, the threat of chaos and violence clearly emanated from the White House. And if there was one thing that Yeltsin was blamed for, it was his slow response in dealing with those who terrorized the city during the next few days.

On 2 October an anti-Yeltsin crowd led by Anpilov clashed with the police in the centre of Moscow, throwing Molotov cocktails and wielding metal rods at them. The following morning Anpilov's mob, numbering some 4,000 people, gathered in October Square, which was dominated by a vast statue of Lenin. The mob easily broke a police chain and marched towards the White House, carrying red flags and portraits of Stalin. Kutsyllo watched in astonishment as the swelling crowd approached the parliament building: 'Nobody tried stopping them.'[51]

The riot police around the White House retreated. 'Either I don't understand something, or they are fleeing,' Kutsyllo wrote. This caused jubilation among the rebels in the White House. Rutskoi emerged from the White House and addressed the crowd: 'We have won! Thank you, dear Muscovites! Men, form fighting detachments! Keep the momentum, forward, to the mayor's office!' Minutes later, two trucks barged through the windows of the mayor's office next to the White House.

The main target of the rebels, however, was not the government buildings, but the television centre. 'We need [television] air waves,' Rutskoi declared. The fighters climbed onto the trucks left by the police and drove at high speed along the empty Moscow streets to Ostankino. As Gaidar wrote, 'The opposition had made an apt choice for its first strike. Its leaders had rightly assessed the potential of television, in this case the most powerful medium for influencing the situation. For as long as Rutskoi, Khasbulatov and their allies were off air, they were rebels and outlaws shouting their slogans in a megaphone whom no military would support. But as soon as they were on air, they were the power in the country.'[52] 'To "take" the Kremlin you must "take" television,' Alexander Yakovlev said a year later.[53]

The attack on Ostankino was led by Anpilov and Makashov, a virulent military commander who intended to clear it of 'Yids' and give the air waves to the 'legitimate president' Rutskoi. The television centre was defended from the inside by thirty or forty soldiers from the Vityaz unit, part of the Dzerzhinsky Division, usually deployed for putting down prison mutinies. Anpilov tried to talk them into laying down their arms, and even succeeded partly, but after the rebels rammed the glass building with trucks and fired a grenade launcher decapitating one of the soldiers inside, the Vityaz soldiers opened fire. Soon a fierce fight raged around Ostankino; tracer bullets cut through the night sky, people ducked and scrambled for the bushes. Within seconds several dozen people, including journalists and onlookers who were caught in the crossfire, were dead.

Just before 7.30 p.m., in the middle of a football match, Channel One, as well as all other channels broadcasting from the Ostankino television centre, went off the air. Television screens had never gone blank in the Soviet Union – not even during the August 1991 coup. One of television's key functions was to show that life just carried on. A sudden blackout on television was a sign of catastrophe and chaos, the collapse of the state.

In fact, there was no reason to stop broadcasting. A plan had been worked out in advance to ensure that the rebels could not transmit from the studio even if they broke into the television centre. Moreover, the actual broadcasting was carried out from a building across the road, which was not under fire. News could have been broadcast from a reserve studio, even if the main ones were damaged. As one of the strategic objects in the Soviet Union, television had several reserve broadcasting facilities, including one that could withstand a nuclear explosion. The idea to switch off the signal belonged to Bragin, the head of Ostankino, who erroneously claimed that rebels were inside, working their way towards the television studios. In fact, Bragin himself was in a different building.

Bruce Clark, the author of *An Empire's New Clothes*,[54] a perceptive and detailed book about those events, argues that the bloodshed in Ostankino as well as the clashes before the White House were not so much, or at least not only, the result of confusion but part of Yeltsin's plan to draw the rebels deeper into the fight and give them a false sense of victory so that they could be dealt with once and for all. Whether or not this was the intention, the television blackout certainly had that effect. Inside the White House parliamentarians started to celebrate victory. Khasbulatov spoke calmly: 'I think that today we must take the Kremlin… Ostankino has been captured. City Hall has been captured. We need to develop a strategy – to complete the victory.'

One reason the attack on Ostankino failed, Nevzorov reflected later, was that it was led by Anpilov and Makashov who were 'as "red" in their views as a flame in hell'. 'They carried statuettes of Lenin in their hearts and spoke in party slogans, which nobody wanted to hear,' he said. Nevzorov himself was not at Ostankino. 'A few hours earlier I was stopped on the approach to Moscow as I led a few dozen armed men who had fought in Vilnius in 1991 to the defence of the White House.' His 'detention' was most probably staged. As Nevzorov recalled twenty years later, 'There was a good reason why I did not go to Ostankino that night, even though I knew about the plan to storm it well in advance.'[55]

While Nevzorov was always in the mood for a bloody spectacle – a coup, a revolution, or a full-out war – as a professional television man he could also see the limitations of the material he was dealing with. Anpilov did not look like Che Guevara or Fidel Castro. 'He looked like a guest from Soviet folklore who prompted immediate questions about whether Soviet people suffer from excessive drinking. The answer was certainly yes,' said Nevzorov.[56]

Anpilov bore an uncanny resemblance to the main character from a popular television adaptation of Mikhail Bulgakov's *Heart of a Dog*, a phantasmagorical novella in which a stray dog is implanted with the half-dead brain of a petty criminal stabbed to death in a drunken brawl a couple of hours earlier. The ruffian produced as the result of this medical experiment, called Sharikov, talks, walks and acts like a new proletarian man. He terrorizes the professor who created him, forcing him to reverse the experiment.

Nevzorov, who fancied himself as a knight and conquistador, had no wish to speak on behalf of Sharikov and of Makashov, a half-mad remnant of the Soviet Empire. 'A month earlier I was still hoping that people's frustration and the humiliation suffered by the army, penniless and disrespected, could have detonated the situation and turned into a vast fire that would have consumed Anpilov and Makashov. But by the end of September I realized that the masses were not catching fire,' he said. 'It was too late to call people to come out under communist flags and too early to call them to come out under nationalist ones.'[57]

The opposite side had a better cast, said Nevzorov. 'Yeltsin looked the part of a tsar. Tall, with sleek white hair, always dressed in a crisp white shirt – he appeared as a man in power – something that Russians respect,' Nevzorov recalled.[58] But if people did not come out on the side of the rebels, they also did not exactly rush to Yeltsin's defence either. Most adopted the role of spectators even if the overall sympathy was on the side of Yeltsin. This political apathy was part of people's self-preservation mechanism. They saw the stand-off between the two sides as a struggle for power and refused to be drawn in.

This made the situation extremely dangerous. As the 1917 Bolshevik coup showed, one did not need vast crowds to grab power if the army and the police were demoralized. Gaidar, whose grandfather had fought in the civil war after the Bolshevik coup, understood the danger better than many. Seeing the blackout of Ostankino, he rushed to the Russia Channel which was broadcast from a different location in the centre of Moscow. Its studio seemed completely improvised with dishevelled reporters reading news from stacked-up sheets of paper. As he walked into the studio, he paused for thought and asked to be left alone for a minute.

> The flush of excitement had suddenly drained away, and in its place came a wave of alarm for those I was about to call out of their quiet apartments and onto the streets of Moscow. What a terrible responsibility for their lives I was taking upon myself. But there was no way around it. In reading and rereading documents and memoirs about 1917, I had often caught myself wondering how it was that tens of thousands of cultured, honourable and honest citizens of Petersburg, any number of military officers among them, could have let a relatively small group of extremists seize power so easily. Why did everyone keep waiting for someone else... to save them? And so, without hesitation, with a sense that I was in the right, I made my speech.[59]

On the night of 3 October, television was the only way to mobilize the public and, most importantly, the army. 'The Russia Channel, the only one that stayed on the air, saved Moscow and Russia,' Yeltsin wrote in his memoirs.[60]

Several thousands of people responded to Gaidar's 'call to the barricades' and turned up in the centre of Moscow, lighting bonfires for the night. These were the same people who had come to defend the White House in August 1991 against the communist putsch, some of whom were now leading a new attack on Ostankino. This display of popular support was addressed first and foremost to the army which, just like in 1991, was reluctant to interfere in a conflict the outcome of which was still unclear, and was waiting to see how events would turn out. Throughout the night, journalists, actors and academics flocked to the improvised studio of the Russia Channel.

Gaidar's appeal was countered not by nationalists and communists but by those who had most benefited from his reforms. The journalists from *Vzglyad* told Muscovites to ignore Gaidar's advice, stay at home, not put themselves in harm's way, leave the politicians and the police to do their jobs, and follow their example and go to bed. Chudakova, a biographer of Mikhail Bulgakov, rebutted this nonchalance: 'Don't believe those who are trying to persuade you to leave it all to the politicians. If you stay at home tonight, you will be ashamed of yourselves – in a few hours, in a few months, in a few years!'[61]

But it was the emotional words of the popular comical actress Liya Akhedzhakova that made the biggest impact on the audience: 'Those who today look at these snarling, bestial faces of the mob and share their anger, have learned nothing in the past seventy years... For the third day in a row innocent people are being killed... And for what? For the constitution? What kind of constitution is this – may it rot in hell! It is the same constitution under which people were imprisoned... Where is our army? Why is it not defending us from this cursed constitution?'[62]

Yeltsin, who watched the Russia Channel in his office, wrote in his memoirs: 'I will always remember Akhedzhakova – shocked, fragile, but firm and courageous.'[63] Yeltsin did not make a television appearance himself that night. At 2.30 a.m., he went to the ministry of defence to 'shake up his generals who were paralysed by stress and hesitance'. He was accompanied by Alexander Korzhakov, his bodyguard and confidant. Everyone had a drink. Then Yeltsin presented them with a plan worked out by one of Korzhakov's men. It was a very Russian plan: to bring in the tanks, position them in front of the White House, fire a few shells 'for psychological effect' and then send in the commandos to clear the rebels out.

At Gaidar's request, Yeltsin also flew to meet army commanders outside Moscow to boost their confidence. It was not clear whether an order from Yeltsin alone would be sufficient to get the officers to clear out the rebels from the White House. On the night of 3 October, Russia's richest businessmen – soon to be known as oligarchs – were called upon by Chernomyrdin, who effectively took charge of the crisis, to help with money. They did not have to be asked twice. Some even went to negotiate with military commanders – cash in hand – although Pavel

Grachev, the defence minister, later denied that this money ever played a part.

Finally, at 9 a.m. on 4 October, Yeltsin came on television and addressed the nation. 'Those who have acted against a peaceful city and unleashed bloody fighting are criminals... I ask you, respected Muscovites, to give your support to the morale of the Russian soldiers and officers... The armed fascist–communist mutiny in Moscow will be crushed within the shortest time limit.'

When tanks appeared in the centre of Moscow, they were greeted with relief rather than resentment and apprehension. As Gaidar wrote, 'Anyone who did not live through the evening of 3 October and did not see the terrible danger that loomed over the country, who did not have to call people out onto the streets of Moscow, may have difficulty understanding my feelings when the first round of tank fire resounded over the White House.'[64]

The tanks were operated by selected officers and personally commanded by Grachev. They fired ten duds and two incendiary shells that set the upper floors of the White House on fire. Nobody was actually killed by the tank fire (those who died on 4 October were killed by a gunfire exchange between the two sides). But the damage caused by the symbolism of tanks firing at the parliament was far greater and more lasting.

The tanks provided a captivating television picture. Russian television relayed live footage from CNN which had its cameras fixed on the nearby rooftops. This created a certain degree of detachment and made the spectacle doubly surreal as if the events were happening not in Russia, but in a foreign country. On a cold, crisp October day, people strolling along Kutuzovsky Prospect were able to watch the spectacle live while Barkashov's snipers on the roof took out people in front of the White House. Theatre critic and historian, Anatoly Smeliansky, called it a 'Russian matinee'. Certainly, people felt like spectators rather than participants in those events.

Within a few hours, the fighting was over. Rutskoi and Khasbulatov, along with the thousands of people inside the White House, were bundled into police vans and taken to jail (though not for long). After many days without any running water or a change of clothes, they had a nasty smell about them. But many of the fighters, including Barkashov, melted away, using underground tunnels and the sewage system as an escape route out of the White House. The nationalist and communist newspapers were briefly banned. Nevzorov's *600 Seconds* was taken off air for 'whipping up national, class, social and religious intolerance'. Alexei Simonov, a documentary film-maker who ran a foundation for the freedom of speech, recalled the vindictive triumphalism of some of the 'democratic' journalists. This triumphalism was ill-placed.

Parkhomenko, who protested against banning nationalist newspapers, wrote a couple of days later: 'Nothing is over. Everything is only starting. The deformed White House is an impressive symbol. But it is only a symbol. The large armed gang that terrorized the city for twelve hours is not destroyed but only dispersed...'[65] The use of tanks against the White House caused more harm to the liberal idea than it did to the nationalists inside the White House. Instead of projecting the image of putting down an armed mutiny against a democratically elected president, it conveyed an image of heavy-handed disregard for the parliament as an institution. It elevated the fighters in the White House from thugs to political martyrs.

Even if the tanks had helped to smoke out the rebels, they could not defeat the nationalist and imperialist ideas that had led to the bloodshed in Moscow. Unlike the events of August 1991, which at least entered history as a failed coup, October 1993 never gained a definition and ambiguously remained in history as 'the events of October 1993'. Just like Barkashov's fighters who escaped through underground tunnels, their ideas and slogans have continued to smoulder under the surface of Russian political life, like a peat fire, occasionally letting off smoke or a nasty smell. The fire was never properly extinguished, but simply covered up in the hope that it would die by itself. Twenty years later it was fanned by Vladimir Putin into the large flames that are consuming not only parts of Ukraine, but also Russia's own future.

In 1993, nationalist and communist ideas seemed defeated not so much by tanks but by life itself. Nevzorov, who was driven in a police car through the centre of Moscow to be put on a plane to St Petersburg, recalled watching Moscow life carry on as normal. 'People walked their dogs, strolled with their children, changed money, bought food, posed for pictures with the blackened White House as a background and I suddenly felt that I was on the margins, that nobody really cared about all these politics any more.'[66] As *Kommersant* wrote at the time, 'The only thing that citizens want from big politics is the possibility of calmly making money and as calmly spending it to their hearts' content.'

As the late Yuri Levada, Russia's leading sociologist, wrote at the time, people minded their own business, their small dacha plots, their incomes and vouchers. 'Perhaps for the first time in the history of our country, daily life scored such a convincing victory over politics.'[67] But as Levada warned, this victory had its reverse side. The dominance of domestic life had a very different nature from Europe where democracy was ensured by political institutions and the elites. In the absence of such institutions and elites, the dominance of private life inevitably brought any important public issue to the level of 'bread and circuses', to simple consumerism, entertainment, game shows and soap operas.

The shelling of the White House was adopted as a 'plot' for an interactive video game. It was featured in a *Vzglyad* programme which was relaunched by Alexander Lyubimov after a four-year break. To compensate the audience for the 'missed-out' years, the well-groomed Lyubimov put together a pastiche of the events that had happened over the previous four years, played in a fast-forward, black-and-white mode accompanied by Scott Joplin's 'Ragtime' tune. It was a new reality, in which ideology no longer mattered and in which Nevzorov and Lyubimov happily coexisted on the same television channel that was soon to be hijacked by Boris Berezovsky, a future oligarch and chief manipulator of Russian politics. Berezovsky immediately reached out to Nevzorov as Russia's best showman, making him an offer Nevzorov readily accepted. 'A mercenary is like a tank: its cannon rotate in any direction,' Nevzorov said.[68]

As Nevzorov said, 'Lenya Golubkov' won over Anpilov and Barkashov and even himself. But this was a poor guarantee against the populism that had manifested in the December 1993 parliamentary elections when millions of Golubkovs voted for Vladimir Zhirinovsky, a charismatic populist and ultra-nationalist. (He too would soon turn into a showman.)

Zhirinovsky's misnamed Liberal Democratic Party won 23 per cent of the votes. The democratic Russia's Choice, led by Gaidar who shunned populism, refusing to make any promises that he could not keep, got 15 per cent of the proportional representation votes (although it did much better in the single-member districts). Sociologists, and much of the Russian political establishment, were stunned. On the night of the elections, state television channels, in anticipation of the Democrats' victory, staged an all-night show, called *The Celebration of a New Political Year*. It was a New Year's celebration come early. There was almost no analysis, but plenty of entertainment from pop singers, actors and folk groups. 'Let us drink to the new constitution,' the main presenter beamed with a smile. 'And let's not talk about politics today.'

Moscow's great and good were sipping champagne and congratulating each other on the new constitution that placed enormous powers in the hands of the president. The main computer that was supposed to relay the results of the parliamentary elections was said to have been infected with a virus. Instead of reading out results, the presenter of the show read out telegrams from the provinces. In fact, the only person who had reason to be in a good mood was Zhirinovsky. When it became clear that he and the communists had got a strong showing, the camera caught the shocked face of a Russian liberal essayist and Dostoevskian scholar, Yuri Karyakin. 'Russia, think hard, you have lost your mind!' he said to the camera.

With hindsight, Zhirinovsky's electoral coup was only natural and the liberals and particularly the media bore a large share of responsibility for it. The media did not try to educate, explain and engage the majority of the country in politics. Despite (or because of) being owned by the state, they performed no public duty. They kept 'Lenya Golubkov' on a diet rich in Latin American soap operas (whose main heroine even made an appearance in one of MMM's commercials) and game shows. The most popular of these was *Pole chudes* (*Field of Miracles*) – a carbon copy of *The Wheel of Fortune*, set up by Vladislav Listyev, a popular TV journalist who in the 1980s was one of the founders and presenters of the *Vzglyad* show. The Russian name of the game show was borrowed from the adaptation of Pinocchio in which a boy made out of wood is fooled by a scheming cat and a fox and buries his coins in a Field of Miracles in the Country of Fools, hoping that more coins will grow overnight. Golubkov's investment suffered the same fate: in 1994 the pyramid scheme finally collapsed. Inevitably Golubkov blamed not those who designed the pyramid scheme, but Yeltsin. The result of the 1993 elections followed the same logic.

The liberals, whose democratic illusions were shattered by the 1993 conflict, also blamed Yeltsin, rather than themselves. The sneering or *styob* was aimed not at the Soviet past, but at Russia's present. In December 1993, after the democrats' defeat in the parliamentary elections, Yeltsin made a strange appointment. He did not turn to Lyubimov or Listyev for support. Instead he turned to the seventy-year-old Alexander Yakovlev, asking him to become the chairman of Ostankino. But the ideologue of Perestroika, who had fought nationalists and communists all his life, suddenly felt powerless.

> 'This was the strangest period of my life... I felt with my skin that something peculiar was emerging in Russian life – very different from what

> was conceived at the beginning of Perestroika. My rosy dreams died when I got myself immersed in the television whirlpool. Chasing money, constantly squabbling about who will get paid more, falsehood, lies. For the first time in my life I saw corruption in action, in its naked form.'[69]

What Yakovlev had dreamt of at the beginning of Perestroika, he wrote, was that once people were given freedom they would elevate themselves and start arranging their lives as they saw fit.

PART II

'IMAGE IS EVERYTHING'

FIVE

Normal Television in Abnormal Circumstances

On 4 October 1993 Igor Malashenko sat in his rickety white Moskvich – a step down from a Lada – watching tanks fire shells and set fire to the White House. His office at the top of the mayor's building – the scene of a battle a day earlier – was sealed off. Malashenko's car, provided by his business partner, the media tycoon Vladimir Gusinsky, was equipped with a satellite phone which he used to call Hollywood Studios to arrange meetings at the Cannes television and entertainment fair where he was planning to buy content for NTV, a new television channel he was setting up.

The people Malashenko was talking to on the phone were watching live CNN coverage of the same dramatic events. 'It must have seemed completely absurd that some Russian guy at this point was calling from Moscow trying to buy movies,' he said later.[1] Malashenko was less concerned with the outcome of the battle – which, he was certain, would end in Yeltsin's victory – than with the programming of the new channel.

NTV's launch had been scheduled for the previous day, 3 October, when the ultra-nationalists and communists had tried to storm Ostankino. But things were not quite ready and it was decided to push the launch back by a week. When NTV finally came on air, on 10 October, its first analytical programme, *Itogi* (*Conclusions*), was almost entirely dedicated to the siege of the White House a week earlier. Gaidar explained to viewers his reasons for calling people out onto the streets at that time. The fact that he was doing so in the comfort of a private television studio was proof of Yeltsin's victory and that life was getting back to normal, or at least so it seemed at the time.

NTV was the first Western-style television in Russia. It was based on an American model, producing its own news and buying everything else from outside. In searching for a name, Malashenko went through a list of similar-sounding abbreviations – along the lines of BBC, CNN, ABC, CBC – until he settled on NTV. Nobody, including Malashenko himself, knew what the abbreviation stood for. Did the 'N' stand for '*nezavisimoe*' (independent) TV, or was it 'new' TV? Perhaps the adjective that reflected Malashenko's intentions best was '*normalnoe*' (normal) TV, the sort that any normal country should have.

In October 1993 Russia had few attributes of such a country. It had no proper banking system, no independent court and, after the shelling of the White House, no parliament. Its police and its army were in a sorry state. Television was supposed to deliver its makers and its viewers to that 'normal' country – Westernized, energetic and bourgeois.

However disturbing the news, it was countered by the calm manner in which NTV reported it. The channel conveyed stability and order. Like *Kommersant*, but on a much larger scale, it programmed and organized life, provided a timetable and a structure. 'When you create a TV schedule, you have to live with your audience, imagine when they get up, how they eat breakfast with the television on in the background, how they are getting their children ready for school, what they do during the day, what time they get back from work,' said Malashenko.[2]

In Soviet times, a television set was a peaceful and domesticated object. People knitted special covers for it and put porcelain statuettes on top. Mass production of TV sets began after Stalin's death and they populated the first separate flats that Khrushchev had had built. After the years of Stalinist mobilization, television worked like a tranquillizer. It provided background noise, like radio. The only threat it emanated was that it might explode (sets often did) and the only drawback was a high electricity bill. Its aim was to sedate rather than excite the audience and make people stay at home. At about 8 p.m. the main Channel One would show a children's programme *Bedtime for Tired Toys*, which would be followed at 9 p.m. by the equally soporific *Vremya* and Soviet feature films – hardly riveting stuff. The programming would usually finish at 11 p.m., which was often a relief. Television-watching was a collective and calming experience. 'Sleep well, the state is looking after you' was its message.

Unlike its Soviet predecessors, NTV was a channel of mobilization of private initiative and existence independent of the state. Its aim was to stop people from falling asleep. As a model of a new country, NTV targeted a 'model' audience: the urban professional class, those who had done well out of Soviet disintegration and benefited from market reforms, the educated, active and on the whole liberal-minded people with the means to buy a car or put their money in a bank – banks were among the biggest Russian advertisers on NTV. It was a channel for clever and successful people.

This audience wanted quality news and good entertainment. NTV provided both. Professionalism and common sense were its top priorities. Privacy – a word that has no equivalent in the Russian language – was its main value. Everything about it conveyed respectability, confidence and optimism, from its sleek logo – a green globe nestled between the letters NTV – to its modern studios and well-dressed young presenters. The green globe bounced and spun and, in children's programmes, morphed into hot air balloons which dissolved into sparkling fireworks. It was unlike anything previously seen on Soviet television – a celebration of private life and personal freedom.

The face and voice of the new channel was its anchor Evgeny Kiselev, who presented the weekly analytical programme, *Itogi*. He was a symbol of solidity and authority. Dressed in a conservative double-breasted suit, sporting a moustache, often pausing for thought and groping for the right word, he spoke in soft, deep, deliberate tones that inspired confidence.

Kiselev did not entertain or lecture the audience – he appealed to its intelligence and common sense.

NTV was sober and serious. Its news and current affairs programmes were devoid of irony or *styob*. Irony was preserved for the weekly non-political programme presented by Leonid Parfenov, NTV's bright and style-conscious young journalist who 'toured' his 'advanced' audience around theatres, exhibitions and fashion shows. While Parfenov's style was closer to that of *Kommersant*, Kiselev carried on the line of the Soviet-era liberals such as Alexander Bovin and Yegor Yakovlev. Kiselev was the man the old intelligentsia and the nascent Russian middle class most trusted and identified with.

Kiselev was born in 1956 – the same year as Yegor Gaidar – and was part of the first post-Stalinist generation. Like Gaidar, he belonged to the Soviet nomenclatura. His father was an aviation engineer who worked at one of the closed Soviet institutes, with a 'postbox' for an address. He grew up in the most comfortable Soviet milieu with none of the fear or hardship that had shaped the previous generation. The times had not demanded heroes or fighters, but bred softer, more flexible and reflective types, capable of compromise and mindful of creature comforts.

'I had a happy childhood. And even if it was not quite settled at first – it was not uncomfortable. We had our own apartment. I went to a good school – a five minutes' walk from home – no thugs, no gangsters,' Kiselev said.[3] Kiselev studied Persian at university and spent a year in pre-revolutionary Iran – where he had access to British and American newspapers and watched Western films. The defining experience for Kiselev's generation was the war in Afghanistan – pointless and costly, both in terms of money and of human life. Kiselev observed it at first hand.

A few months before the Soviet invasion of Afghanistan, Kiselev was sent to Kabul as a military interpreter – a job which involved close co-operation with the military intelligence service and the KGB. He saw how the KGB prepared a coup in Afghanistan, how they staged the storming of President Amin's palace. The natural thrill of being part of a spy movie plot was mixed with a nudging sense of the stupidity, futility and opportunism on the part of the Soviet government. Unlike the Soviet invasion in Czechoslovakia, the invasion of Afghanistan did not crush any illusions because there were none left.

Kiselev's stint in Afghanistan was followed by three years in the KGB school where he taught Persian to young spooks. This was not a matter of choice – turning down a proposal from the KGB was not an option. The fact that Kiselev came through the KGB school was not unusual – many of those who enjoyed successful careers had KGB connections one way or another. So did many businessmen.

When he was finally released from service, Kiselev joined Radio Moscow – the Soviet foreign language service that broadcast communist propaganda around the world and which also worked closely with the KGB. None of the people who worked there believed their own propaganda. Nor did they expect it to be heard. 'It was a common grave for an unknown journalist: a shortwave station that nobody wanted to listen to broadcasting to a foreign audience,' Kiselev said.[4] Yet what the job lacked in terms of professional fulfilment it made up for by providing plenty of free time and access to information. In the late 1980s it supplied ready-made cadres for Perestroika television. Kiselev ended up in the foreign department of the *Vremya* news programme.

It was here that he met Oleg Dobrodeev – a man who was to play a similarly important role in the creation of Russia's first independent television channel and an even greater one in its subsequent demise. The first head of news and current affairs at NTV, Dobrodeev subsequently climbed to the pinnacle of the Russian propaganda machine – under Vladimir Putin – a journey that passed through the destruction of NTV.

Dobrodeev was part of the same generation as Kiselev, but he grew up in a family of the artistic intelligentsia. Even more than Vladimir

Yakovlev, Dobrodeev was a 'son' of the *shestidesiatniki*. His father was a film scriptwriter and secretary of the Film-Makers Union, a mecca of the liberal artistic intelligentsia in the 1960s. Dobrodeev Sr was an author of a documentary film about the early years of Karl Marx and belonged to the same circle as Yegor. The Dobrodeev family lived in a house for writers in the north of Moscow. His co-author shared a flat with Evgeny Primakov, a future head of the Russian intelligence service and prime minister. A fluent French speaker and historian by background, Dobrodeev Jr was erudite, clever and extremely hard-working. He moved to television in 1983, but did not participate in boisterous Perestroika conversations that started a few years later and kept himself to himself, Kiselev recalled.

'He had a very systematic brain. Facts and quotes were on the right shelves ready to be retrieved,' said Kiselev. 'He did not show off, kept a modest appearance, but he appreciated the trappings of power – an office with a secretary, a chauffeur-driven car, a special government telephone line, the ability to talk informally to those in power. We could be having some important meeting and suddenly there would be a call from the Kremlin. Oleg would say: "Sorry old chap – I'm being called to the Kremlin. Got to go. We'll continue tomorrow." He savoured it, like one savours wine – its smell, its taste, its aftertaste,' said Kiselev,[5] a connoisseur of good wine himself who was also not indifferent to the trappings of power.

Dobrodeev had an unmistakable sense for news and trends; he sensed the mainstream and knew how to put himself at the head of it. In terms of his intellect and his work ethic, Dobrodeev was way above anyone at Ostankino and he quickly became one of Yegor Yakovlev's favourites. Malashenko, Dobrodeev's boss for many years, said he was a workaholic. 'Nothing interested him apart from work. He read every text, watched every news bulletin. When he went on holidays abroad, he made his secretary put a telephone receiver next to a TV set, so that he could at least listen to the news, if not watch it.'[6] On 5 January 1992, ten days after the Soviet Union ceased to exist, Dobrodeev and Kiselev went on air with *Itogi* – a forty-five-minute analytical summary of the week's news.*

In terms of prominence, *Itogi* filled the place vacated by *Vremya* as a trend-setting (or trend-explaining) programme. Foreign ambassadors often based their Monday morning dispatches on *Itogi* which came out on Sunday evenings. Kiselev invited news-makers and experts to 'try to work out what is going on'. The measure of *Itogi*'s success became apparent a year later when they decided to celebrate its first anniversary and invited everyone who had featured in *Itogi* over the past year. 'To our complete astonishment, they all came, apart from Yeltsin of course.'[7]

The happy days of *Itogi* ended with the firing of Yegor Yakovlev and the resignation of Malashenko. Bragin, who replaced Yakovlev, was an insult to human intelligence, a 'clinical case', as Dobrodeev put it. For an erudite man, the crème de la crème of the Soviet establishment, the idea of answering to a provincial party apparatchik who had hastily rebranded himself as a 'democrat', was humiliating. Ten years later, Dobrodeev himself would turn into the Kremlin's chief propagandist, but in 1992 he found the idea of using television as a means of propaganda distasteful. 'Information as such is not needed by the authorities; they see it as an instrument of instantaneous influence and rapid reaction,' he complained.

Kiselev, too, was unhappy – not so much because of censorship, but because he realized that he was sitting on a gold mine and getting paid peanuts. Everyone around him was making money by turning programmes into independent production companies which then sold the programmes back to the state channel, pocketing the profit. *Itogi*, however, remained part of state television and Kiselev was a state employee on a modest salary that was being wiped out by raging inflation. Kiselev decided it was time to walk away from Ostankino and take the programme

* *Itogi* started on Channel One but moved under the same name to NTV.

with him. When Dobrodeev, once again, came into his office to moan about the pressure, Kiselev told him it was time to act.

The speed with which the events unfolded in the next few hours was typical of 1990s Moscow. Kiselev picked up the phone and called Sergei Zverev, an old acquaintance who worked for Vladimir Gusinsky, the owner of a bank, a newspaper and radio station Echo Moskvy. 'I am here with Oleg,' he told him. 'We've been reading your paper. Big success. Have you thought of doing something similar in television?' 'Who would do it?' Zverev asked. 'We would.' 'Come over now,' Zverev told him.[8] Less than two hours later Dobrodeev and Kiselev were discussing their idea with Gusinsky, a theatre director turned oligarch.

The Oligarch and the Intellectual

'The oligarch was a special species which could only have been born in Russia in the late 1980s. We came out of the Soviet system, but we overcame that system and the remarkable criminality in the country. We were the people with fangs growing from the back of our necks,' Gusinsky said in the mid-2000s, several years after being kicked out of Russia.[9]

The business world of the early 1990s was a jungle in which only the fittest survived and Gusinsky was among those. He did not come from a privileged background, like Kiselev or Dobrodeev. The story of his family was fairly typical: grandfather shot in 1937, grandmother sentenced to seven years in the Gulag. Gusinsky was born in 1952 – a few months before Stalin's death – and grew up in a single-room, 18-square-metre (21.5-square-yard) flat with his parents. He received his first education on the street, fighting with other boys in the courtyard who picked on him as a 'little Yid'.

At school he wanted to be a physicist, but ended up studying engineering at an oil and gas institute – a fairly typical downshift for someone who was marked down as a 'Jew' in his Soviet passport. (High-profile university departments had secret, but strict, quotas for Jews and physics was enormously popular.) But he was not an academic type and after he had served his two-year conscription in the Soviet army, his boisterous temperament and his taste for theatrics guided him to GITIS, a Moscow drama school, where he studied to be a theatre director. He staged a couple of shows in the provincial, industrial Russian town of Tula, but left no mark on the theatre.

To make a living, he drove a gypsy cab ferrying foreigners to and from airports, pushed blue jeans and American cigarettes he bought from foreigners on the black market and traded foreign currency – all of which was illegal. In his excellent and thorough book *The Oligarchs*, David Hoffman describes Gusinsky as a *fartsovshchik* – a huckster.[10] As someone who was buying stuff from foreigners, he came to the attention of the KGB, which caught him trading foreign currency. He was brought in, though never charged, and had an audience with Filipp Bobkov, the head of the KGB's fifth directorate that dealt with dissidents. As Hoffman suggests, Gusinsky may have been a useful source for Bobkov who kept tabs on the intelligentsia.

In the late 1980s Gusinsky founded a co-operative that made bogus, vaguely oriental 'healing' bracelets out of copper wire that he bartered for a few bottles of vodka from a tramway depot. He also used copper to cover fake figurines made out of moulded plaster – copies of Russian art – and persuaded a senior man at the Central Committee to give him permission to export them for hard currency.

Connections mattered and nowhere more so than in the construction and real estate business in Moscow – another of Gusinsky's ventures. Gusinsky struck up a friendship with Yuri Luzhkov, the bald, stout and fiercely energetic future mayor of Moscow who, at the time, oversaw vegetable distribution and co-operatives in Moscow. Gusinsky's friendship with Luzhkov bordered on partnership – a private–public partnership of a very Russian sort which resulted in Gusinsky's company setting up its headquarters on top of the Moscow mayor's office.

Almost all big business in Russia grew out of this nexus between state and private interests. Gusinsky's construction company received city land and permits with miraculous ease. But the real trick was latching onto the cash flow of state enterprises or the government itself. All Russian oligarchs did so. Gusinsky latched onto the Moscow government which channelled its operational capital into a consortium of banks led by Gusinsky himself.

The difference between Gusinsky and others was in how they used the state capital. While most of the oligarchs used it to privatize state assets, effectively bidding for state companies with the state's own money, Gusinsky prided himself in using city hall cashflow as starting capital for building his own business from scratch, including newspapers and now a television channel. He felt that while most oligarchs were simply scrounging off the state, he was creating something new. None of the businesses that he owned had existed in Soviet days.

By the standards of the early 1990s, Gusinsky's business was still on a small scale. But what he lacked in terms of industrial assets he made up for in appearance and in status. Along with Boris Berezovsky, who managed to work himself into Yeltsin's inner circle and take charge of Channel One, he was the ultimate Russian oligarch. A man of the theatre who did not fulfil himself on stage, he did not just live the life of an oligarch with all its trimmings, including private jets, yachts and bullet-proof cars, but he also acted it.

One of the key attributes of a Russian oligarch in the early 1990s was a large security service that could fend off gangsters and racketeers. Instead of paying for protection, they recruited policemen and KGB staff. Gusinsky's security services, however, amounted to a small army, numbering 1,000 people. And although he sometimes deployed it for business purposes (he once helped Luzhkov to reclaim dozens of petrol stations that had been raided by gangsters), it was mainly a status symbol. It was as though Gusinsky was playing soldiers.

At one point Gusinsky had a proud collection of five top KGB ranks in his employment, including Bobkov, who had questioned Gusinsky when he was brought in just a few years back. What kind of work Bobkov did for Gusinsky was never entirely clear, but it certainly flattered Gusinsky's ego. Gusinsky's media interests fell into the same category. When he bankrolled the newspaper *Segodnya*, he did not do it as a business proposition. It was largely an ornament on the façade of his business empire, a symbol of status and influence. A television channel, however, would move him to a different league.

So when Kiselev and Dobrodeev came through his door with their idea of a television production company, he was ready and waiting, but he was thinking on a completely different scale from Kiselev, who simply was looking to sell his programme. Half an hour later, Gusinsky's office was swarming with aides and lawyers who were told that they were setting up a new private television channel. It was like a scene out of a 1950s Hollywood movie. Money was not an issue.

With the state being poor and pitiful, oligarchs created their own parallel infrastructure which substituted for a state. Gusinsky's holding, called Media Most, comprised a small army, a bank, a foreign service, his own newspaper, radio and a television channel. In time he would also try to get hold of an airline and his own telecommunications business. He was driving around Moscow in a cortège of cars with blue flashing lights, using a lane reserved for senior state officials.

Had the Soviet Union survived, Kiselev would have likely gone on to become the main commentator on foreign affairs in Soviet television and Dobrodeev would have climbed into the chair of the head of Soviet television. Like the older generation of ideologues, they were part of the Soviet elite. But unlike their Perestroika predecessors who had lost their status in the process of economic liberalization, they seized opportunities generated by the destruction of the Soviet command economy. The privileges and perks that were earlier provided by the party were now provided by Gusinsky. They got free flats in special houses, country dachas, chauffeur-driven cars and pay cheques well above market rates. They emerged as the winners because they were not burdened by communist principles – like Anpilov or Nina Andreeva – or obsessed with the Russian national idea or its past. They were professionals who lived in the present, free of any state ideology. They had education, skills and confidence in their own abilities and, as a result, made a seamless transition from the Soviet to the Russian elite. It was only natural that when Gusinsky asked Kiselev and Dobrodeev who would be the best person to lead the new channel, both named Igor Malashenko – their former boss who had served as the deputy head of the state-owned Ostankino and was widely considered to be one of the smartest and most able people in television.

Malashenko's first encounter with Gusinsky, the man who changed his life, was a meeting of two parallel universes which, had it not been for the end of the Soviet Union, would probably never have collided. 'He made a strange impression on me, and I am sure I made a strange impression on him,' Malashenko said.[11] A son of a Russian general and a member of the nomenclatura, he certainly had little in common with a Jewish millionaire, a former huckster, who had a strange way of showing off by hiring senior former KGB officers. Accidental as it was, there was an historic logic in this encounter.

It was a union of two different social milieux: big business that grew out of co-operatives and Soviet-era meritocracy. Malashenko, who despised the notion of the 'intelligentsia' as a measure of liberal and moral values, was nonetheless a quintessence of the intelligentsia as a professional, educated and skilled class bred by the Soviet system. He had studied philosophy at university and eschewed Marxism and Leninism in favour of Dante's political philosophy. He wrote a dissertation on *De Monarchia*, a work that dealt with the relationship between religious and secular powers. A proud and ambitious man, he soon realized that the field was too narrow for him, so he started to climb the career ladder of secular power. He got a job at the US and Canada Institute, harbouring no illusions about socialism with a human face. 'All this stuff that Lenin's ideas were being distorted – I never bought it.'[12]

Malashenko was no dissident. Solzhenitsyn did not interest him much. The book that made the strongest impression on him was Orwell's *Nineteen Eighty-Four*:

> Psychologically, it rang completely true. This country, this galaxy [described by Orwell] was not supposed to exist in reality, but it did. I lived in it, I tried to learn its double-speak in order to talk coherently and convincingly about the Soviet Union, but it was impossible. Our official dogma said that two plus two was ten. At the more liberal US and Canada Institute we were (informally) allowed to say that two plus two was eight, sometimes that it was seven. But in the end it did not matter as both were lies.[13]

Like many smart, energetic and ambitious people in the Soviet Union, Malashenko was faced with a problem: how to use his energy and talents without losing his self-respect. A talented mathematician or Latinist could carry on their studies with the minimum of sacrifices – the state did not interfere unless they tried to challenge it politically. But what if your energy and talents were in politics, media, or public relations? 'I understood very clearly that either I would waste my life or the system had to change.'[14]

Thirty years old when Andropov died and Chernenko was given office, Malashenko 'felt that we did not deserve this humiliation'. So when Gorbachev started to dismantle the system, Malashenko felt like joining in and giving him a hand. At the time when many, including Yeltsin, were heading out of the Central Committee, Malashenko went in. This was a peculiar career move – and it was underpinned by Malashenko's realization that his future depended on the dismantlement of the Soviet system. Yet, when on 25 December 1991 Malashenko stood in the Kremlin along with Yegor Yakovlev, watching Gorbachev sign his resignation, he was dumbstruck:

> In front of me, the last ruler of Russia in its imperial borders of the Soviet Union was signing off the empire to history. I was hypnotized by it. I did not try to say or do anything – I just watched. It was like being in a dream, watching a huge cliff coming down on you. I knew that the Soviet Union was going to collapse sooner or later – this was inevitable. But when I realized that what had been produced by several generations of the Russian elite was coming down, I could not jump up and down in joy.[15]

When the dust settled, it became apparent that the landscape looked like ground zero, a barren place. It did not have a grand design (nor did it need one after a seventy-year-long experiment), but it did not have as much as a simple blueprint. 'Yet, there was also a feeling that things would work out, that despite all the demoralization and ruin, something new would grow in its place,' Malashenko said.[16] What would grow in place of Soviet ideology depended largely on people like him.

Malashenko did not believe in a state or in ideology. He believed that an individual, himself or herself, valued dignity and freedom. Perhaps it was his studies of medieval and Renaissance philosophy that infected him with the idea of individual will and self-respect as the base of European civilization. He was not typical of his generation. He had an odd combination of cynicism and idealism, of misanthropy and respect for other people (perhaps as a form of respect for himself). He did not share the ideas of the 1960s generation, but nor did he want to settle scores with it. He valued the bright, independent-thinking people like Yegor Yakovlev who had invited him to work as his deputy at Ostankino, not as members of a generation but as individuals.

When Yegor got fired, Malashenko publicly stuck up for him and, a few months later, handed in his own resignation. 'I don't like my own generation,' he told a Russian newspaper. 'I found working with Yegor easy, simply because I myself have traits which I too consider anachronistic. And although I understand the sarcasm… about the '60s generation, many of these people are close to me – at least the strong and bright figures like [Yegor] Yakovlev.'[17]

He was unwilling to participate in the corrupt schemes that permeated Central Television, not because he was indifferent to money, or because he had high morals, but because he considered it beneath his sense of self-worth. His state job as the deputy head of Ostankino offered a choice: 'Either you steal and take bribes, or you live in relative poverty.' He wished for neither, but when his former journalists pitched the idea of launching a private television channel, he jumped at it.

Malashenko was much more than the general director of NTV. He was its main ideologue and creator, a man who, to a large degree, inherited the role played by Alexander Yakovlev in the Soviet Union – albeit for a much shorter period and with very different results. However, unlike Alexander Yakovlev, who believed in social democracy as a way of transforming Russia into a normal, free and Westernized country, Malashenko believed that the way to political freedom and the West lay through laissez-faire, individual freedom and private ownership.

Both Alexander Yakovlev and Malashenko agreed on the essential power of free information flow. News was not what the state wanted its citizens to believe, but what NTV decided it was. Malashenko's slogan was 'News is Our Profession' – a variation on the motto of General Curtis LeMay, the legendary head of America's Strategic Air Command, whose B-52 bombers carried on their tails the words: 'Peace is Our Profession'. The combative origin of NTV's slogan was fully justified by the battles that accompanied its birth and which it waged for much of its existence for as long as it stayed independent of the state.

NTV did not have a full licence and was considered an 'experiment'. Security men, better known as '*siloviki*', tried to thwart it from the very start, rightly seeing in it a threat to their own power. But every time, throughout the 1990s, NTV came out the winner. The battles varied in subject and in pretext, but they were invariably part of the same conflict between the private and the state, between competition – however imperfect – and restriction, between individual rights and statism, and, in the end, between war and peace.

NTV made its name at a pivotal and, as it later turned out, ill-fated point in Russia's history – the war in Chechnya. The first Chechen war (1994–6) was partly the result of the December 1993 parliamentary elections that brought up Zhirinovsky with his ultra-nationalist rhetoric and a shift in the balance of power within the Kremlin.

As was always the case with Yeltsin, he thrived in a crisis, mobilizing himself in the face of a threat, and flagged when the danger passed. Periods of high concentration were followed by periods of depression and drinking. This happened when he disappeared from sight after the defeat of the August 1991 coup and again after October 1993. 'Yeltsin had become more isolated, angry and vengeful,' Sergei Shakrai, Yeltsin's close aide, recalled.[18] In his memoirs, Gaidar called the chapter about the period that followed the October 1993 crisis 'The Time of Lost Opportunities'.

In early 1994, Yeltsin was absent for five weeks and when he was around, he was almost invariably in an awful mood and often drunk. After the December elections, Gaidar lost his influence and, three months after being reappointed to the government, had to resign. Yeltsin allowed himself to be surrounded and influenced by scheming, crude and thuggish lackeys who played up to his worst habits. His inner circle included Alexander Korzhakov, his bodyguard, and Mikhail Barsukov, the head of the security services – 'toadies' and 'half-brains' as Gaidar called them. By the summer of 1994, the changes in Yeltsin's entourage started to show.

Yeltsin was obviously drunk when he attempted to conduct an orchestra during an official ceremony in Berlin marking the withdrawal of Russian troops from Germany. He failed to emerge from the presidential plane when it landed in Ireland on the way back from America. In the minds of many ordinary Russians, this was far worse than shelling the White House. Not only was Russia withdrawing its troops, but it also had a drunkard for president. And the perception of Russia by the outside world often mattered more than the conditions the Russians were prepared to put up with at home. Hardship was one thing – humiliation, quite another.

Korzhakov, who had always stood behind Yeltsin's back as his bodyguard, was suddenly sitting next to him at Security Council meetings in the Kremlin. Kiselev spotted the change while watching the Kremlin footage and turned it into news. 'The rumours about the growing influence of Korzhakov have been confirmed,' he explained on *Itogi*. 'The head of presidential security is taking part in important and confidential state affairs.' This would have been alarming in any event, but in the autumn of 1994 it became lethal. Trouble in the North Caucasus republic of Chechnya was brewing and Yeltsin's advisers, Korzhakov and Barsukov, saw it as a perfect opportunity for a small victorious war that could steal Zhirinovsky's thunder, boost Yeltsin's rating that had been falling as the result of economic difficulties and strengthen their own positions. Chechen separatism was part of a chain reaction set off by the collapse of the Soviet Union and Yeltsin decided to end it by force.

NTV seized on Chechnya several months before the war actually started. 'Starting from June, there was hardly an *Itogi* programme that did not mention Chechnya,' Kiselev recalled.[19] In September, NTV's future war reporter, Elena Masyuk, reported from a southern Russian region neighbouring Chechnya that field hospitals were being set up. In November 1994, Malashenko ran into Evgeny Savostyanov, the soft-spoken head of the Moscow KGB whom he knew from his days at the Central

Committee. 'He told me in his carefree way: "Igor, listen, forget about Chechnya for a couple of weeks. We will finish it all off and then I will tell you all about it." I realized that they really didn't understand what they were doing.'[20]

At the time of this encounter, Savostyanov had signed a contract with forty-seven tank crews, behind their commander's back, to lend President Dudaev's disparate and weak opponents in Chechnya a helping hand. But when the Russian-contract soldiers reached Grozny, the capital of Chechnya, they came under intense fire from Dudaev's army. Most of them fled and some were captured. Chechen 'opposition forces' broke ranks and started to loot Grozny. While the state media peddled the official line that Dudaev was fleeing and that there were no Russian soldiers on the ground, NTV exposed the operation for what it was – a humiliating debacle.

Malashenko had no sympathy for Dudaev – a paranoid and narcissistic dictator. In fact, his biggest problem with the war was not what it might do to Chechnya, but what it would almost certainly do to Russia. The war was not just an assault on separatists, it was an assault on everything that NTV stood for: professionalism, respect for individual rights, normal life and common sense. 'I realized that the war in Chechnya would inflate the role of the army and security services and that it would change the rules of the game in Russia, because once you start shooting people in Chechnya, you can shoot them anywhere, the hand almost involuntarily reaches for the gun or a truncheon,' Malashenko said.[21] So Malashenko and Dobrodeev decided that NTV would show the war in its full and gruesome details. Its correspondents reported it from both sides. They went behind the Russian lines and interviewed Chechen commanders, inciting the outrage of the Russian army chiefs.

When the government said there were no prisoners, NTV showed a line-up of captured young conscripts, disarmed and helpless. When the government kept silent about its losses, NTV showed a downed Russian helicopter and bodies of Russian soldiers. When state TV channels said that civilians had left Grozny, NTV showed wounded civilians bombed out of their houses, old people desperately looking for cover, a woman whose face was just a bloody wound. The Kremlin was not only losing militarily; it was also losing the information war to NTV.

The images of devastating military action, blood and destruction provided by NTV's own correspondent and particularly by its star war reporter, Elen Masyuk, were invariably more powerful than written statements supplied by the Kremlin or even official footage of Russian tanks driving down a dusty road. 'In Grozny we use *no* other sources apart from what [our reporters] directly see,' said Oleg Dobrodeev, NTV's news director.[22] In the winter of 1994–5, the majority of Russians, according to polls, were on the side of NTV against the war. Polls also showed that it was television that commanded attention during the war in Chechnya and it was NTV that was in the lead. Nearly 30 per cent of the television audience chose NTV news for objective coverage of the war, compared with 12 per cent for the pro-Kremlin Ostankino/Channel One news.[23] NTV was changing the Kremlin's agenda.

The beginning of the war in Chechnya also coincided with the launch of NTV's satirical show *Kukly* (*Puppets*). Based on Britain's *Spitting Image*, it featured rubber latex puppets of all Russia's top politicians and was unabashedly irreverent. The idea of the programme came from a Russian producer who lived in France. The scriptwriter was the former actor and satirist Viktor Shenderovich who knew Gusinsky from the days of drama school. Each *Kukly* skit was based on a famous book or film rewritten to fit in with the reality of the day. One of the first skits stylized Mikhail Lermontov's *Hero of Our Times*, making the most of the parallels with the nineteenth-century war in the Caucasus. The puppets parodied the voices of Russian politicians. It was decided that Yeltsin should be left out of the show – at least to start with. 'We thought that would be too much of a shock and we should prepare the audience,' Malashenko said.[24]

Russia had a long tradition of political satire, but not of turning its leaders into funny puppets. The Kremlin rulers could be hated or loved, feared or despised, but they had always preserved some mystique of power and were never laughed at in public. It was that mystique that NTV deliberately sought to destroy, de-sacralizing state power at a time when the state was trying to justify its brutal war in Chechnya.

In one of the skits, Vyacheslav Kostikov, Yeltsin's press spokesman, introduced Pavel Grachev, the defence minister, as 'the brain behind the Chechen operation'. He then knocked on Grachev's puppet head producing a hollow wooden sound. 'We have many soldiers here who have experienced defeat in Afghanistan,' Kostikov said. 'Yes, and we are using their experience to the fullest.'

As Yeltsin's bodyguards, Korzhakov and his men saw their task not just in providing physical security but also in dealing with his critics and shielding him from political attack. The first *Kukly* programme went on air on 19 November 1994. The same day an article appeared in the state newspaper *Rossiyskaya gazeta*, portraying Gusinsky as an evil media mogul from a James Bond film. 'Now the Most group has its sights set on the pinnacle of power... For this purpose the Most group is gradually "taking over" the most influential media outlets.'[25] Gusinsky knew the article was a black mark, a threat from Korzhakov.

Two weeks later Korzhakov's men, in unmarked fatigues, clashed with Gusinsky's security guards outside his office in the Moscow mayor's building. Pointing their guns at Gusinsky's men, they ordered them to lie on the ground, face down in the snow, while they roughed up the head of security, breaking several of his ribs. This 'special operation' became known in Moscow as 'mugs in the snow'. Malashenko called around the foreign television bureaux and asked them to send their crews which arrived just in time to capture images of Korzhakov's men forcing Gusinsky's security guards onto the ground and kicking them even when they were down.

Watching the whole scene from his office at the top of the tower, Gusinsky called in the Moscow KGB, headed by his friend Savostyanov. Soon, a team of Moscow state security agents arrived at the scene and pointed their weapons at Korzhakov's men whom they mistook for gangsters. After a brief clash, Savostyanov's men retreated. Korzhakov quickly reported the whole incident to Yeltsin and within two hours Savostyanov – the last man who was hired to work at the security services from outside the KGB – was fired.

Soon after the raid, Gusinsky was summoned to the Kremlin and told that he would lose his television channel unless it stopped its damaging coverage of Chechnya. Gusinsky refused, but thought it would be safer to send his family to London where he soon joined them. In a newspaper interview, Korzhakov boasted that his favourite sport was chasing geese – wordplay on Gusinsky's nickname 'Gus' which means goose in Russian.

After a few months of shuttling between Moscow and London, Gusinsky's business and media partners, including Malashenko, Kiselev and Dobrodeev, gathered in the dimly lit wine bar in the basement of London's exclusive Lanesborough Hotel in Park Lane – a favourite hang-out of Russian oligarchs – to discuss the situation. Gusinsky, who presided over the long wooden table, let his partners on the banking side speak first. They told him that NTV was jeopardizing their business and so it had to be either sold or transformed into a non-political channel. Then it was Malashenko's turn to speak. 'Your partners are wrong,' he told Gusinsky. 'NTV is your only defence.' Malashenko called it the principle of 'explosive reactive armour' used to protect tanks against artillery fire. Reactive armour is stuffed with elements that counter-explode when hit by a charge. 'So, if you close down NTV, they will consider you a weakling and that will be the end,' Malashenko said. 'If they attack you – we will counter-explode.'[26] Gusinsky thought for a moment and sided with Malashenko.

What gave Malashenko and his journalists confidence was the knowledge that they and not the military and security services were on the right side of history. They were clever, skilful and Westernized. They held out the promise of a normal life that most people craved. The state was weak, dysfunctional and unattractive. The slogan Malashenko came up with was simple and powerful: 'News is power. Power is in truth.' Behind this statement, as armour, was the large and growing empire of one of Russia's top oligarchs.

As Malashenko predicted, the Kremlin did not shut down NTV, although not for the want of trying. Chernomyrdin's government considered revoking its licence, but Alexander Yakovlev, who now headed the Federal Commission for Television and Radio – his last official post – came to the rescue. 'I realized we had to save NTV. To a great extent, it was a question about the fate of democracy.' Without telling Chernomyrdin, he prolonged NTV's licence. 'You've made a mistake,' Chernomyrdin told him that evening. 'It did not even occur to me that you could do it over the head of the government.' He demanded that Yakovlev cancelled his decision. 'It is your error – you correct it.' But Yakovlev, a former member of the Soviet Politburo, put Chernomyrdin, a junior member of the Central Committee, in his place: 'Don't raise your voice to me, Viktor Stepanovich. I had no legal excuse to refuse them a licence.'[27] Moreover, in May 1995, Gusinsky decided it was safe enough to return from his London exile. He carefully timed his return to coincide with Bill Clinton's official visit to Moscow for the Second World War Victory Day celebration. Harassing the owner of an independent television channel while America's president was in Russia discussing financial aid with Yeltsin would be too daring even for Korzhakov. Shortly after Gusinsky's return, NTV put out a *Kukly* skit which he had considered to be risky a few weeks earlier. The skit was called 'Don Quixote and his Bodyguard' and portrayed Yeltsin as a drinking knight in a nightcap and Alexander Korzhakov as Sancho Panza.

'How could I live without your simple wisdom, Sancho?' (Yeltsin/Don Quixote asks.)

'I know a lot of things. Do you want me to tell you how to trade oil? I will write you a memo.'

'I did not know you could write.'

'Yes, although I can't read yet.'

'Well, that is not necessary.'

Astride a donkey, Korzhakov/Sancho shouts down a radio to his officers: 'I am an ass, I am an ass, receive.' Towards the end, Sancho falls asleep, dreaming of turning into Yeltsin's master and Yeltsin turning into his servant. Yeltsin/Don Quixote tries to wake him up. 'Was that a dream?' Sancho asks. 'No, that was a nightmare,' Yeltsin replies.[28]

Seeing that NTV not only got away with its coverage, but was actually getting stronger, other television channels started to follow its critical reporting of the war. NTV doubled its number of viewers. In Moscow the share of NTV's audience was nearly 50 per cent, shaping the public perception of the war and eventually leading to an anti-war sentiment. Malashenko's party was winning. Not only was NTV setting its own agenda, it was also changing the behaviour of the government, as the first major terrorist attack by Chechen fighters made apparent.

When, on 14 June 1995, one of Chechnya's most notorious field commanders, Shamil Basayev, with 200 men, bribed his way through various Russian checkpoints and took 1,600 people hostage in a hospital in the small town of Buddenovsk, demanding an end to the war, the Russian government initially responded with a familiar mix of cover-ups and heavy-handedness. With Yeltsin on his way to a G7 meeting in Halifax, Nova Scotia, Chernomyrdin, who was left in charge, dispatched the heads of police security agencies to Buddenovsk.

Their first step was to ban journalists from attending a news conference called by Basayev. Furious, Basayev executed five of the hostages.

On the fourth day of the crisis, Russian special forces attempted to storm the hospital which resulted in total mayhem. Basayev was interviewed live by NTV, defending his position: 'We don't need anything – not ammunition, not clothes, not food – only to stop the war in Chechnya... If [Russia's war in Chechnya] over the past six months is not terrorism, then this is not terrorism either. I am not a terrorist, I am a saboteur.'[29] Gaidar called on Chernomyrdin to start immediate negotiations. After a couple of botched attempts to storm the hospital, with more than 100 people already dead, Chernomyrdin agreed to negotiate with Basayev.

If Basayev used television cameras, so did Chernomyrdin. He invited journalists into his office and let them film his telephone conversation with Basayev. Chernomyrdin looked composed and resolute, taking responsibility for the lives of people in front of the cameras. The country watched an extraordinary scene: the prime minister talking on the phone to the prime terrorist: 'Shamil Basayev, can you hear me? I am at work and I am responsible for everything that is happening in the country at the moment. I am ready. Tell me how much time you need...' Chernomyrdin promised a ceasefire in Chechnya from 8 p.m. that day and safe passage for the terrorists back to Chechnya. His agreement was broadcast on television, along with footage of the burials of the hostages who had died in the attack.

Buddenovsk was a turning point in the war. For the first time since the start of the war, the Kremlin bowed to public pressure and began serious talks. Television and NTV in particular helped to break the pattern of lies and cover-ups by the Kremlin. It was, arguably, NTV's finest hour.

In the mid-1990s, any attempt to 'do something with NTV' invariably failed. When prosecutors launched a case against *Kukly* for 'the conscious and public humiliation of the honour and dignity of high officials, expressed in an indecent way' they only boosted *Kukly*'s fame. Malashenko and Kiselev, flanked by the puppets of Chernomyrdin and Yeltsin, held a press conference which was as embarrassing for the Kremlin as it was helpful to NTV's rating.

When they realized that they could not beat NTV, the smartest members of the government decided to join them. Chernomyrdin came to the channel's studios to meet his own puppet. To the disbelieving laughter and applause of NTV journalists, Chernomyrdin joked with his 'double', showing himself once again to be a real person and winning the sympathies of journalists and viewers alike. 'Why have you got such a fat mug?' he laughed to the cameras, in the way that any Western politician would do. For a second, Russia seemed almost like a normal country where the ability to criticize and ridicule politicians is a sign of a healthy democracy.

Yet, there was one fundamental problem. In contrast to 'normal' countries where freedom of expression is guaranteed by institutions such as parliament, civil society, the media itself and, above all, by the consensus of the population, in Russia freedom of speech rested on the goodwill of just one man – Yeltsin – who, for some reason, believed it to be a valuable thing. As Alexander Yakovlev testified, 'Not once did he complain about a single programme, although he had plenty of reasons to do so... His tolerance towards criticism... went beyond any measure.'[30]

Whether Yeltsin needed to be unequivocally supported or unequivocally criticized simply because it was 'healthier' for democracy was at the heart of the debate which unravelled among the Russian intelligentsia as soon as Yeltsin became Russia's president.

Back in October 1991, in a heated exchange with a scholar of the Renaissance, Leonid Batkin, in the pages of the *Literary Gazette*, Marietta Chudakova, scholar and Yeltsin supporter, argued against those who thought it was the job of the intellectual to attack any government. 'There are plenty of reasons to be disappointed [in the government] but I insist that it is the democratically oriented journalists and publicists who are shaping this disappointment, putting it into talented formulations, without much thought about the aims and consequences.'

Of course Yeltsin and his government made plenty of mistakes – how could they not – but one must not lose sight of the historic circumstances in which they were acting, Chudakova argued:

> Is it not too early for us to copy the tough grip of Western journalists? They have a long tradition of keeping a vigilant control over people in power, catching them out on anything, including their private lives. They don't have to deal with such nerve-racked politicians who did not go to public schools to learn how to run a democratic system and with an exhausted nation. There people reading a morning paper over coffee can have a good laugh and forget all about it by lunchtime. Here, people pore over a newspaper, finding in it an expression of their own frustration and anger.[31]

The paradox was that programmes such as *Kukly* and the media more generally took an easy swipe at Yeltsin and helped to drive down his rating, which, by the end of 1995, was in single digits, but they also owed their existence to him. Journalists were not only protected, but empowered by Yeltsin who saw them as his natural allies against nationalists and communists, retained a Soviet-era relationship with the intelligentsia that allowed it to bite a feeding hand and considered it his role to patronize it. When television talked about his health or poked fun at him, Yeltsin preferred to switch it off, rather than call its owners. Never before or after did journalists in Russia have such a high status and command as much power as they did in the 1990s.

But if Russia had freedom of speech and private property in the 1990s, it was not because there was an inbuilt tradition or craving for it, but because Yeltsin allowed it. Malashenko recalled asking American officials why they supported Yeltsin almost unconditionally instead of paying more attention to democratic institutions. 'Yeltsin is your only democratic institution' came the answer. Malashenko said: 'I knew this could not last. If Yeltsin was the only guarantor of our freedom, then we would be finished sooner or later.'[32]

Fighting for the President

In 1996 the Russian liberal media rallied behind Yeltsin when he faced presidential elections, challenged by the communist leader Gennady Zyuganov. The war in Chechnya, the growing gap between the rich and the poor, and the continuing economic slump had brought Yeltsin's rating close to zero. Yeltsin was also suffering from serious heart problems and to many, including Gaidar, he did not seem fit to fight – either physically or spiritually. Gaidar wrote Yeltsin a letter, arguing he should not run at all. The problem was, as Gaidar soon realized, there was nobody else who could. The communists were riding high, exploiting economic hardship, accusing Yeltsin of acting against the interests of Russian people and promising to restore equality and Russia's status as a superpower and to kick out (Jewish) tycoons. In practice, Zyuganov's victory would mean the end of all the economic reforms and freedoms that Yeltsin had fought for so fiercely since 1991. He decided to run.

One of the biggest threats, however, was not even that the communists would come to power, for it was highly unlikely that Yeltsin would have ceded this power to them, but that the party of war led by Korzhakov would persuade Yeltsin to postpone or cancel the elections altogether and use force instead, as he had done in October 1993. At the very least this would have deprived Yeltsin of legitimacy, isolated him from the West and made him completely reliant on Korzhakov and the security men who would quickly put an end to any reforms.

In charge of Yeltsin's official election campaign was Oleg Soskovets, the first deputy prime minister and a friend of Korzhakov, who presented Yeltsin with his low rating as proof positive that the only way to defeat the communists was to ban them. The reformers needed Yeltsin to win – openly and fairly.

The Russian business tycoons who observed Zyuganov schmoozing and hobnobbing with the Western elite in Davos, trying to present himself there as a social democrat rather than as the Stalinist and anti-Semite that he was at home, agreed to throw their energy and media resources behind Yeltsin. A fight against the communists was a proxy fight for Yeltsin against a war party inside the Kremlin. Yet, far from paying for Yeltsin's victory, the oligarchs saw it as a way of making money.

The idea of forming a coalition of the seven largest business tycoons belonged to Boris Berezovsky – the archetypal Russian oligarch who epitomized the 1990s with all the opportunities, ruthlessness, colour, individualism and utter lack of morals. A mathematician by background, Berezovsky specialized in the theory of decision-making and in optimization, using applied mathematics to model how choices are made. He also applied models to his life and to the country, as though it were a giant chessboard where he moved the pieces. He 'optimized' the hangovers of the Soviet Union and the inadequacies of the emerging market economy.

Berezovsky thrived on uncertainty and crisis, surviving several assassination attempts, and expanded his influence. Unlike other oligarchs who wished to own their assets and be able to pass them on, Berezovsky did not formally own much of what he controlled. He operated not through share registers, but through people he appointed as managers of his key enterprises, gaining control over cash flow. Berezovsky saw money not as a goal in itself, but as a by-product of his main activity: scheming and playing politics.

He fashioned himself (and often persuaded others to see him) as the chief manipulator of Russian politics: not the first politician, but the man who manipulates the first politician – an image he cherished and poeticized. He cultivated myths about his influence and power and exploited them to obtain real power, money and influence. A man of demonic energy, he was always in ten places at once, always plotting and on the move. The process was as pleasing to him as the result. Like an alchemist, he turned personal connections into money and money into influence. He spoke fast, quietly and articulately. As a Jew, he was a gift to anti-Semites.

Having made his first fortune by selling cars, he worked his way into Yeltsin's circle after the collapse of the Soviet Union, through the president's ghost writer and future son-in-law. Berezovsky paid for the publication of Yeltsin's memoirs and regularly delivered the royalties from sales in other countries – whether real or not, nobody knew. At the end of 1994 – just as Russia headed into war with Chechnya – he persuaded Yeltsin and his family to hand him effective control over Channel One, promising to turn it to their service. He then convinced the Kremlin to sell him and his partners Sibneft, an oil company, at a knockdown price, in order to finance Channel One, which he used as a blunt and effective tool of propaganda. 'I never saw the media as a business, but as a powerful instrument in a political struggle,' he said in one television interview. He also deployed Channel One in his wars with business competitors, as did Gusinsky with NTV.

Until 1996 Gusinsky and Berezovsky were at loggerheads, fighting fiercely for the accounts of Aeroflot, the loss-making national carrier. Gusinsky believed (for good reason) that it was Berezovsky who had bad-mouthed him to Korzhakov and Yeltsin and who put up Korzhakov to raid his office in the winter of 1994. In 1996, faced with the threat of Zyuganov's victory or cancelled elections, the two men put their feud aside and joined resources for Yeltsin's re-election. They decided to hire Chubais, who had been fired from the government a couple of months earlier, largely thanks to Korzhakov, to lead Yeltsin's campaign. Chubais, who had the reputation of a highly effective manager, accepted their offer with great enthusiasm: 'I was planning to fight for Yeltsin anyway and was certainly ready to join forces with them.'[33]

In fact, Chubais had already tied the knot between the oligarchs and the Kremlin. Business tycoons had a strong incentive for bringing Yeltsin to victory. A few months earlier Chubais had endorsed an audacious scheme devised by one of the oligarchs, Vladimir Potanin, that would transfer control over Russia's natural resources to a select group of tycoons in exchange for their political support. It was known as the 'loans-for-shares' privatization and was the worst example of insider trading and outright sham that the world had ever seen; and it has haunted Russian capitalism ever since. According to this scheme, tycoons would lend money to the cash-strapped government and in exchange be allowed to manage the state's shares. The loans would run out in the autumn of 1996 – after the election. At that point, in theory, the government could repay the oligarchs and get the shares back to be sold in an open auction. But this was just a smokescreen for a quiet transfer of shares to the hand-picked oligarchs. In practice, the government had neither the money nor the intention to buy the shares back. Foreigners would be excluded and the oligarchs' banks that managed the shares would auction them to themselves.

Worse still, not only were the auctions fixed, but the money with which the tycoons had bought the most lucrative assets had come from the state itself. The state, or its agency, would deposit its money in one of the tycoons' banks which would then use this money to bid for a company, while its workers' wages and payments to suppliers would be delayed for months. The deal was a political pact between the oligarchs and Yeltsin's government since the second part of the deal – the actual exchange of loans for shares – depended on Yeltsin's victory. 'It was a small price to pay for averting a communist revanche,' Chubais said.[34] In fact, the loans-for-shares scheme was so unfair that it undermined its main purpose of reforming Russia into a normal, civilized country.

What is more, the deal was hardly necessary. The government did not owe any favours to tycoons. The risk of losing their wealth and influence

– if not their freedom – in case of Yeltsin's defeat was enough of an incentive for them to rally behind Yeltsin.

The biggest help provided by the oligarchs was not money, but ideas. The oligarchs put together a rival campaign headquarters that was headed by Chubais and included Yeltsin's own daughter Tatyana Dyachenko and her husband Valentin Yumashev, a former journalist and Yeltsin's ghost writer. Igor Malashenko was seconded from NTV to the Kremlin to lead the media campaign. The team told Yeltsin that despite his dismal 5 per cent rating he could still win the election, if he entrusted the campaign to them. Yeltsin was suspicious. Faced with the prospect of losing power to people whom he had literally shelled out of the White House three years earlier, Yeltsin felt the risks were too high to experiment with 'election games' run by private businessmen and their brainy men.

This is what Korzhakov told him: 'You will only lose time with all these election games, and then what?' Like any Russian politician in a moment of crisis, Yeltsin naturally leaned towards the security services. 'Comparing two strategies offered to me by two teams different in their mentality and approach, I felt I could not wait until the election results in June. I had to act now!' he wrote in his memoirs.[35]

Yeltsin told his aides to draft a decree banning the Communist Party, dissolving parliament and postponing elections for two years. The idea horrified Chubais's team. Yeltsin's aides leaked his secret plans to Kiselev, who torpedoed them by breaking the news on *Itogi*. Dyachenko persuaded Yeltsin to hear out Chubais, who told him the situation was completely different from 1993, and dissolving parliament would be equal to a coup. Yeltsin shouted a lot but succumbed to the pressure. 'I reversed a decision I had almost made,' he recalled in his memoirs.[36]

A day or two later, Dyachenko brought Malashenko before her father. Malashenko felt confident that Yeltsin could win the elections honestly as long as he ran a proper campaign. This confidence was based on a simple assumption that however bitter people might feel about Yeltsin himself, the majority of Russians did not wish to return to the communist past which Zyuganov represented.

'I told him that there was a big gap between his low rating and the anti-communist sentiment which could be turned into votes, if he campaigned,' Malashenko said. Yeltsin seemed relieved. 'It was as though I had told him something that he had thought about himself and wanted to hear from someone else. He was clearly tired, but his eyes suddenly lit up. He got everything I told him extremely quickly and he engaged. It was like a game of ping-pong.'[37] Sensing the scent of a genuine political fight, Yeltsin sprang back to life. Gaidar, who came to see Yeltsin around the same time, could barely recognize him. 'He was crisp, focused, energetic and quickly grasped the essence of his interlocutor's thoughts and asked the right questions. It was as though the past five years were erased and we were back in October 1991, at our first meeting.'[38]

Malashenko had never run an election campaign in his life. All he knew – from his time at the US and Canada Institute – was how it was done in America and he built the campaign with the vigour and aggression suitable for an American presidential candidate. During this time he formally remained the head of NTV. To step down from NTV or to get a formal secondment would have been hypocritical: in the Russia of the 1990s nobody would have believed in this separation.

Malashenko told Yeltsin that he needed to generate news every day which television could report. Yeltsin's first trip to Krasnodar – a communist stronghold – was a disaster. The president and his entourage walked down an empty street that had been cleared by his security and waved at the crowd of people that had been cordoned off. When Yeltsin returned to Moscow, Malashenko and Chubais put two photographs in front of him. One showed Yeltsin in 1991 in the midst of a jubilant crowd – a true people's president. The other one was of his visit to Krasnodar where he looked like a Soviet-era boss. 'Yeltsin got it. The staged Soviet-style visits stopped straight away and he started to work,' Malashenko recalled.[39]

Within a few weeks Yeltsin had shed nearly 10 kg (22 pounds) and stopped drinking. He regained his charisma and sparkle. He criss-crossed the country holding American-style election rallies. He went down mines in Vorkuta, a horrific Gulag town in the north whose coal miners went unpaid for months; in a crisp white shirt he danced the twist, in sweltering heat, in the southern town of Rostov, swaying his hips and flapping his elbows. Over the three months of the election campaign Yeltsin flew to twenty-six regions across nine time zones.

The main strategy of Yeltsin's campaign was to mobilize the anti-communist votes, presenting the election as a final and decisive battle between the Soviet communist regime and anti-Soviet democratic reforms. The media's job was to stoke and exploit the fears of a communist comeback. The threat was somewhat exaggerated, not least because the communists did not seem that desperate to gain real power in the country, but it provided the best consolidation ground for Yeltsin's electorate.

An agitprop-style propaganda sheet headed *Ne dai Bog* (*God Forbid*) illustrated the spirit of the campaign. It was published by Vladimir Yakovlev, the founder of *Kommersant*; 10 million copies were distributed for free across provincial Russia. It played on the common fears and memories of empty shelves and long queues in shops. It drew parallels between Zyuganov and Hitler; it ran interviews with famous artists who spoke of their fears of bloodshed and ruin in the case of a communist victory. The paper's budget (apparently $8 million) and the source of money were a closely guarded secret. But while newspapers were small weaponry, television was the heavy artillery.

To mobilize the young voters who normally did not vote, Yeltsin's media campaigners came up with the slogan 'Vote or Lose', adapted from Bill Clinton's 'Choose or Lose'. What the voters stood to lose was illustrated by videos and animated cartoons. 'If your fridge is empty, all television channels show the same programme and you receive only one newspaper, then the "happy tomorrow" is here,' a voice warned in one such cartoon. An even more important slogan was 'Vote with Your Heart' and was aimed at older and more reliable Russian voters. With melancholic music in the background, election advertisements showed ordinary old Russian men and women calmly talking about their families and their experiences of living under the communists, of repressions and collectivization, of their reluctance to go back to the Soviet era and their hopes for Yeltsin. 'If the communists come to power, they will take my land – just like before,' a Russian farmer said. 'Let Yeltsin finish the good things that he has started,' a woman in a headscarf insisted. Whatever the motives, Yeltsin's campaign appealed to the sensibility and the best instincts in Russian people.

It began with a summary of Yeltsin's heroic political career, followed by extensive coverage of his campaign. Yeltsin was shown visiting the ancient city of Yaroslavl', promising to give its cash-strapped citizens 'everything and to take back nothing'. He was shown in the newly restored Cathedral of Christ the Saviour near the Kremlin, 'ruined under the communists and restored under Yeltsin'. Gennady Zyuganov, Yeltsin's main communist rival, was depicted hobnobbing with the oligarchs in Davos or in international airport VIP lounges.

TV critic Irina Petrovskaya lamented NTV's metamorphosis. 'NTV, my sorrow and my pain! Where did its objectivity and even-handedness go? What happened to its European correctness? Evgeny Kiselev resembled in his manners and his tone political commentators of [Soviet] Central Television.' She saw far enough into the future to pose the key question of that fraught time: 'If they manage [to get Yeltsin elected], will television be able to return to those democratic principles? Will the new (old) power allow it? Or will it turn a temporary love affair with the media into a compulsory admiration?'[40]

Yet, while some media executives saw Yeltsin's campaign purely as a money-making opportunity, most journalists who participated in the election campaign did so because they too had much to lose. The return of the communists or the victory of Korzhakov's clan would have spelled the end to free journalism and its special status in Yeltsin's Russia. As Kiselev said, 'Yes, we were biased, but we genuinely believed – and still believe – that Yeltsin's victory would save the country and that Zyuganov would throw it back. We were defending ourselves. When a house is in flames you don't worry about spoiling books and carpets by throwing water on them.'[41]

Judging by NTV's own standards in previous years, the Yeltsin coverage was clearly biased. By the standards of Russian television in the late 2000s, when it became nothing but propaganda, it was an example of restraint and moderation. Even more crucially, Malashenko and his journalists campaigned not just for Yeltsin per se, but for a Yeltsin who would end the war in Chechnya, carry on with reforms and bring Russia closer to the West. NTV continued its highly critical coverage of Chechnya. 'Every time NTV showed something about Chechnya – they looked at me in the Kremlin as though I was a traitor,' Malashenko recalled. 'But I kept telling them: if you want it to look different on the screen – do something about Chechnya itself – don't try to doctor the picture.'[42]

On 31 March, Yeltsin went on television and announced he was ready for peace talks and promised a 'political solution to the crisis'. A few weeks later, on 21 April, Dudaev was killed and Yeltsin flew to Chechnya to meet the elders and to thank the soldiers for their service. 'Peace in Chechnya has been restored,' Yeltsin declared, effectively admitting that the army was unable to end the insurgency. Pressing his pen and paper against the side of an APC, Yeltsin theatrically signed an order to decommission soldiers. Opinion polls showed Yeltsin's rating climbing steadily while Zyuganov's figures were either flat or falling. Yeltsin was clearly ahead of Zyuganov in Moscow and St Petersburg and in other large cities. He was overwhelmingly supported by the educated, the well-paid and the young. This was NTV's prime audience.

But apart from mobilizing the general public, television also communicated the 'party line' to all regional bosses who controlled election registers. Although many of them were natural communist supporters, they took their instructions from the state media. By the end of spring 1996, Malashenko's team was clearly winning over Korzhakov's group inside the Kremlin. On the eve of the first round of elections, Kiselev published an article in the weekly news magazine *Itogi* – the namesake of his television programme and part of Gusinsky's media empire. 'Yeltsin will win, despite the shameful [fact] that an ex-KGB bodyguard with the rank of a major has become the number-two man in the country... Korzhakov and his men won't forget and forgive those who pushed them aside. And they won't forget us journalists for the way we covered this campaign.'[43]

On 16 June, in the first round of elections, Yeltsin got 35 per cent of the votes, Zyuganov 32 per cent. Another 15 per cent went to Alexander Lebed – a gravel-voiced and charismatic army general, a sparring partner promoted by Yeltsin's team to split the communist vote. The calculation was that in the second round Lebed's votes would go to Yeltsin.

A few days later the battle between Malashenko's and Chubais's analytical group and Korzhakov's group broke into the open. Korzhakov's people arrested two men from Chubais's team, one of whom was the author of the slogan 'Vote or Lose', who were carrying a cardboard box with $500,000 in cash out of the White House. The cash had been earlier taken out from the ministry of finance: state money was being used to pay for Yeltsin's campaign, including the 'God Forbid' news-sheet. Korzhakov knew about this. In fact, he was supposed to provide security for transporting the money, but instead set a trap.

Gusinsky, Malashenko and Chubais were at Berezovsky's lavish 'House of Receptions' in central Moscow when the news came. They were furious. This was a clear set-up by Korzhakov designed to foil the second round of elections and reassert control over Yeltsin. While Chubais was unsuccessfully trying to raise Yeltsin from his bed in the middle of the night and

Berezovsky was summoning Dyachenko on the phone, Malashenko mobilized his journalists. He called Kiselev, told him the news, and asked him to go on air immediately. At two o'clock in the morning, NTV interrupted its night programming with an 'emergency' news bulletin. The country, Kiselev told the audience, was on the brink of a political catastrophe and an attempted coup by Korzhakov, Barsukov and Soskovets. An hour later, Lebed also went on air to say that 'any mutiny will be crushed and crushed with extreme severity'. Television declared Yeltsin's chiefs of security traitors while they still held their positions.

Two hours later Korzhakov blinked and the two men detained with the box were released. In the morning Chubais went to see Yeltsin to tell him that Korzhakov had just jeopardized Yeltsin's campaign for the sake of his own position. Chubais also showed Yeltsin a blackmail letter that Korzhakov had sent to Kiselev a few days earlier. In his letter Korzhakov addressed Kiselev as a 'colleague', implying Kiselev's affiliation with the KGB. 'Why such contempt for our joint profession, colleague... Be sensible...' Attached to the letter was a copy of Kiselev's article in *Itogi* magazine and a facsimile of the first page of a KGB personal file with Kiselev's photograph and his secret name, Alekseev, that identified him as an agent. The letter was signed with the military-style 'on my honour, Alexander Korzhakov'. 'He has no honour,' Yeltsin grumbled, picked up the phone and told Korzhakov he was fired. Having seen the proof of Malashenko's and Chubais' work in the first round of elections, Yeltsin no longer needed Korzhakov.

Yet, the tussle and the exertion of the campaign took their toll on Yeltsin. Less than two weeks before the second round, he suffered his fifth heart attack. That day he was supposed to record his last election broadcast to the nation. He was clearly unfit for the job. Yeltsin's family kept the news secret, even from members of his election team. After a few days, Malashenko decided the recording could wait no longer. He realized Yeltsin was too weak to go to the Kremlin, so the recording had to be done at his country residence. But to make it look as though he was speaking from the Kremlin, Malashenko ordered that Yeltsin's office furniture and wooden panelling be moved to the country.

When Malashenko arrived at the recording, he saw Yeltsin sitting at a table with the Kremlin wooden panelling behind his back, looking straight ahead, his face frozen, almost unable to move. Chernomyrdin sat next to him, but Yeltsin did not see him. 'Yeltsin was using all his energy for sitting up straight,' Malashenko recalled.[44] Yeltsin spoke slowly and often inaudibly, leaving words and sentences unfinished. It was a sorry sight. The tape had to be heavily doctored, retouched and edited to make Yeltsin look less wooden and sick. 'Reality' was not something that occurred in real life, but instead was something that television portrayed, and which therefore could be edited and improved. It turned the genuine historic figure that Yeltsin was into a television character.

As Malashenko said, 'I would rather have elected Yeltsin's corpse than Zyuganov as Russia's president.'[45] Although Malashenko never told his journalists about what had actually happened to Yeltsin, rumours about Yeltsin's heart attack, or even stroke, spread through Moscow. Journalists knew Yeltsin was gravely ill. Yet none of the TV channels, including NTV, said anything about the president's health. On 3 July – the day of the second round – Yeltsin appeared on television at a polling station set up near his country residence. He could barely slot his ballot paper into the box. The two doctors in white coats behind his back were edited out of the picture. Yeltsin was elected with 53.8 per cent of the vote – a result that had seemed impossible only a few months earlier.

Yeltsin's presidential inauguration a few weeks later was conspicuously short. He could hardly walk. He managed to take a few steps towards a microphone and said thirty-three words in total. It was clear that Yeltsin was only half alive. The central idea of defeating the communists through elections rather than by force, noble in its intentions and effective in its results, did not alter the fact that behind Yeltsin's victory was not a broad coalition of democratic forces and parties but a narrow alliance of oligarchs and media managers. The actual democratic movement that brought Yeltsin to power in 1991 was virtually extinct. The main democratic parties, including Russian Democratic Choice, led by Yegor Gaidar, were weak and at best played the role of a chorus, rather than protagonists in the 1996 drama. As Gaidar wrote, 'Given Zyuganov versus Yeltsin, we, as the party of democracy, were simply obliged to back Yeltsin.'[46]

Yeltsin's victory, therefore, was not a triumph for democratic institutions, the rule of law and property rights. Rather it was the triumph of those who had invested in and stood to benefit most from it – the tycoons and media chiefs. As Kirill Rogov, a political essayist and a founder of one of the country's first internet news sites, noted, control over the media and its technology allowed the oligarchs to reach a goal which had little to do with public good.

The 1996 elections and the loans-for-shares privatization turned business tycoons into oligarchs and journalists into spiritual leaders. Berezovsky boasted about it in an interview with the *Financial Times*. He spoke on behalf of the seven bankers who had participated in the Davos pact to have Yeltsin re-elected. 'We hired Chubais and invested huge sums of money to ensure Yeltsin's election. Now we have the right to occupy government posts and enjoy the fruits of our victory.'[47] With Yeltsin only semi-functional, the oligarchs felt they would be the ones ruling Russia.

'Berezovsky's logic was very simple: if we are the richest, we must be the smartest. And if we are the smartest and the richest then we should be ruling Russia,' said Chubais.[48] They nominated Potanin, the author of the loans-for-shares scheme, to be Russia's deputy prime minister. Within a few months, Berezovsky was appointed the deputy secretary of the Security Council. However, the main tool of power in the hands of the oligarchs was not their official jobs, but the media and, in particular, television. Yeltsin's election persuaded the oligarchs that control over the media equalled political power. 'At some point I realized that the thing we created had become too powerful and I was trailing behind,' said Malashenko.[49] It certainly was not 'normal' television as Malashenko had initially designed it.

Gusinsky showered his journalists with bonuses and privileges, giving them free credit and buying them flats and cars. Paid well above their peers in other media outlets from the very beginning, they were incorporated into the oligarchic clan. They dined in Moscow's most expensive restaurants. Kiselev, who had earned the nickname *barin* ('landlord', a master), received a free house – as did Malashenko and Dobrodeev – in Chigasovo, a fenced country settlement built by Gusinsky. It was known as 'Russian Switzerland'.

In the opening credits to *Itogi*, Kiselev walked through the Kremlin. A kaleidoscope of pictures and fragments of phrases were flashed onto the screen: Thatcher, Gorbachev, Yeltsin, Nixon. The last snatched phrase was spoken by the Patriarch of the Russian Orthodox Church: 'a spiritual image of Russia', he was heard saying as Kiselev swaggered across Red Square. The scene was recorded before the election, but after the election it gained a new meaning.

'Kiselev in his *Itogi* programme is preaching, rather than broadcasting,' critic Irina Petrovskaya wrote less than a year after the election. 'He is speaking, not even on behalf of the presidential team, but as one of its fully accepted members.'[50] *Itogi* shaped the political process more than it reflected it. Kiselev could get almost any information he wanted. 'It became very difficult for Kiselev to distance himself from the Kremlin,' Malashenko admitted.[51] Kiselev turned from being a political commentator into a political figure, whose rating was followed by newspapers along with other politicians.

In recognition of Malashenko's role in the election campaign, Yeltsin asked him to be his chief of staff – one of the most important posts in the Kremlin. But Malashenko did something that was unprecedented: he turned Yeltsin down – a decision he would regret for the rest of his life. He did not do it out of false modesty or even humility. On the contrary, Malashenko believed that being in charge of a private television channel was far more important than being in charge of one of the Kremlin's towers, as Yeltsin's election campaign had just proved.

Having defeated the communists and demolished the party of war in the Kremlin, Malashenko and Gusinsky felt invincible. The victory of liberalism in Russia seemed complete and final – whoever would come after Yeltsin. 'I did not see a political task. Now I understand that the central question in Russian political history is one of succession. If, back in 1996, I realized that Yeltsin's succession would determine Russia's future direction, perhaps I would have acted differently. But at the time this did not occur to me,' Malashenko said years later.[52]

There was another reason for his refusal, however. Having observed Gusinsky and Berezovsky during the election campaign, having fought on their side against the 'statists', he knew that if he accepted Yeltsin's offer, they would treat him as 'their' man in the Kremlin, a tool of their influence rather than a source of power. The only way he could be his own master would be to declare a war on the oligarchs – something that he was neither willing nor able to do.

Yet, for all the brashness and the questionable origins of their wealth, he saw the oligarchs generally, and Gusinsky in particular, as private businessmen whose individualism and initiative could keep state power in check, something that Malashenko strongly believed in. An extreme individualist and misanthrope, Malashenko, the operator of one of the most important mass media channels in the country, had a low opinion of the masses. Liberalism and democracy were not synonyms to him, but antonyms. Fascinated by Spanish history, he fully subscribed to the ideas of Ortega y Gasset, who argued that democracy is no guarantee of liberalism and of individual rights and that any state – democratic or despotic – will seek to extend its powers and therefore needs to be countered with alternative sources of power that can be mustered only by private barons.

In the corner of Malashenko's office at NTV stood a suit of genuine Toledo armour. His motto, displayed on his computer screensaver, was a quote from Ortega: 'These towers were erected to protect an individual from the state. Gentlemen, long live freedom!' The most important one was a television tower.

After seventy years of Soviet socialism, feudalism seemed like a step forward and the oligarchs were a lesser evil than those who had sacrificed millions of lives in the name of a strong state. With their taste for castles and private armies, the oligarchs seemed a good fit for the role of feudal barons.

As it soon turned out, Malashenko had miscalculated. His idea that the oligarchs would defend private liberties and counter the power of the state suffered a fiasco. A few years later, the oligarchy of the 1990s brought a KGB statist to the presidential post. The baronial identities that the oligarchs tried upon themselves were fake, but they behaved as though they owned the country, treating the rest of the population with contempt and arrogance. Their lack of historic perspective and above all responsibility meant that they used their money and power not to install rules and build institutions but to enlarge their fiefdoms and fight wars with one another and with the state.

The Bankers' War

The first war between the oligarchs broke out in 1997 – less than a year after the elections. That war consumed not only the oligarchs, but also the government of young reformers appointed by Yeltsin after the election. The 1996 election assured the oligarchs that the future belonged to them and they began to turn this future into money and assets.

As a reward for his services, Gusinsky was given a full licence for one of the main channels, Channel 4, for a symbolic price and with no tender. This transformed NTV from a temporary 'experiment' into a permanent channel. But Gusinsky's ambitions were now far greater. He decided to launch a satellite channel – along with the satellite itself – that would make his television omnipresent and autonomous of the state. It was the stuff of a James Bond movie. After relentless schmoozing, he got approval from Russia's military and space industry chiefs and persuaded America's State Department to give its blessing. He commissioned Hughes Space & Communications to build the satellite with the backing of America's Export-Import bank.

To finance his new venture, he sold 30 per cent of NTV to Gazprom, Russia's natural gas monopoly, run by the jovial, red-faced Soviet industry man, Rem Vyakhirev, who saw NTV as a deterrent against predators, including Berezovsky who had set his eyes on Gazprom. 'NTV was like a gun hanging on the wall. If anyone attacked Vyakhirev, he could use it against them,' said Gusinsky.[53] Gazprom also provided Gusinsky with a $40 million loan on extremely lenient terms.

Half in jest, Malashenko, highly sceptical of the whole venture, advised Gusinsky to privatize an oil firm or some other natural resource company to pay for this indulgence. But Gusinsky had other plans. He was eyeing Svyazinvest – a telephone communications company that consisted of dozens of regional providers which jointly controlled 22 million crackling telephone lines. Gusinsky's grand vision was to consolidate all these communication assets in the country into one vast private holding that could then be floated on the New York Stock Exchange.

Before the 1996 elections, Gusinsky was the only Russian oligarch who did not participate in the privatization of state assets. Now Gusinsky was certain that Svyazinvest belonged to him by right. Media and communications were his fiefdom and fellow oligarchs, including Berezovsky, agreed and encouraged him. 'Some even tried to persuade me that I should get it for free,' said Gusinsky.[54] It seemed only fair: other oligarchs had already got their spoils, so why shouldn't he?

He felt all the more entitled to it since he had spent six months wining and dining military generals and security services chiefs to get their agreement to allow private owners, including foreigners, into telecoms – a zone of strategic military importance since Soviet times. 'The amount of alcohol which I had to drink with them over those six months inflicted serious damage to my liver.'[55] Gusinsky then went to Chubais, who had been appointed a deputy prime minister after the 1996 presidential election, to agree the terms of the auction. Foreigners would be allowed in and no state money was to be used in the bidding process.* 'We agreed that it would be an honest auction that would draw a line under the loans-for-shares privatization. This was an absolute consensus,' recalled Gusinsky.[56]

Gusinsky's understanding of an 'honest' auction had one important caveat, however: all other oligarchs who had participated in previous privatizations were supposed to stay away from Svyazinvest, allowing him to win the auction 'honestly', although he was prepared to pay real money for it. The oligarchs decided that Chubais was on their side.

Chubais had his own political agenda, however. He saw Svyazinvest as a chance to assert power over the oligarchs who considered him 'their' man. 'I had a very simple picture of the world. If you want to beat someone, you need to consolidate resources. In 1996 I consolidated with the oligarchs against the communists.'[57] Now the main political task had shifted. The new target was the oligarchs. 'If it was not Svyazinvest, it would have been something else,' said Chubais.

The problem was that in his affront to the oligarchs, Chubais 'consolidated' resources with one of their kind – Vladimir Potanin – who devised the loans-for-shares scheme and who also served as a government

* Gusinsky formed a consortium of investors including Mikhail Fridman, another oligarch, Credit Suisse First Boston and, most importantly, Spain's Telefonica, which was supposed to manage Svyazinvest.

minister while handling the government's money: his private bank held the account of the state's Customs Agency which maintained a balance of about $1 billion.

When the government announced that the auction for 25 per cent + 1 share of Svyazinvest would be open to all bidders, Potanin, who had left the government shortly before the auction, said he would participate. 'I thought we had agreed that Potanin was not allowed to take part,' Gusinsky recalled, 'but suddenly Chubais told me there was no such deal.'[58] From Gusinsky's point of view, this was a brazen breach of agreement.

Chubais's pledge to make the auction fair was either hypocrisy, Gusinsky decided, or part of a secret deal with Potanin. 'Chubais had upset the balance by pumping Potanin with [customs accounts] money,' said Malashenko.[59] The situation was made worse by Gusinsky's personal relationship with Chubais. He had been enchanted by the charismatic Chubais and did not even mind when other people told him so. Now he felt betrayed.

Berezovsky was there to console him. Although he had no obvious commercial interest in Svyazinvest, he inserted himself into the conflict and sided with Gusinsky against Chubais. Any war was positive for him. Like Chubais, he saw the auction as a battle for political control. Its outcome would determine his own status as Russia's chief oligarch, a man who could rule Russia from behind the scenes. The conflict between Chubais and Berezovsky was least of all about democracy: neither side believed that ordinary people should be trusted with important decisions. In a poor country like Russia, democracy would always lead to populism and ultimately to authoritarianism. And only the rule of the few – who had resources and intellectual power – could launch the country on the right path. The whole question was who would be the ruling minority.

Chubais subscribed to the idea that the top priority was to build a market economy that would make the country richer, which would then create the right conditions for democracy. He never had to worry too much about the political base for their reforms – Yeltsin took care of that. 'Our market approach was completely unsuitable for building a democracy. But we believed that a market economy and the creation of the middle class would result in a democracy,' Chubais reflected later.[60] The oligarchs and the loans-for-shares privatizations were a necessary evil to avert a communist comeback and ensure the continuity of reforms. The auction of Svyazinvest would therefore be a necessary correction.

Two days before the auction, Berezovsky, Gusinsky and Potanin flew on Gusinsky's private Gulfstream to the south of France where Chubais was on holiday. They told him that they had come to an agreement: Gusinsky would get Svyazinvest and Potanin would get the next asset to be sold by the state. Chubais dithered for a moment but refused to cave in. To him, it was not about who got what in a privatization, but who gets to set the rules. Berezovsky felt the same way. 'You can't just break the system over your knee. You are igniting a war,' he told Chubais.[61]

On 25 July 1997, Potanin, backed by the money of international financier George Soros, won the auction by offering $2 billion, a record amount of money by the standards of Russian privatization, but only slightly more than Gusinsky. The next day a media war broke out. The first shot was fired by Berezovsky's Channel One. The man who delivered it was Sergei Dorenko, a good-looking, shamelessly cynical but effective anchor with a deep, penetrating voice and an overt lack of scruples. Dorenko accused Potanin of planning to siphon profits out of Svyazinvest. He and George Soros, Dorenko said, were *spekulianty* (speculators), effectively black marketers, 'people with a scandalous, tarnished-to-doubtful reputation', who had benefited from a sweetheart deal arranged by Alfred Kokh, the man who had been in charge of conducting the auction on the government's behalf.

Both Malashenko and Kiselev were on holiday abroad when the 'bankers' war' broke out. Gusinsky summoned them back to Moscow. Malashenko, who was no longer running NTV but oversaw all of the television projects, including the satellite one, argued strongly against getting NTV involved. 'I could see that Gusinsky had every reason to be furious – they did screw him over – but at the same time I was against waging any wars or fighting any vendetta. I thought we just needed to cut our losses and move on,' said Malashenko.[62] But this was not Gusinsky's style. He was not an oligarch for nothing. Just as he could not cave in to gangsters, he could not submit to the government. 'There was an informal block on saying anything negative about the young reformers of the new Yeltsin's government. All we had to do was to remove it,' Gusinsky said.[63]

Gusinsky's first target was Kokh. Through his own contacts in Switzerland, Gusinsky dug up information that Kokh had received a 'book advance' of $100,000 – a vast sum of money by the standards of most ordinary Russians – from a mysterious Swiss company, Servina, which, on closer inspection, appeared to have links to Potanin. Kokh had to resign.

A week into the war, Chubais gathered the oligarchs in his office, hoping to put pressure on Gusinsky and Berezovsky to stop fighting. Those who had no interests in the auction, including Mikhail Khodorkovsky, were called to arbitrate and ruled that Gusinsky should have got Svyazinvest. Gusinsky offered to match Potanin's price. Chubais, however, refused to reconsider the result of the auction. 'He was certainly breaking an informal agreement,' said Khodorkovsky.[64] At the same time Chubais told Yeltsin, 'We need to sock them in the teeth for once in our lives! We won't achieve anything if we don't do this.'[65] But if Chubais wanted to fight, so did Berezovsky and Gusinsky. Buoyed by the support of his peers, Gusinsky doubled his effort.

As the war got more intense, Yeltsin grew increasingly nervous and gathered the oligarchs in the Kremlin. On the face of it, the meeting went well. But as Yeltsin wrote in his memoirs, 'Despite their assurances, I sensed that these men had not really become my allies. After the meeting there was an unfamiliar silence in the room… It was as if I were dealing with people of a different race, people made not of steel but of some kind of cosmic metal... There was no area for compromise.'[66]

Two weeks later, Chubais and his fellow deputy prime minister, Boris Nemtsov, persuaded Yeltsin to fire Berezovsky as the deputy secretary of the Security Council. This achieved nothing: Yeltsin took away Berezovsky's title, but left him with the main source of his power – Channel One. A few days later Gusinsky and Berezovsky fired back at Chubais with such force that it knocked out the entire government. On 12 November 1997, Gusinsky's radio station, Echo Moskvy, reported that Chubais and five of his deputies had received $90,000 each in book advance fees from a publisher owned directly by Potanin.

The story was immediately picked up and amplified manifold by both NTV and Channel One. 'The government no longer has to worry about its [moral] authority. It has none,' Dorenko stated bombastically.[67] Then, as though by magic, Dorenko's sources in the prosecutor's office started to leak documents, bank transfer details, contracts. There was little doubt that this was the fruit of Gusinsky's efforts. To any ordinary viewer, it seemed that the young reformers, who preached to the oligarchs and the country about honesty and fair competition, were at it as well.

Chubais first dismissed the whole story as slander, then, after being given a dressing-down by Yeltsin, admitted that the fee was, perhaps, too large. A few days later Chubais offered his resignation. He was stripped of his post as finance minister, though he formally remained in the government. Gusinsky, somewhat tongue-in-cheek, justified himself by saying that what NTV told its viewers about the book scandal was true: 'We did not lie, we did not make up the story. It was simply that we allowed it to be aired'. The story was dug out and cynically used by the oligarchs to destroy Chubais. As Chubais later admitted, the book was conceived to cover the transfer of money left over from Yeltsin's election campaign to his team as a reward for their service. Effectively, it was no better or worse than the 'box money'. Both Gusinsky and Berezovsky knew this.

One person who did know about it, but who was also turned into a target, was Boris Nemtsov, a young, bright and charismatic reformer who had moved to Moscow in the spring of 1997 from Nizhniy Novgorod, an old Russian merchants' town on the Volga where he had served as governor. Yeltsin groomed Nemtsov – a brainy former physicist with a vast frame, curly black hair and oozing charm – as his successor and even introduced him to world leaders as such. In many ways Nemtsov was part of the Perestroika-era dream of Russia as a liberal, Western-oriented, dignified country driven by energetic, well-educated and decent people. Yeltsin first met Nemtsov in 1990 when the thirty-one-year-old democrat was elected to Russia's first parliament. Nemtsov shunned communist ideology not because it was communist, but because it was ideology. Instead of ideology, he had values and ideas. He stood by Yeltsin in August 1991 and in October 1993 – despite criticizing Yeltsin's decision to dissolve the parliament.

Nemtsov and Chubais – the two deputy prime ministers – were the core of Yeltsin's government of young reformers who, after the communist defeat in 1996, were supposed to finally launch the country on a path of reforms. Nemtsov reflected the optimism of the 1990s, when everything seemed possible for those who had energy and brains – and he had both. Unlike most people of his generation he also had integrity and an inherent understanding of right and wrong. Stealing, betraying, killing were wrong. Thinking, loving, living were good. Of all the people who served in the Russian government, Nemtsov was the most scrupulously honest and untainted by connections with oligarchs. In fact, it was Nemtsov who coined the word 'oligarchs' and took them on. In January 1998, Nemtsov organized a public debate called 'Russia's Future: Oligarchy or Freedom?' 'I had the idea of a normal European Russia and the oligarchs did not fit into it. They had privatized most of the state institutions – including the police, security services and the courts. So my first thought was that we should "re-nationalize" the state, take away their special passes to the

Kremlin and their special blue flashing lights, which allowed them to break traffic rules, remove the system of banks entitled to state money,' said Nemtsov.[68]

The privatization of Svyazinvest was expected to highlight Nemtsov's independence from the influence of the oligarchs and turn it into his political capital. But if the oligarchs did not fit into Nemtsov's picture of Russia, neither did he fit into theirs. Although he clearly had nothing to do with the book scandal, he was an obvious target. To attack Nemtsov, Dorenko hired prostitutes who, for a modest price of about $200, would say that Nemtsov used their services but forgot to pay. 'I am a [TV] killer and they wrote a contract out on you,' Dorenko apparently told Nemtsov a few years later when they bumped into each other at an airport.[69] (Dorenko said the prostitutes' tape was simply given to him and he did not think it necessary to verify their story.)

NTV peddled Nemtsov's gaffes, including his appearance in white chinos at an official ceremony greeting the President of Azerbaijan. Kiselev tracked Nemtsov's rating, which he himself helped to drive down, until it reached single digits. He then gleefully placed a large graphic cross over Nemtsov's face and 'sent' his portrait into a dustbin.

In fact, the talk about anyone's electoral rating a year after the presidential elections was meaningless. But as Maxim Sokolov sarcastically wrote at the time, television channels thrived on election campaigns just as a military industrial complex thrives on a war. 'A war guarantees demand for arms. Election campaigns create the same demand for information weapons.'[70] By constantly hyping up the subject of rating, NTV was reminding the politicians of its powers.

The 'revelations' were addressed to one spectator – Yeltsin – and were supposed to persuade him to sack the government of young reformers with little idea of who would replace them. Yeltsin took NTV's attack on his reformers, and Nemtsov in particular, to heart. A couple of weeks after the Svyazinvest auction, Yeltsin called Nemstov in. 'I am tired of defending you,' he said. Nemtsov stayed in the government for another year, but he was weakened and demoralized and in the end handed in his resignation.

What started as a war between bankers had turned into a major political crisis.

Chubais rightly likened the scandal stirred up by television in 1997 to 'exploding an atomic bomb'. The abbreviation NTV now stood not for 'normal' or '*nezavisimoe*' (independent), but for 'nuclear' television. The bankers' war left no winners, destroyed everything in its range and left the field polluted with radiation for years to come. The point of ultimate victory and triumph, which NTV and Gusinsky reached in 1996, marked the beginning of a decline. Surviving victory turned out to be a far greater challenge than achieving it.

The irony was that the oligarchs who sided with Yeltsin against the communists and nationalists managed to do what the parliament in 1993 failed to achieve: the oligarchy destroyed the government of liberal reformers and discredited the idea of liberal media. Yet, unlike in 1993 and 1996, the information war of 1997 contained no ideology or even an idea about the country's future. But it did contaminate television and NTV in particular.

Powerful media magnates behaved not like the elite they claimed to be, but like small-time co-operators with sophisticated weapons in their hands. They dressed like a Westernized elite, spoke like one, sent their children to Western schools, but they lacked the most important attribute of an elite – a sense of responsibility for, and historic consciousness of, their own country. They behaved like caricatures of capitalists in old Soviet journals. Having helped Yeltsin to win in 1996, they did not use the chance to make Russia better. Nor did they care about public good, or the well-being of the Russian people. 'We did not match the historic task which was in front of us,' Malashenko admitted.[71] The same could be said of Chubais, though.

Giddy with their own wealth and power, the oligarchs did not realize that, along with Chubais and Nemtsov, they were also destroying their own futures and the future of the country. Arrogance and narrow-mindedness on both sides of the conflict got the better of common sense. The ultimate irony was that the asset, which the oligarchs fought for so furiously, turned out to be worthless. Having sold 25 per cent of the firm, the government did not privatize it further and Potanin never got real control over the company. George Soros called it the worst investment he had ever made.

The breakout of the 'bankers' war' coincided with a dramatic event in the life of NTV which had an equally lasting consequence on the country's narrative. On 10 May, Elena Masyuk, the channel's intrepid war reporter, and two members of her crew were kidnapped in Chechnya, which had received de facto independence as a result of the 1996 peace accord aimed at improving Yeltsin's chances for re-election and was allowed to hold its own presidential elections.

Chechnya's new president, Aslan Maskhadov, was a moderate but ineffective former military man, who could barely control his own field commanders. Chechnya turned into a black hole, sucking in money allocated by the Kremlin, siphoning off oil from a pipeline that went through Chechnya, and kidnapping journalists and aid workers for ransom.

Masyuk was not the first journalist to be kidnapped in Chechnya, but of all Russian television reporters, she was arguably the most sympathetic towards the Chechen independence cause. She also had the best access to its field commanders, including Shamil Basayev. In 1995, days after Basayev had led the attack on the hospital in Buddenovsk and was then allowed to 'vanish' in Chechnya as part of the deal for freeing the hostages, the Kremlin claimed that he had gone abroad. Masyuk managed to find and interview him on camera, embarrassing the Russian security services. Her reporting, much of it from the Chechen side, tested the limits of objectivity and Malashenko effectively banned her from travelling to Chechnya. This did not stop Oleg Dobrodeev, who had assumed day-to-day control of NTV, from sending Masyuk to interview one of the field commanders who had taken responsibility for an explosion at a railway station a few weeks earlier.

In July 1997, in the midst of NTV's frenzied attempts to free its journalists, Yeltsin held a dinner for those who had worked in his election team. Yeltsin talked about the great successes over the past year – both in the economy and in settling for peace in Chechnya. Yeltsin's forced optimism could barely conceal his worries. Then Malashenko asked to speak.

He told Yeltsin that the situation in Chechnya was not as radiant as the president had painted and that sooner or later Russia would face a choice: either to start another war or to capitulate, in which case Chechnya would rule Russia, because it had a will and Russia did not. The government, he asserted, could not provide safety for its own people. He spoke for ten or fifteen minutes. 'I don't know what came over me, but it just burst out. It was wrong, of course – one cannot speak for that long, and in that way, to the president.'[72]

After Malashenko's monologue, silence fell over the dining table. 'Yeltsin said nothing. He just continued to eat in complete silence. After a long pause Yeltsin started to tell us again how everything was getting better in the country, how salaries and pensions were being paid on time.'

When Yeltsin finished, Malashenko spoke again: 'Forgive me, Boris Nikolaevich, but I just raised a subject which I consider to be of extreme importance. You may disagree with me and tell me that I am completely wrong, but you can't just ignore it.' At that point Yeltsin became white with anger. Malashenko later said: 'I suddenly remembered the story I heard at university explaining why a bear is so dangerous. It is because a bear's facial muscles are weak, so he always looks as though he is smiling. There is no way to tell when he is turning angry, but by the time he does, it is usually too late.' Barely able to control his temper, Yeltsin turned to Malashenko: 'I speak. You speak. But we will not have a discussion.'[73] The dinner ended in awkward silence with everyone staring at their plates.

Shortly afterwards, Gusinsky paid the ransom of $1.5 million through Berezovsky's business partner, and on 17 August 1997, after three months in captivity, Masyuk was released – to coincide with a visit by Aslan Maskhadov to Moscow. Two days later, Malashenko, Dobrodeev and Kiselev gave a press conference at the Slavyankaya Hotel, where NTV usually celebrated its birthday. Malashenko announced that NTV had paid a ransom and pointed a finger at Maskhadov and his government. 'We have every reason to assert that Maskhadov is well aware of the kidnapping business in Chechnya which is conducted by his lieutenants, including his vice-president Vakha Arsanov...' Then, after a pause, Malashenko added: 'I don't know whether Yeltsin realized that [when he met with Maskhadov] he was talking to their main captor: I am convinced that only the captor could dovetail his visit to Moscow with the release of the journalist.'[74] Malashenko concluded that the state was incapable of performing its constitutional duties and defending its own citizens.

Masyuk spoke about her experience in captivity where she had been guarded by drug-inhaling Chechens. 'Sometimes we had an urge to kill them. There were situations when we could have simply stretched out our arms [to reach the weapons] and pulled the trigger... Today there is nothing for journalists to do in Chechnya. Let them sit there with no journalists. I don't judge the whole of the Chechen people, but there are people I hate,' she said angrily.[75]

The day after the press conference, Yeltsin publicly answered Malashenko. At a meeting of his Security Council, he said the peace process was taking place in Chechnya and some ill-informed people like Malashenko, who knew nothing about Chechnya, were trying to blacken it. Yeltsin was thinking about his own succession and was desperately eager to close the Chechen question and move on – hence his fury with Malashenko's attempt to stir up the subject. Talks with Maskhadov were necessary because, however weak the Chechnya president was, he provided the only alternative to the war that NTV berated Yeltsin for.

After Yeltsin's angry comments, Berezovsky came up to Malashenko to cheer him up. '"Don't worry, Igor", he told me. "The fact is that now, after Masyuk, we can do what the hell we like with Chechnya."'[76] Nobody incited the hatred towards Chechnya and criticized Yeltsin for his peace deal with Maskhadov more than Berezovsky's Channel One, which put out a weekly programme presented by Nevzorov, who was hired by Berezovsky, called *Dni* (*Days*) – a reference to the ultra-national newspaper *Den'* (*Day*), edited by Prokhanov. In the summer of 1996, Nevzorov's programme showed Russian paratroopers brandishing the sun-cured ears of Chechen fighters, and mentioned crucifixions of federal soldiers that those fighters had performed.

In 1997 the disturbing images moved to the news slots. Soon after the release of Masyuk, NTV and Channel One showed gratuitous footage of public executions in Chechnya of people sentenced to death by the shariah law. 'Now you see how the two convicted people are being led to a wall covered with black cloth,' a good-looking Channel One female presenter explained calmly.[77] 'The execution is being set up in a way traditional for some Eastern countries.' Both channels showed the actual moment of shooting in their prime-time news. This was clearly different from reporting a war. The purpose of the video was not to inform the public but to incite its repulsion and outrage.

The confluence of these two events – the demolition of the government of young reformers and the shift in the public attitude towards Chechnya – made stabilization in the country all but impossible. But stability was the last thing that television needed. Instability allowed television to exercise influence and keep the audience entertained. A fast succession of political faces on television meant the audience did not get bored. Politics followed the rules of consumerism: Lebed was the flavour of the month one day, gone another. So was Nemtsov.

The year 1997 was supposed to herald the beginning of a new country. It did not. The problem was not just the behaviour of the media or the shallowness of the elite. The problem was the lack of a new project or vision of the future that could unite the country. The threat of a communist revanche that helped Yeltsin's side to consolidate his electorate, had been used up in the 1996 elections. Communist leaders now seemed more interested in cashing in on their 'threat' than realizing it. The defeat of the communists revealed the lack of further purpose. Nobody in Russia had any sense of direction, true identity, or history – and nobody cared.

Old Songs about Important Things

Russia's post-communist constitution stated that no ideology could be imposed by the state. Yet, after the 1996 elections, the vacuum of a unifying idea became self-evident. Yeltsin charged his aides to come up with an answer to 'what national idea or national ideology is most important for Russia'. As *Kommersant* wrote in 1997:

> The search for a national ideology has become the Kremin's idée-fixe. This is understandable. In the election of 2000, you can't attract voters by saying 'vote, or things will get worse'... The hitherto foggy wish of the rulers of our vast and muddled country to gain, at last, a national idea is starting to take practical shape. There is nothing objectionable in this wish. Any citizen would welcome a nice, clear and truly national unifying idea. But in an enlightened state – such an idea is not an object of first necessity. Quite the opposite – it is a luxury and it would be nice to be able to afford it.[78]

A special group was put together and even produced a pamphlet on the subject, but it did not amount to much. The very way in which this search was conducted was slightly comical. Like a tsar from a Russian fairy tale, Yeltsin was instructed to 'go I know not whither and fetch I know not what'. The only possible idea could be a nationalist one, but Yeltsin who saw Russia's future as a Western-style democracy did not go in that direction.

The lack of a new big project or idea was also evident in the lack of any coherent style. So the media turned to history – not by way of a serious examination, but as a form of entertainment. Having thwarted the communists, the young and bright stars of the media looked at the past as a fashion accessory or an artefact; Soviet civilization – whatever the merits of its political regime and ideology – had left behind a vast reserve that could be tapped to fill a stylistic void.

A wave of nostalgia swept Russian popular culture and television. Old Soviet plays, songs and films attracted large audiences. The Soviet era was treated with ironic sentimentality as a source of sincerity and meaning. In fact, the first signs of this nostalgia began to emerge soon after the Soviet collapse. In the 1994 New Year's Eve NTV television show, young and carefree journalists appeared on the screen sporting red Young Pioneer ties as a tribute to their own childhoods and singing a song from the classic Soviet comedy of 1956, *Carnival Night*. The show's host was Leonid Parfenov – one of NTV's brightest stars with an impeccable sense of style and period. He wore a dinner jacket and black tie and brought a technological novelty into the studio – a karaoke box. 'It allows you to sing in your own voice to recorded music,' Parfenov explained with a smile.

In contrast to Kiselev and Dobrodeev – golden Moscow youths with good connections – Parfenov, in his early thirties at the time, came from the small provincial town of Cherepovets, and conquered Moscow with his light and sincere touch. One of Parfenov's first documentaries made for Central Television was called *Deti XX s'ezda'* (*The Children of the 20th Congress*) and was dedicated to the *shestidesiatniki*. Standing on the Sparrow Hills above Moscow, Parfenov spoke to the camera: 'We need to understand their rise, their drama, maybe even their tragedy and their second wind. Because without them, we would not be here and without their bitter experience – we can do nothing. Nothing. That is it.' Parfenov posessed an acute sense of his own roots, Soviet history and its aesthetics.

The casual name of Parfenov's programme on NTV, *Namedni* (an obsolescent form of 'recently' in Russian), implied the past and, in 1996, Parfenov turned to the stylistically coherent Soviet period and its popular culture, relaunching *Namedni* as a series of programmes about the past thirty years of Russian history. He defined historic periods not so much by political events, but by their sound, smell, rhythm and tone, mixing high and popular culture. Parfenov used montage and inversions liberally, and occasionally 'mixed' himself into historic documentary footage. There he was shooting ducks with Khrushchev, chatting with Hollywood actor Tom Hanks, lighting Fidel Castro's cigar, kissing Marilyn Monroe. Behind Parfenov's light-hearted project stood a serious perspective on Russia's reconciliation with its own past and on turning history from a political minefield into an aesthetic object, providing people with a much-needed sense of continuity and stability.

Parfenov was not the only person trying to make a connection with the past. In 1995, Parfenov's friend Konstantin Ernst, who had just been appointed the 'chief producer of Channel One', launched an advertising campaign called 'The Russia Project', which consisted of a series of one-and-a-half-minute films in which famous Soviet actors played ordinary people, war veterans, bus drivers, cosmonauts, or alcoholics. The purpose was to promote simple feelings: love, friendship, memory, kindness. In one episode, an old man walks through a Metro station and hears the sound of a wartime march; he stops and remembers his youth and his love when he was a young soldier. Each episode ended on a tag-line: 'We remember' or 'It is my city' or 'Home is always better'.

This was a precursor to a much more resonant project that Ernst and Parfenov produced in December 1995. It was called *Starye pesni o glavnom* (*Old Songs about Important Things*). In it, Russian pop stars, dressed in 1930s fashion, performed popular songs of that decade in a pastiche show inspired by the Soviet socialist musicals and paintings such as the 1937 *Celebration in a Collective Farm*. It worked like a karaoke machine. 'I had a very acute postmodernist feeling that everything has already been said, that it just needed to be revived. We couldn't just waste it. Yes, these songs were written in the Stalinist years, but they were good songs,' said Parfenov.[79] To make the film, Parfenov and Ernst resurrected an old pavilion at Mosfilm Studios (Moscow's equivalent of London's Ealing Studios) and dusted off its old props, trucks and costumes. Yet *Old Songs* was shot using the best Kodak film and ended up costing $3 million – a vast sum of money by Russian standards at the time. It was sleek and modern.

The film appealed equally to the sense of nostalgia among older Soviet people – many of whom had voted for the communists – and to a younger audience that could barely remember Soviet culture, but danced to Soviet songs in expensive Moscow nightclubs, bought Soviet memorabilia in trendy flea markets and put on old Soviet clothes for fancy-dress parties. None of the participants could imagine that within three years the Kremlin would revive the most important old song of all – the Soviet national anthem – which would signal the start of restoration, or that a fancy-dress party would soon turn into a neo-Soviet parade of state nationalism.

However, in 1997, the young, urban NTV audience saw Parfenov's *Old Songs* as proof that Russia could never return to the Soviet system and ideological wars. Parfenov's programmes were saturated with the feeling of warmth that people experience when visiting the home where they grew up, picking up and smiling at their old toys or records. 'We had parted with the Soviet regime, life around us was very different. We could sit in front of a Samsung TV, drink Absolut vodka, decorate our flats in a "European" style, but the soul demanded some harmony. What other songs could we sing?' said Parfenov.[80] Neither he nor Ernst had any political agenda when they made *Old Songs*: they made it for fun and their own pleasure, but they accurately sensed the public appetite.

It was also a natural reaction to several years of overdosing on popular Western culture which had swept over Russian television after the Soviet collapse and to a relentless bashing of anything Soviet under the slogan 'We are the worst and useless'. It was only to be expected that, a few years later, an inferiority complex would engender feelings of wounded pride. As Parfenov told the *New York Times* in 1995, 'It's about admitting that there were things that were good… that there is nothing to be ashamed of, and that we don't have any other history. What else can we reflect? Why should we struggle with ourselves?'[81] (Five years later Vladimir Putin would repeat the same words almost verbatim.) Parfenov's work provided a sense of continuity and soothed the trauma of fractured history. In that sense his programmes acted like a tranquillizer, removing symptoms of anxiety.

Later, when nostalgia for the Soviet past morphed into a restoration of Soviet political practices, liberal critics pointed to Parfenov's project as the original sin of stirring up nostalgia in the first place. This was hardly fair. The revival of old Soviet instincts was caused not by *Old Songs*, but by the lack of immunity against those instincts and the absence of a nation-building project and institutions.

One politician who tried to remake the past and turn *Old Songs* into a new ideology was Yuri Luzhkov, the all-powerful mayor of Moscow whose presidential ambitions were manifested in the reconstruction of the late-nineteenth-century Cathedral of Christ the Saviour that had been blown up by Stalin in 1931.* At the same time as Parfenov's *Namedni*, Luzhkov celebrated the 850th anniversary of Moscow's foundation. The date itself

* Luzhkov was also one of the first acting Russian politicians to exploit the subject of Crimea and Ukraine. He travelled to Sebastopol to declare that the city of Russian glory should never have been passed to Ukraine.

was chosen rather randomly, since nobody knew precisely when Moscow was founded, but it marked the fiftieth anniversary of the last lavish celebration in 1947.

The celebrations made use of all periods of Russian history as long as they contributed to Russia's glory. Russian princes beheaded by the tsars, the tsars shot dead by the communists, the communists overthrown by Yeltsin – they all coexisted harmoniously and rejoiced triumphantly in Luzhkov's extravaganza. Soviet and pre-Soviet icons were bundled together and fused into a peculiar new ideology of nationalism and patriotism.

As Andrei Zorin, a historian of state ideologies, wrote at the time in an essay, 'Are We Having Fun Yet?', history was being replaced by mythology.[82] A quotation from an old Stalinist song 'Moscow – you are my favourite' decorated banners stretched across the city's main streets. Television channels churned out Soviet retro films and songs about the good old days. A statue to Peter the Great, who moved the Russian capital to St Petersburg, was placed in the centre of Moscow – a tribute to Luzhkov 'as a great reformer', according to its maker Zurab Tsereteli. Historic conflicts were not reconciled but obliterated. The unifying idea was consumerism, legitimated by the history of the Russian Empire and by the Russian Orthodox Church.

One of the most elegant squares in the city – between the Kremlin and the old Moscow University – the site of mass political rallies in the late 1980s and early 1990s – was turned into an underground shopping centre and an overground amusement park. Its globed glass roofs rose up from the ground like bubbles from the earth. A few hundred metres away, the Cathedral of Christ the Saviour, reconstructed with lavish donations from the oligarchs, gleamed with its gilded cupolas. The purpose of this remake was not to atone for the past sins of the regime, but, on the contrary, 'to create an illusion that the demotion never happened. We have to believe that all these buildings were always present, that nothing bad was ever done to them.'[83]

The idea of a collective repentance vanished. A serious examination of the Soviet past would have raised the question nobody wished to be asked, let alone answer: who was responsible for the Soviet experiment and the suffering it brought? The only honest answer would be 'everyone'. Several Russian artists who wrestled with that question inevitably arrived at the grim conclusion that Stalinism was an act of self-destruction rather than an external force.

But Moscow was having too much fun for such dark matters. The Russian stock market was booming, money was flowing into the country, attracted by crazily high interest rates; Moscow restaurants were full. The fact that much of the country was still suffering from chronic wage arrears, that poverty was reaching its post-Soviet peak and that the majority of the population was barely getting by, hardly registered in Moscow.

Meltdown

While Moscow was revelling and the oligarchs savouring their victory over the government of young reformers, thousands of miles to the east in Asia a major financial crisis on the scale of the Great Depression was unfolding and investors began to withdraw money from emerging markets. The Russian government, however, was too demoralized by the bankers' war and the oligarchs too euphoric to think about the financial tsunami heading Russia's way. Gusinsky was preparing to float his company for $1.2 billion on the New York Stock Exchange to pay for the new satellite he was planning to launch.

Meanwhile, Russia's economy was in a sorry state. The country was running a large budget deficit; the oligarchs used every loophole to avoid paying taxes. To finance itself, the government had been issuing short-term high-yielding bonds. By the spring of 1998 the interest rate on those bonds was exceeding 50 per cent. To repay bondholders the government was issuing more bonds with even higher yields. The oligarchs and foreign speculators were all piling in. Effectively, it was a debt pyramid of vast proportions and, as with all pyramids, it was only a matter of time before it started crashing.

Politics was hardly more stable. In early 1998 Yeltsin sacked Chernomyrdin, who had faithfully served him as prime minister since 1993. The most popular explanation was that Yeltsin had grown suspicious of Chernomyrdin's presidential ambitions. The opposite explanation, supported by the oligarchs and Yeltsin himself, was that Chernomyrdin had exhausted his potential, was unelectable as Yeltsin's successor and therefore had to be disposed of. The oligarchs, along with Yeltsin's daughter Tatyana Dyachenko and her husband Valentin Yumashev, held counsel about who should replace Chernomyrdin.

At one such meeting, Berezovsky suggested Malashenko. Everyone seemed to like the idea, apart from Malashenko himself. Furiously, he turned to Berezovsky: 'And do you know what my first decision will be? I will kick you out of the country the very next day.' 'Why is that?' Berezovsky asked, taking it as a joke. 'Because outside this building, virtually, stands the whole country demanding for you to be kicked out.' Berezovsky was taken aback. 'I was not joking,' Malashenko said years later. 'If I were to act as a politician I would have had to maximize power, which is what Putin did a few years later. But this is precisely why I did not want to do it – I just did not like the idea of a country like that.'[84]

After the 'bankers' war', Yeltsin, too, realized that the oligarchs were getting too powerful and he was looking for a man who would be efficient, economically literate but also distant from the oligarchs – a new face altogether, untainted by previous scandals. Yeltsin's choice for Chernomyrdin's replacement was Sergei Kiriyenko, a baby-faced, smiling, thirty-five-year-old former banker from Nizhniy Novgorod – a protégé of Nemtsov's, quickly dubbed 'Kinder Surprise'. But while Kiriyenko may have been a good technocrat to serve as a government minister in calm times, he was appointed when, in the words of Gaidar, 'a mine had not only been planted, but its fuse had also been lit'.[85] The idea of Kiriyenko being able to stand up to the oligarchs was wishful thinking as the oligarchs were keen to prove.

In May 1998, the miners from the Kuzbas region – unpaid for months – went on strike. Some blocked railways. A few hundred came to Moscow, banging their helmets on the ground in front of the White House and refusing to leave. Miners' strikes had happened before, but this one was clearly stoked and egged on by television, which showed it with great sympathy as the main event in the country, thus sustaining it over weeks and mobilizing other miners to join in. As Yeltsin wrote in his memoirs, the strike became an excuse for attacking Kiriyenko's government. When Yeltsin asked television executives to stop this information attack, they pretended to be indignant. 'Not to notice that half of the country is cut off by the miners' strikes, to pretend that it is not happening and accuse the media – that is something we've seen before,' said Dobrodeev.[86] This was the height of cynicism.

Meanwhile Channel One was entertaining its audience with a game show that captured the crazy spirit of those pre-crisis days. It was called *Zolotaia likhoradka* (*Gold Rush*). The audience was ushered into the studio, resembling a dimly lit vault, by a dwarf in a golden cloak. The host, pretending to be Satan, and demonically laughing, asked the audience general knowledge questions and selected a finalist – usually some middle-aged, balding man with bags under his eyes. If the finalist answered the questions correctly, he was offered a slab of gold and showered with banknotes. If not, a suitcase of gold melted away in front of his eyes. 'What a remarkably nasty thing to do: tempting people with money they have not earned. How tactless, in a country which officially has no money, to play for gold and to throw banknotes into the air on the screen,' Petrovskaya, the TV critic, wrote.[87] Within weeks, the entire country was to observe its savings, along with Russia's gold reserves, melt away.

On 17 August 1998 the Russian government, unable to repay or roll over its debt with a yield of 150 per cent, declared itself bankrupt. It simultaneously defaulted on its rouble-denominated debt and devalued its currency. Countries sometimes default on their local debts in order not to devalue the currency, and sometimes they devalue their currency in order to repay their debt. Russia did both. To protect the oligarchs, the government also declared an official moratorium on their payments to foreign investors, allowing Russian banks not to repay $16 billion worth of debt owned to foreigners.

Less than a week after the default, Kiriyenko and Nemtsov were gone. The day Yeltsin counter-signed their resignation, they walked out of the White House with a bottle of vodka and went over to the striking miners to drink it with them. Three months after the crisis, in November 1998, Gusinsky watched his American satellite blast off from Cape Canaveral. It was the first-ever American satellite ordered by a private Russian client. Gusinsky swelled with pride. There was one problem: his potential viewers – the nascent middle class – were no longer ready to subscribe to it. People cut back on anything that was not essential, including Gusinsky's satellite channel. Television advertising plummeted.

Gusinsky's plans to float the company on the New York Stock Exchange were scrapped. Foreign investors also had little appetite for Russian assets. Yet Gusinsky was still full of enthusiasm. He turned to his friend Rem Vyakhirev, the head of Gazprom, and they agreed on a loan of $260 million. A year later, Gusinsky took another loan of a similar size – also guaranteed by Gazprom. At the time Gusinsky could barely imagine that he was putting a noose around his neck. Whatever the events that were taking place in the country, he believed that his future was protected by his media machine.

The long-lasting impact of the crisis, however, went beyond economics. The economy – as it happened – started to grow only a year later, buoyed by the weak currency that made Russian exports more competitive, and the middle class got back on its feet. The main impact was political. It was not just the government of liberal reformers that was blown up by the crisis, but their entire model of turning Russia into a 'normal' country. Their hope that Russia's transformation into a functioning market democracy could be achieved by monetarism and privatization turned out as ephemeral as the Perestroika generation's idea that democracy and freedom of speech would automatically bring prosperity.

There was a bitter irony in this turn of fortunes. Seven years earlier, in 1991, the ideologues of the Russian liberal reforms, the generation of *Kommersant* and NTV, had declared their parents – those who had initiated Perestroika and believed in socialism with a human face – bankrupt both morally and financially. Now they were in the same position.

Having failed to build their own political foundation, the reformers and the oligarchs alike relied on Yeltsin for political cover. Now he was in a precarious position both physically and politically. Yeltsin never understood the workings of the market economy, but he had put his trust in the knowledge and ability of the Soviet-era meritocracy that controlled the economy and the media to deliver Russia into a better state. That trust was now gone. The question of succession and 'continuity of power', however, remained.

SIX

Lights, Camera, Putin

In Search of a Spy

In September 1998 NTV aired its first big project of the new television season. It was produced and presented by Leonid Parfenov and was dedicated to the twenty-fifth anniversary of the iconic Soviet television spy film – *Semnadstat' mgnovenii vesny* (*Seventeen Moments of Spring*). The series' main character is the Soviet spy Maxim Isaev who infiltrates the Nazi high command at the very end of the Second World War under the name of Max Otto von Stierlitz – a well-regarded SS Standartenführer. His task is to find out who in the German Reich is leading backdoor peace negotiations with America and to foil their attempt to undercut Stalin's Soviet Union. Stierlitz learns about Himmler's secret communications with Allen Dulles, the director of the CIA, and leaks the details to Hitler and reports it to Stalin, thus torpedoing America's 'treacherous' plans.

The twelve-part television series was released in 1973 and became an instant hit gathering between 50 and 80 million viewers every night. No Russian film before or after has attracted such an audience. At 7.30 p.m. when the film was shown on Channel One, the streets of Soviet cities emptied out, the crime rate fell and electricity consumption surged. It was shown every year before and after the Soviet collapse.

Stierlitz was a cult figure who spawned an entire Soviet folklore – he was the subject of popular jokes and kids' war games. Favourite lines from the film and its soulful theme tune were as popular as those from any James Bond film.

The Nazi officers were played by the most popular and best-loved Soviet actors. They were human and likeable and nobody more so than Stierlitz himself, who was played by the heart-throb Vyacheslav Tikhonov. Tall and handsome, with perfect cheekbones, a chiselled nose and piercing blue eyes, he was calm and unflappable. The sleek and shiny Nazi uniform, tailored in the Soviet defence ministry workshops, seemed to have been shaped on him. He was a perfect Russian 'German', more Aryan in his appearance and style than any of the 'real' Nazis in the film.*

The film was part of a propaganda campaign launched by Yuri Andropov, who became the head of the KGB in the late 1960s. Its aim was to improve the image of the KGB from a dark, secret police – a synonym of political repression – and to attract young, bright recruits into a 'glamorous' secret service. The novel by Yulian Semyonov, on which the film was based, was commissioned personally by Andropov to glorify Soviet secret agents serving abroad.

In his two-part stylized documentary about *Seventeen Moments of Spring*, Parfenov presented and partly enacted the story of the film's creation. In a sober 1970s dark suit and tie, he walked into one of the KGB's offices, 'which was designed in such a way that it made a visitor look smaller and the owner of the office larger', and sat behind the desk, with a portrait of Andropov on the wall and a row of telephones by his side. Parfenov picked up one phone which had a hammer and sickle in place of a dial, and 'summoned' Andropov's deputy who handled the writer of the novel and consulted the makers of the film.

* One of the film's unintended consequences was that it inspired Russian neo-Nazi youths, who even adopted the names of the film's characters.

As TV critic Irina Petrovskaya wrote at the time:

> Almost every line of the film corresponds to the contemporary Russian situation – especially the theme song about 'moments which swish by like bullets'. All political actors, all experts on all television channels say that Russia is on the verge of an [economic] disaster and the time is counted in hours, minutes, moments. And those who sit on this side of the television screen are trying to catch a glimpse of light at the end of the tunnel. But there is no glimpse, just as there is no Stierlitz who can find a way out of the most difficult position.[1]

Less than two months before Parfenov's documentary came out, a new chief of the FSB – the post-Soviet successor to the KGB – had taken over Andropov's old office. His name was Vladimir Putin, a former colonel who had served in Dresden in Eastern Germany in the 1980s. Putin was one of the 'young and educated' recruits who had been targeted by Andropov's propaganda campaign. He was twenty-one years old, a law student in Leningrad, when *Seventeen Moments of Spring* was first released. Two years later, in 1975, he joined the service.

As fate would have it, Putin's first appearance on the television screen was in 'the character' of Stierlitz. In 1992 the St Petersburg mayor's office, where Putin served at the time, commissioned a documentary series about the city's government. The only part of it that actually got made was about Putin – on his own initiative. Putin used the film to declare himself a former KGB operative. To make the film more entertaining, its director, Igor Shadkhan, set Putin up as a modern version of Stierlitz. 'I decided to stage the last episode of the film where Stierlitz is driving a car,' Shadkhan recalled.[2] Driving a Volga, Putin 're-enacted' the last episode of the film in which Stierlitz drives his car back to Berlin. The famous theme tune from *Seventeen Moments of Spring* played in the background. Putin was a perfect fit.

The public longing for a real-life Stierlitz who could deal with any crisis calmly and efficiently was not a fanciful notion. In early 1999 *Kommersant* commissioned a public opinion survey asking which film character Russians would like to see as their next president. Stierlitz was runner-up to Second World War Marshal Zhukov, a real historic figure. *Kommersant*'s weekly supplement put Stierlitz on the cover with the caption 'President-2000'. This was not, strictly speaking, a surprise. For all its history, the KGB had a mystique, an aura of knowledge and professionalism. Like secret agents anywhere else, KGB spies in Russia were seen as dashing, clever and protective of their motherland. In the public's eye the KGB was a pragmatic, if also ruthless, force that supported economic modernization. After all, it had been Andropov who championed Gorbachev in the early 1980s.

Having lost faith in liberals, the country was searching for its Stierlitz. Yeltsin, too, looked towards the former and present members of the military or security services for a possible successor. Opinion pollsters told Yeltsin that his successor had to be young, ethnically Russian, a former member of the security services and non-drinking. Yeltsin, a man of great political instinct, agreed. 'For some time now, I had been sensing the public need for a new quality in the state, for a steel backbone that would strengthen the whole government. We needed a man who was intellectual, democratic, and who could think anew, but who was firm in the military manner.'[3] A year later such a person did appear, and was greeted with enthusiasm: Vladimir Putin. In September 1998 nobody had yet heard of him.

Goodbye America

In September 1998 Yeltsin appointed Evgeny Primakov, a sixty-nine-year-old foreign minister and veteran of Soviet politics, as Russia's prime minister. It was more of a necessity than a wish. The oligarchs, including Berezovsky, who, a few months earlier, had helped to get Chernomyrdin fired, lobbied for his return, seeing him as a guarantee of continuity.

Yeltsin twice submitted Chernomyrdin's nomination to the communist-dominated parliament and twice he was vetoed. It was a battle Yeltsin felt he could not win and in the end he was forced to nominate Primakov – a wily and experienced member of the Soviet nomenclatura, a candidate for the Politburo and an old spymaster who headed the first post-Soviet intelligence service. He was supposed to be a consensus figure, fulfilling the same role that Chernomyrdin performed in 1992: he would be loyal to Yeltsin, could lead a left-leaning government and satisfy communists in the parliament who could not possibly object to him as a liberal Westernizer.

Primakov was two years older than Yeltsin and had come into politics at the end of the Stalinist era. He started in state Soviet television, which often provided cover for 'spooks', worked at *Pravda* newspaper and specialized in foreign affairs which meant frequent trips abroad. His connections with the KGB were never formally declared, but always taken for granted. Primakov was an Arabist, a personal friend of Saddam Hussein and Yasser Arafat. But he had also worked with Gorbachev.

Primakov's appointment had a therapeutic effect on the country, which had been shaken by the financial crisis. His slightly slurred speech and his Soviet manner were reassuring without being too threatening – at least not to ordinary people. He was measured and conservative and had an air of solidity and unhurried wisdom. Most people felt relieved – as though an old and steady hand was taking over the levers of power after a team of young and reckless pilots had nearly crashed the plane. 'Don't worry, the experiments and the turbulence are over,' Primakov's demeanour said. In public he spoke about a greater role of the state in the economy and played to the paternalistic sentiments in the country. At the same time he oversaw some budget cuts and took advice from American economists.

He took no revolutionary steps. In fact, his biggest achievement was that he hardly took any action at all, letting the economy run its own course, which soon turned into growth. Primakov's popularity rating shot up – not because of what he did or did not do, but because of the image he projected of a statist.

In fact, Primakov was more concerned with the media than he was with the economy. He obsessively read newspapers and watched television programmes, often calling editors and owners to complain. In his memoirs, Yeltsin recalled how Primakov brought him a special dossier which contained newspaper cuttings that criticized his government, with words and sentences highlighted with a marker pen. Yeltsin, who had always tolerated all the mud that was thrown at him, found it odd. 'Evgeny Maximovich, I am used to this. Every day newspapers write such things about me. But what can you do? Close newspapers?'[4]

Russian liberal journalists, those who had taken Yeltsin's side in 1993 and who had set the narrative for much of the 1990s, saw Primakov as an alien figure. They took against him in a way that sometimes seemed almost irrational. They were put off by his Soviet manners more than his actions (or the lack of action). They considered him a Soviet-era dinosaur. The best he could offer Russia, they felt, was stagnation. At worst, he could take the country in the direction of Stalinism-lite. Primakov's instincts were far from being liberal, but he was a pragmatic and rational politician with real knowledge of the country. Alexander Yakovlev felt that 'democrats are wrong to be so antagonistic towards Primakov, calling him a conservative! He simply does not rush to his conclusions. He prefers not to say anything today that can be said tomorrow.'[5]

But it was also a question of power. Throughout the 1990s journalists had enjoyed a highly privileged position and status. Primakov, on the other hand, eschewed journalists whom he thought to be untrustworthy and antagonistic. As a statist, he naturally relied on the old-style Soviet nomenclatura: the security services, bureaucracy and diplomats. He instantly made the government less accessible to journalists and gave a dressing-down to television executives for distorting and blackening its image, telling them what and how they should report. Journalists found this more of a snub and a humiliation than a threat. They associated the loss of their dominance with Primakov. As Yeltsin wrote in his memoirs: 'Willingly or not, Primakov consolidated anti-market and anti-liberal forces and infringed on the freedom of the press.'[6] Primakov's premiership also coincided with a shift in Russia's attitude towards the West.

The biggest event of Primakov's short term in office was the bombing of Yugoslavia by NATO forces. On 23 March 1999 – the eve of the NATO strikes – Primakov was in the air, on his way to Washington to negotiate financial aid for Russia, when he learned that the air-strike on Belgrade was imminent. In a powerful gesture, loaded with symbolism, Primakov ordered his plane to turn around over the Atlantic and fly back to Moscow.

The next morning *Kommersant* came out with a short front-page article which reflected the rage of most of its journalists. Its emotional pitch was not typical of *Kommersant*'s usual sarcastic and detached style. 'RUSSIA HAS LOST $15 BILLION THANKS TO PRIMAKOV' the headline screamed. The figure was derived from the sum of contracts and credit lines Primakov *could* have signed in America, but

> as a true Bolshevik he decided to sacrifice the interests of his own country for the sake of some 'internationalism' which only he and other former members of the Communist Party can understand... There is only one conclusion that one can draw: supporting Milosevic's regime, which is so close to Primakov's heart, is more important to the needs of his country. But when the prime minister gets back to Moscow he will have no right to look in the eyes of the old people to whom he promised to pay out their pensions.[7]

Primakov's U-turn was not just an expression of the government's frustration with America's policy towards Serbia and its disregard for Russia's opposition to air-strikes. It captured something far more significant – a general change in attitude towards America and the West among the Russian general public. In 1988, when the Soviet era was drawing to a close, the Russian rock band Nautilus Pompilius had recorded a 'Farewell Letter' that captured Russia's image of America as a promised land:

> Goodbye America, oh! Where I have never been
> Farewell forever… I've outgrown your sand-stoned jeans
> They have taught us to love your forbidden fruits
> Goodbye America, where I will never be.

The idea of America as a utopia, literally a no-place, a dream, had long been engrained in Russian culture. In Dostoevsky's *Crime and Punishment*, one of the characters, Svidrigailov, who is about to commit suicide, says to a guard: 'When you are asked, you just say he was going, he said, to America.' He then puts the revolver to his right temple and pulls the trigger. America was the other world.

For much of the 1990s America served as a model, an inspiration and an anchor. The 1998 crisis showed the futility of the dream. The bombing of Serbia crashed the dream itself. The West ceased to be an anchor. It turned out that there was no one happy post-Soviet space, that Russia was on its own. America turned into a scapegoat for all the troubles that the Russian people had experienced over the previous decade.

The outburst of anti-Americanism and nationalism was shrill. Massive rallies were staged outside the American Embassy in Moscow. Someone tried to fire at it from a grenade launcher, which luckily did not work, and then opened fire with automatics. A mob of football fans pelted the embassy with paint and eggs. Three men urinated on its door.

This did not so much reflect Russians' concern for the 'brotherly'

Slavic nation – most people had little knowledge about what was actually going on in Kosovo – but the need to take out the pent-up frustration, irritation and humiliation on traditional adversaries, America and NATO. It was as though the bombing of Serbia unleashed something that had been building up for years. It was a delayed reaction to the 1998 crisis, the bankers' war or even deeper – to the Soviet collapse and the loss of Russia's imperial status.

Some of the media went into a nationalistic overdrive. State television channels began to talk about American hawks and NATO aggressors. More surprising was the initial coverage by NTV. Its first news bulletins seemed anti-Western, made no mention of Kosovo refugees and drew parallels between NATO's air-strikes and German bombings during the Second World War. 'For the first time since 1941 there are German bombers with black crosses on their tails in the sky over Belgrade,' an NTV news presenter said. The idea belonged to Oleg Dobrodeev who was in charge of news and current affairs. Both Gusinsky and Kiselev were shocked by the change of NTV's tone that was as sudden as Primakov's U-turn over the Atlantic.

When Kiselev confronted Dobrodeev a few days later, Dobrodeev was wound up and unapologetic. 'He told me that I didn't understand anything; that the situation in the country had changed, that public opinion was against NATO's strikes and that we had to reflect that change or be left behind,' Kiselev recalled.[8] Dobrodeev's outbursts of 'statism', said Kiselev, coincided with Primakov's offer to move over to the government. He argued that if Malashenko was allowed to work for Yeltsin's campaign, why should not he, Dobrodeev, be seconded to work for Primakov. Gusinsky, however, did not look favourably on the idea.

In the following *Itogi* programmes, Kiselev showed Kosovo refugees and reminded its audience of the ethnic cleansing which Kosovan Albanians had been subjected to. America might have lost a sense of reality and acted arrogantly, *Itogi* asserted, but this did not warrant the anti-American hysteria unleashed by Russia, which historically paid little attention to international norms. Using black-and-white footage from the 1950s and 1960s, *Itogi* reminded the audience how Soviet forces had pulled Eastern Germany into the socialist camp in 1953, how they had broken up the Hungarian uprising in 1956 and how they had invaded Prague in 1968. 'The Soviet Union killed people where it wanted and how it wanted. Is America guilty of this? Of course it is. It is guilty that it lives better than us, that it has become richer than us and works harder than us, which makes it stronger than us. And we have spent all our energy looking for a third way – and we have found it in our boundless, vicious love for Serbia.'[9]

Yet, Dobrodeev, who had an unmistakable sense of the country's direction, rightly assessed the shift in public mood. Russia was unable to match America, but it no longer wanted to hear that America was stronger, richer and better. Anti-Americanism would prove to be one of the most lasting and effective ideological narratives over the next decade and a half. America, as an unreal country, could be blamed for any trouble at home. A symbol of Russian hopes, it easily flipped into a symbol of their default. Utopia turned into an anti-Utopia.

Primakov's U-turn over the Atlantic pushed his rating to new heights. In April 1999 he was the most popular politician in the country – while Yeltsin's rating dropped to single digits, as a result of the crisis, disillusionment with the West and corruption scandals. Without any constitutional change, Russia was evolving into a parliamentary republic with a strong prime minister supported by the parliament. Primakov, as the head of the government, started to behave as an independent politician.

Even before the Balkan crisis in December 1998, Yeltsin, who had been in and out of hospital, had been sufficiently worried about losing levers of power to Primakov and his government for him to reaffirm his control over the power ministries, including the ministry of justice and the tax police. At the same time he met with the heads of television channels. 'You can ask why the president is once again showing interest in the mass media,'

Yeltsin said. 'It is because you are the fourth estate, you are *siloviki*,' he said with a charismatic smile. 'This is why you are under the president, under the president's protection. This is super-important.'[10]

In January 1999, Channel One, which was effectively run by Berezovsky, launched a weekly *Vremya* programme presented by Sergei Dorenko. 'We are witnessing a redistribution of power – the highest power in the country,' Dorenko said alarmingly. 'Primakov is trying to deprive Yeltsin of his right to sack him as prime minister... He is trying to take control over *siloviki* and the media, instead of dealing with the economy which is heading towards a new crisis.' Primakov said he had no intention of introducing censorship, but Dorenko juxtaposed his comments with the old Soviet footage showing a Congress of the Communist Party, suggesting that this was where the country was heading.[11]

Less than a week after the programme, Primakov attacked Berezovsky. Commenting on a decision by the Duma to amnesty nearly 100,000 prisoners, Primakov said Russia needed to free up some space in prisons so that it could jail people who had committed economic crimes. A few days later, firms linked to Berezovsky were raided by camouflaged police with guns and in skiing masks. Berezovksy was fired as the secretary of the Commonwealth of Independent States and soon faced an arrest warrant in connection with siphoning money from Aeroflot. Primakov also tried to retake control over Channel One.

For Primakov, who had served as a candidate member to the Politburo and had started his career in television, Channel One and its iconic *Vremya* programme were main staples of the state power. The idea that the national channel had been hijacked by Berezovsky who turned it into a tool of personal influence was nonsense. Primakov offered Channel One a state subsidy of $100 million on the condition that Dorenko was removed from the air. Dorenko also came under investigation by the tax police.

Berezovsky, who was forced to flee the country, launched a counter-offensive on Primakov, portraying him as a force darker than the communists and stoking and exploiting the fears of the liberal media about Primakov's style. 'Communists want to bring back the communist system. Primakov wants to build the empire. From the first day [in office] he started fighting for control over the media, security services... He has succeeded in his fight for the security services. For ten years they were quietly lying low. When they saw one of their own men [in power], they started coming out of their hole,' Berezovsky said.[12]

On 12 May 1999, Yeltsin sacked Primakov, invoking jubilation among liberal journalists. 'It is the departure of the last big figure of the Soviet era and the fact that he was incapable of governing post-Soviet Russia speaks only about one fact: the country has changed and the point of return to the bright Soviet yesterday has passed,' read an article in the pro-Western and liberal *Itogi* magazine – part of Gusinsky's media empire.[13] The media placed Primakov into the context of an old battle between the Soviet past and the Westernized future that shaped the 1996 elections. But unlike in 1996, this was not a battle of ideas or even directions. It was a battle for power and for survival within the Kremlin. It had little to do with the public good of the country, but everything to do with the interests of those who had been empowered and enriched by Yeltsin's rule and who had much at stake in the question of his succession.

Operation 'Successor'

Vlast'. The untranslatable Russian *vlast'* is listed in the *Oxford English Dictionary* as 'political power in the countries of the former Soviet Union'. In Russia and its former republics, *vlast'* is inseparable from *sobstvennost'* or ownership, property, assets. Lacking legal property rights, Russian ownership can be backed only by state power. So for the oligarchs who received their main assets as a result of the highly dubious loans-for-shares privatization, the continuity of *vlast'* meant the preservation of *sobstvennost'*.

'We were obsessed with the idea of *vlast*',' said Gleb Pavlovsky, who had been working for the Kremlin since 1996. 'Preserving Yeltsin's "rule" while letting him leave safely at the end of his second term was the horizon of our planning.'[14] All this was done in the name of saving Yeltsin from a possible retribution and protecting his legacy. In fact the legacy of Yeltsin as Russia's first democratically elected president who parted with communism and launched reforms was the last thing on the minds of those who planned his succession and in the end caused more damage to his legacy than anyone from the outside could have done. Yeltsin's own safety was not under threat, but the safety of his entourage was.

Yeltsin's daughter Tatyana Dyachenko and her husband Valentin Yumashev had been implicated in several financial scandals, including alleged kickbacks for a contract to renovate the Kremlin. It was the subject of a probe by Yuri Skuratov, Russia's prosecutor general, who threw dirt at Yeltsin's family and was implicitly supported by Luzhkov. Luzhkov was an oligarch in his own right, he controlled one of the most profitable 'corporations' in Russia – Moscow itself. On the one hand, Luzhkov epitomized Russia's regional feudalism. On the other hand, he considered his Moscow fiefdom a nucleus of a more centralized country. He could be a new prince Yuri Dolgoruky, the founder of Moscow. As Yeltsin wrote in his memoirs, 'After the incredibly pompous and overblown 850th anniversary of Moscow, the mayor evidently became dizzy with success.'[15]

In the summer of 1999 Luzhkov teamed up with Primakov, whose sacking was opposed by 80 per cent of the population and whose rating jumped from 20 per cent to 32 per cent. Luzhkov quickly drew Primakov to his side. Luzhkov's 'Fatherland' Party and Primakov's 'All Russia' Party forged a coalition: 'Fatherland–All Russia'. Their likely victory in the parliamentary elections in December 1999 could make one of them president and the other prime minister. In either case, a redistribution of assets, the sidelining of Yeltsin's family and the banishment of rival oligarchs including Berezovsky and Roman Abramovich (his junior partner in 1999–2000) would be inevitable. Luzhkov openly called for the revising of the result of the privatization and Russia's agreement with its former republics. 'Sebastopol is a Russian city,' he stated. 'And will belong to Russia. It can be achieved by force. But I am an advocate of a peaceful solution.'[16]

Luzhkov's mouthpiece was a well-equipped Moscow television channel, Central Television, which he controlled and which he turned against Yeltsin's entourage. (One of its presenters was the little-known Dmitry Kiselev who would later turn into the most audacious of propagandists even by the Kremlin's own standards.) Every day, it lobbed populist-loaded shells at the Kremlin. 'The Yeltsin regime has sold the motherland to foreign capital... It created the system of corruption. It arranged for the "genocide of Russian people." And it is to blame for the fall in the birth rate, the catastrophic state of science and education, medicine and culture. A Mafia-like family, a real gangster clan, has formed around the president,' Luzhkov's media trumpeted.[17]

Yeltsin's clan, which apart from his daughter and her husband, also included Alexander Voloshin, Yeltsin's chief of staff and Berezovsky's former business associate, and Roman Abramovich, Berezovsky's junior business partner, now needed their own, obedient Primakov. In the autumn of 1998 – shortly after Primakov's appointment as prime minister – Pavlovsky wrote in a memo to the Kremlin: 'Any new head of state will be a Primakov. Either we get onto this process or it will unfold without us.'[18] In the late spring of 1999, the Kremlin 'got onto this process'. While Berezovsky blamed Primakov for relying on the security services, the Kremlin engaged in the extraordinary exercise of substituting Primakov with a political 'double' – a loyal and obedient man of a similar background who could appeal to the same electorate.

The short list included Sergei Stepashin, the former interior minister, Nikolai Putin, the head of the FSB, and Nikolai Aksenenko, the minister of railways. In the end, the choice fell on Putin. 'Putin and Primakov were two former intelligence officers, two representatives of the security services, and they occupied the same niche in the public mind,' Yeltsin wrote in his memoirs.[19]

Yeltsin's family had their own reasons to like Putin. He had faithfully served Anatoly Sobchak, the democratic mayor of St Petersburg, and when Sobchak got entangled in a corruption scandal and was effectively banned from leaving the country, Putin managed to smuggle him to a hospital in France. Yeltsin's 'family', who heavily promoted Putin, calculated that if Putin had not given up Sobchak, he would stick to Yeltsin. Putin also proved his loyalty to Yeltsin's family by helping to deal with Skuratov, the troublesome prosecutor general, who had been secretly videotaped in bed with prostitutes. Putin, who was put in charge of the inquest into the tape's origins, confirmed its authenticity and is believed to have authorized that the footage be shown on television, which led to Skuratov's dismissal.

Berezovsky had his own relationship with Putin. He had befriended Putin in the 1990s and invited him to go skiing in Switzerland. In the spring of 1999, when Berezovsky's conflict with Primakov was at its peak, Putin came to a birthday party Berezovsky organized for his wife, even though he was not invited. 'Primakov will never forgive you this gesture,' Berezovsky told Putin. 'Friendship is friendship,' Putin apparently replied. Several other similar accounts of Putin's remarks exist, but all of them point to Putin's loyalty to friendship. Berezovsky, who had always exercised control and reaped benefits through people, rather than formal positions, believed that Putin was his man.

The media were to play a key role in this game of substitution, just as they played a key role in getting Yeltsin re-elected in 1996. The difference, however, was that Yeltsin was a genuine politician of historic proportions. Neither Malashenko nor Chubais, nor anyone else, 'created' Yeltsin. All they had to do was to galvanize him and persuade the majority of the country that he was the only one who could stop the communists from coming to power.

—

But Yeltsin's victory in 1996 convinced his entourage that the trick, performed with the help of television, could be repeated without Yeltsin; that any candidate – however negligible – could be turned into a successor, given the right technology.

In 1999 politics was replaced by political technology, citizens by spectators, reality by television. 'Media became a branch of state power,' Pavlovsky said.[20] The idea that by means of television a group of 'political technologists' and media managers could create a president out of someone nobody ever heard of seemed incredible. This time, however, Gusinsky's NTV, which had led the 1996 campaign, found itself on the wrong side of the Kremlin.

Gusinsky did not object to the principle of creating a presidential candidate as such. He objected to being treated as a branch of state power, rather than a power in its own right. In 1996 he was a partner who chose to back Yeltsin and got his dividends from it. Now he was told to fall into line or to get lost. It was partly a question of money and partly of kudos. Gusinsky demanded that NTV should receive the same $100m that was given by the government to Channel One. Instead, Alexander Voloshin, Yeltsin's chief of staff, backed by Berezovsky and Abramovich, told him to get lost. Gusinsky, who was notorious for his bad temper, flew off the handle. Whether this spat was an accident or a deliberate provocation by rival oligarchs, is hard to say, but the result was a feud. Neither Gusinsky nor Malashenko, who had been offered the job of Yeltsin's chief of staff, was prepared to put up with Voloshin's insolence.

While Gusinsky was having his spat with Voloshin, Yumashev tried a softer approach with Malashenko. In June 1999 Dyachenko and Yumashev, who had a house in Gusinsky's Chigasovo village, dropped in on Malashenko for tea, trying to persuade him to back Putin. To make up his mind, Malashenko asked his friend, Peter Aven, a former trade minister and a banker who knew Putin personally, to arrange a meeting with Putin. A casual dinner was held in Aven's dacha which had once housed the famous Soviet writer Alexei Tolstoy. Putin arrived with his two daughters. Malashenko's own daughter was on her way to London for the last term at her English boarding school. The dinner lasted nearly three hours and revealed little, apart from one small detail.

Towards the end of the dinner, Malashenko's daughter called from Heathrow where she had just landed. The school car was not there to pick her up, so she was calling to see if she should wait or get a taxi, Malashenko's wife told the dinner guests, and she had said her daughter should take a taxi. Suddenly, Putin intervened in the conversation. 'You gave the wrong advice to your daughter. She was right to wait for the school car. You can't be sure that the taxi she will get is a real taxi.' Malashenko's wife, who had arrived late and had hardly registered Putin, looked at him in surprise. London taxis, she explained, are not some gypsy cabs – they are black cabs with taxi signs and meters. 'You can't be sure that it would be a real taxi,' Putin repeated calmly. 'He was effectively saying that our daughter could be kidnapped,' Malashenko recalled.

The conversation moved on. 'Afterwards, my wife told me that this comment was a distilled Putin, a KGB officer. I laughed it off at first, told her she was exaggerating. But then I thought – she was right, because the KGB was not about repression at that time, it was all about control. Anything you control is safe. Anything you don't control by definition represents a threat – it is in their mental set-up and a KGB officer is always a KGB officer.'[21] Malashenko was no idealist. He had dealt with plenty of KGB people in his life. One of the KGB's top people, Bobkov, was working for Media Most. He was not worried about terror, but he resented the very idea of the state's exercising control over private lives through its security service.

Guarding the state as a dominant power was the KGB's top proclaimed goal. It was not called the 'Committee for State Security' for nothing. It was the quintessence of that state, its main embodiment after the collapse of the Communist Party. As someone who believed in keeping the state in check, Malashenko did not like the idea of the KGB coming to power. A few days after that memorable dinner, Malashenko dropped by Yumashev's dacha to tell him that he could not support Putin. 'I told him that the KGB was the KGB for ever.' That was, as Malashenko reflected, NTV's last chance to jump on Putin's train.

Instead, it came out with an *Itogi* programme that exposed Yeltsin's 'family' as a narrow circle of people who made all the decisions in the country and manipulated the president himself. The story was illustrated with a diagram of 'family' members. This was a shot against Yeltsin's 'family' and, by extension, Putin himself, their preferred choice as successor. The notion of the 'family' had hardly been used before, although some strange billboards had started to appear around Moscow – probably as part of Luzhkov's anti-Yeltsin campaign. One such billboard carried a reference to the tycoon Roman Abramovich – widely rumoured to be 'the family's cashier'. The text on the billboard, surrounded by golden coins, read: 'Roma looks after the family. The family looks after Roma.'

In the minds of the Kremlin's political technologists, Gusinsky's attack on the 'family' and that of Luzhkov had merged into one coordinated campaign. Yeltsin took the NTV programme as a stab in the back:

> The photographs [of the members of the 'family'] shown on TV reminded me of wanted posters I used to see at factories, bus stations, or movie theatres in Sverdlovsk. The posters usually depicted the faces of drunks, thieves, murderers, and rapists. Now, the 'police', in the person of NTV, was talking about my so-called Family – myself, Tanya, Voloshin and Yumashev. All of these people were accused of everything under the sun – bribery, corruption, the hoarding of wealth in Swiss bank accounts, and the purchase of villas and castles in Italy and France.[22]

What shocked Yeltsin most were not the actual revelations, but the fact that this was done by people who knew him and his immediate family personally and who had spent time with them. He saw this as a personal betrayal of trust.

NTV's journalists were barred from important Kremlin meetings. There was a strict and concerted decision that no Kremlin official should appear on NTV, said Pavlovsky, who was responsible for the media in Putin's presidential campaign.[23] NTV was left with Primakov and Luzhkov. 'We got marginalized,' Kiselev recalled. *Itogi* magazine was paid a visit by the tax police.

Berezovsky, who championed Putin, exploited the situation to his own ends by persuading the Kremlin that NTV had switched sides and was working for Luzhkov and Primakov. This was not strictly speaking true. Gusinsky and Malashenko did not support Luzhkov. Gusinsky had fallen out with Luzhkov and it was Malashenko who had ruled him out as a possible prime minister in his conversation with Yeltsin back in September 1998. Nor did they see Primakov as 'their' man – at least not initially. In fact, their main weakness was that they did not have a candidate of their own and did not think this was important. As the owners of the country's most influential television channel, they considered themselves to be the power to be reckoned with, whoever the president.

On 9 August, Yeltsin named Putin as prime minister and his 'successor' – the only man who could 'consolidate' the country. Berezovsky was in a celebratory mood. With Gusinsky out of the way, most probably with his help, he was the sole kingmaker – the most indispensable man in Russia, who controlled the main television channel. Despite Berezovsky's public objection to Primakov as a security man, Putin's background didn't bother him in the least.

To the world outside the Kremlin walls, this seemed like one of Yeltsin's eccentric antics. His previous prime minister, Sergei Stepashin, had lasted less than three months. Most people had never heard of Putin and would not have recognized him in a photograph if they had seen one. The majority did not even notice his appointment. His rating hardly registered in sociologists' polls, falling into the margin of error – below 2 per cent. He rarely appeared in public or gave interviews. Meantime, Primakov's rating was 32 per cent. Gusinsky had every reason to think that the odds of 'defeating' the family were in his favour.

But while the barons were getting agitated in anticipation of political battles for Yeltsin's succession, forming alliances, getting ready for information wars and loading their media weapons with explosive revelations and compromising material, the rest of the country felt more and more alienated from politics. The majority did not feel responsible for the actions of their government and felt they had little influence on the direction of the country. 'Nothing depends on us and everything is decided behind the stage' – this was the most popular attitude of Russian voters.

According to Alexander Olson, a sociologist who worked for Yeltsin in the 1996 election and carried out work for Putin's election campaign, the population recognized familiar political actors – such as Yeltsin, Luzhkov, or Primakov – but looked at politics as someone else's game in which they were just spectators. This attitude to politics, instilled in the population by the media themselves, perfectly matched the format of television-watching. Nobody enjoyed staging television spectacles more than Berezovsky.

The rules of the game were different this time. In 1996, however biased the media was, Yeltsin was still ready to compete with Zyuganov. His little-known 'successor' had no chance of winning fairly against such heavyweights as Luzhkov and Primakov. To make Operation 'Successor' work, Luzhkov and Primakov had to be removed from the presidential race, to leave Putin the only real contender. To perform this task, Berezovsky turned to the man who was known in Russian television as the assassin: Sergei Dorenko.

The Gunman

Dorenko, the son of a military pilot, grew up in garrison towns, moving from one part of the country to another. He had a suitably colourful career for a showman. As a boy he had dreamt of a military career but ended up in television because of bad eyesight. He learned Spanish and Portuguese and served as a military interpreter in Angola during the civil war that pitched the Soviet Union against America. He had frequent contacts with the KGB, but said he was never formally recruited. 'Whenever they talked to me – I would tell everyone else, so they did not think me reliable.'[24] In the early 1990s he moved freely between different channels and freelanced for the Spanish service of CNN, reporting on the shelling of the White House and the war in Chechnya. But in Dorenko's own mind, his two careers – in the military and in television – merged into one. He called himself *pulemetchik* – a machine-gunner. The territory in which he felt most comfortable was war. Any war. Political or military.

Dorenko belonged to the same breed as Nevzorov. He was a perfect mercenary. Stylistically, he was the antithesis of Kiselev. Whereas Kiselev was a symbol of respectability and bourgeoisie, an icon of the middle class, Dorenko addressed a broader and less sophisticated audience. He had none of Kiselev's deliberations. He was not asking his audience to think for itself – as Kiselev did – but told it what to think and to feel, skilfully manipulating its instincts and prejudices.

Berezovsky first 'fell in love' with Dorenko while recovering from an attempted assassination in 1994, when his Mercedes was blown up. From his hospital bed he watched Dorenko telling the audience that, although there was nothing wrong with oligarchs blowing each other up, it would be better if they found a special area for doing this, so that ordinary people would not get hurt.

Berezovsky then went to see Dorenko in his office. Dorenko said he was busy. Berezovsky waited for a while, was fed some watermelon by Dorenko's assistant and left without seeing his 'hero'. 'Why should I've seen him? He was just an oligarch,' Dorenko recalled.[25] Dorenko's 'stunt' of not seeing Berezovsky only strengthened Berezovsky's appreciation of Dorenko's showmanship. When they finally met, in a Japanese restaurant in the monstrous Rossiya Hotel opposite the Kremlin, Berezovsky offered Dorenko the job of presenting the country's main television news programme, *Vremya*. 'In the middle of the conversation he ran to the Kremlin to clear my appointment with the administration.'[26]

Berezovsky loved Dorenko's style. 'I am a big fan of Dorenko. I think he is an outstanding journalist... I watch him not as a political analyst – I don't need to. I watch it as a brilliant show in which my point of view coincides with his. The form is particularly important to me. I can't read books written in poor language. But I can read books about nothing that are written in brilliant language,' Berezovsky said in an interview at the time.[27] Dorenko said Berezovsky would call him after every other programme. 'He always started the conversation by saying, "You are a genius". He then quoted lengthy passages from my own programme back to me.'[28]

Dorenko was a Russian version of America's Rush Limbaugh – a right-wing tyro who moved seamlessly between earnest lecture and political vaudeville. Presenting the *Vremya* programme in 1997–8, Dorenko transformed it into a show of damning revelations, a sermon turned inside out. It lowered the tone, agitated and inspired outrage and hatred, but most importantly it captivated the audience and removed taboos. He did not appeal to reason, like Kiselev did. He penetrated people's minds through sensations, repeating evocative words and phrases, heavily rolling his 'Rs' when talking about 'Russia' or 'betrayal', modulating his voice in bemusement, juggling words and showing images that conjured up associations even if they had no direct relevance to the subject. Facts were irrelevant.

It was pure circus and mischief – the kind that Koroviev, a character from Bulgakov's *The Master and Margarita*, engages in as part of Satan's band. Koroviev famously performs acts of 'black magic' in a variety show, uncovering adultery and greed among members of the public. Dorenko acted in much the same way, poking fun and terrorizing his victims whom he was hired to destroy. Asked how he would define his profession in those years, Dorenko replied: '*Peresmeshnik*' – a mocking-bird, a jester, a fool.

In fact, said Dorenko, the 'Sergei Dorenko' that appeared on the screen was a creation, a fiction:

> He existed only for as long as I was on stage, in front of the camera. Some powerful people, including Yumashev and Dyachenko, often invited me to their dacha, but I never went. They wanted to meet 'Sergei Dorenko' from the television screen, but he did not exist in real life... He died every time the cameras were switched off. Away from the stage there was an introvert person who shunned big company and despised the oligarchs. I often told Berezovsky: 'Listen, when I am fighting against Potanin, I am, in fact, fighting against all of you.' I was setting them off against each other.[29]

On stage, he was so shameless in his demagoguery, so cynical in his groundless, over-the-top allegations – that it was almost breathtaking. Like some fairground act it could prompt gasps of disbelief among critics and spectators: 'How does he do it?' or 'How can he get away with it?' The more 'unbelievable' and 'outlandish' Dorenko's revelations were – the greater their entertainment value.

People believed what they saw, not because they were persuaded by factual evidence, but because it confirmed what they thought anyway: that everyone was a liar and a thief. 'I did not "programme" anything. I simply whispered what people wanted to hear,' said Dorenko.[30] Berezovsky courted and cultivated Dorenko for some time, recognizing in him an enormous television talent with few principles attached.

In August 1999, Berezovsky, who returned to Russia after a short self-exile, which Primakov had forced him into, was once again in hospital – this time with hepatitis. He summoned Dorenko, who turned up with a bag of tangerines. 'He was lying in a palatial two-room ward. There were drips all over him and he told me we would "fuck" them all [Primakov and Luzhkov].'[31] It was there that Berezovsky also first shared his plan to set up the Kremlin's own Unity Party which was to provide Putin with loyalists in the parliamentary elections in December. 'Its emblem is going to be a bear – can you draw a bear?' he asked Dorenko.

Dorenko needed little persuading to attack Primakov and Luzhkov. A few months earlier he had been kicked out of his job at Channel One on Primakov's instructions. Dorenko was also the subject of a tax investigation in Moscow, which he blamed on Luzhkov and Primakov. The investigation ended on the day that Primakov was fired as prime minister. The adrenaline of a battle excited him: 'I told Borya [Berezovsky], the result will be this: they will hang you among the first five people on Red Square. And they will hang me among the next ten. And we will both be hanging in Red Square. "So?" asked Berezovsky. "So, let's have a good smoke and go for it – with God's help."'[32]

Dorenko's new programme started to come out in September on Sunday evenings – the same time slot as Kiselev's *Itogi*. Like Kiselev, Dorenko was now wearing glasses – to appear more respectable and authoritative. He made fifteen programmes and called them 'fifteen silver bullets'. Watched in sequence, these fifteen 'analytical' shows worked like a soap opera which used documentary footage, but in such a way that it turned into fiction. It had a set of villains and heroes and a loose plot peppered with conspiracy, murder stories, sex, intrigue and titillating images. Like any soap opera, it was shown at the same time every week and combined the repetition of situations, familiarity with the main characters and new twists in the plot. As Boris Dubin, a sociologist, wrote at the time, the repetition created a calming sense of order while new twists provided the entertainment.

Appropriately, the opening titles of Dorenko's series consisted of industrial cog-wheels and the sounds of grinding metal and hammering. Primakov and Luzhkov – the main characters of the show – were ground into mincemeat by Dorenko's television machine. The machine was primitive, crude and extremely effective. The themes and even some formulations were fed to Dorenko by Putin's election campaign staff, but the presentation was self-inspired. Primakov was to be portrayed as 'old', 'weak' and 'Soviet'; Luzhkov as one of the oligarchs with bloodied hands and connections to the North Caucasus Mafia. Dorenko cultivated the image of Luzhkov as a comic inversion of a Godfather figure: a short, bald and plump man under the heel of his wife, Yelena Baturina, Russia's richest oligarchess.

In one programme, Dorenko alleged that Luzhkov's family was receiving money from a Swiss firm, Mabetex, which was involved in a scandalous renovation of the Kremlin. He showed bank transfers for hundreds of millions of dollars from its German sister firm into various offshore bank accounts held by a man with the same family name as Luzhkov's wife. As it happened, the man was of no relation to Baturina and Dorenko never even spoke to him. But none of this mattered to Dorenko. Luzhkov – hardly an example of integrity – was forced to justify and defend himself and his wife, but the more he spoke, the deeper he dug himself into a hole.

'My wife has a brother, but his name is Viktor and not Andrei, and he is her only business partner,' Luzhkov tried to explain in exasperation. 'Sorry, we have to stop the mayor here before he says something that he would later regret,' Dorenko said with a mischievous sparkle in his eyes. 'We never said that Andrei was the only business partner of his wife. Anyway, if Luzhkov were a real man, he would not involve his wife in it. This is not our Sicilian way. You and I, Yuri Mikhailovich,' Dorenko addressed the absent Luzhkov, 'we are two Dons: Don Sergio and Don Georgio. We must not involve your wife. You see, Don Georgio, I am still trying to defend your honour.' For the rest of the programme, Dorenko referred to Luzhkov as only a 'member of his wife's family'.[33]

He also accused Luzhkov of killing an American businessman, Paul Tatum, who was gunned down three years earlier in a murky dispute over the Radisson Slavyanskaya Hotel in central Moscow.

> Sensation. The family of Paul Tatum has filed a legal suit against Luzhkov in an American court. I am sure that Luzhkov won't be able to bribe the American courts at least for now, which means for the first time he will be tried by an independent court,' Dorenko announced on his television show. He then read out a press statement prepared by Tatum's lawyers as though it were a high court verdict. 'Luzhkov is responsible for committing the murder of Paul Tatum and is guilty of expropriating his property in Russia.[34]

The main point of Dorenko's show, however, was to ridicule Luzhkov and turn him into a laughing stock. 'I have a feeling that Luzhkov will soon be hunted by the law-enforcement agencies and will be put on the Interpol list. But our programme will come to his rescue. Let me make an official statement,' Dorenko said with a deadpan expression on his face. 'I will personally run away with Luzhkov. We will try to cross the border between Argentina and Paraguay – incognito. I don't need to disguise myself – nobody knows me anyway. But the member of his wife's family will have to change his appearance. We will dress him up as a man. Here are the options...' Dorenko then showed Luzhkov with a Fidel Castro beard and in a Che Guevara beret. And 'since none of those suited Luzhkov', he portrayed him with Monica Lewinsky's hair – 'in case he has to hide in America'. It was political assassination.[35]

Dorenko's treatment of Primakov was equally mesmerizing. In one of his most memorable programmes, he first accused Primakov of organizing an assassination attempt on Eduard Shevardnadze, Georgia's president, then – without much of a link – he showed bloody surgery being performed on someone in a Russian hospital. This, he said, was the kind of operation that Primakov was supposed to undergo in Switzerland. All Primakov had, in fact, was a standard hip replacement, but Dorenko turned it into a lengthy and graphic report in an operation theatre. It was not even Primakov's leg that was being cut up on television – but that hardly mattered.

For the appetizer, Dorenko told the audience, whose average income was $200 a month and most of whom had to put up with decrepit Soviet hospitals, that Primakov's treatment in an elite hospital in Berne could cost $45,000. 'Nobody here asks about the origins of the money. If any of you is planning to have the same operation the hospital will accept these tens of thousands of dollars in any convertible currency...' Then, for the main course, Dorenko produced gory details of the surgery itself and the risks it carried. 'First the doctors remove the top of the hip. As you can see it is fragile and easily crumbles. Then they replace it with an artificial joint. Part of this artificial hip is joined to the pelvic bone by screws. Then, as you can see, doctors widen the hollow space inside the hip bone and connect the second part of the artificial hip which is then fixed with cement.'

The camera showed a bloodied leg and surgeons drilling and banging on the bone with a hammer, while casually discussing the latest football results. Bang, bang, bang. 'This operation makes quite a morbid impression on a lay spectator,' Dorenko's correspondent told the audience, 'but the drill and the hammer are absolutely necessary for such surgery.' As a final nail, Dorenko argued that if one of Primakov's hips had given way, the other one would have to be replaced soon as well. The second operation, however, might wait until after the presidential elections, which meant Primakov would be masking problems with his health. 'But once he becomes president, he can leisurely take care of his health – for the next four years.' Dorenko's programme left no doubts:

Primakov was as old and unfit as Yeltsin. 'Since Primakov wants to be our leader, a full analogy with Yeltsin is completely justified,' Dorenko concluded cheerfully.[36] With Yeltsin's rating deteriorating along with his health, such an 'analogy' was more damaging to Primakov's political form than any surgery.

Primakov was so outraged by this demagoguery that he felt compelled to call and complain to Kiselev, Dorenko's rival at *Itogi*. Kiselev was on air and Primakov's call was put straight through to the studio. 'I am glad you are still on air, I have a chance to respond to the programme I just watched,' Primakov said. 'Do you mean our programme?' Kiselev asked, pleased with such a high-profile response. 'I mean Dorenko's programme – known for its "truthfulness, benevolence and integrity",' Primakov said. Kiselev was taken aback by this tactlessness, but Primakov continued: 'He said I was gravely ill and awaiting a serious operation. I want to reassure everyone that this is untrue... And also did you see that episode with Shevardnadze?' 'Unfortunately, I have not,' said Kiselev, live, 'I was myself on air.' 'Never mind,' sighed Primakov. If Dorenko did not finish off Primakov, Primakov did so himself. The call made him look ridiculous and weak.

If anyone was watching Kiselev's *Itogi*, it was certainly time to switch over to Dorenko's show. Kiselev, with his slow, deliberating manner, was no match for Dorenko's circus. It was like using a sword against a machine gun.

When he was not destroying Primakov and Luzhkov, Dorenko was interviewing and extolling Putin in every other programme, presenting him as the only alternative for the post of the president. At the beginning of Dorenko's anti-Luzhkov and anti-Primakov campaign, Primakov's rating was 32 per cent. Fifteen programmes later, it had fallen to just 8 per cent. Luzhkov's rating fell from 16 per cent to 2 per cent. Putin's rating rose from 2 per cent to 36 per cent.

Berezovsky praised Putin for providing the 'continuity of power' that would enable him, Berezovsky, 'to fulfil himself in Russia'. What attracted him to Putin, he said, was Putin's pledge not to reopen the question of privatization. 'Many people are unhappy about how property has been distributed. Even the billionaires are unhappy, because they think that a neighbour-billionaire got more than his peer. But Putin understands that any redistribution of property will result in real bloodshed.' He likened the situation with Putin to the 1996 elections when the oligarchs put their differences aside and agreed to support Yeltsin. 'Today there is a clear understanding that Putin is a man who should be supported by society, including the oligarchs.'[37]

Chubais, Berezovsky's old nemesis, agreed, stating on NTV's *Itogi*: 'If elections were held today, there is no other candidate other than Vladimir Vladimirovich Putin. There is no point in anyone else putting himself forward.' The impression was partly created by the media: Pavlovsky planted the idea of 'Putin's majority' in the media – even when Putin's rating was below 50 per cent. But one thing was clear: Putin, who had no political programme, clear ideology, or political party, hit key expectations and responded to frustrations which had been building up in Russia for some time. Kiselev on *Itogi* stopped showing Putin's rating altogether. Olson recalled Kiselev telling him: 'I don't understand these figures. And what I don't understand cannot be.'[38] Kiselev was not the only one, however, who found Putin's rating incomprehensible. How could this unremarkable man with no charisma, unmemorable features and a weak voice be seriously seen as a successor to Yeltsin?

But it was precisely the contrast with Yeltsin that made Putin 'sellable' to the Russian public. The popular support for Yeltsin, boosted by the threat of the communist victory in 1996, started to decline as soon as that threat was removed and was completely undermined by the 1998 crisis. Nearly half of the country felt that Yeltsin's years in power had brought nothing good to the country; what they had brought was economic crisis, inflation and the collapse of the Soviet Union. Only a quarter of Russians credited him with freedoms and democracy. The majority wanted him to go.

The trick was to transform Yeltsin's negative rating into Putin's positive one. In order to do so, Putin had to be portrayed at once as Yeltsin's opponent but also as someone who was anointed by him. 'Our aim was first to mobilize the remaining Yeltsin electorate and then the anti-Yeltsin electorate which was split between several parties. Putin was in an ideal position – he was already in power, which always appeals to Russian voters – but also looked opposite to Yeltsin,' Pavlovsky explained.[39]

He provided both 'continuity' and 'contrast'. Yeltsin was old, ailing and increasingly divorced from reality. Putin was young, sharp and energetic. Yeltsin had a large frame, a swollen face and grey hair. Putin was short, had chiselled features and thin hair. Putin could fly a military jet, pose on a warship, fight on a judo mat. He spoke clearly, calmly and decisively. After Yeltsin, who was quintessentially Russian – emotional, a drinker, impulsive – Putin seemed almost un-Russian. He was secretive, restrained, sober, unemotional and almost pedantic. In opinion-focus groups people described him as Germanic, a true Aryan character – an ideal Stierlitz.

The fact that Putin seemed to have come from nowhere, had no political 'baggage', was not associated with Perestroika or the communists, worked in his favour. Even in April 2000, when he was already elected as president, two-thirds of the Russian population said they knew little about Putin, despite his round-the-clock presence on the television screen. He could be ascribed any qualities. Putin was a man with no features, a perfect spy.

The close association between Putin and Yeltsin's family was the only line of attack left to our opponents, said Pavlovsky. The most effective way to free Putin from this association was for Yeltsin himself to resign early. This was a crucial part of the Putin 'succession' plan and Yeltsin agreed to it. However, he decided to wait until the December parliamentary elections to make sure that the pro-Putin Unity Party did well. The party itself was a purely artificial creation. It had no political agenda other than Putin himself. The job of the Kremlin spin-doctors was to link Putin with the Unity Party.

The party's fortunes were sealed the moment when Putin 'casually' appeared next to the party leader, Sergei Shoigu. The 'appearance', which lasted only a few seconds on the television screen, was carefully staged by his media managers, according to Pavlovsky, as was Putin's 'off-the-cuff' response to the question of 'whom he was planning to vote for in the parliamentary elections'. As a state official with no party affiliation, Putin said he was not supporting anyone, but, as an individual, he was planning to vote for Unity.

On *Itogi*, Kiselev protested that 'as a private person' Putin should speak in a '*banya* [bathhouse] or in a kitchen' rather than on television. But Putin's endorsement fitted in with the logic of a television game show and was worth more than any political programme or statement. 'Putin asked the audience to support him in his pursuit of power. In the popular imagination he was a [television] hero who was getting ever closer to his ultimate goal but might not succeed unless the "audience" gave him a baseball bat to club his enemies with,' Pavlovsky explained.[40]

The 'audience', used to this format – in which they pressed buttons or dialled a number in support of one character or another – obliged. In the December general elections, the Unity Party, which had been created only a few months earlier, won nearly 24 per cent of the votes. As the sociologist Yuri Levada wrote, 'In Soviet days the only party in the country declared itself in power. Now the state power declared itself the only right party in the country.'[41] Luzhkov's and Primakov's Fatherland–All Russia alliance was in third place with just 13 per cent. Within a year it would merge with Putin's Unity Party to form United Russia. Both Primakov and Luzhkov agreed not to stand in the presidential elections.

Yet to say that Putin's popularity was the result of media games or that Gusinsky's NTV lost out because it was less effective than Berezovsky's Channel One would be as untrue as to deny it. Victories have many parents. The oligarchs' idea that a few men could decide on the future president actually worked. But while the oligarchs, the media and political technologists fought battles, claimed victories and engaged in cunning projects, thinking they were the prime players, real events were taking place in the country which were outside their control but not beyond their ability to exploit in their own interests. As a politician, Putin may have been a media invention, but the events that turned him into a president were not.

A day before Putin's appointment as prime minister, a group of Chechen rebels led by Shamil Basayev staged an incursion into neighbouring Dagestan as part of his grand plan to create a Caucasus emirate. After an exchange of fire between Russian troops and Chechen rebels, Putin, with Yeltsin's blessing, ordered a military invasion of Chechnya, thus starting the second war in five years. As Putin said on 8 September, 'Russia is defending itself. We were attacked. And we must cast away all syndromes, including the syndrome of guilt.'

That night Moscow was shaken by the first in a series of explosions in residential apartment blocks which killed over 300 people and spread terror throughout the country. Nobody ever claimed responsibility for the bombings.

Malashenko was on his way to an airport in Spain to fly back to Moscow when he learned about the explosion.

> When the first apartment block was bombed, I did not want to believe this was the work of Chechen terrorists. But after the second bombing, I realized that this was the end, that the whole situation had changed, that there would be no more "normal" television, that everything we had worked towards was over... It was like watching an avalanche moving towards you with the speed of a train when you know you can neither stop it nor jump aside.[42]

The bombings, he understood, would give Putin and the security services complete carte blanche in restoring the state. In 1994 NTV was able to counter it. This time, public opinion was against them.

Malashenko's fears were fully borne out. The apartment explosions were a turning point both towards Putin and also towards the war in Chechnya. Its impact on people's minds was similar to the bombing of the New York Twin Towers two years later. Until that moment Chechnya was seen as a black hole, a lawless territory where people got kidnapped and killed by bearded terrorists. Only four days earlier, a similar explosion had ripped through a residential block in the small town of Buynaksk in Dagestan, killing sixty-four people, twenty-three of whom were children. But even that was 'somewhere over there', behind the television screen.

On 9 September, shortly after midnight, the 'television screen' got shattered. Millions of people momentarily experienced the same emotion of fear and danger in their own lives. This was not something happening on television. It was happening to them. They came out of their houses, organizing watch groups to stand guard and look for suspicious clues. Conspiracy theories started to circulate almost immediately.

This was prompted by the discovery of bags with explosives in Ryazan', a city south of Moscow. The residents who spotted the bags called the police, who initially confirmed they contained an explosive. The Russian interior minister told the parliament that a terrorist attack had been foiled. Then, half an hour later, the head of the FSB said this was, in fact, a civil defence exercise and the suspicious bags contained sugar not hexogen, a white crystalline explosive. Many people smelled a rat. Perhaps the FSB was behind the previous bombing and had just botched this one, or maybe the terrorists were assisted by Berezovsky who wanted to boost Putin's rating. Warranted or not, the desperate search for conspiracies revealed one thing: people were prepared and willing to think that everything happening in the country was orchestrated by someone behind the stage. NTV hosted a discussion about the Ryazan' incident, which irked the Kremlin. Yet, however warranted or not the conspiracy theories were, they did not change the fact that the explosions were real.

Putin was away in New Zealand when the first explosion ripped through a block of flats. When he came back, a few days later, he appeared on television, making a statement, looking shell-shocked. This, said Olson, who was measuring Putin's rating every week, was the moment when people first 'saw and recognized Putin'. When he came to pay his respects to the victims, he said what everyone felt: 'Incredible. Unbelievable. Inhuman cruelty.' The explosions, he said, were a threat to the existence of the Russian state. 'We have to use force, there is no other way.'

It was not what Putin said and what he did. It was the way he looked and sounded that allowed people to identify themselves with him. His appearance resonated with the feelings of millions of people, causing something of a 'short circuit' moment, according to Olsen. Suddenly, Putin, a bland, 'accidental' man, the joker in a pack of cards, turned into an ace. He was a 'hero' that people did not even know existed before. People turned to Putin as their only hope, a man who was capable of defending them whatever it took. He was offering to take responsibility and deal with a problem which they were unwilling and unable to deal with. A few weeks later Putin delivered the words which became his hallmark for years to come: 'We will pursue them everywhere. If it is in the airport, then in the airport. If we catch them in the toilet, we'll wipe them out in the shit-hole. That is it. Subject closed.'

Putin was different from other politicians; in fact, he did not behave or talk like a politician at all – he talked like an ordinary man, like the guy next door. 'The meaning of Putin's words was not just that we are going to be tough, but also "who are these Chechens for us to be afraid of"' Pavlovsky explained.[43] In his streetwise talk and his readiness to fight against Chechens who terrorized the country, he matched a character from one of the most important post-Soviet films. It was called *Brat* (*Brother*) and told the story of a young, open-faced, charismatic Russian, Danila

Bagrov, who after serving his two-year conscription in Chechnya, returns to a criminalized St Petersburg. His older brother, a small-time gangster, asks Danila to help him eliminate competitors – ethnic Chechens – who control street-market trade in the city. Danila turns into a hitman who administers justice like Robin Hood, helping the poor and homeless along the way and eliminating the 'dirt' from the streets.

In one of the opening scenes of the first *Brat* movie, Danila confronts two swarthy, heavily accented men – obviously from the Caucasus – who cockily refuse to pay a fine for riding on a trolley-bus without a ticket. Danila takes out a gun and points it at the crotch of one of the loud-mouths. 'Don't shoot, brother,' says the terrified Caucasian man. 'I am not a brother to you, you black-arsed shit,' Danila replies. He then takes his wallet, pays the fine, drops it on the floor and tells them to run. Danila was Russia's first real hero – strong, charismatic, sincere, simple and organic.

The film was released in 1997 – the same year as Elena Masyuk, the NTV journalist, was kidnapped in Chechnya. It was a huge success, mainly because it captured the shift in the mood towards Chechnya and the first, almost unconscious, signs of rising nationalist resentment towards the outside world. When, in the spring of 1999, Putin's spin-doctors surveyed the attitude of the Russian public towards different fictional characters, Danila from *Brat* was up there along with Stierlitz.

Like Danila, Putin came from 'nowhere' into this ugly and cruel world to protect his 'brothers'.* Just like *Brat*, Putin effectively licensed and justified the use of extra-judicial force. Like Danila he was a strong and positive character unconstrained by political correctness and Western convention. Dorenko, in his programmes, also appealed to the image of Putin as a 'brother', contrasting him with Primakov. 'I was whispering to the audience: "Look, we have a father, Primakov, who while he may mean

* A member of a criminal gang in Russia was often described as '*bratok*' – a diminutive of 'brother'.

well, is too ill and can't fight, but we have a brother, a bro, who is strong, decisive and will defend us."'[44]

Dorenko, who regularly travelled to Chechnya with the Russian army, had a message for Putin, whom he interviewed every couple of weeks. 'Every time I saw him we talked about Chechnya: "The army wants more, more fighting, heavier, more aggressive, please, let's advance deeper into Chechnya," I told him. And every time Putin's eyes lit up. "Are you prepared to say it on air?" he asked. "Me – I am screaming about it every week!" I told him. Bomb it, burn it with napalm along with the people, destroy, kill. We had to press a button and destroy it.'[45]

The button in Dorenko's hands belonged to television and he used it to the same effect. He was among the first reporters into Grozny when the Russian military finally took it over after levelling it to the ground. Dressed in black, he reported from the central square of Chechnya's capital, with Russian APCs driving around in the background. He leaned over military maps as the commander of the Russian forces explained his army's disposition and showed the minefields where hundreds of Chechen soldiers had met their death. He interviewed Russian soldiers who told him that Chechen fighters should not be allowed to return to their cities. Those who had stopped the war in 1996 were traitors. Putin, who allowed them to finish the job, was obviously a hero.

On *Itogi*, Kiselev tried to say something about an 'excess' of force and human rights abuses in Chechnya, about the criticism from the West – as though the West still mattered. His words drowned in the general support for the war. The coverage of the second Chechen war could barely have been more different from the first one. One practical reason was that journalists were barred from entering what the Kremlin described as a 'counter-terrorist zone' without special permission from the Russian security services. Whereas in the first war much of the reporting had been done from the Chechen side, the only footage emerging from Chechnya in the second war was from the Russian army side. While in the first war even soldiers, interviewed on camera, had talked about the senseless violence they themselves had perpetrated, in the second war soldiers talked about 'Russian unity'. 'It is our land. Our core is our *vlast* [state power],' one soldier told an NTV correspondent.

A minority made up of old Soviet intelligentsia types and human rights activists opposed it. Grigory Yavlinsky, the leader of the liberal Yabloko Party, called for negotiations with Maskhadov, the Chechen president. But most of those who were still called young liberal reformers were firmly on Putin's side. As Chubais said in response to Yavlinsky: 'The war in Chechnya is the rebirth of the Russian army; it reinforces faith in the army and any politician who thinks otherwise... is a traitor.'[46]

Gusinsky and Malashenko, who were against the war, could barely control their own television. Malashenko recalls watching video footage on NTV which showed the beheading of a Russian hostage by Chechen fighters. 'The image had enormous power and I called Dobrodeev to ask him why he had decided to show it without even warning us. He told me that Rushailo [the interior minister] asked him to do it. It was clear that Dobrodeev engaged in war propaganda.'[47] Dobrodeev understood the change of mood and not only 'jumped aside' from the approaching avalanche, but decided to ride its wave.

Shortly after the beginning of the war, Dobrodeev gave an interview entitled 'The Army: These Are Our Brothers and Sons' to *Krasnaya Zvezda* (*Red Star*), an army newspaper, saying, 'When in real time the defence ministry generals are giving you information, you don't have to ask anyone for anything else...' The army and the media, he asserted, are doing one job and anyone who tried to create an impression that there is a wall between us – is wrong. 'It is clear that Russia will soon enter a new stage of its development. We cannot live like we lived before,' he said.[48] A few months later, Dobrodeev left NTV, which he had helped to set up, and was appointed the head of the state television. It was from this high and comfortable chair that Dobrodeev observed Putin destroy NTV and expel its founders. The time of the pro-Western individualists who had put themselves above the state was coming to an end.

SEVEN

Remote Control

On New Year's Eve 1999 Boris Yeltsin, by way of the traditional televised seasonal greeting to the nation, announced that he was stepping down as president and was passing the reins of power to Vladimir Putin. 'Russia has to enter the new millennium with new politicians, with new faces, with clever, strong and energetic people. And we, who were in power for many years, we must leave. I am leaving... Russia will never go to its past. Russia will always move only forward. And I must not stand in the way of history.'

It was an emotional and moving speech. Yeltsin asked to be pardoned by those who 'believed that we could, in one big swing, in one thrust, jump from a grey, totalitarian past into a bright, rich and civilized future. I believed this myself... It seemed one thrust and we would do it. We did not... I've done all I could. A new generation is coming to replace me – a generation of those who can do more and better.'

Yeltsin's speech was followed, without as much as a pause, by Putin's greeting. 'Today I am entrusted with acting as the head of state... There will be no vacuum of power in the country – not for one minute. Any attempt to move outside the constitution will be decisively put down.'

A few hours earlier, Yeltsin had left the Kremlin for the last time. Handing over a case with nuclear codes and the pen with which he had signed his resignation and Putin's appointment, he told Putin: 'Take care... Take care of Russia.' Television showed the two men standing shoulder to shoulder in Yeltsin's office – a tall, towering figure with grey hair on his way out, a slim, short one on his way in.

The transfer of power seemed seamless. The ritual was unmistakably staged – the New Year's address by the leader of the country had greater symbolic value than any election. Putin *was* the president. The actual presidential election three months later only confirmed the fact. Putin's appointment represented continuity but also a visual contrast. By the time the country watched Yeltsin's successor make his New Year's statement, Putin was already in Chechnya. Celebratory programmes that night were interrupted by images of Putin in a parka, flanked by men in military uniforms, handing out awards to Russian soldiers. 'This [war] is not just about restoring the honour and dignity of the country. It is about putting an end to the disintegration of Russia,' Putin said.

In contrast to Yeltsin, who for better or worse saw Russia as a nation, Putin saw it first and foremost as a state and himself as its guardian, *gosudarstvennik* or statist. Two days before Putin was formally entrusted with Russia, Putin published his manifesto 'Russia on the Threshold of the New Millennium', that hailed the state as a key driver of Russia's success and a force of consolidation. Russia did not need state ideology, the manifesto argued. Its ideology, its national idea, was the state. Personal rights of freedom were all well and good, but they could not provide the strength and security of the state. Russia, he asserted, would never become a second edition of Britain or America where liberal values had deep historic traditions. Russia had its own traditional, core values. These were patriotism, collectivism and *derzhavnost* – a tradition of being a great geopolitical state power that commands the attention of other countries – and *gosudarstvennichestvo*, the primacy of the state.

> For Russians, a strong state is not an anomaly to fight against. Quite the contrary, it is the source and guarantor of order, the initiator and the

> main driving force of any change. Society desires the restoration of the guiding and regulating role of the state. In Russia, a collective form of life has always dominated over individualism. It is also a fact that paternalism is deeply grounded in Russian society. The majority of Russians associate the improvement in their lives not so much with their own endeavours, initiative and entrepreneurship but with the help and support of the state... And we can't ignore them.[1]

It is tempting to project our knowledge of the current state of Russia and Putin onto the early years of Putin's presidency; to describe Russia's descent into a nationalistic corporatist state as part of a premeditated plan. In fact, few people paid attention to Putin's statement at the time. Even fewer were alarmed by it.

Putin's millennium message, drafted by Pavlovsky, reflected not just what Putin thought but also what people wanted to hear from him. An opinion poll conducted in January 2000 found that 55 per cent of the Russian population expected Putin to return Russia to the status of a great and respected *derzhava* and that only 8 per cent expected him to bring Russia closer to the West.[2] As a man with a KGB background, Putin was clearly a statist, but he was also free of any ideology and in the minds of most Russians this did not contradict the idea of capitalism. Quite the opposite.

Many Russian liberals perceived Putin as an authoritarian modernizer who would restore the functioning of the state and economy. The media saw Putin as a blank sheet onto which they could write their own narrative. The corridor of opportunities, which was quite wide, was to be narrowed by those who were in charge of that narrative. The educated, well-off, Westernized middle class saw him as a centre-right, economically liberal president – a Russian version of Augusto Pinochet.

Five days after Putin's formal election as president, Peter Aven, the head of Alfa Bank, Russia's largest private bank, and a long-term acquaintance of Putin's, evoked Pinochet as a model in an interview with the *Guardian*. 'I'm a supporter of Pinochet not as a person but as a politician who produced results for his country. He was not corrupt. He supported his team of economists for ten years. You need strength for that. I see that parallel here. There are similarities in the situation.'[3] If the president had to use authoritarian means to further reforms, so be it, Aven argued. Putin's KGB past did not worry Russian liberal journalists much. Stigmatizing Putin because of his former intelligence work seemed like a form of social discrimination. Those who did object to Putin on the basis of his KGB past were considered marginal dissidents, intelligentsia, or *demshiza* or *demskitz* – a pejorative shortening of 'democratic schizophrenics'.

The Union of Right Forces, a liberal economic party led by Gaidar, Nemtsov, Chubais and businesswoman Irina Khakamada, and which received a respectable 8.5 per cent in the parliamentary elections in 1999, campaigned under the slogan 'Putin to the Kremlin, Kiriyenko to Parliament'. Nemtsov, who voted against supporting Putin, was overruled. The night after the December parliamentary elections of 1999, Putin attended a post-election party held by the Union of Right Forces and raised a toast 'to our common victory'.

The next day, Putin gathered the leaders of all the winning factions in his office and joined in a toast to Stalin raised by the communist leader, Gennady Zyuganov, on the occasion of the 120th anniversary of the tyrant's birth. Putin, whose grandfather had been a cook in Stalin's court, did not cringe. To Putin, Stalin was not a symbol of repression, but the ultimate expression of state power. Putin was neither a Stalinist nor a liberal. As a man who had been trained to be a spy, he was nondescript and had skills for mimicry. He could assume whatever personality best suited the situation to win the trust and sympathy of his interlocutor. His ability to perform and to blend in made people who talked to him feel that he shared their views.

As someone who had observed Soviet economic failure, who, as a KGB officer in Dresden, understood the advantages of the capitalist West Germany over the socialist East Germany (the GDR) and was exposed to business as a deputy mayor in St Petersburg in charge of foreign trade, Putin had few illusions about the planned economy. His early economic programme, including a low flat-rate income tax system, was arguably more liberal than anything Russia had had in the past. His economic adviser, Andrei Illarionov, was a convinced libertarian and his Finance Minister, Alexei Kudrin, a member of Chubais's and Gaidar's circle. Putin did not set out to dismantle capitalism – far from it.

The first years of Putin's rule filled the Russian middle class with optimism, even exuberance. The oil price started to rise; Russian economic growth surged at 10 per cent; disposable incomes were growing even faster. The central and simple message of Putin's rule was: we will give you security, stability and a sense of pride, shops full of goods and the ability to travel abroad without bothering you with ideology. It was the dream of the late 1980s come true. All that the Kremlin asked in return was for people to mind their own business and stay out of politics – something that they gladly did. Lifestyle changes were more interesting than politics. The first IKEA store had just opened in Moscow and middle-class Russians, like everyone else in Europe, were too busy assembling their Scandinavian-style homes to care about politics.

Suddenly there were coffee shops where people could sip cappuccinos while reading *Vedomosti* – a Russian business daily part-owned by the *Financial Times* and the *Wall Street Journal*. There were new Western-style cinemas, home-grown musicals, skating rinks and fitness clubs. To guide people through the new lifestyle opportunities there was a new glossy weekly called *Afisha* (*Playbill*). It was conceived as Russia's equivalent of *Time Out* but, as ever in Russia, it was more than that. In the same way that *Kommersant* had 'programmed' the 'new Russians' and NTV had shaped the tastes and values of the middle class and self-reliant businessmen, *Afisha* drafted the image of a young, educated, urban and Europeanized class of people – the children of the intelligentsia, who shunned the very word along with the preoccupations of their parents.

As Ilya Tsentsiper, one of the founders and first editors of *Afisha*, said, his readers were somewhere in between a creative media class and young urban professionals – yuppies. *Afisha* described Moscow as a European capital city – no different from, say, Berlin or Madrid. 'In many ways *Afisha* itself was a confirmation that Moscow was the same [European] city as others,' Tsentsiper argued. 'All this coincided with Putin's era – everyone around us started to get richer and some different narrative emerged after the years of chaos and uncertainty. People started to think about their long-term future. People started to have children and dogs and all this "live fast, die young" lost its attractions. On the ruins of an empire a new life started to grow, full of extraordinary energy.'[4] Soon *Afisha* started to publish guidebooks for mobile, English-speaking and independent travellers. The readers of *Afisha* and *Vedomosti* and the voters of the Union of Right Forces considered themselves liberals, but they wished for the state to provide their liberties, comforts and stability.

Essential to the narrative of 'stabilization' was the portrayal of the 1990s as an era of total chaos and banditry. The irony was that this image was formed as much by the television of the 2000s as it was by the reality of the Yeltsin era. In May 2000, NTV aired one of its most popular soap operas called *Banditskii Peterburg* (*Gangsters' Petersburg*) about organized crime bosses, known in Russia as 'crowned thieves-in-law', contract killings and bent cops. It was a true carnival of banditry in which the only positive figure was a local journalist who tried to solve crimes but ended up getting people killed. Russia in the 1990s had certainly provided rich material for crime fiction – the Soviet collapse opened up opportunities for colourful gangsters – but it was the TV dramas of the 2000s that turned crime into the dominant characteristic of the 1990s. The fact that Putin was the flesh-and-blood of the 1990s and had served in the St Petersburg administration precisely at the time in which *Gangsters' Petersburg* was set was negated by the narrative of stabilization.

One of Putin's first symbolic steps as president was the restoration of the Soviet national anthem which was originally composed in 1938 – the height of Stalin's great terror – as a hymn to the Bolshevik Party and later adopted as an anthem. Yeltsin abandoned it along with other Soviet symbols, replacing it with Mikhail Glinka's wordless 'Patriotic Song'. After meeting Russian sportsmen, who apparently complained that they could no longer sing along to the national anthem, Putin proposed bringing back the old tune, albeit with new lyrics that were promptly supplied by the author of two previous Soviet versions. To say that the Russians were longing for the restoration of the Soviet anthem was untrue. Most people did not care.

The act of restoring something that had been once abolished for ideological reasons carried its own meaning. Alexander Yakovlev saw it as a sign of disrespect for the country's past, of a lack of 'Christian feeling of repentance'. 'For as long as I live I will neither sing nor stand up to this music. This is not my anthem. It is the anthem of a different country – different not just in name but in its substance. We are a new country, a free Russia, and we want to be free people.'[5] In fact, neither Yeltsin nor Putin saw Russia as a new country, but as a continuation of the old one. But while Yeltsin and his ideologues searched for symbols of Russia's statehood in the pre-Revolutionary era, rejecting the Soviet period as something ideologically alien, Putin made the next logical step: he incorporated the Soviet past into a narrative of Russia as a great state.

The liberals who rejected Soviet history and demanded repentance were cast as sectarians. 'Perhaps I and the people [of Russia] are mistaken, but I want to address those who disagree with this decision [to restore the Soviet anthem]. I ask you not to dramatize events and not to build unbreachable barriers, not to burn bridges and not to split society once again,' Putin told the Duma.[6] Putin's formulation, 'I and the people', was, in fact, more alarming than the anthem.

The revival of the old Soviet anthem, previously known as the hymn of the Bolshevik Party, coincided with the consecration of the Cathedral of Christ the Saviour, which had been destroyed by the Bolsheviks and was restored by Luzhkov. The clash of symbols did not bother Putin. Both were symbols of Russian statehood. This is why, perhaps, one person who did not object to Putin's decision was the Russian patriarch, Alexei II. The media-savvy middle class, the readers of *Afisha*, cringed, but saw in it the spirit of a postmodernist political game where nothing could or should be taken seriously, since everything was just an imitation, be it the cathedral or the anthem. The revival of the Soviet anthem did not signal a return to the Soviet Union, but it signalled the beginning of restoration as a historic trend that usually follows a revolution.

So, on the eve of the new millennium and the tenth anniversary of the Soviet collapse, the country clinked glasses to the tune of the Soviet anthem. It was also a powerful statement that Putin did not see freedom and post-Soviet political order as the essence of the new country called Russia, but only as a decoration that could be dismantled as easily as a theatrical set. As the astute columnist Kirill Rogov wrote at the time, like any symbolic act, the restoration of the Soviet anthem had practical consequences that were beyond the will of its authors. The symbol was first. The meaning came later.[7]

Unlike Yeltsin, Putin felt no alienation from the Soviet past. A year earlier he had unveiled a plaque and laid flowers to Yuri Andropov, who had been the head of the KGB at the time when Putin as a young man joined the organization. Andropov, who died only nineteen months after becoming the head of the Soviet Union, was seen as an enlightened and authoritarian modernizer. His short stint at the helm of the country contributed to a myth that he could have transformed the Soviet Union into a functioning economy, while keeping the country together, had he not died prematurely at the age of seventy.

It was not just the liberals who tried to wind back the tape of history and find the point where things had gone wrong – so did the *siloviki* who saw Putin's promotion to the top post in the country as a chance to fulfil Andropov's ideas.*

Like most people who served in the KGB, Putin had little respect for Gorbachev and saw him not as a man who gave Russia freedom, but as someone who had lost the country and the job as a result of his weakness. As Putin said many years later, a person who does not regret the collapse of the Soviet Union has no heart and one who wishes to restore it has no brain. Putin certainly had a brain. He did not try to restore the Soviet Union; he saw his mission in preventing further disintegration. And since it was Gorbachev's liberalization of the media that had undermined the Soviet system, he had no intention of repeating that mistake.

'Magic TV Comb'

Boris Nemtsov recalled visiting Putin in his office soon after his election as president. It was the same office Nemtsov had visited many times when Yeltsin was president. 'We had a conversation and in the middle of it, Putin asked me if I minded watching the 3 p.m. news. It was odd. I looked around the familiar office. Nothing seemed to have changed there. Apart from one thing. The only object that had been on Yeltsin's otherwise empty desk was his pen – it was the pen that he gave to Putin when he signed his own resignation. Putin's desk was also empty, but the

* Soon after being appointed prime minister, Putin half-jokingly told an assembly of intelligence officers on the anniversary of the foundation of the Soviet secret police: 'The intelligence operatives planted inside the Russian government have successfully completed the first stage of the operation.'

pen was gone. Instead, Putin had a TV remote control on his desk,' said Nemtsov.[8] (Nemtsov could hardly have imagined that he would fall victim to the hatred that this remote control of television would incite in Russia a decade and a half later.)

That remote control was to become one of Putin's tools, the sceptre of his power. Unlike Yeltsin, who had rarely watched himself on television and simply turned off the channels he disliked, Putin developed an obsession with television. At the end of each day he watched how the different channels covered him. Having observed the role played by television in his own coming to power and the destruction of Primakov and Luzhkov, Putin knew that the power of the oligarchs lay in their control over the media and he did not wish to leave it in their hands.

In January 2000 NTV showed a scathing *Kukly* sketch based on E. T. A. Hoffmann's novella *Klein Zaches, genannt Zinnober* (1819) – the story of a small town that blindly takes an ugly dwarf Zaches for a beautiful youth, thanks to the magic spell cast by a fairy who has pity on Zaches. Whatever little Zaches does elicits adulation and he turns into a minister. In the end, one of the characters finds that Zaches's magical power is contained in the three hairs on his head. The hairs are pulled out and Zaches loses the spell and drowns in a chamber pot. *Kukly* showed a puppet Yeltsin cradling a dwarf with Putin's face. Berezovsky was cast as the 'fairy' who combs the dwarf's hair with a 'magic TV comb', thus turning him in the eyes of all Russian officials into a wise and handsome president.

The *Kukly* skit was aired a few months before the presidential elections – just as the state television channels showed Putin, with great adulation, flying a military jet from his residence in Sochi to Grozny, posing on a submarine and inspecting a farm. The parody cut too close to the bone, particularly given Putin's lack of height. According to Russian media reports, Putin took it personally.

A few weeks later, a Soviet-style letter was published in a small St Petersburg newspaper denouncing *Kukly*'s programme as a criminal act.

'*Kukly* has evoked a feeling of deep outrage and indignation by misusing the freedom of speech,' the letter said.[9] One of the signatories was promptly appointed by Putin as his 'trusted representative' in the presidential campaign. Soon, prosecutors opened an investigation against Gusinsky and his Media Most group.

Viktor Shenderovich, the scriptwriter of *Kukly*, received a message – apparently from the Kremlin – saying that the attack on Media Most would stop if NTV fulfilled three conditions: changed its coverage of Chechnya; halted its criticism of the 'family'; and removed 'the first person', that is, Putin, from *Kukly*. In response, Shenderovich publicized the message and made an even more provocative skit based on the Bible, in which Putin was portrayed as God. His puppet did not make an appearance, though: he was represented by a burning bush and a stormy cloud. Chief of Staff Voloshin was Moses conveying the Ten Commandments: 'Don't kill anyone, except people of Caucasus nationality in a shit-hole' and 'Don't have any other gods apart from Him – at least for two terms' and 'Don't steal unless it is federal property'. Asked how 'He' should be referred to, Voloshin said: 'Just call him Lord God, abbreviated as GB.' In Russian, GB stood for KGB.

If that was not enough, on 24 March, just two days before Putin was elected president, NTV aired a talk show called *Nezavisimoe rassledovanie* (*Independent Investigation*) that questioned the official version of the apartment block explosions in the autumn of 1999. It focused on the foiled apartment bombing in Ryazan. The programme's host interviewed former and present FSB officers and tenants of the apartment block who had discovered the bags of a white substance that was first identified as hexogen, but which the FSB later claimed was sugar. While the programme did not prove anything definitively, it certainly raised the strong suspicion that the FSB was concealing the truth and had actually tried to blow up the apartments for real. Putin saw this as a deliberate and subversive attack timed for the elections.

On 11 May, only four days after Putin's pompous inauguration, the offices of Media Most were raided by armed men in camouflage uniform and in black ski masks. There was little doubt that the raid had received a green light from Putin, who was shown that day on television talking about democracy and the freedom of speech to Ted Turner, the founder and owner of CNN. The raid reminded everyone of the winter of 1995 when Gusinsky's security guards were made to lie face down on the snow by Korzhakov's men. At the time, however, NTV was on the ascent and history was on its side. This time NTV was sailing against the wind.

On 13 June 2000 Gusinsky was arrested and put into one of Moscow's oldest, flea-ridden jails without any clear charges and with no connection made to previous investigations. Malashenko was on holiday in Spain where Putin was about to begin his first post-election tour. Despite the Russian security services' best efforts, Malashenko called a press conference in Madrid in a hotel across the street from the one where Putin was staying. 'Today Russia got its first political prisoner,' Malashenko announced to a room packed with journalists who were supposed to be covering Putin's visit. 'His name is Vladimir Alexandrovich Gusinsky.' As Putin moved to Berlin, so did Malashenko. 'I was sitting in Gusinsky's small Challenger on the runway in Madrid and we had to wait to let the presidential jet take off.'[10] The double-act continued: Putin talked about the investment climate in Russia, Malashenko about the politically motivated case against a private company.

Foreign journalists loved the drama that was unfolding in front of them. Instead of Putin, newspapers made a splash with Gusinsky. Putin said he knew nothing about the case. 'I hope the prosecutor has sufficient reasons for this step,' he said, adding that he could not get through to him on the phone. Everyone knew Putin was lying and Putin knew that they knew, but this was within the remits of his power: as a former spy, a modern-day Stierlitz, Putin had a licence to use decoy and deceit as his fighting tactic – especially in Berlin. NTV, on the other hand, fell back on its tactic of 'explosive armour', putting on a special edition of a popular talk show to discuss Gusinsky's arrest. The most unexpected guest on the television progamme was Dorenko.

> We thought that the old system was broken over these ten years. We dumped the robots. They have been lying there. And they have stirred and started moving again, as if they have heard some music. Today the security structures throughout the whole country are taking a message from Putin's rise to power... They hear music that we don't hear, and they get up like zombies and walk. They surround us. And they will go far if there is silence... We need to bash them over the head every day.[11]

Coming from Dorenko who had extolled Putin, such a level of solidarity seemed odd. Putin was so put off by Dorenko's appearance that he called him in for a chat a few days later. 'We want you on our team,' he told the 'TV killer'. In answer, Dorenko said, 'I am not part of anyone's team. You and I have a relationship – let's just keep it this way.' But he also told Putin that by attacking Gusinsky he was sending the wrong signal to security men throughout the country. When Putin indicated that Dorenko could be handsomely rewarded for his services, Dorenko felt belittled. He recalled walking out of Putin's office shouting on his mobile phone to Berezovsky: 'What have you done, Borya? What the fuck have you done?'[12]

The reasons for the stand-off between NTV and the Kremlin went far deeper than the Kremlin's dissatisfaction with NTV's programmes. It was a fundamental conflict between individualists and private barons on the one hand and statists on the other. Television channels controlled by the oligarchs may not have been objective, but they were independent of the state. Whatever Gusinsky's faults, he had used his brain and energy to create something from scratch. As Gaidar warned back in 1994, a bureaucrat is always a greater source of corruption than a businessman. 'A businessman can enrich himself honestly. A bureaucrat can only enrich himself dishonestly. The carcass of a bureaucratic and punitive system can become a carcass of a mafia state – the only question is the goals of its actions.'[13]

In relation to Gusinsky, the state certainly behaved like a mafia. While Gusinsky was in jail, the Kremlin dispatched Press Minister Mikhail Lesin, a former seller of NTV's airtime, to negotiate with Malashenko about the 'ransom' of his boss. The Kremlin's condition for dropping charges and releasing Gusinsky was that he sold NTV to Gazprom, the state-controlled gas monopoly, for $300 million and a debt write-off. If he disagreed, he would share a cell with prisoners infected with AIDS and TB. Gusinsky agreed to sell and three days later walked out of jail on the further condition that he would not leave Moscow until he signed the deal.

After several weeks of intense talks, Gusinsky signed the sales contract, though not before secretly telling his American lawyers that he was acting under duress. Cunningly, Gusinsky also demanded that Lesin attach an appendix guaranteeing his freedom to the contract, which Lesin did, thus providing Gusinsky with crucial evidence of political pressure that was later used in the European Court of Human Rights. On 26 July 2000, a few days after his signing the papers, the prosecutors, without any explanation, dropped all charges against Gusinsky. The same day he and Malashenko boarded a plane and left Russia, hoping to return before too long. (Malashenko returned after nine years; Gusinsky is still waiting.)

The attack on Gusinsky reopened an old debate between 'fathers and sons'. The old intelligentsia recognized the old Soviet methods in the actions of the Kremlin. *Obshchaya gazeta*, first printed during the August 1991 coup when the putsch leaders shut down all independent press, and revived by Yegor Yakovlev as a reincarnation of his old *Moskovskie novosti*, argued that Gusinsky was fighting not just for his business, but also for dignity and justice which had been trampled on by the Kremlin. The 'children' – those who had started *Kommersant* – responded with contempt and derision.

Alexander Timofeevsky, who assisted Putin in his election campaign, said a few weeks later: 'What dictatorship, what terrors? I can't see a single sign of terror. I see chimeras of the intelligentsia's consciousness, but no terror.' Timofeevsky, who praised *Kommersant* for modelling reality, now accused NTV of twisting it: 'Gusinsky's media did not describe reality, but created it and sold its creation.' Timofeevsky ridiculed Gusinsky's intelligentsia as 'all those throbbing hearts that so love the small, distant but proud people of Chechnya'.[14] In fact, the main reason Gusinsky's NTV opposed the war in Chechnya both in 1994 and in 1999 was based on the premise that a state that kills its own people in Chechnya would break any laws.

Maxim Sokolov, who personified the values of liberalism in *Kommersant*, wrote on the day of Gusinsky's departure: 'Those who fight against the state and its deadly interference (much exaggerated in the case of freedom of speech) are right that there is nothing pleasant in such interference. They assume that the alternative to such interference is the individual, independent of the state both economically and spiritually.'[15] But, Sokolov argued, Media Most had cynically used the notion of freedom of speech to defend its own right to interfere, dictate and regulate. So, in the end, Sokolov concluded, it is all a matter of taste. Timofeevsky and Sokolov, who so despised the Soviet era, acted in its finest tradition: denouncing someone who had been forced out of the country. This time it was not a question of ideology but of simple ethics.

Soon after Gusinsky's departure, an NTV correspondent who worked in the Kremlin pool asked Putin about his relationship with the tycoon. 'I can talk to him now, if you like. Do you have his number?' Putin asked playfully. Seconds later, Putin was talking to Gusinsky in front of several other journalists. There was a rich history of 'theatrical' telephone calls made by the country's leader to disgraced artists, starting with Stalin's famous call to Mikhail Bulgakov, but unlike the playwright who was struggling to survive in Moscow, Gusinsky was sailing on his yacht in Spain. Putin agreed to meet with Gusinsky, implying he could return to Moscow after the summer holidays. It seemed like a good sign.

But August is a dangerous time in Russia and when the rest of the world goes quiet, things start happening: political coups, financial defaults, wars in the Caucasus. That year was no exception. On 12 August, two powerful explosions ripped through the Russian nuclear submarine the *Kursk* with 118 crew members on board. Most of the men died instantly, but 23 members of the crew managed to seal themselves off in a rear compartment of the vessel while it sank into sand 350 feet (106.5 m) below the sea's surface.

The Russian military responded in a familiar way – it lied, tried to cover things up, and arrogantly refused foreign help. The navy, which at first said nothing at all, provided contradictory accounts. It claimed that it was communicating with the crew by knocking on the hull of the submarine, that it was providing the crew with oxygen through special tubes, that its rescue operation was obstructed by storms and a strong current – all of which later turned out to be untrue.

On the day of Russia's worst ever submarine catastrophe, Putin went to Sochi on holiday. He decided not to interrupt his vacation and kept silent for four days. Stories about the suntanned Putin jet-skiing with his family and 'scaring off fish' clashed with the footage of the distraught relatives of the *Kursk* sailors. NTV questioned the official line and demanded answers to why the military was refusing offers of foreign rescue assistance. 'When a country thinks about the lives of its soldiers and sailors, national pride does not usually suffer,' NTV's correspondent bitterly told the viewers. Channel One drew parallels between the Kremlin's handling of the *Kursk* disaster with the shameful attempts to cover up the Chernobyl nuclear explosion in 1986. Putin was furious.

While the lies about Chernobyl in the end triggered the opening up of the media, the *Kursk* disaster had the opposite effect. Television journalists were barred from entering the garrison town, Vidyaevo, the base of the submarine crew. Even when Putin, dressed in black, came to Vidyaevo to meet the relatives on 22 August, only a handful of reporters was let into the hall. No recording equipment was allowed. The only television camera was placed behind soundproof glass in the top gallery. The sound was relayed separately into a television van and apparently edited by plain-clothed FSB specialists. A full record, secretly taped by one of *Kommersant*'s journalists, showed that Putin was more furious about the television coverage than he was about the attempts to cover up the incident. He saw the role of the media not in informing the audience, but in keeping things from it.

'Television? They are lying! They are lying! They are lying!' he fumed. He blamed the dire state of the army and the navy on the oligarchs. 'There are people in television who shout louder than anyone today [about the state of the navy] and who over the past ten years have destroyed that same army and navy where people are dying today. And today they pose as the army's biggest defenders in order to discredit and ruin it completely. They have stolen so much money that they are buying everyone and everything.'[16]

After his return from Vidyaevo, Putin met with the journalists from the Kremlin pool. 'I don't want to see or talk to Gusinsky. He does not respect agreements,' Putin told Alexei Venediktov, the editor of Echo Moskvy radio station who acted as a go-between for Putin and Gusinsky.[17] Putin saw NTV's coverage of the *Kursk* as a clear sign that Gusinsky was reneging on his word and breaking their informal deal. In the same conversation with Venediktov, Putin explained the difference between enemies and traitors. Gusinsky, who had never been on his side, was an enemy. Berezovsky was a traitor.

—

The relationship between Putin and Berezovsky had began to sour a few months earlier, when Berezovsky had tried to advise his 'protégé' to negotiate a peace deal in Chechnya. Berezovsky also wrote Putin an open letter, which resembled (in its ambition rather than its content) Solzhenitsyn's letter to the Soviet leaders and contained his advice on how to run Russia. The laws proposed by Putin, Berezovksy argued, infringed on the civil society and individual liberties that were the main achievement of Yeltsin's years.

Berezovsky also wrote a private letter to the president, addressing him in a familiar way by his shortened first name, Volodya. 'I told him he was an idiot to write to Putin like that,' Dorenko recalled. 'I said, "You don't understand – Putin is a Russian tsar, not a European leader. In Russia a tsar is not a leader, a tsar is a high priest. You can't write letters to a high priest. You need to crawl, kiss the carpet and kneel before the throne. Because he is not Volodya – he is the throne of the Russians, a mystical, ancient throne."'[18]

According to Dorenko, in April 2000 Berezovsky went to talk to Putin and presented him with his four points on running Russia. First, Russia would need a proper president by 2004; second, it would need a proper party system – like in America; third, one of the leftist parties could be headed by Putin; fourth, the right-wing party would be headed by Berezovsky. 'When Berezovsky told me all this, my hair stood on end. I asked what Putin had replied to him. "He told me – it was very interesting and that we should try," Berezovsky said. "Borya, you are fucked! This is your end. You might as well buy yourself a strong rope,"' Dorenko told Berezovsky in a tragically prophetic turn of phrase.[19] Any reader of Machiavelli's *The Prince* would have told Berezovsky the same – disposing of people who helped you on your way to power and who consider you to be indebted to them is rule number one.

'I have read Machiavelli. But I have not discovered anything new for myself,' Berezovsky said years later in his London exile. He had more time for Lenin: 'Nobody had a better perception of what was possible. He had a unique sense of the moment and events.' Berezovsky believed there was no limit to what was possible for him, but he misjudged both the moment and events.

The relationship between Putin and Berezovsky completely snapped after Channel One's coverage of the *Kursk*. Not only did it blame Putin for carrying on with his holidays, but Dorenko openly called Putin a liar and accused him of 'immorally' paying off the widows of the submarine sailors. Coming from Dorenko, the word 'immoral' sounded like mockery, but Dorenko grew up in a garrison town and felt a strong affinity with the people in Vidyaevo. In his usual forceful and judgemental manner, Dorenko on his programme played extracts from Putin's interview and dissected them with his own killer commentary: 'What Putin says contradicts facts,' he said. Like Nevzorov, Dorenko was a mercenary 'whose cannon rotated in any direction'. But as a professional hit-man, he took pride in his work and worked off his contract to the end. He did not turn against Berezovsky even when it would have been expedient to do so.

That was Dorenko's last programme. A few days later he was fired. Berezovsky was told that either he gave up his shares in Obshchestevnnoe Rossiiksoe Televidenie (Russian Public Broadcaster), as Channel One was formally known, or he would follow in Gusinsky's footsteps. In his thorough book about the oligarchs, David Hoffman describes a conversation between Berezovsky and Putin. After reading a list of accusations which seemed to have come straight from Primakov, Berezovsky's old nemesis, Putin told him: 'I want to run ORT... I personally am going to run ORT.' 'This is ridiculous, at a minimum. And second, it is unrealizable,' Berezovsky retorted. Putin told him, 'ORT covers 98 per cent of Russian territory, of Russian households,' and he left the room.[20] Unwilling to follow in Gusinsky's footsteps, Berezovsky sold the shares in ORT to Roman Abramovich, his younger partner, and left the country. Years later he tried to sue Abramovich in the London courts, but lost. Soon after, he died, allegedly committing suicide.

At the beginning of September, Putin gave an interview to Larry King on CNN. Asked what had happened to the *Kursk*, Putin answered with a half-smile on his face: 'It sank.' In the same interview, he likened his former job at the KGB to that of a journalist. 'Intelligence people are very close in their duties to the staff in mass media. They have the same purpose of gathering information, synthesizing it and presenting it for the consumption of decision-makers.'[21] But this time he was the top decision-maker in the country. Controlling the flow of information was the prerequisite of his power.

Gusinsky had his own decisions to make. He held a meeting with his junior partners, including Malashenko and Kiselev, in London to decide whether to honour his deal to sell his shares in NTV. Everyone at that meeting had a sense of déjà vu. Five years earlier, also in London, the same group had met to decide whether or not to give in to pressure and sell NTV. At the time, Malashenko was the only one who said NTV should fight back. This time he was one of the few to argue for the sale of NTV. Kiselev, on the other hand, suggested that NTV should continue to fight back. Gusinsky sided with Kiselev and told Gazprom that he was pulling out of their agreement, that he had signed under pressure. The war was on and it was played out on the screen. Each side used its professional tools. The Kremlin used a mixture of pressure and bribery. The journalists used their cameras.

But while kicking Gusinsky out of the country and stripping him of assets was a fairly straightforward task, changing the 'software' of the channel and bringing to heel its 'unique journalistic team' was more delicate.

In January 2001, Tatyana Mitkova, a popular NTV presenter, was called in for questioning by prosecutors. Her colleagues went along, filming themselves. Svetlana Sorokina, the host of a popular talk show, looked straight into the camera, and appealed directly to Putin: 'Vladimir Vladimirovich, please listen to us, find time to meet with us. We are not the oligarchs, we are journalists, those who make NTV... but if tomorrow we all get summons to the prosecutors' office, we will also consider it an answer.'[22] The same day Sorokina received a friendly telephone call from Putin and an invitation to come to the Kremlin for talks along with ten other journalists, including Kiselev.

The 'chat' between Putin and a dozen NTV journalists went on for more than three hours. Putin was clearly well briefed and occasionally quoted from the documents supplied by the prosecutors. After listening to Putin for the first thirty minutes of the general discussion, Sorokina scribbled on a piece of a paper and passed it to her colleagues: 'It is all useless.' Putin clearly did not believe that the NTV journalists were speaking for themselves. As a professional KGB man, he believed in conspiracies – not people's free will. 'You are getting all your instructions from Gusinsky,' he told Kiselev, looking straight in his eyes. 'Don't deny it. I know all about the hours and hours of conversations with Gusinsky,' Putin said, effectively admitting that Kiselev's phone was tapped.[23]

On 4 April, Gazprom staged a corporate coup, replacing NTV's management and forcing out Kiselev as general director of the channel. In crushing Gusinsky and NTV, the Kremlin skilfully relied on the television channel's past by setting off its former 'victims' against it. It appointed Alfred Kokh, the former member of Chubais's team who had been demolished by NTV in 1997, as the head of Gazprom's media arm which was supposed to take over NTV. Boris Jordan, an American banker of Russian descent, who had helped raise money for Potanin's winning bid for Svyazinvest, was appointed the general director instead of Kiselev.

While the Kremlin, working through its state television channels, tried to portray its attack on NTV as a business dispute, NTV tried to present it as a fight for freedom of speech and democracy. Neither was true – at least not entirely.

Gusinsky was indeed in a vulnerable position. He owed a total of nearly $500 million to Gazprom, stemming from two loans he had taken on to finance NTV Plus, the satellite television business. The loans could have been converted into Gazprom's shares in Media Most but the Kremlin ordered Rem Vyakhirev, the Gazprom chairman, who had plenty of reasons to fear for his own past, to dump Gusinsky. But Gusinsky was also in a vulnerable position in terms of his 'credit history' with the Russian public. The enormous credit which NTV received in 1993 when it first came on air had been largely used up.

Few people in Russia, including those who defended it, were prepared to think about NTV as a standard-bearer for civil liberties and freedom of speech. NTV journalists tried to draw parallels between their protests and those that had unfolded in the Czech Republic a few months earlier, where journalists from public television had gone on strike against the appointment of new managers, prompting mass demonstrations across the whole country and enlisting the support of Vaclav Havel. But the parallels were not convincing.

Tempting as it may be to portray NTV journalists as altruistic defenders of freedom of speech, it would be as misleading as to present their opponents as stewards of justice and state interests. The Kremlin attacked NTV not for its faults, but because of its merits, yet in doing so it relied on its weaknesses. Many of the journalists, spoiled and compromised by their inflated status, and their own cynicism, which they saw as an asset during the times when they were in power, evoked moral values in their time of need.

NTV's transformation into a protest movement seemed unnatural. Journalists flew an NTV flag out of the window at the Ostankino television centre. News programmes started coming out with the NTV green logo crossed out by the word 'protest' in red. The slogan 'news is our profession' turned into 'protest is our profession'. NTV reduced its programming to news. The rest of the air time was filled with a live feed from inside NTV's studios and offices. This was a Big Brother reality show before the format even appeared in Russia.

The sight of Kiselev, in a dapper black coat, addressing the crowd at a public rally in his usual respectable television manner, holding hands with other correspondents and waving along to a song, seemed odd. Parfenov cringed at this stylistic clash. He published an open letter to Kiselev in the *Kommersant* newspaper, offering his resignation. 'I can no longer hear your preaching in the newsroom – these ten-minute-long outbursts of hatred – and I can't just ignore them as long as I work here,' he wrote.[24]

The same day as his letter was published, Parfenov went to NTV's studio to participate in the talk show *Anthropology*, which consisted entirely of NTV staff. 'You are a traitor!' NTV's flamboyant night talk-show presenter, Dmitry Dibrov, shouted at him on air: 'You have betrayed our battle for the freedom of speech! You have betrayed people who are working here!' Ever ironic, Parfenov asked his fuming colleague: 'Do you really think that the words "traitor", "freedom of speech" and "battle" should be pronounced with three exclamation marks?'[25] Parfenov's stand would have looked more principled had he not accepted a generous pay offer from NTV's new owners.

In fact, the conflict with NTV was much more about the freedom of speech than people realized. After all, freedom did not automatically imply objectivity or even quality, but merely the right to say something different without the fear of persecution. What NTV provided was not objectivity, but pluralism. Had Russia had ten other powerful private news channels with the same reach as the state ones, the fate of NTV would have mattered less. But Russia had only two state or quasi-state channels whose finances were far murkier than NTV's. By taking over NTV, the state was not just disposing of a defiant oligarch; it was disposing of competition.

The people who realized this were not NTV's young audience, but the very same 'relics' of the Soviet intelligentsia who had seen it all before. A group of Russian intellectuals – poets, artists and journalists – published a letter in defence of NTV under the headline: 'IT IS TIME TO GET WORRIED'. 'The political motive of the persecution [of NTV] is clear: suppression of dissent in the country... Meantime, Russian society watches everything that is going on with cold detachment, creating the impression that defending freedom of speech is a private problem for NTV. This is a dangerous misconception. We have no doubt that the political consequences of NTV passing over to state control will affect everyone.'[26]

The letter, both in its language and its arguments, firmly belonged to the tradition of the 1960s generation. It was signed, among others, by Yegor Yakovlev and published in *Obshchaya gazeta*, which he edited. A decade after its first emergency issues in August 1991, it printed 300,000 copies of another 'emergency' issue entirely dedicated to the takeover of NTV.*

In his own article, Yegor blasted Putin's cynicism. 'First of all Vladimir Putin is not a man of his word. He swore his sympathy for an independent media and he has blessed its crucifixion... There are many people of my profession – not to mention members of the Duma – who would prefer to stand aside. Believe me – I have witnessed this more than once: you think you are just washing your hands of something and then you end up to your ears in shit.'[27]

The paper was distributed freely among some 20,000 people who came to protest against NTV's takeover in Moscow and St Petersburg. The atmosphere of those demonstrations was reminiscent of the democratic marches of the late Perestroika years held in front of *Moskovskie novosti*.

* Yegor was also one of NTV's trustees, as were Alexander Yakovlev and Mikhail Gorbachev.

The 1960s generation which NTV came to replace was the one that rushed to its defence, while its target audience – the young, smart, energetic, self-sufficient capitalist crowd – 'kept their cool' and watched the conflict over NTV as though it was a reality show. This is what NTV had taught them to do over the years. After all it was 'normal television' for a 'normal country' that propagated the idea of a calm, private, bourgeois life.

The television drama culminated in a showdown at 4 a.m. on 14 April 2001 and resembled a military takeover. The eighth floor of the Ostankino television centre, where NTV's studios were based, was sealed off by tough private security men. Some members of Kiselev's team were barred from entering the studios, but the cameras kept rolling, capturing Oleg Dobrodeev, one of the founders of NTV, and now head of state television, trying to calm down his former colleagues. Most refused to speak to him or shake his hand. After a sleepless night, the team of NTV journalists, including Sorokina and Shenderovich, walked out, taking with them their own photographic portraits that had hung in the corridors. They crossed the street and reported the night's drama from a borrowed studio. NTV itself came out with the usual, calm morning bulletin. The takeover of NTV was just one of the news items.

One could end the narrative of NTV here, blaming its destruction purely on Putin and leaving the few last honest NTV journalists as noble knights fighting for their freedom, but the picture would be incomplete. 'The unique journalistic team' first took refuge at a small cable channel owned by Berezovsky and then migrated to TSN, a channel that was owned by the Kremlin-friendly oligarchs, including Roman Abramovich. Kiselev, who became its editor-in-chief, trod the line carefully this time. When the channel folded a few months later through a lack of financing nobody batted an eyelid. The 'unique journalistic team' expired with a whimper. The Kremlin broke NTV not just financially, but morally. The victory had been shockingly easy to achieve. Grilled by foreign journalists about the freedom of speech in Russia, Putin answered crudely: 'A real man always tries. A real woman always resists.'[28] To extend the metaphor, many Russian television journalists did not resist the embraces of the new powers.

The attraction of highly paid jobs, celebrity status and influence turned out to be stronger than the desire for free expression. 'Ten years ago Russian journalists thought they were the fourth estate, but they have now been told by the president that they are the world's oldest profession,' Petrovskaya said at the time.[29] Many of those who stormed out of NTV's studios in 2001 soon flocked back, offering their services to the new powers and ultimately turned NTV into one of the most malicious channels even by the standards of state television.

It was NTV that in the 2010s harassed opposition leaders and foreign diplomats, slinging mud at liberals such as Boris Nemtsov. It was NTV's Andrei Norkin – one of those who had stormed out of NTV's studio in 2001 – who just hours after Nemtsov was killed in February 2015 hosted a twisted talk show that portrayed him as a source of all evil. But that was later.

Dolce Vita and Blood, Sweat and Tears

In 2001 the transition was not immediately visible. In fact, if anything, the channel became livelier, more entertaining and sleek. NTV continued its critical coverage of the Chechnya war and showed no more reverence for the Kremlin than any Western television channel did at the time. It even launched a talk show called *Freedom of Speech*. Parfenov returned to the channel, replacing Kiselev as its main political anchorman.

The protest rhetoric and moralizing vanished. *Namedni* replaced Kiselev's *Itogi* as the main political programme of the week. Where Kiselev had preached, Parfenov informed and entertained. Where Kiselev had used meaningful pauses to underscore the gravity of his subject, Parfenov used half-squinting irony and sarcasm to show that no subject was too grave for a good pun.

The makers of *Namedni* put together a written set of rules which they referred to as the 'bible'. The programme, it prescribed, should keep a balance between '*dolce vita*' and 'blood, sweat and tears'. It must not look too rich: 'Yes, we are urban and well-to-do, but we also know how others live.' However, the element of '*dolce vita*' dominated and when *Namedni*'s correspondents travelled to the depths of Russia, it seemed like an exotic travelogue feature about the life of an indigenous population.

A dull business story about Putin and Silvio Berlusconi opening a new factory line of Italian washing machines in Russia was illustrated with the washing machine itself brought into the studio. Speaking to the camera next to the washing machine, Parfenov looked like he was advertising it (advertising became one of Parfenov's main trades after he left television). The main object of Parfenov's 'advertisements', however, was Russian liberalism and its middle-class lifestyle. And like any advertisement it made it look far more attractive than the reality. 'We portrayed Russia as more liberal than it really was,' he said later.[30]

In his contract with NTV Parfenov's official job description had been mistyped as 'chief programmer' (instead of 'programme chief') and in many ways *Namedni* did programme Russia as the liberal country he wished it to be – one where people don't climb barricades and talk about politics but enjoy individual freedoms to consume and to travel. Liberalism, he used to say, was not in political slogans, but on the Internet, in coffee shops, in fashion boutiques, in trips abroad and pedestrianized streets. In this sense, Russia was certainly getting more liberal. NTV fitted perfectly into this picture, showcasing Russian capitalists, praising their initiative and individual talents.

This agenda matched that of the Kremlin. Boris Jordan's appointment had been supposed to appease the Kremlin's critics at home and abroad, and reassure Russia's middle class that it had been right to keep its cool during the conflict. Regardless of what people thought of Gusinsky, public opinion was not ready for an overt clampdown on the media and the Kremlin did not try to force it. On the contrary, it used NTV as its calling card that was meant to prove its economic liberalism, safe in the knowledge that it had ultimate control over it.

The limits of the Kremlin's licence started to show a year later, during a theatre siege in Moscow. On 23 October 2002 a group of Chechen terrorists took more than 900 people hostage during the performance of a musical called *Nord-Ost*. There was a macabre theatricality in the siege itself. When the first terrorist clad in military camouflage and a ski mask walked on stage, fired in the air and declared everyone hostages, the audience thought it was part of the show. That Chechen fighters who were part of a different reality could burst into the comfortable life of the Moscow middle class seemed incomprehensible.

As in 1995, during the hostage-taking in Budennovsk, terrorists demanded an immediate end to the war in Chechnya. But this time nobody was willing to put the lives of hostages above the interest of the state. While negotiations with the terrorists were still going on, Channel One, now firmly under Kremlin control, poured oil onto the flames. Its commentary programme showed the old footage of Chernomyrdin negotiating with Basayev. 'For all these seven years we have been paying a price for Budennovsk, for the unprecedented shame of political negotiations with bandits and degenerates,' the programme said. 'We have no intention of telling the Russian government and security services how and what should be done, because we have no reason to doubt that they are doing everything right...'[31] The camera cut to Putin.

At the end of day three of the siege, the Russian security services pumped a mysterious narcotic gas into the auditorium and stormed the building, killing all the terrorists and poisoning to death more than 120 hostages. The security services then released a video of the dead terrorists. It showed some still sitting in their chairs, others lying on the floor, their faces covered in blood. The camera zoomed in and paused on their dead, disfigured faces; it showed the leader of the terrorists lying dead on the floor in a corridor with a bottle of Hennessy which had been apparently planted next to him by a journalist from Russia Channel who had previously worked at NTV. Television was changing reality even after death. State television kept showing the explosives which the terrorists could have used. Its central message was – thank God (and the Kremlin) for a successful operation. In fact, the evacuation took more than four hours. By the time the ambulances reached the hospital, many hostages, including children, were dead. Doctors did not know what they were dealing with because the security services refused to name of the gas they had used, claiming it was a state secret.

NTV's reporting stood out. It showed the crisis unfold in real time, providing blanket coverage that included the storming of the theatre. It was the only channel that was allowed – in fact, demanded – by the hostage-takers to film inside the theatre. It aired an interview with the defiant terrorists' leader Movsar Barayev who, as NTV pointed out, had been reported as dead only two weeks earlier by the state news agencies. It showed the protests of the hostages' relatives, demanding an end to the Chechnya war. It hired a lip-reader to transcribe the soundless video of Putin provided by the Kremlin press service. It questioned the official line: had everything possible been done to avoid the storming of the theatre and to save the lives of the hostages?

As the death toll of hostages climbed, Putin made a televised statement – asking forgiveness for not having been able to save everyone. The terrorists, he said, had no future, 'but we have'. None of those who planned or executed the rescue operation was reprimanded. As in the *Kursk* disaster, he shifted the blame onto television, accusing NTV of endangering the lives of hostages by showing the preparations for the storming of the theatre. Putin summoned news executives to the Kremlin and angrily told them that 'journalists should not ply their trade on the blood of their own citizens – if, of course, those who do this consider these citizens to be their own'. The remark was clearly addressed to NTV's general director Boris Jordan, who was poignantly not invited to the meeting. A pragmatic investment banker, Jordan resigned with a handsome pay-off from Gazprom.

The head of the FSB, Nikolai Patrushev, held regular meetings with media chiefs. 'The meetings which we have had before have yielded results: we have a mutual understanding and a certain trust. At the end of the day we are doing one job: working for society, working for the state,' he declared.[32]

Parfenov stayed on at NTV for another couple of years. 'I knew it was a matter of time before *Namedni* would get shut down. But I continued to chirrup for as long as I could,' he said.[33] Parfenov's 'chirruping' was entertaining and ultimately projected optimism. However serious or grim the subject matter was, his style was playful and ironic. When Mikhail Khodorkovsky, Russia's richest tycoon and Putin's opponent, was arrested in 2003, Parfenov called it 'Khodorkost' and invited a popular stand-up comedian to come on the programme to parody Putin's angry speech in which he had told his ministers 'to stop the hysteria and speculations and not to interfere in the case'. The comedian mimicked the speech and commented on Putin's psychological state. *Namedni* called the item 'Starting Hysteria'.

The last straw, perhaps, was *Namedni*'s coverage of Putin's inauguration in 2004 that mixed images of the actual ceremony with scenes from *The Barber of Siberia*, a kitsch fiction film set in the time of Tsar Alexander III. Putin's arrival at the Kremlin in a black limousine was mixed with the arrival of Alexander III on a white horse; when Putin addressed the Kremlin guards, he got a reply from Alexander III's soldiers. Playfully, *Namedni* was putting across a serious message: Putin's ceremony was a coronation of a new monarch, rather than the inauguration of a president.

Yet, however 'clever' this interchange between documentary and fiction was, it was a very postmodernist attitude to reality – not as something fixed, but as something that could be constructed and deconstructed, cut and pasted. Parfenov used the device to deliver a true message. But there was nothing to stop his followers from using it to deliver a fake one. It was all relative. In June 2004 Parfenov was sacked and *Namedni* was shut down. Parfenov's 'chirruping' was out of tune with the new order that started to emerge in Putin's second presidential term. The time for jokes and jokers was over. The events that were taking place in the country, including the arrest of Khodorkovsky, the destruction of the Yukos oil company and the occasional of acts of terror, were too serious and complex to be described through the wordplay and sarcasm that Parfenov had turned into his house style. Parfenov admitted that much, but not until six years later, when he delivered an explosive speech which was filled with sincere civic pathos.

He spoke at an elegant black-tie ceremony, where he received an award set up in memory of Vladislav Listyev, an iconic Russian journalist and showman, who was murdered in 1995. Standing in front of Russia's powerful TV executives, Parfenov told them what he thought about the state of their industry. 'Our television is getting more sophisticated at exciting, enticing, entertaining and making [the audience] laugh, but it can hardly be called a civic or public political institution.' For a reporter on Russian state television, said a visibly nervous Parfenov, 'top bureaucrats are not newsmakers, but his boss's bosses'. This means that 'journalists are not journalists at all but bureaucrats, following the logic of service and submission'.[34]

In the past, Parfenov would have cringed at words such as 'civic institution'. Now, he was delivering them with dead seriousness. The TV executives who had turned Russia's state television channels into a mixture of entertainment and propaganda looked at Mr Parfenov with deadpan expressions on their faces. Among them were Dobrodeev, Parfenov's long-time colleague at NTV, and Konstantin Ernst, his old-time friend and co-producer of *Old Songs about Important Things*, who was now in charge of Russia's Channel One.

The Survivor

Ernst was no Soviet apparatchik. With his long, flowing hair, he was a Hollywood-crazy television journalist and producer who had stayed the course and arrived at the top, presiding over the country's main national television channels that broadcast to its eleven time zones. Born in 1961, he was among the brightest and most ambitious members of the generation that was created both by the Soviet Union and by the reaction against it, who most despised the restrictions of that period and who benefited most from their removal. He was a blue-blood of the Soviet intellectual establishment; his father was a professor of biology and Ernst himself had a doctorate in biochemistry. His real passion was cinema, though, and like many talented and energetic people of his generation he was drawn to television. He started with the *Vzglyad* programme, which was at the forefront of Perestroika television, but soon launched his own programme called *Matador*.

The show had nothing to do with bullfighting: Ernst simply liked the sound of the word. He took his viewers into the world of Hollywood studios, film stars and the Cannes film festival. Its format was similar to Parfenov's early, non-political *Namedni*. As Ernst said at the twentieth anniversary of *Namedni*, both *Matador* and *Namedni* tried to articulate a time that had not yet arrived. 'We wanted this time [to look like our programmes] and to be ahead of it,' he said.[35]

In one memorable episode of *Matador*, Ernst told the story of the creation of Francis Ford Coppola's film *Apocalypse Now*. Dressed in an US Air Force uniform for effect, Ernst seemed intoxicated by the energy of the scene where US helicopters bomb the Vietcong to the soundtrack of

Wagner's 'Ride of the Valkyries'. Francis Ford Coppola seemed a natural role model for the young Ernst.

In 1995, Berezovsky singled Ernst out for his determination and ambition, appointing him general producer of Channel One which went under the name of Ostankino or Public Russian Television (ORT) at the time. Ernst was not so much an ideologist, but an *organizer* and a *producer* of the channel. Entrusted with the largest channel in terms of its reach, he produced not just news and popular shows, but common experiences for the country. They were invariably sleek and watchable. Ernst's first big hit as a producer was *Old Songs about Important Things* which seamlessly connected the Soviet past and Russia's present.

Four years later, in September 1999 just as Putin was being promoted as Yeltsin's successor, Ernst was appointed the head of Channel One. Under Ernst, the word 'One' referred not so much to the number of the television broadcasting frequency, but its position in the ratings and influence. While Putin restored the Soviet anthem as the country's 'most important song', Ernst restored *Vremya* with its familiar Soviet-era tune as the most important prime-time news programme which articulated the country's narrative. What he was most interested in, though, was not news, but fiction. In the late 1990s and early 2000s Ernst and Channel One became one of the biggest producers of film and TV serials.

As Lenin said, 'of all the kinds of arts the most important for us is cinema'. Images could get through to people's consciousness in a way that words could not. They could also sell in a way that words could not. The ability of a film to influence the minds of the audience in Russia was far greater than in America, simply because there was less noise in the marketplace. Ernst did not set out to sell an ideology – he did not really have one – but he used ideology to sell the films he produced.

After the 1998 devaluation of the rouble, import substitution became one of the main factors behind Russian economic growth. It was also the main factor behind the growth of the Russian film industry. In the same way as people swapped imported goods for domestic equivalents they substituted locally produced dramas for American soap operas. 'Russia' became a brand.

Few people sensed the demand for patriotism as acutely – and supplied it as profitably – as did Ernst. He used Russian patriotic slogans, in addition to the weight and resources of the state-controlled television channel, to promote films which were modelled on Hollywood blockbusters. In 2004 Ernst produced the most successful post-Soviet blockbuster called *Nochnoi Dozor* (*Night Watch*), a special effects-filled fantasy-thriller. Ernst sold the distribution rights for the film to 20th Century Fox and in the first four weeks the film collected more than $16 million, breaking box office records and in Russia even putting it ahead of *The Lord of the Rings: The Return of the King*.

Based on a fantasy novel by Sergei Lukyanov, *Night Watch* was the Russian answer to *The Matrix*. It is set in contemporary Moscow where ordinary people have parallel other-worldly existences as vampires, shamans and witches. They are divided into 'light ones' and 'dark ones' and have been fighting with each other since life began.

The 'light' ones in the film are closely connected to their Soviet past, whereas the 'dark' ones clearly belong to the world of Russian capitalism. The two sides are fighting for the soul of a twelve-year-old boy – 'the great other' – who in the end chooses the dark. As the boy tells his estranged father, who is one of the 'light ones': 'You are no better than the dark. You are even worse. You lie and only pretend to be good.'

In his interviews Ernst explained that the 'dark' ones, for all their aggression, do not equal evil and the 'light' do not equal good. 'The "dark" are much freer, they let themselves be as they want to be. The "light" are more frustrated, they have too many duties, and feel responsible for a lot of people. The "dark" have eschewed constraints, they live for themselves, while the light look like neurotics who are trying to be good to everyone.'[36] Ernst identified himself with the dark ones.

He threw in the entire resources of Channel One, including its news programmes, to promote the film, which ensured its commercial success. The makers tried to load the film with extra meaning, which soon evaporated, but the precedent of a Hollywood-scale Russian blockbuster stayed. In an interview that Ernst gave after the film, he lamented the inability of Russians to live in the present moment.'Our people live either in the past or in the future,' he said.[37] Ernst, who descended from an old German family that had settled in Russia, lived in the present and shaped it.

Ernst did not suffer from cognitive dissonance. News and fiction were not two separate parts of his life but harmoniously complemented and interacted with one another. *Night Watch* featured a scene from Channel One's nine o'clock news programme *Vremya* with a cameo appearance by one of its smooth-talking presenters who informs his audience about an approaching cataclysm.

Vremya was an antidote to chaos and disorder – a source of stability and routine, a matrix. Every programme followed the same repeated pattern – like a lullaby – starting with Putin travelling around the country or receiving ministers in his office, followed by examples of Russian resurgence and ending with (bad) news from abroad. Unlike any other programme on the channel, *Vremya* was (and still is) broadcast uninterrupted by commercials.

Strictly speaking, *Vremya* did not report news. Instead, it created a virtual reality according to the hierarchy of the state with Putin at the top. As a state news programme, *Vremya* did not allow itself any scorn, irony or ridicule. The tone of the presenter was always stern and serious. Its aim was to assure viewers that they could sleep peacefully in the knowledge that the country was being governed and guarded by a wise and caring president who would make the right decisions; that criminals and terrorists would be punished and champions of labour rewarded. 'Any stabilization makes news calmer. If news works like a constant nerve irritant – as it did in Russia in the 1990s – it is a sign of instability rather than of the freedom of speech,' Ernst explained.[38]

In fact, TV news did not reflect the country's stabilization – it emanated an illusion of stability just as the violent crime dramas that flooded Russian television created an illusion of total lawlessness. Both news and soap operas were artefacts and they worked together to create a balance between dark and light as the plot of *Night Watch* would have it. While news was supposed to calm the audience, the violent crime dramas raised the level of adrenaline and aggression in the national bloodstream. As one high-powered Russian official and former FSB general explained, this deluge of graphic violence was not a response to high spectator demand, but a conscious policy formed in the high echelons of the Russian power structure, to create the impression that only the strong state portrayed in the news could protect the vulnerable population from the violence on the screen.

The question of what was good or bad for the audience was not decided by its tastes. 'A doctor does not ask the patient under the knife what is good for him,' Ernst said.[39] It was his and Dobrodeev's job to prescribe and administer the medicine.

The Battle Between Light and Darkness

Night Watch was released in Russia in early July 2004. A few weeks later, on 1 September, real horror struck the country – a school in Beslan in North Ossetia, with over 1,000 children, was taken hostage by Chechen terrorists. It was the worst terrorist attack in Russia's history, more cruel and deadly than any other. Throughout the crisis the Russian media reported official figures fed by the Kremlin which put the number of hostages at 354. This was almost certainly a deliberate falsehood that infuriated the terrorists so much that they started to deny the children water and barred them from going to the toilet, forcing them to drink their own urine. According to one surviving hostage, the terrorists were listening to the news on radios. When they heard the number, one of them said: 'Russia says there are only 300 of you here. Maybe we should kill enough of you to get down to that number.'[40]

After two days and three nights of negotiations, when independent Russian journalists and activists, including the courageous Anna Politkovskaya,* who commanded respect among Chechen fighters, were prevented from helping with negotiations, the security services began to storm the building.

On 3 September, at 1.03 p.m., two explosions were heard from the school's gym where most of the hostages were being kept. As it later turned out, the explosions were caused by a thermobaric grenade fired by the Russian special forces. The terrorists started shooting the children, mayhem broke out and fighting began. Foreign networks such as CNN and the BBC broadcast the events live. In Russia, on the two state-controlled TV channels, normal programming continued. An hour later, they switched to what by then was turning into a massacre, but their coverage was confusing and brief. Channel One spent ten minutes on Beslan before returning to a Brazilian soap opera called *Women in Love*. Echo Moskvy, the city's liberal radio station, kept its viewers up to date by watching events unfold on CNN.

Throughout the day, both state channels featured news bulletins on the hour, repeatedly reporting the official line: the authorities did not plan to storm the school; the terrorists had started the shooting; the siege was the work of an international terrorist organization whose numbers included ethnic Arabs and even an African (he later turned out to be Chechen).

* Politkovskaya was poisoned with mysterious toxins while on a plane as she flew to Beslen to negotiate with hostage-takers. Two years later, on 7 October 2007, she was killed outside her Moscow apartment.

Several hours into the clash, Russia Channel gave the impression that the fighting was over and that most of the hostages were now safe. Viewers saw children being carried by their parents and heard a relieved voice behind the camera saying: 'They are alive, it is OK, they are alive, alive.' As some were reunited with their parents, a correspondent commented: 'There are tears here again, but this time these are tears of joy.' A presenter gave figures of those taken to hospital, but carefully avoided giving estimates of the number of people killed. 'According to the latest information,' he said, 'the fighting in the school is over. There are no dead or wounded there... we can't give more exact figures of the injured... er... the precise figure of how many hostages were freed.'[41]

Then, at about 9 p.m., after more than 300 children and parents had died, and as the gunfight between the hostage-takers and special forces was still going on, viewers were treated to extraordinary programming. Russia Channel showed brave Russian soldiers fighting bearded Chechen bandits who were hiding in caves and shouting 'Allahu Akbar!' These were scenes from the military drama *On My Honour!* Channel One meanwhile showed *Die Hard*, a film in which Bruce Willis saves hostages in a New York high-rise. The actors on the screen seemed to be taking fictional revenge on behalf of those who in Beslan were still dying.

Dobrodeev and Ernst were the demiurges who created myths and explained reality. As Ernst said afterwards: 'Our task number two is to inform the country about what is going on. Today, the main task of the television is to mobilize the country. Russia needs consolidation.'[42] Unlike Soviet television, which was closely guarded by censors, Ernst mostly made his own decisions. 'Nobody calls me and orders me to do anything,' he insisted.[43] This was probably true. But even if it were not, he did not slavishly take instructions from the Kremlin, but willingly put his talent and imagination at its service.

'I am a statist, a liberal statist,' said Ernst a decade later.[44] Throughout his years as the head of Channel One he has put his energy into consolidating the nation around spectacular television projects and creating common experiences based on a narrative of the state, removing any need for doubt, reflection or repentance. Unlike Dobrodeev, who turned into a political apparatchik and the master of the Kremlin's propaganda, Ernst considers himself an artist, a creator, or, to use television language, a producer of the country.

Like any good producer, he unmistakably sensed the demands of his audience and in the 2000s the country craved a show of resurgence. People whose incomes kept going up because of the increase in the price of oil, rather than because they had to work harder, had plenty of free time for entertainment and demanded a display of Russia's greatness to explain and supplement their improving fortunes. In the mid-2000s, this demand was largely satisfied through sport, entertainment and parades.

In June 2008 the Russian football team won a quarter-final against the Netherlands in the European championship. Nearly 80 per cent of the country watched the match – a record rating in Russian television history. At night, Moscow erupted into a mass patriotic frenzy with cars hooting, flags waving and bikers parading – the same ones who would a few years later wave Russian flags in Crimea. At first glance, it seemed a copy of European football events, but while in Europe sport has long turned into a substitute for war, in Russia it was only a starter.

The victory was number one news on Russian television. Popular talk shows could not get enough of sport. 'Russia – forward!' became a national slogan. The celebration of victory coincided with an escalation of a propaganda campaign against Georgia which was portrayed as America's proxy. A few weeks later Russian tanks and aeroplanes invaded Georgia. It was Russia's first fully televised war, scripted as a copy of NATO's action in Kosovo, and it produced a similar reaction to the one after the football match.

This was the ultimate show of Russia's resurgence. Television channels were part of the military operation, waging an essential propaganda campaign, spreading disinformation and demonizing the country Russia was about to attack. The war started on 7 August 2008 – the day of the opening of the Summer Olympics in Beijing – with Georgian forces responding to fire coming from the Russian-backed breakaway region of South Ossetia with heavy artillery. According to the Russian propaganda, Georgia was a reckless and dangerous aggressor and Russia had an obligation, as a peacekeeper, to protect the victims. Russian television talked about genocide, 2,000 civilian deaths and tens of thousands of refugees. (The real figure of South Ossetians killed in the conflict was 133.)

Putin, in a light sports jacket, talking to South Ossetian women, performed the role of superman in a special effects drama staged by Ernst and Dobrodeev. He flew to the Russian side of the Caucasus mountain range straight from Beijing to hear hair-raising stories from refugees:

> *First woman*: They burnt our girls when they were still alive.
>
> *Putin* (surprised): Alive?
>
> *First woman*: Yes, young girls! They herded them like cattle into a house and burnt them...
>
> *Second woman*: They stabbed a baby, he was one and a half. They stabbed him in a cellar.
>
> *Putin*: I cannot even listen to this.
>
> *Second woman*: An old woman with two little kids – they were running and a tank drove over them.
>
> *Putin*: They must be crazy. This is plain genocide...

The rumours spread by Russian television – of Georgian troops targeting women and children and performing genocide – later proved to be untrue, but at the time they inspired ethnic cleansing of Georgian villages by South Ossetian irregulars. The main target for attack by Russian television, however, was not Georgia – which was an obvious enemy – but Russia's own audience which was bombarded with anti-American propaganda.

Judging by the picture, Russia was fighting not against a tiny, poor country that used to be its vassal, but against a dangerous and powerful aggressor backed by the imperialist West. One Russian Duma deputy reflected the mood in a television interview: 'Today, it is quite obvious who the parties in the conflict are. They are the US, the UK, Israel who participated in training the Georgian army, Ukraine who supplied it with weapons. We are facing a situation where there is NATO aggression against us.'[45]

In the following few years, as America proposed the so-called 'reset' – a form of détente policy – and Dmitry Medvedev, who acted as Russian president, talked about modernization under the slogan 'Russia – Forward!', patriotic urges were satisfied by military parades and song contests. On 9 May 2009, fresh from watching the annual Second World War victory day parade, Putin went to inspect the readiness of the Eurovision Song Contest that was staged by Ernst and opened three days later. The two events occupied equally important places in Putin's schedule and in the Kremlin's narrative of resurgence. As Ernst said at the time, it was the 'external political effect' that mattered. The main 'geopolitical show' of Ernst's television career was still to come.

Ernst was entrusted with staging one of the crowning moments of Vladimir Putin's rule – the 2014 Sochi Winter Olympics – a project that Putin cared about deeply and which was supposed to legitimize his return to power as Russia's president in 2012. No expenses were spared for the Olympics – $50 billion was thrown at the project. A special arena was built for the opening and closing ceremonies; the world's top technicians, designers, architects, riggers and musicians worked around the clock. The result was the most grandiose pageantry Russia had ever seen, a staggering display of the country's comeback, staged with panache, style and imagination.

Ernst called the show *Dreams about Russia*. The 'dreams' defied the forces of gravitation as the show unfolded both on stage and in the air

– the heavy sets were suspended and moved along rail tracks attached to the roof of the stadium. The sky was no limit. Seven islands – each representing a piece of the country – drifted through the air like clouds, accompanied by a song from the opera *Prince Igor* about a promised land of the free where 'the sun shines so brightly', where 'roses bloom luxuriously' and where 'nightingales sing in the green forests and sweet grapes grow'. It was a captivating and grandiose utopia.

At the centre of the show's narrative was a history of the empire and the state – not of its people. Rather than celebrating the diversity of the country's population, as the Olympic rules prescribe, it celebrated unity under the state flag. A troika of horses made of white light floated through the sky; the colourful domes of St Basil's Church (balloons filled with hot air) bounced joyfully along with jesters and acrobats in a medieval fayre; subtle engravings of Peter the Great's construction of St Petersburg morphed into a choreographed display of the Russian imperial army; a captivating ball scene from *War and Peace* gave way to a constructivist study of the Bolshevik Revolution drowned in red light. A steam engine, suspended in mid-air, pulled along the wheels and clogs of Stalin's industrialization. The scene was set to a tune called '*Vremya Vpered*' ('Time, Forward!') which has long been used as the theme tune of the *Vremya* television programme. Time moved seamlessly on to the optimistic and humane 1960s filled with humour and nostalgia – as though inspired by Ernst's and Parfenov's project *Old Songs about Important Things*.

Ernst exceeded himself. No country had ever staged such a technically complex show in the air. He watched the opening in the command centre. At the sound of the final firework, Ernst jumped from his seat, shouting in English 'We've done it!' The country that Ernst had conjured up on the stage was not a place of Russian dolls and Cossack dances, but one of avant-garde artists, great ballet, Tolstoy, Nabokov and Gogol; a sophisticated European country proud of its culture and its history: 'the country I want to live in,' tweeted Ksenia Sobchak, a socialite and journalist. The only problem was that there was no such place.

'I wanted to create a matrix that would indirectly affect the whole country,' said Ernst.[46] This was the invention of Russia. It had the same mythological function as Stalin's 1930s Exhibition of People's Achievements (VDNKh) that served as a matrix of Soviet life. The exhibition, which turned into a permanent display of Soviet achievements, presented a model of a cornucopia and fertility in a country where farmers had been eliminated as a class. Live bulls were paraded on the site, supposedly to inseminate growth. It was no accident that a year after the Olympics opening ceremony, its sets were displayed at VDNKh.

Receiving the Man of the Year award in 2014 from the Russian edition of GQ, a men's fashion and style magazine, Ernst said that his opening of the Olympics was the happiest and scariest moment of his life. 'I got a chance to confess my love to the country in front of three billion people on earth and what is probably even more important, for two hours to bring my compatriots together in one emotion, even though many of them cannot be brought together in one emotion...'[47] The question is what kind of emotion.

For all its technological modernity and scenes of the avant-garde, Russia's present was its past. There was no sign of Perestroika or the 1990s or the 2000s. It was as though the Soviet Union never collapsed. Ernst effectively stopped the story of the country in the early 1960s, the time of Krushchev's Thaw and when Ernst was born. 'The time after the war is the time we live in,' Channel One commentators told their television audience.

As Grigory Revzin, an architecture critic and columnist, noted, the choice of Krushchev's Thaw as the last 'historic' period reflected the spirit of the time when the ceremony was conceived – in the short period of Dmitry Medvedev's presidential rule, which was perceived as a brief 'thaw' and which proposed 'modernization' as its main goal. Yet when the show opened the times had changed and its optimistic mood clashed with the tone of a military-style mobilization created by Ernst's television news. Channel One rebranded itself as 'First Olympic', and dressed its presenters in the Russian team's uniform. Any critic of the Olympics who dared to mention corruption during its construction was deemed an enemy. Every Russian medal was celebrated as though it was a military victory.

Parallel with the show in Sochi, another far more dramatic but no less colourful show was unfolding in Kiev. Thousands of people on Maidan Nezalezhnosti (Independence Square) rose against a kleptocratic, dysfunctional and authoritarian post-Soviet order that was personified in Ukraine by the thuggish, corrupt president Viktor Yanukovych. People waved EU flags as a symbol of the dignified life they wished to have. Riot police tried to disband protesters who set up a camp in the square after Yanukovych dumped an agreement with the EU under pressure from Russia.

At night, faced with the very real prospect of being beaten up or killed, the people in Maidan came together in one emotion. On the illuminated stage, projected on a screen, protest leaders called for calm and defiance, priests read out prayers and Ruslana, a popular Ukrainian singer and the winner of the 2004 Eurovision Song Contest, led the national anthem: 'Ukraine has not yet perished, nor her glory, nor her freedom.' Thousands of Maidan protesters struck up the chorus line: 'Souls and bodies we'll lay down, all for our freedom.' It looked like the birth of the nation.

By the time the Sochi Olympics had finished, blood had been spilled in Kiev. Riot police stormed Maidan. Officers threw percussion grenades taped up with nails and bolts at protesters, who responded with Molotov cocktails. Snipers shot protesters with live ammunition. The centre of Kiev went up in flames and Yanukovych flew to Sochi to consult Putin. The picture of Kiev's inferno spoilt Putin's spectacle in Sochi. He was furious. The revolution in Kiev, he was convinced, was staged by the West which wanted to undermine him and turn Ukraine away from his sphere of influence. 'The Olympics', Ernst said, 'goes well beyond sport. It is geopolitics. We staged a good Olympics and it produced a strong counter-reaction. One day we will turn up all kinds of documents and write a true history of 2014.'[48]

Three days after the closing ceremony of the Sochi Olympics – also staged by Ernst – Russian 'polite green men' in unmarked military uniforms staged a coup in Crimea. Russian naval vessels that guarded the coast around Sochi set course towards Sebastopol. The Kremlin began the annexation of Crimea and stirred a war in the east of Ukraine. Television was at the forefront of that attack and Ernst and Dobrodeev were commanding the information forces. It was a television show whose cost was no longer calculated in billions of dollars but in thousands of lives.

Epilogue: Aerial Combat

In May 2000, two months after Vladimir Putin became Russia's president, Danila Bagrov, the main character of Russia's most popular blockbuster *Brat* (*Brother*) returned to the screen in *Brat* 2. If *Brat* had been an instant hit, its sequel became an instant cult.

The film follows Danila and his brother as they travel to America to take revenge for the death of a friend, Konstantin, whose twin brother was being blackmailed by an American businessman who also deals in drugs and violent sex. Danila spares the life of the Russian banker who was responsible for Konstantin's murder, and instead decides to track down the banker's American partner and deliver justice. After killing a few Ukrainians and 'niggers' and saving a Russian prostitute, Dasha, the Russian Robin Hood shoots his way through the American's office. 'Tell me, American,' says Danila, putting his gun on the table, 'do you think power is in money? I think power is in truth. The one who has truth is stronger.'

Made according to the canon of a Hollywood thriller, the film discerned and accurately captured Russian national instincts, thoughts and prejudices. When Danila's brother, before shooting a Ukrainian gangster, shouted: 'You will answer to me for Sebastopol!' audiences in Russia erupted in a slightly embarrassed laughter of recognition and approval. This and many other lines instantly turned into popular catchphrases.

'Are you gangsters?' an American woman asks Danila and Dasha as they barge into her flat. 'No, we are Russians,' Dasha, the Russian prostitute, replies.

The film had the charisma of Quentin Tarantino's *Pulp Fiction* and Danila shot people with the calm coolness of the character played by John Travolta. But it also made some serious points. It divided the world into 'ours' or 'brothers', and 'others' or 'aliens'. 'Brotherhood' was established through blood rather than ideology or values.

Preparing to fight for justice, Danila buys his weapons in Moscow from a freak collector of Second World War trophies who dresses in an old Nazi coat and goes under the nickname 'Fascist'. 'Willing or not, we are all brothers,' he says to Danila, who meekly tells him that his grandfather died in the war. 'It happens,' the 'Fascist' replies peacefully.

After years of futile search for a national idea and common values, *Brat 2* provided a simple and highly enticing answer: Russians are strong because they are moral and have truth behind them, while Americans are weak and hypocritical because they are all about money. Russians who were sucked into America, like Konstantin's twin brother, were corrupted morally. Just like the Soviet maxim, 'the teaching of Marx is all-powerful, because it is right', it required no further proof. Russians are better simply because they are.

At the end of the film Danila and Dasha fly back home. An airport official checking their passports tells the Russian woman in astonishment: 'But your visa expired years ago! You will never be able to return to America.' By way of reply, she gives him the finger. The closing credits of the film were accompanied by the soundtrack of 'Goodbye, America', sung by a children's choir.

The film was a product of art, not ideology. It did not tell people what they should think, rather it told them what they thought. It was not made to order by some official body. It was made to order by the public and appealed to some deeply rooted sense of injustice and humiliation that demanded satisfaction. Directed by Alexei Balabanov, the film had the strength, clarity and directness of a powerful beam that projected the country's future. Danila did not live long enough to see it.

In 2002, two years after the film was made, Sergei Bodrov, the actor who played Danila, died in a freak accident. He was filming in the Caucasus when a block of ice fell from Mount Dzhimara and dislodged a glacier that moved down the ravine, burying the film crew alive under the mud and boulders it brought with it. A decade later some Russians retrospectively imputed symbolism to his tragic end, as though it had contained a warning about the dangerous forces that Danila had set into motion. At the time it was made, however, the country was in the grip of a postmodern malaise, in which nothing was real, particularly politics, and the film was not taken as the prophecy that it turned out to be.

One man who was in charge of constructing Russia's political life in the 2000s was Vladislav Surkov, Putin's political adviser, who created a system of make-believe that dominated the country's political reality. Surkov had trained as a director of mass theatrical events and had worked as a PR man for the tycoon Mikhail Khodorkovsky, before moving to the Kremlin administration where he occupied the office that had belonged to the chief Soviet ideologists. Unlike his predecessors, however, he had no ideology. He was a master of an 'as if' world that consisted of simulacra and manipulations.

On the face of it, Russia had all the trappings of democracy: it had political parties and elections. But most parties were controlled by the Kremlin and elections – which are supposed to be a mechanism of orderly transfer of power – turned into a mechanism of retaining power. It worked like a house of mirrors. Those trying to challenge the Kremlin ended up fighting their own distorted reflection.

In 2003 Surkov set up and ushered into parliament a fake left-wing nationalist party called Rodina (Motherland) led by the demagogue and populist Dmitry Rogozin, who campaigned against immigrants and oligarchs. The party got 9 per cent in the parliamentary elections. Putin and his United Russia Party were marketed as the only alternative to the dark forces of nationalism.

Behind all these political games, which Surkov called 'sovereign democracy', was not a vision of Russia's future or an ambition to restore an empire, but something far more primitive: personal enrichment, comforts and power. Money was the only ideology the Kremlin subscribed to. Unlike Danila, who believed that truth was more powerful than money, the Kremlin believed there was no such thing as 'truth' and that strength was in money, that there was no such thing as values and that the only difference between Russian and Western officials was that Western ones could hide their cynicism better. If the new Russian elite had money, it could buy itself a Western lifestyle and the loyalty of the population, without bothering with all those 'values' which it considered to be no more than just wrapping.

Whereas Yeltsin's era bred the oligarch, Putin's introduced a far more dangerous type – the bureaucrat-entrepreneur who used the powers of the state for personal enrichment. 'Entrepreneurs' who work for the security services or the police have done especially well, because they have the ultimate competitive advantage: a licence for violence. The arrest of Mikhail Khodorkovsky and the appropriation of his vast oil firm Yukos was the biggest coup these men achieved and marked a turning point for the country, from one where universal human values were at least proclaimed to be at the centre of everything, to one where the state was proclaimed the top priority and people acting in its name had complete power over any individual, however rich or powerful. To justify their racketeering, Putin's people portrayed themselves as great 'patriots' who served the interest of the state. And since they *were* the state, helping themselves to its riches seemed only fair. The public, which resented the oligarchs, approved.

For all his authoritarianism, Putin derived his legitimacy from popular support and while he did not believe in fair elections, he paid careful attention to public opinion.

Opinion polls in 2004 showed that the number of Russians who considered themselves no different from people in other countries had fallen, while the opinion that Russia was surrounded by enemies had grown stronger. 'It is as though an invisible wall still counterpoises everything that is "ours" to everything "foreign",' wrote sociologist Yuri Levada.[1] One of Russia's oldest ideological constructions – the 'besieged fortress' – was also one of the most durable ones.

As a professional KGB operative, Putin 'recruited' people by telling them what they expected to hear. He told his core, traditionalist electorate that the state was the only provider of public good and that it was surrounded by enemies. But he also had a message for the middle class: don't involve yourself in politics and enjoy life while we, in the Kremlin, deal with the dark and uneducated plebs which have neither desire nor taste for Western democracy.

While the Kremlin pumped people with anti-Western tripe, its close friends, who had enriched themselves, shopped in Milan, holidayed in France, kept their money in Switzerland and sent their children to the top private schools in England. Money and corruption, many thought, would prevent the Kremlin from nationalist ideology and serious confrontation with the West. High oil prices allowed Putin to satisfy all: his friends became billionaires, the traditionalist paternalistically minded electorate got wage increases, while the middle class enjoyed low taxes and personal freedoms. Although money was the main mechanism of ruling the country, it was supplemented with entertainment: the show of Russia's resurgence, be it a football match or a war in Georgia, was enthusiastically received by all.

By the end of the decade the middle class had grown to 25 per cent of the population and nearly 40 per cent of the workforce – and those proportions were higher in big cities. In less than ten years Russia had transformed into a mass consumer society. Most of what it consumed, however, was imported. Russians in big cities drove the same cars, wore the same clothes, bought the same iPads, ate the same food, saw the same films, worked in the same open-plan offices and hung out in the same stylish bars as their counterparts in the West. Moscow acquired all the trimmings of a normal European city, but something was missing: a sense of security and justice, respect for one's achievements, the rule of law, property rights and healthcare – and none of these could be imported.

After the 2009 financial crisis, which exposed the fundamental weakness of Putin's economic model, the middle class became restless and started to talk about 'shoving off' from the country. This was not so much a statement of intention but a sign of an approaching crisis. The frustration was exacerbated by a false expectation created by the Kremlin among the Russian public. In 2008, in order to circumvent a constitutional rule that prevented him from serving for more than two consecutive terms as Russia's president, Putin made himself prime minister by installing the obedient sidekick and former lawyer Dmitry Medvedev as Russia's president. This was another of the Kremlin's simulacra. Medvedev talked about modernization and freedom, tweeted and recorded video blogs creating an illusion of change. The purpose of this illusion, however, was to leave everything intact and allow Putin to reclaim the title of the president four years later. But when Putin broke the illusion of change by saying that he would simply retake his job as president, making Medvedev prime minister, the frustration of the middle class boiled over. Medvedev's announcement that the 'job swap' had been planned all along added insult to injury. Many Russians felt duped and humiliated. By returning to the Kremlin, Putin was moving against the flow of time.

In December 2011, after the Kremlin rigged parliamentary elections, tens of thousands of Muscovites took to the streets. It was the biggest protest since the early 1990s and it marked not a revolution, but the transformation of the middle class from consumers to citizens. They demanded to be treated with the same respect by the state as they received as consumers. It seemed like a carnival rather than an uprising. People wore white ribbons and carried white balloons with the slogan 'If you blow us out again we will burst'. There were students, businessmen, journalists, pensioners, teachers and managers of different backgrounds and views. Some sported ski jackets previously worn on European slopes; others wore Russian felt boots and sheepskin coats.

Putin's rating started to slide and the trust in the media wobbled. Surkov's system of imitations was clearly failing. People who came out on the streets were real. Worse still, Putin with his PR stunts, which included his flying with cranes or diving for (planted) amphorae, evoked laughter. He had turned into a butt of jokes – just like the old Soviet leaders. He was out of fashion.

Putin was angry and rattled. He likened the protesters to the tribe of unruly monkeys from Kipling's *The Jungle Book* and ridiculed their ribbons and balloons by comparing them to condoms. The people who came out on the streets chanting 'Russia without Putin' were once his supporters and owed everything they had to his ten-year rule.

The protest was driven not by opposition politicians – they were largely caught by surprise – but by civil activists, journalists, writers and Internet bloggers. These were the ideologists of the protests who set its agenda and articulated its demands and slogans. They spread the ideas through social networks, mainly Facebook.

Afisha, a popular fashion and entertainment magazine that set the fashion and tastes of Moscow's creative class and which constructed the image of Moscow as a European city, became one of the voices of the protest movement. Its young editors – the children of the Soviet-era intelligentsia – found themselves in the same position as their parents had done thirty years earlier.

Like the intelligentsia of the 1970s that had been fostered in closed research institutes, Moscow's creative class grew up in the folds of an oil-rich authoritarian state. For much of the 2000s this creative class eschewed politics for the make-believe world of fashion. Now politics became the fashion. Russia's most fashion-sensitive television journalist, Leonid Parfenov, who had ridiculed Evgeny Kiselev for climbing the barricades a decade earlier, addressed his audience of successful, Westernized professionals frustrated by the lack of prospects for personal fulfilment in Russia from the stage of a street rally.

What the middle class wanted was institutions and lifestyle, not another political leader or a revolution. In fact, they mistrusted all political parties and organizations. They were happy to organize themselves into civil-society groups, and monitor the elections, but they were not prepared to delegate their power to any party or politician, including Alexei Navalny, a popular anti-corruption blogger turned politician who galvanized the protest in the first place.

A young, charismatic and blue-eyed lawyer in jeans and a white shirt with rolled-up sleeves, he was a Russian version of an American-style grass-roots politician whose style and tactics were inspired by *The Wire*, an American television drama. He used the Internet to circumvent the state monopoly over television and turned his social media followers into real crowds.

Navalny was born in 1974 into a military family and grew up in the semi-closed garrison towns around Moscow. He was an ardent supporter of Chubais and the team of radical market reformers of the early 1990s and rejected them as 'failures' in the 2010s. He represented the first generational shift in Russia since Putin's generation seized power. For all their differences – in age, background, status and values – Navalny struck at the same two issues as Yeltsin did in the 1980s: corruption (the unfair privileges of the party bosses in Yeltsin's days) and nationalism (independence from the rest of the empire). Navalny was no liberal and his appeal was far broader than the creative middle class. He positioned himself as a European-style nationalist and took part in their marches against immigrants from Central Asia and the Caucasus. Russia, he insisted, must shake off its imperial legacy and build a nation-state. He played on popular resentment of Chechnya, now ruled by Putin's protégé Ramzan Kadyrov, formerly a rebel fighter.

But his main line of attack was the Kremlin's kleptocracy and lies. He exposed the riches of Putin's elite, published photographs of their palaces and the names of the English schools where they sent their children. He described the Kremlin nomenclatura not as dark villains or even gangsters, but as parasites who had hijacked power in the country and used it for personal enrichment. He branded the ruling United Russia Party as 'the party of crooks and thieves' – thereby deliberately lowering the tone. Despite the Kremlin's tight control over the television, the term spread throughout the country like a rash.

The protest in the cities started to resonate within the provinces. The fastest decline in Putin's support was among poorer people over fifty-five years of age who felt Putin had not honoured his promises, and who were tired of waiting. They were also aggrieved by the impudence of United Russia Party bosses who grabbed land and built large mansions. It was losing legitimacy across different social strata and risking a broader discontent. The revolution was happening not in the streets but in people's heads, and that could not be stopped by the police force.

To dissuade ordinary people from joining their protests, Russian security services orchestrated clashes between protesters and the police, who threw ordinary and mostly innocent protesters into jail. But repression was limited in scale. Using real force against protesters as China had done in 1989 would have made things worse. Violence would have deprived the Kremlin of the remains of its legitimacy. Putin needed to defeat protesters ideologically. He had to change the narrative of the country and trump the political agenda set by the leaders of the protest movement.

Putin countered the idea of Russia as a modern, European-style nation-state by inciting traditionalist values of the state and the church. By prosecuting Pussy Riot, the young women punk singers who performed obscenely in front of the altar of Russia's main cathedral, banning the promotion of homosexuality and barring the adoption of Russian children by American couples, the Kremlin was able to present the liberals, who protested against all this, as a bunch of homosexual, blasphemous mercenaries ready to sell Russian children. Having lost the loyalty of the middle class, Putin tried to cement his core, paternalistic and traditionalist electorate. He moved towards a personalized Franco-style rule, sidelining the elites whom he deemed opportunistic and unreliable, and appealing directly to the people.

He turned to anti-Americanism as the only ideological tenet that had survived the collapse of the Soviet Union. Russia no longer aspired to be like the West, or sought its approval and recognition. Instead, it trumpeted its difference. Maxim Shevchenko, a TV journalist and a Kremlin-approved crusader against liberalism, argued in a newspaper column headlined 'WE ARE NOT EUROPE? AND THANK GOD FOR THAT!' that 'Russia and the West are at war... There is a growing feeling that most Western people belong to a different humanoid group from us; that we are only superficially similar, but fundamentally different.'[2]

Putin's tactic worked, but only partly: it discredited protesters and dampened the mood for coming out on the streets, but it did not boost his own rating. The mistrust of the Kremlin and its rhetoric seemed too deep. And whereas the protest in 2011 was about rules and elections, by 2013 it became more overtly political. Navalny attacked the regime not because of the way it counted votes, but because it was corrupt and morally bankrupt and therefore illegitimate. Putin responded in kind. He defended his rent-seeking, crooked, post-Soviet system of governance by claiming moral superiority over the West. 'We see how many Euro-Atlantic countries are in effect turning away from their roots, including their Christian values,' Putin said. Russia, by contrast, 'has always been a state civilization held together by the Russian people, the Russian language, Russian culture and the Russian Orthodox Church'.[3]

Words had to be backed up with actions. A crisis in Ukraine, which in February 2014 turned into a revolution, presented both a threat and an opportunity. Revolution in Kiev, Russian state television claimed, was part of America's plan to encroach on and emasculate Russia and to throw it back behind the Urals. The Kremlin had to fight back. The basic idea of the propaganda was the same as it was during the August 2008 war with Georgia, but the intensity and scale was unlike anything seen before.

In preparation for its offensive against Ukraine, the Kremlin cleared out the last pockets of independent media in Russia, including popular Internet news sites, personal blogs and the liberal cable TV channel, TV Rain. To be effective, propaganda had to be total. Dmitry Kiselev, the main anchor on the Russia Channel, run by Oleg Dobrodeev who had once set up NTV's news, was put to work.

Wearing a tight-fitting suit, he paced up and down the studio, operatically gesticulating, squinting his eyes and accentuating his words, drilling the message home with a sadistic smile. 'Here are fighting brigades,' he said of the middle-class Kiev protesters who came out under EU flags. 'There is fear and emptiness in their eyes; and here they are preparing food, a dish for gourmands: a piece of lard fried on the side of a rusty tin.'[4] Kiselev's weekly analytical news programme was close in style to Orwell's two minutes' hate, stretched to an hour. As part of their Soviet-era military service, many Russian television executives had been trained in 'special propaganda', which sought to 'demoralize the enemy army and establish control over the occupied territory'.

In 1999 Kiselev had moralized about journalistic ethics: 'People will, of course, swallow anything. But if we keep lowering the bar and drop morals we will, one day, find ourselves splashing in the dirt like pigs and eating each other, along with this dirt, and then we would not be able to sink any lower.'[5] Kiselev's programmes have now reached that state.

—

The unexpected fall of Viktor Yanukovych, the authoritarian and thuggish president of Ukraine, allowed Putin to execute an audacious plan long harboured in his mind – the annexation of Crimea. It provided the same miraculous 'short-circuit' effect as Putin's response to the bombing of the apartment blocks in Moscow in 1999. It turned Putin into a historic figure who had revised post-Soviet history and had succeeded in returning to the country, suffering from phantom pain, a limb it had lost in 1991. Corruption – the main subject only two years earlier – receded into the background.

Putin's rating jumped from 60 per cent to 80 per cent. Many of the affluent Russians who had protested against Putin a few years earlier moved to his side. Unmet hopes of personal fulfilment were assuaged by a symbolic victory for the state. The annexation of Crimea was a substitute for modernization. It gave people a sense of purpose without their having to make any effort. Only 3 per cent of Russians disapproved of the annexation. Crimea has long been the nerve centre of Russia's imperial nostalgia and its annexation had been an *idée fixe* of Russian nationalists ever since the end of the Soviet Union. They now celebrated the triumph of their idea.

Announcing the annexation of Crimea in the Kremlin's gilded Hall of St George on 18 March 2014, Putin repeated, almost verbatim, the words which twenty years earlier were printed in the nationalist newspaper *Den'* by Igor Shafarevich, one of the ideologists of Russian nationalism. 'Everything in Crimea speaks of our shared history and pride. This is the location of ancient Khersones, where Prince Vladimir was baptized... The graves of Russian soldiers whose bravery brought Crimea into the Russian empire are also in Crimea.'[6] While it had been Prince Vladimir who was baptized in Crimea, it was President Vladimir who brought it back into Russia's fold. In October 1993 Russian nationalists had tried to storm Ostankino television centre to air their ideas. Now these ideas were articulated by the president of Russia and broadcast by all central television channels without a single shot being fired.

In fact, very few Russians were even aware of Vladimir's baptism in Crimea. For them, the peninsula was linked to hedonism rather than spirituality. It was a place for holidays, summer romances, state sanatoria and dachas, but to make the annexation look legitimate, Putin had to ground it in Christian mythology. The true symbolism of the annexation of Crimea was that Putin was reversing the course of history and elevating Russians to their past imperial glory – something that the nationalists and communists could only dream about.

However, the red–brown coalition that had formed in the early 1990s had undergone a change. Communists were dumped along the way. Nina Andreeva, who wrote the infamous letter 'I Cannot Forsake Principles', today lives in a shoebox-sized studio flat near St Petersburg, studying the works of Lenin and 'commanding' the Central Committee of the All Union Communist Party of the Bolsheviks – a party that consists of her and a few other pensioners. The old communist Viktor Anpilov, who led the siege of Ostankino, nestles on the outskirts of Moscow in a basement that reeks of body odour and sour cabbage, surrounded by portraits of Stalin and old Soviet flags.

The new coalition emerged in 2013 – between nationalists and the party of 'crooks and thieves'. The annexation of Crimea, performed by an extraordinary sleight of hand, cemented their union. Even Alexander Nevzorov, Russia's first television stuntman who experimented with Russian fascism in the 1990s but became 'disillusioned' by the idea, cringed: 'If Crimea was taken from a strong, rich and brave country, it would have been an honest and noble victory. But it was taken from a wounded, bleeding and motionless country, and that was looting,' he wrote.[7] Yet it was the television techniques that Nevzorov had used in the 1980s which allowed Russia to take Crimea without a battle.

Events on the ground unfolded according to a script created by television, which ran something like this: the Ukrainian revolution brought to power America-sponsored neo-Nazis. The descendants of those who had collaborated with Hitler during the Second World War now vandalized Soviet war memorials and threatened to annihilate the Russian language and history in Crimea. The Russian population of Crimea turned to Vladimir Putin for help, which he duly provided. The plot was enacted on 27 February when the Russian military seized airports, government buildings and broadcasters within hours, blockaded Ukrainian military bases and installed its marionettes in government.

Russian soldiers were portrayed as liberators, rather than occupiers. Videos were uploaded on the Internet showing a Russian soldier in Crimea holding a small child in his arms – a reference to the giant statue of the Soviet Liberator Soldier erected in Berlin in 1949. In Sebastopol, home to Russia's Black Sea fleet, local people celebrated their liberation. There was only one thing missing: the enemy.

While the military were at work, Moscow PR men, coordinated by Vladislav Surkov, turned former local crooks and racketeers into the 'freedom-seeking government' of Crimea. One of these PR men was Alexander Borodai, the son of an orthodox nationalist philosopher, who had participated in the nationalists' uprising against Yeltsin in 1993 while studying philosophy at Moscow State University. He was particularly interested in the ideology of the ultra-nationalists who fled Russia after the Bolshevik Revolution and had strong sympathy for (and influence over) the rise of fascism in Europe.

As a nineteen-year-old in 1992, Borodai went to fight in Transnistria to defend ethnic Russians against Moldovan 'fascists' and a year later turned up at the White House in Moscow. He claims to have led some twenty armed men in the siege of the Ostankino television centre in October 1993. He managed to escape from Ostankino unscathed and continued his studies while also writing for the nationalist *Zavtra* newspaper. But he made money by consulting private oil companies, both Russian and foreign. He epitomized the union between the party of 'crooks and thieves' and the nationalists. While Putin believed he was using the nationalists, the nationalists were convinced that they were using Putin. Crimea was just the start. Russia also planned to create a protectorate in the east of Ukraine that would stop the country drifting towards Europe and the West.

Borodai's job was to help stir the situation in the Donbass region of eastern Ukraine in the hope that it would set off a chain reaction of separatism in the east of the country. They called it 'the Russian Spring', analogous to the Arab Spring. Putin promoted the idea of the 'Russian World' and Novorossiya (New Russia), an historic term that described the southern part of the Russian Empire that contained the territory of modern Ukraine, including Odessa, though, ironically, not Donetsk, the capital of the region. To help Novorossiya into being, Russia funnelled money, weapons and agents provocateurs into Donetsk, helping a ragtag of thugs, opportunists and jobless to take over the local administration, which quickly turned into an unruly and smelly squat rather than a revolutionary headquarters.

But while the region smouldered, it did not burst into flame. To set off a big fire, a generous helping of petrol and a firelighter were needed. Enter Igor Girkin, an old friend of Borodai, who arrived in Crimea shortly before the annexation. Girkin, who went under the pseudonym Strelkov (Shooter), first fought in Transnistria in the early 1990s, then in Bosnia – on the side of the Serbian army – and finally in Chechnya, where he was responsible for the 'disappearances' (secret executions) of several alleged rebels. He claimed to have served in the Russian security services. Far more important, though, was his passion for reconstructing past wars. A graduate of the Institute of History and Archives, he belonged to a group of aficionados who dressed in historic costumes and staged theatrical re-enactments of famous battles. Strelkov was particularly keen on the Russian Civil War of 1917–22, in which he would dress as a White Army officer. The scripts of his most recent military historic games concerned the actions of the Russian volunteer army in the south-west of Ukraine in 1920. In the summer of 2014, Strelkov got the chance to re-enact the Russian Civil War with real weapons.

In April 2014 Strelkov, with a group of men backed by the Russian military, stormed the town of Slavyansk in eastern Ukraine. The first thing they did was to seize the television transmitters. Ukrainian channels were taken off the air and replaced by Russian state channels. Within a few days fierce fighting was raging across the region.

Had it not been for Russian television, the war probably would not have started. The notion of television as a weapon lost its metaphorical sense. It *was* the real weapon causing real destruction.*

Wars have been televised before. But never before have wars been conducted and territory gained primarily by means of television and propaganda. The role of the military was to support the picture. The Russian media have not just distorted reality – they invented it, using fake footage, doctoring quotes, using actors (sometimes the same actor would impersonate both the victim and an aggressor on different channels). 'Our psyche is set up in such a way that only an artistic form can explain the time [we live in],' Ernst once said.

On 12 July 2014, Channel One 'interviewed' a Ukrainian woman with a heart-wrenching story. The woman said she had witnessed the public execution of a three-year-old boy, who was crucified in the crowded main square of Slavyansk when Ukrainian forces retook it. She provided the gory details: the Ukrainian 'animals' – descendants of the fascist collaborators during the Second World War – cut into the little boy's flesh and made him suffer for an hour before he died. The woman added that the boy's mother was then tied to a tank and dragged along until she too

* Konstantin Ernst, the head of Channel One, has long had an affection for military hardware but none had as wide a range as television.

was dead. The story was a fake. By planting stories about children crucified or tortured by Ukrainians, Russian propaganda deployed the same time-tested mechanism of arousing hatred as the one used in Jewish pogroms in pre-revolutionary Russia.

Russian television worked like a psychoactive agent, a hallucinogen. As Nevzorov wrote, 'Patriotic hallucinations are aggressive, hysterical and persistent... One must remember the ideological drug [of patriotism] is injected into the country's veins for one main purpose: so that, at the first click of the fingers of any idiot in military stripes, crowds of boys voluntarily agree to turn into burnt and rotting meat.'[8]

The point of the information war unleashed by Russia was not to convince someone of Russia's point of view, but to ignite the fighting and draw the civilian population into the conflict, and this is what it achieved. Many of those who joined the fight were jobless and disenfranchised, some were paid pittances in illegal coal mines, many were former Soviet soldiers who felt abandoned by their Soviet motherland when the Soviet Union collapsed. Russian television exploited their weaknesses and lured them into a fight for a country that had ceased to exist nearly a quarter of a century earlier. Russia's 'hybrid' war lifted them from their miserable, anonymous and hopeless existence onto the television screen, told them they were victims and heroes, provided them with weapons and pointed to an enemy. Russian propaganda also mobilized thousands of Russian volunteers who flocked to take part in a bloody battle against 'fascism' in Ukraine.

Those who produce Russian propaganda are not driven by the idea of the notional 'Russian World' or empire rebuilding – they are too pragmatic for that. They acted not out of conviction or a sense of reality but out of a disrespect for it. The hallucinations they produced took on a life of their own and started to behave in an unscripted way, unaware they were only part of a television show. Five days after the airing of the story about the crucified boy, the Russian-backed separatists brought down Malaysian flight MH17, killing all 298 passengers on board.

For the vast majority of Russians, however, the war in Ukraine was just a show provided by television. For most of 2014, news programmes, often twice as long as usual, were entirely dedicated to Ukraine, as though life in Russia itself stopped. The war was 'serialized' into hour-long episodes filled with blood, violence and suspense. News programmes used cinematic devices and special effects: clips, dramatic flashbacks, montage, music. Television channels competed for the largest share of the audience (and advertising market) by selling the war drama, which they had staged. For the first time in Russian history, news programmes consistently topped the viewing tables, overtaking soap operas and serials. As ever, Channel One and its *Vremya* came first.

For the Russian audience the show was largely free of charge. The sanctions imposed by the West on Russia did not affect the majority of the population, at least initially. And the deaths of Russia's own soldiers who were sent to fight in Ukraine were carefully covered up and concealed. The popularity of the show transferred into Putin's rating, pushing it close to 90 per cent approval. But this also suggested that as soon as the show ended, the rating would fall. Mobilization, therefore, was the only resource available to Putin.

To sustain the audience's attention, the plot had to evolve to produce new virtual enemies and raise the level of aggression and hatred. The narrative of war has now moved beyond Ukraine to the West in general. The claim that Russia is at war with America and the West has been drilled into the minds of ordinary Russians. Those who protested against the war have been labelled as national traitors and collaborators with Western-sponsored fascism.

All television channels attacked liberals, but NTV did it with particular zeal, perhaps compensating or taking revenge for its own past. One of its regular targets was Boris Nemtsov – a man who once symbolized Russia's hopes for becoming a normal, civilized and above all free country of which NTV was supposed to be a part. In May 2014, the state of the country filled him with despair:

> I can't remember such a level of general hatred as the one in Moscow today. Not in 1991, during the August coup, not even in 1993. Aggression and cruelty are stoked by the television while the key definitions are supplied by the slightly possessed Kremlin master. 'National traitors', 'fifth column', 'fascist junta' – all these terms are coming from the same Kremlin office... The Kremlin is cultivating and rewarding the lowest instincts in people, provoking hatred and fighting. People are set off against each other. This hell cannot end peacefully.[9]

Less than a year later, Nemtsov was shot dead next to the Kremlin.

After Nemtsov's murder, Vladimir Yakovlev, the founder of *Kommersant*, made a public appeal to everyone who worked in the media. He spoke not just for himself, but also on behalf of his father, Yegor Yakovlev. 'Stop teaching people how to hate. Because hatred is already tearing the country to pieces. People live in a crazy illusion that the country is surrounded by enemies. Boys get killed in a war. Politicians are executed by the walls of the Kremlin. It is not Europe and America that stands on a verge of social catastrophe. The information war is first and foremost destroying ourselves.'[10]

Television images work like drugs, creating a sense of elation, destroying judgement and intelligence, lowering moral barriers and suppressing inhibitions and fears. No enemy of Russia could cause as much harm to the country as has been inflicted by those who pump out these drugs into the bloodstream of the nation.

The vast majority of Russians now contemplate the possibility of a nuclear war with America and 40 per cent of the younger ones believe that Russia can win, as though it were a video game in which people have lives in reserve. Few Russians are prepared to pay for it with their lives or their suffering.

Just as in any trade in drugs, television propaganda exploits people's weaknesses and cravings. The main reason Russian propaganda works is because enough people want to believe it. Many of those who crave it are not poor and ignorant – but affluent and well informed. They are deceived because they want to be deceived. Opinion polls show that almost half of the Russian population knows that the Kremlin is lying to the world about the absence of Russian troops in Ukraine, but approves of these lies and sees them as a sign of strength. More than half think it is right for the media to distort information in the interest of the state.

This propaganda feeds not so much on ignorance, but on resentment – a mixture of jealousy and hostility. Having an imagined but mighty enemy, America, makes people feel noble and good; it compensates for personal weaknesses and failures, and frees them from the need to justify themselves to anyone and above all to themselves. Russia is running the risk of overdosing on hatred and aggression. The euphoria and nationalist frenzy cannot just be switched off like a television set – energy does not simply vanish. History cannot be rewound like a tape and the choices that brought it to this state cannot be unmade. But the future is not predetermined either.

The only consistent feature of Russia's history is its unpredictability. As Yegor Gaidar, who chronicled the collapse of the Soviet empire, once said, big changes happen later than we think but earlier than we expect. Putin's war in Ukraine is aimed at modernity and the future. The forces that it has awoken are not the forces of imperial expansion – Russia does not possess the energy or vision required for empire-building – but forces of chaos and disorganisation. They may plunge the country into darkness or Russia may rid itself of its post-imperial syndrome and emerge as a nation state. But history does not have a will of its own and what kind of place Russia becomes depends on the next generation that will come to invent it.

Notes

Anyone dealing with Russian language sources and names comes across the problem of transliteration. The existence of several systems makes it difficult to be entirely consistent in rendering words from the Cyrillic alphabet into the Latin one. In the main text of the book Russian names and titles are presented in the form used by most English language newspapers, so Yeltsin not Eltsin, Yegor not Egor, *Novy Mir* not *Novyi Mir*. However, in transliterating references and citation sources provided in the endnotes I use the Library of Congress system of transliteration adopted by most English language library catalogues. This makes locating the sources easier. For example, the Cyrillic letter *е* is transliaterated as *e*, *й* as *i*, *у* as *u*, *х* as *kh*, *ц* as *ts*, *ч* as *ch*, *ш* as *sh*, *щ* as *shch*, *ю* as *iu* and *я* as *ia*. Russian soft and hard signs ь and ъ are indicated by '.

The titles of Russian literary works that have been translated into English are given only in English. When a book that has not been translated is mentioned, its title is given both in Russian and in English. The translations of Russian texts are my own unless otherwise noted in the endnotes. The names of cities that have changed their names after the Soviet collapse are given in their historic context, so Mikhail Gorbachev visited Leningrad in 1985 but Vladimir Putin worked for the mayor of St Petersburg.

Some institutions have changed their name more than once. Channel One used to be known as ORT (Public Russian Broadcaster) and also as Ostankino (the name of the television centre from which it was broadcasting). To spare readers from confusion, I refer to it as Channel One throughout. The *Moskovskie novosti* newspaper had foreign language editions including an English one called *The Moscow News*, but since I only refer to the Russian language newspaper, I use the Russian name: *Moskovskie novosti*.

PROLOGUE

1. Michal Kacewicza, 'Final Interview with Boris Nemtsov', *Newsweek*, 28 February 2015. http://www.newsweek.com/2015/03/13/final-interview-boris-nemtsov-310392.html
2. 'End of the Soviet Union', Gorbachev's farewell address, *New York Times*, 26 December 1991.

3. Ivan Pavlov, 'Ob ume voobshche, o russkom ume v chastnosti'. http://www.gumer.info/bibliotek_Buks/History/Article/pavl_russum.php
4. Quoted in Ellen Mickiewicz, *Changing Channels: Television and the Struggle for Power in Russia* (Durham, NC: Duke University Press, 1999), p. 10.

Part I

CHAPTER ONE

1. Documentary film, SSSR. *Krusheniie*, part 1, Channel Rossiia 1, 2011.
2. Andrei Grachev, *Kremlevskaia khronika* (Moscow: Eksmo, 1994), p. 392.
3. Alexander Yakovlev, *Omut pamiati*, 2 vols (Moscow: Vagrius, 2001), vol. 2, p. 83.
4. Nikita Sergeevich Khrushchev, *Dva tsveta vremeni: Dokumenty iz lichnogo fonda N.S Khrushcheva*, 2 vols (Moscow: Mezhdunarodny fond 'Demokratia', 2009), vol. 2, p. 465.
5. Alexander Bovin, *XX vek kak zhizn'* (Moscow: Zakharov, 2003), p. 108.
6. Otto Latsis, *Tshchatel'no splanirovannoe samoubiistvo* (Moscow: Moskovskaia shkola politicheskikh issledovanii, 2001).
7. Documentary film *Khvost komety*, Moscow, TVS, 2003. I am grateful to Sergei Kostin, the maker of the film, for letting me read the complete transcript of his interviews with Yegor Yakovlev.
8. Alexander Yakovlev, *Sumerki* (Moscow: Materik, 2005), p. 33.
9. Alexander Yakovlev, *Omut pamiati*, vol. 1, p. 17.
10. Ibid., p. 447.
11. *Pravo perepiski* (Moscow: Memorial, 2014).
12. Joseph Brodsky, *Less than One* (London: Viking, 1986), p. 457.
13. *Fireglow* was first published in 1965, in *Znamia*, a literary journal; the book appeared a year later. Yuri Trifonov, *Otblesk kostra* (Moscow: Sovetskii Pisatel', 1966), p. 5.
14. Lichnoe delo Yegora Yakovleva [Yegor Yakovlev's personal file], Moscow, Izvestia Archive, fond 1, opis' 5, MS 1549.
15. Moscow, Russian State Archive (GARF), Yegor Yakovlev's archive, uncatalogued.
16. Ivan Bunin, *Cursed Days: A Diary of Revolution*, trans. by Gaiton Marullo (London: Phoenix Press, 2000), p. 89.
17. Ibid., p. 81.
18. Yegor Yakovlev, *Ia idu s toboi* (Moscow: Molodaia gvardiia, 1965), p. 127.
19. Irina Yakovleva, interview with the author, May 2012.
20. Yegor Yakovlev, *Ia idu s toboi*, pp. 89–90.
21. Andrei Sakharov, *Vospominaniia*, 3 vols (Moscow: Vremia, 2006), vol. 1, p. 362.
22. Ibid., p. 276.
23. Inna Solovyova, interview with the author, November 2012.
24. Yegor Yakovlev, *Ia idu s toboi*, pp. 56–7.
25. Alexander Yakovlev, *Omut pamiati*, vol. 1, p. 177.
26. William Taubman, *Khrushchev: The Man and His Era* (London: Simon & Schuster, 2003), p. 278

27. Ibid., p. 276.
28. Bovin, *XX vek kak zhizn'*, p. 56.
29. Yegor Yakovlev, *Ia idu s toboi*, pp. 110–11.
30. Yegor Yakovlev in *Khvost komety*, a documentary film (see endnote 7, p. 356).
31. Alexander Tvardovsky, *Chestno ia tianul moi voz. Stikhi. Proza. Dnevniki. Pis'ma. Dokumenty. Golosa sovremennikov*, ed. by A. Turkov (Moscow: MIK, 2010), p. 10.
32. C. P. Snow, 'Introduction', in Alexander Tvardovsky, *Tyorkin and the Stove Makers* (London: Carcanet Press, 1974), pp. 7–16 (p. 13).
33. Alexander Solzhenitsyn, *The Oak and the Calf* (London: Collins/Harvill Press, 1980), pp. 14–15.
34. Alexander Tvardovsky, *Novomirskii dnevnik, 1961–1966* (Moscow: PROZAiK, 2009), p. 111.
35. Latsis, *Tshchatel'no splanirovannoe samoubiistvo*, p. 63.
36. Bovin, *XX vak kak zhihn'*, p. 123.
37. Ibid., p. 126.
38. Ibid., p. 109.
39. Alexander Borin, 'Da zdravstvuiet privereda!', *Zhurnalist*, 4 (1967), p. 54.
40. *Pressa v obshchestve (1959–2000). Otsenki zhurnalistov i sotsiologov. Dokumenty* (Moscow: Moskovkaia shkola politicheskikh issledovanii, 2000), pp. 470–2.
41. *'Prazhskaia vesna' i mezhdunarodnyi krizis 1968 goda: dokumenty*, ed. by N. Tomilina, S. Karner and A. Chubarian (Moscow: Mezhdunarodnyi fond 'Demokratiia': 2010), p. 197.
42. Bovin, *XX vek kak zhizn'*, p. 184.
43. Ibid., p. 189.
44. Alexander Galich, *Kogda ia vernus'* (Frankfurt am Main: Posev, 1981), p. 29.
45. Quoted from Leonid Parfenov's film *Deti XX s'ezda*, Moscow, 1987.
46. On Karpinsky, see David Remnick, *Lenin's Tomb: The Last Days of the Soviet Empire* (New York: Random House, 1993), pp. 169–79.
47. L. Okunev (Len Karpinsky), 'Words are Also Deeds' in Stephen F. Cohen (ed.), *An End to Silence: Uncensored Opinion in the Soviet Union from Roy Medvedev's underground magazine, Political Diary* (New York: W. W. Norton, 1982), pp. 300–310 (p. 306).
48. Mikhail Fedotov, 'Zakon SSSR o pechati kak iuridicheskoe litso', *Novoe literaturnoe obozrenie*, 83 (2007), p. 115.
49. Okunev (Len Karpinsky), 'Words are Also Deeds', p. 308.
50. Alexander Yakovlev, *Sumerki*, p. 312.
51. Alexander Yakovlev, *Omut pamiati*, vol. 1, p. 256.
52. Alexander Tvardovsky, *Novomirskii dnevnik, 1961–1966*, p. 471.
53. Alexander Yakovlev, 'Protiv antiistorizma', *Literarurnaya gazeta*, 15 November 1972, p. 5. For detailed discussion on the subject of the nationalists in the Communist Party, see Nikolai Mitrokhin, *Russkaia partiia. Dvizhenie russkikh natsionalistov v SSSR 1953–1985* (Moscow: NLO, 2003).
54. Alexander Yakovlev, *Omut pamiati*, vol. 1, p. 272.
55. Vasily Grossman, *Life and Fate* (New York: Random House, 2011), p. 379.
56. Alexander Yakovlev, *Omut pamiati*, vol. 1, p. 45.

57. Ibid., p. 305.
58. Ibid., p. 306.
59. Alexander Solzhenitsyn, 'Live Not by Lies', *Washington Post*, 18 February 1974, p. 26.
60. Alexander Solzhenitsyn, 'Obrazovanshchina', *Novy Mir* 5 (1991), pp. 28–46.
61. Andrei Amalrik, *Will the Soviet Union Survive until 1984?* (New York: Harper & Row, 1981), p. 24.
62. Irina Yakovleva, interview with the author, May 2012.
63. Documentary film *Khvost komety*.
64. Latsis, *Tshchatel'no splanirovannoe samoubiistvo*, p. 173.
65. Arkady Ostrovsky, 'Echoes in the Cherry Orchard', *Financial Times*, (*Weekend FT*), 30 May 1998, p. 8.

CHAPTER TWO

1. Anatoly Smeliansky, *Mezhdometiia vremeni*, 2 vols (Moscow: Iskusstvo, 2002), vol. 1, p. 79.
2. Yuri Burtin, '"Vam, iz drugogo pokoleniia..." K publikatsii poemy A. Tvardovskogo "Po pravu pamiati"', *Oktiabr*, 8 (1987), pp. 191–202 (p. 200).
3. Mikhail Gorbachev and Zdeněk Mlynář, *Conversations with Gorbachev – On Perestroika, the Prague Spring, and the Crossroads of Socialism* (New York: Columbia University Press, 2003), p. 77
4. Alexander Yakovlev, *Omut pamiati*, vol. 1, p. 319.
5. Ibid., p. 367.
6. Ibid., p. 367.
7. Ibid., p. 390.
8. 'Otravlennoe oblako antisovetizma', *Moskovskie novosti*, 11 May 1986, p. 1.
9. *V Politburo TsK KPSS: 1985–1991*, ed. by A. Chernyaev, A. Veber and V. Medvedev (Moscow: Alpina Bizness Books, 2006), pp. 64–5.
10. Ibid.
11. Yegor Yakovlev, Speech to the Communist Party organization at *Moskovskie novosti* [K dokladu na partsobranii], 25 September 1987, MS, Russian State Archives (GARF).
12. Alexander Lyubimov, interview with the author, 2004.
13. Latsis, *Tshchatel'no splanirovannoe samoubiistvo*, p. 213.
14. Mikhail Shatrov and Stephen Cohen, 'Vernut'sia, chtoby idti vpered', *Moskovskie novosti*, 14 June 1987, p. 9.
15. Nina Andreeva, 'Ne mogu postupit'sia printsipami', *Sovetskaya Rossiya*, 13 March 1988.
16. Quoted in Remnick, *Lenin's Tomb*, p. 76.
17. Ibid., p. 77
18. Stephen Cohen and Katrina vanden Heuvel, *Voices of Glasnost: Interviews with Gorbachev's Reformers* (New York: Norton & Company, 1989), p. 210.
19. *V Politburo TsK KPSS*, p. 249.
20. Leon Aron, *Yeltsin: A Revolutionary Life* (New York: St Martin's Press, 2000), p. 222.
21. Ibid., 233.
22. Cohen and vanden Heuvel, *Voices of Glasnost*, p. 211.

23. Alexander Kabakov, 'Unizhenie', *Moskovskie novosti*, 12 March 1989, p. 5.
24. A. Craig Copetas, *Bear Hunting with the Politburo: American Adventures in Russian Capitalism* (Lanham, MD: Madison Books, 2001), p. 13.
25. Andrew Higgins, Guy Chazan, Alan Cullison, 'Secretive Associate of Putin Emerges As Czar of Russian Oil Trading', *Wall Street Journal*, 11 June 2008. http://www.wsj.com/articles/SB121314210826662571
26. Mikhail Zygar and Valeriy Paniushkin, *Gazprom: Novoe russkoe oruzhie* (Moscow: Zakharov, 2008), p. 18.
27. Yegor Gaidar, *Vlast' i sobstvennost': Smuty i instituty. Gosudarstvo i evolutsiia* (St Petersburg: Norma, 2009), p. 280.
28. Yegor Gaidar and V. Yaroshenko, 'Nulevoi tsikl. K analizu mekhanizma vedomstvennoi ekspansii', *Kommunist* 8 (1988), pp. 74–86.
29. Yegor Gaidar, 'Chastnaia sobstvennost' – novyi stereotip', *Moskovskie novosti*, 8 October 1989, p. 11.
30. Igor Malashenko, interview with the author, September 2010.
31. Ibid.
32. Mickiewicz, *Changing Channels*, p. 10
33. Sakharov, *Vospominaniia*, vol. 3, p. 655.
34. Ibid., p. 717.
35. Sergei Averintsev, *Moskovskie novosti*, 31 December 1989, p. 2.
36. Andrei Sakharov, 'Poslednee vystuplenie', *Moskovskie novosti*, 31 December 1989, p. 10.
37. 'Speaking Truth to Power', *The Economist*, 9 August 2008, p. 11.

CHAPTER THREE

1. Marietta Chudakova, 'Pri nachale kontsa: Zapiski nabliudatelia i kommentarii istorika, okazavshikhsia odnim i tem zhe litsom', *Novoe literaturnoe obozrenie* 84 (2000), pp. 533–56 (p. 533).
2. Alexander Nevzorov, interview with the author, 2004.
3. A. Kabakov, *Nevozvrashchenets* (Moscow: Vagrius: 2003), p. 67.
4. Natalia Gevorkyan, interview with the author, March 2012.
5. Natalia Gevorkyan, Natalya Timakova and Andrei Kolesnikov, *First Person: An Astonishingly Frank Self-Portrait by Russia's President Vladimir Putin*, trans. by Catherine A. Fitzpatrick (New York: PublicAffairs, 2000), pp. 71–2.
6. Natalia Gevorkyan, '"Otkrovennost'" vosmozhna lish kogda za toboi zakroetsia dver', *Moskovskie novosti*, 24 June 1990, p. 11.
7. Natalia Gevorkyan, 'Gosbezopasnost': prazhskii variant', *Moskovskie novosti*, 29 July 1990, p. 16.
8. Natalia Gevorkyan, interview with the author, March 2012.
9. *V Politburo TsK KPSS*, p. 543.
10. Unpublished diaries of Sir Rodric Braithwaite.
11. Ibid.

12. Yegor Yakovlev, 'Vozrozhdenie partii v rukakh levykh sil', *Moskovskie novosti*, 22 July 1990, p. 4.
13. Ibid.
14. Nikolai Shmelev, 'S kem i kuda idti "Moskovskim novostiam"', *Moskovskie novosti*, 29 July 1990, p. 6.
15. *V Politburo TskKPSS*, pp. 617–19.
16. Ibid.
17. Tengiz Abuladze, Ales Adamovich, Evgeny Ambratsumov, Yuri Chernichenko, 'Strana ustala zhdat'', *Moskovskie novosti*, 18 October 1990, p. 1.
18. Anatoly Chernyaev, *Sovmestnyi iskhod. Dnevnik dvukh epokh. 1972–1991 gody* (Moscow: Rossiiskaia politicheskaia entsiklopediia, 2010), p. 887.
19. Unpublished diaries of Rodric Braithwaite.
20. Quoted in Remnick, *Lenin's Tomb*, pp. 374–5.
21. Alexander Nevzorov, interview with the author, January 2015.
22. Ibid.
23. Ibid.
24. Alexander Nevzorov, interview with the author, 2004.
25. 'Prestuplenie rezhima, kotoryi ne khochet ukhodit' so stseny', *Moskovskie novosti*, 20 January 1991, p. 1.
26. Remnick, *Lenin's Tomb*, p. 390.
27. Quoted in Yevgenia Albats, *Mina zamedlennogo deistviia* (Moscow: RUSSLIT, 1992), p. 405.
28. Alexander Yakovlev, *Omut pamiati*, vol. 1, p. 429.
29. 'Slovo k narodu', *Sovetskaya Rossiya*, 23 July 1991.
30. Remnick, *Lenin's Tomb*, p. 455.
31. Boris Yeltsin, *Zapiski prezidenta* (Moscow: Rosspen, 2008), p. 88.
32. Yevgenia Albats, *Mina zamedlennogo deistviia (Politicheskii portret KGB)* (Moscow: RUSSLIT, 1992), p. 241.
33. Vasily Rozanov, *Apocalipsis nashego vremeni* (Moscow: Zakharov, 2001), p. 7.
34. Alexander Yakovlev, *Sumerki* (Moscow: Materik, 2005), pp. 123–4.
35. General Alexei Kondaurov, quoted in 'The Making of a Neo-KGB State', *The Economist*, 25 August 2007, pp. 25–30 (p. 25).
36. Latsis, *Tshchatel'no splanirovannoe samoubiistvo*, p. 371.
37. Yegor Gaidar, *Gibel' imperii* (Moscow: Rosspen, 2007), p. 388.
38. Alexander Kabakov, 'Ten' na piru', *Moskovskie novosti*, 1 September 1991, p. 3.
39. Sergei Averintsev, 'Da ogradit bog nas ot prizrakov', *Literaturnaya gazeta*, 25 September 1991, p. 15.
40. Ibid.
41. Ibid.

CHAPTER FOUR

1. Remnick, *Lenin's Tomb*, pp. 374–8.
2. Andrei Malgin, 'Smotrite, kto ushel', *Stolitsa* 4 (1993), pp. 6–12.

3. Yegor Yakovlev, 'Razgovor s synom', *Moskovskie novosti*, 8 September 1991, pp. 8–9.
4. Copetas, *Bear Hunting with the Politburo*, p. 79
5. Vladimir Yakovlev, interview with the author, September 2014.
6. The 'hard sign' (the 28th letter of the Russian alphabet), used at the end of words, was part of Russia's pre-revolutionary orthography. It was abolished as part of the Bolshevik reforms in 1917–18.
7. Quoted in Copetas, *Bear Hunting with the Politburo*, p. 177.
8. Vladimir Yakovlev, interview with the author, September 2014.
9. Marietta Chudakova, 'Pri nachale kontsa', p. 547.
10. Maxim Sokolov, interview with the author, July 2013.
11. Maxim Sokolov, 'Desiat' let spustia', *Novoe lieraturnoe obozrenie* 41 (2000), pp. 292–5 (p. 292).
12. Maxim Sokolov, 'Slava Bogu Perestroika zakonchilas'', *Kommersant*, 19–26 August 1991, p. 1.
13. Pavel Astakhov, Dmitri Avkhimenko, 'Budet ugol', zerno i strashno dorogaia vodka', *Kommersant*, 26 August–2 September 1991, p. 18.
14. Alexander Timofeevsky, 'Puzyri zemli', *Stolitsa* 46–47 (1991), p. 19.
15. Yegor Gaidar, *Dni porazhenii i pobed* (Moscow: Vagrius, 1996), p. 153.
16. Interview with Vladimir Yakovlev from a documentary by Leonid Parfenov: *S tverdym znakom na kontse*, Moscow, Studia Namedni, 2009.
17. Elena Nusinova, interview with the author, June 2013.
18. Vladimir Yakovlev, interview with the author, September 2014.
19. Copetas, *Bear Hunting with the Politburo*, p. 245.
20. Vladimir Yakovlev, interview with the author, September 2014.
21. Ibid.
22. Yuri Levada, *Ot mnenii k ponimaniiu* (Moscow: Moskovskaia shkola politicheskikh issledovanii, 2000), p. 18.
23. Quoted in Mikhail Khodorkovsky and Natalyia Gevorkyan, *Tiurma i volia* (Moscow: Howard Roark, 2012), p. 151.
24. Quoted in David E. Hoffman, *The Oligarchs: Wealth and Power in the New Russia* (New York: PublicAffairs, 2003), p. 230.
25. Andrew Higgins, 'Insufficient Funds: How a Russian Banker Outfoxed Creditors to Rebuild an Empire', *Wall Street Journal*, 4 October 2000, p. 1.
26. Quoted in Arkady Ostrovsky, 'Father to the Oligarchs', *Financial Times Magazine*, 13 November 2004, pp. 14–15.
27. *Kommersant Daily*, 6 October 1992.
28. The comparison between *Pravda* and *Kommersant* was made by Natalia Ivanova in *Nostaliashchee* (Moscow: Raduga, 2002), p. 14.
29. Ksenia Makhnenko, 'Chto khoroshego?', *Kommersant Weekly* 12, 19 October 1992, p. 1.
30. Opinion poll by VTsIOM, 1992.
31. Maxim Sokolov, 'Tak kakuiu zhe voinu my proigrali?', *Oktiabr* 4 (1992), pp. 165–72 (p. 171).

32. Natalia Narochitskaya, 'Rossiia i Evropa', *Nash sovremennik*, 12 (1993), pp. 94–113 (p. 101).
33. Igor Shafarevich, 'Tretia oborona Sevastopolia', *Den'*, 28 March–3 April 1993, p. 3.
34. Quoted in Alexander Yanov, *Posle Yeltsina. Veimarskaia Rossiia* (Moscow: Moskovskaya gorodskaya tipographiia Pushkina, 1995), http://www.lib.ru/POLITOLOG/yanow.txt
35. Alexander Yanov, 'Istoriia odnogo otrecheniia. Pochemy v Rossii ne budet fashisma?', *Snob*, 15 December 2011, http://snob.ru/selected/entry/44335#comment_437933
36. Igor Malashenko, interview with the author, September 2010.
37. Irina Petrovskaya, 'Nam vsem dali poshchechinu. Konets romana s vlast'iu, *Nezavisimaya gazeta*, 28 November 1992, p. 3.
38. Viktor Anpilov, interview with the author, December 2014.
39. Viktor Anpilov, *Nasha bor'ba*. http://1993.sovnarkom.ru/KNIGI/ANPILOV/ogl.html
40. Vladimir Nadein, 'Tol'ko soobshcha mozhno ostanovit' programmu pogromov', *Izvestia*, 19 June 1992, p. 1.
41. Natalia Gevorkyan, 'Chto esli zamolchit Ostankino', *Moskovskie novosti*, 21 June 1992, p. 8.
42. Boris Yeltsin, *Zapiski prezidenta* (Moscow: Rosspen, 2008), p. 286.
43. Alexander Yanov, 'Istoriia odnogo otrecheniia'.
44. 'Tsitata dnia', *Rossiyskaya gazeta*, 13 August 1993, p. 1.
45. Alexander Nevzorov, interview with the author, January 2015.
46. Sergei Parkhomenko, 'Partizanskaia respublika Belogo doma', *Segodnya*, 2 October 1993, p. 2.
47. Veronika Kutsyllo, *Zapiski iz Belogo doma: 21 September–4 October 1993* (Moscow: Kommersant, 1993), p. 40.
48. Interview with Sergei Parkhomenko from a film by Maria Slonim, *Eto tiazhkoe bremia svobody*, Internews, 2001.
49. Sergei Parkhomenko, interview with the author, July 2014.
50. Veronika Kutsyllo, *Zapiski iz Belogo doma*, p. 6.
51. Ibid., p.113.
52. Gaidar, *Dni porazhenii i pobed*, pp. 286–7.
53. Quoted in Mickiewicz, *Changing Channels*, p. 10.
54. Bruce Clark, *An Empire's New Clothes: The End of Russia's Liberal Dream* (London: Vintage, 1995).
55. Alexander Nevzorov, interview with the author, January 2015.
56. Ibid.
57. Ibid.
58. Ibid.
59. Gaidar, *Dni porazhenii i pobed*, p. 290.
60. Yeltsin, *Zapiski prezidenta*, p. 362.
61. Quoted in Aron, *Yeltsin: A Revolutionary Life*, p. 545.
62. Ibid., p. 549.

63. Yeltsin, *Zapiski prezidenta*, p. 362.
64. Gaidar, *Dni porazhenii i pobed*, p. 293.
65. Sergei Parkhomenko, 'V nachale byl miatezh', *Segodnya*, 7 October 1993, p. 2.
66. Alexander Nevzorov, interview with the author, January 2014.
67. Levada, *Ot mnenii k ponimaniiu*, pp. 29–30.
68. Alexander Nevzorov, interview with the author, January 2011.
69. Alexander Yakovlev, *Omut pamiati* , vol. 2, p. 152.

Part II

CHAPTER FIVE

1. Igor Malashenko, interview with the author, September 2010.
2. Ibid.
3. Evgeny Kiselev, interview with the author, May 2012.
4. Ibid.
5. Ibid.
6. Igor Malashenko, interview with the author, September 2010.
7. Evgeny Kiselev, interview with the author, May 2012.
8. Evgeny Kiselev, interview with the author, March 2013.
9. Vladimir Gusinsky, interview with the author, 2006.
10. Hoffman, *The Oligarchs: Wealth and Power in the New Russia* (New York: Public Affairs, 2003).
11. Igor Malashenko, interview with the author, September 2010.
12. Ibid.
13. Ibid.
14. Ibid.
15. Ibid.
16. Ibid.
17. Olga Kuchkina, '"Ia ukhozhu v otstavku"', *Komsomol'skaia pravda*, 23 February 1993, p. 6.
18. Sergei Shakhrai quoted in Peter Aven and Alfred Kokh, 'Revolutsiia Gaidara' (Moscow: Alpina Publisher, 2013), p. 288.
19. Evgeny Kiselev, interview with the author, August 2013.
20. Igor Malashenko, interview with the author, September 2010.
21. Ibid.
22. Quoted in Mickiewicz, *Changing Channels*, p. 246.
23. Ibid., p. 255.
24. Igor Malashenko, interview with the author, September 2010.
25. 'Padaet sneg', *Rossiyskaya gazeta*, 19 November 1994.
26. Igor Malashenko, interview with the author, September 2010.
27. Alexander Yakovlev, *Omut pamiati*, vol. 2, pp. 161–2.
28. 'Don Kikhot i ego telokhranitel', *Kukly*, NTV, 29 April 1995.
29. *Itogi*, NTV, 18 June 1995.
30. Alexander Yakovlev, *Omut pamiati*, vol. 2, p. 170.

31. Marietta Chudakova, 'Blud bor'by', *Literaturnaya gazeta*, 30 October 1991, p. 3.
32. Igor Malashenko, interview with the author, September 2010.
33. Anatoly Chubais, interview with the author, December 2013.
34. Ibid.
35. Boris Yeltsin, *Prezidentskii marafon* (Moscow: Rosspen, 2008), p. 29.
36. Ibid, p. 31.
37. Igor Malashenko, interview with the author, September 2010.
38. Gaidar, *Dni porazhenii i pobed*, p. 361.
39. Igor Malashenko, interview with the author, September 2010.
40. Irina Petrovskaya, *Sto odna nedelia s Irinoi Petrovskoi* (Moscow: Monolit, 1998), pp. 95, 116.
41. Quoted in Arkady Ostrovsky, 'Broadcast Views', *Financial Times Magazine* 76, 9 October 2004, p. 22.
42. Igor Malashenko, interview with the author, September 2010.
43. Evgeny Kiselev, 'Pobeda Yeltsina eshche ne pobeda demokratii', *Itogi* 5, 11 June 1996, p. 38.
44. Igor Malashenko, interview with the author, September 2010.
45. Ibid.
46. Gaidar, *Dni porazhenii i pobed*, p. 362.
47. Chrystia Freeland, John Thornhill and Andrew Gowers, 'Moscow's Group of Seven', *Financial Times*, 1 November 1996, p. 17.
48. Anatoly Chubais, interview with the author, December 2013.
49. Igor Malashenko, interview with the author, September 2010.
50. Petrovskaya, *Sto odna nedelia s Irinoi Petrovskoi*, p. 27.
51. Igor Malashenko, interview with the author, September 2010.
52. Ibid.
53. Vladimir Gusinsky, interview with the author, October 2013.
54. Ibid.
55. Ibid.
56. Ibid.
57. Anatoly Chubais, interview with the author, December 2013.
58. Vladimir Gusinsky, interview with the author, October 2013.
59. Igor Malashenko, interview with the author, September 2010.
60. Anatoly Chubais, interview with the author, September 2014.
61. Quoted in Hoffman, *The Oligarchs*, p. 382.
62. Igor Malashenko, interview with the author, October 2013.
63. Vladimir Gusinsky, interview with the author, October 2013.
64. Mikhail Khodorkovsky, interview with the author, March 2015.
65. Yeltsin, *Prezidentskii marafon*, p. 92.
66. Ibid, p. 98.
67. *Vremya*, Channel One, 15 November 1997.
68. Boris Nemtsov, interview with the author, June 2014.
69. Boris Nemtsov, *Ispoved' buntaria* (Moscow: Partizan, 2007), p. 26.

70. Maxim Sokolov, *Poeticheskie vozzreniia rossiian na istoriiu*, 2 vols (Moscow: Russkaia panorama, 1999), vol. 1 (Razyskania), pp. 270-1.
71. Igor Malashenko, interview with the author, September 2010.
72. Ibid.
73. Ibid.
74. Iulia Papilova, 'Malashenko naekhal na chechentsev', *Kommersant Daily*, 20 August 1997, p. 1.
75. Ibid.
76. Igor Malashenko, interview with the author, September 2010.
77. *Vremya*, Channel One, 3 September 1997.
78. Mikhail Novikov, 'Ne dai zasokhnut' Rodine svoei!', *Kommersant Daily*, 8 August 1997, p. 1.
79. Leonid Parfenov, interview with the author, October 2013.
80. Ibid.
81. Alessandra Stanley, 'Russians Begin to Gild the Communist Past', *New York Times*, 30 December 1995. http://www.nytimes.com/1995/12/30/world/russians-begin-to-gild-the-communist-past.html
82. Andrei Zorin, 'Are We Having Fun Yet?'. http://web.stanford.edu/group/Russia20/volume-pdf/zorin.pdf
83. Ibid.
84. Igor Malashenko, interview with the author, September 2010.
85. Yegor Gaidar, 'Protalkivanie reform. Statia tretia', *Russkaya mysl*, 29 October–4 November, p. 6.
86. Irina Petrovskaya, 'Ne streliaite v perevodchika', *Izvestia*, 30 May 1998, p. 6.
87. Ibid.

CHAPTER SIX

1. Irina Petrovskaya, 'Tetia Asya uekhala', *Izvestia*, 5 September 1998, p. 6.
2. Igor Shadkhan in 'Sluchainoe interv'iu Putina porazhaet svoei otkrovennostiu', NTV, 27 March 2007. http://www.ntv.ru/novosti/106187/
3. Yeltsin, *Prezidentskii marafon*, p. 231.
4. Ibid., p. 220.
5. Quoted in Grigorii Voiskoboinikov, 'Vtoraia molodost' "pozhilykh reformatorov"', *Itogi* 36, 15 September 1998, pp. 15–17.
6. Yeltsin, *Prezidentskii marafon*, p. 269.
7. Vladislav Borodulin, '15,000,000 dollarov poteriala Rossiia blagodaria Primakovu', *Kommersant Daily*, 24 March 1999, p. 1.
8. Evgeny Kiselev, interview with the author, August 2013.
9. *Itogi*, NTV, 28 March 1999.
10. ITAR-TASS, 24 December 1998.
11. *Vremya*, Channel One, 23 January 1999.
12. Quoted in Elmar Guseinov, 'Ia slabo pokhozhu na zhertvu', *Izvestia*, 9 April 1999, p. 2.
13. Alexander Golts, Dmitry Pinsker, 'Poslednii prem'er imperii, *Itogi* 20, 18 May 1999, p. 20.

14. Gleb Pavlovsky, interview with the author, June 2014.
15. Yeltsin, *Prezidentskii marafon*, p. 288.
16. *Avtorskaia programma Sergeia Dorenko*, Channel One, 7 November 1999.
17. Yeltsin, *Prezidentskii marafon*, p. 287.
18. I am grateful to Gleb Palvovsky for showing me this memo.
19. Yeltsin, *Prezidentskii marafon*, p. 282.
20. Gleb Pavlovsky, interview with the author, June 2014.
21. Igor Malashenko, interview with the author, December 2011.
22. Yeltsin, *Prezidentskii marafon*, p. 292.
23. Gleb Pavlovsky, interview with the author, June 2014.
24. Sergei Dorenko, interview with the author, June 2014.
25. Ibid.
26. Ibid.
27. Natalia Gervorkyan, '"Ia po prezhnemu sam s soboi"', *Kommersant Daily*, 27 November 1999, p. 1.
28. Sergei Dorenko, interview with the author, June 2014.
29. Ibid.
30. Ibid.
31. Ibid.
32. Ibid.
33. *Avtorskaia programma Sergeia Dorenko*, Channel One, 3 October 1999.
34. *Avtorskaia programma Sergeia Dorenko*, Channel One, 15 January 2000.
35. *Avtorskaia programma Sergeia Dorenko*, Channel One, 3 October 1999.
36. *Avtorskaia programma Sergeia Dorenko*, Channel One, 26 December 1999.
37. Natalia Gervorkyan, '"Ia po prezhnemu sam s soboi"', p. 1.
38. Alexander Oslov, interview with the author, June 2014.
39. Gleb Pavlovsky, interview with the author, June 2014.
40. Ibid.
41. Levada, *Ot mnenii k ponimaniu*, p. 200.
42. Igor Malashenko, interview with the author, December 2010.
43. Gleb Pavlovsky, interview with the author, June 2014.
44. Sergei Dorenko, interview with the author, June 2014.
45. Ibid.
46. *Polit.ru*, 12 November 1999. http://polit.ru/news/1999/11/12/539713/
47. Igor Malashenko, interview with the author, December 2010.
48. 'Oleg Dobrodeev: 'Armiia – eto nashi brat'ia i synov'ia', *Krasnaya zvezda*, 29 September 1999, p. 4.

CHAPTER SEVEN

1. Vladimir Putin, 'Rossiia na rubezhe tyciachiletii', *Nezavisimaia gazeta*, 30 December 1999. http://www.ng.ru/politics/1999-12-30/4_millenium.html. For a full study of Putin

as a 'statist', see Fiona Hill and Clifford G. Gaddy, *Mr Putin: Operative in the Kremlin* (Washington: Brookings Institution Press, 2013).

2. Opinion poll by VTsIOM, 21–24 January 2000. http://www.temadnya.ru/spravka/29dec2000/96.html
3. Ian Traynor, 'Putin Urged to Apply the Pinochet Stick', *The Guardian*, 31 March 2000. http://www.theguardian.com/world/2000/mar/31/russia.iantraynor
4. Ilya Tsentsiper in *Istoria russkikh media*, 1989–2011, ed. by Alexander Gorbachev and Ilya Krasilshchik (Moscow: Afisha, 2011), p. 215.
5. Alexander Yakovlev, *Newsru*, 10 December 2000. http://www.newsru.com/itogi/10Dec2000/artpeople_about_gimn.html
6. Vladimir Putin's speech to the Duma, 4 December 2000. http://archive.kremlin.ru/text/appears/2000/12/28432.shtml
7. Kirill Rogov, 'So Stalinym v serdtse. Rossiya snova budet pet' kholuiskuiu pesniu' in *Za Glinku! Protiv vozvrata k sovetskomu gimnu*, ed. by M. Chudakova, A. Kurilkin and E. Toddes (Moscow: Shkola 'Yazyki russkoi kultury', 2000), p. 58.
8. Boris Nemtsov, interview with the author, June 2014.
9. Viktor Shenderovich, *Zdes' bylo NTV* (Moscow: Zakharov, 2004), p. 11.
10. Igor Malashenko, interview with the author, December 2010.
11. *Glas naroda*, NTV, 13 June 2000.
12. Sergei Dorenko, interview with the author, June 2014.
13. Yegor Gaidar, *Vlast' i sobstvennost'*, p. 323.
14. Olga Kabanova, 'O chem govoril Timofeevsky', *Russkii zhurnal*, 15 August 2000. http://old.russ.ru/culture/textonly/20000815-pr.html
15. Maxim Sokolov, 'O vvedenii edinomysliia v Rossii', *Izvestia*, 26 July 2000, p. 9.
16. 'Vstrecha s rodnymi', *Kommersant Daily*, 29 August 2000. http://www.kommersant.ru/doc/17499
17. Alexei Venediktov, interview with the author, June 2014.
18. Ibid.
19. Sergei Dorenko, interview with the author, June 2014.
20. Quoted in Hoffman, *The Oligarchs*, p. 488.
21. *Larry King Live*, CNN, 8 September 2000. http://edition.cnn.com/TRANSCRIPTS/0009/08/lkl.00.html
22. *Glas naroda*, NTV, 26 January 2001.
23. Quoted in Hoffman, *The Oligarchs*, p. 484.
24. *Kommersant Daily*, 9 April 2001, p. 1.
25. *Antropologiia*, NTV, 9 April 2001.
26. *Obshchaya gazeta*, 7 April 2001.
27. Ibid.
28. Putin's press conference, 23 December 2004.
29. Quoted in Ostrovsky, 'Broadcast Views', p. 22.
30. Leonid Parfenov, interview with the author, 2004.
31. *Odnako*, Channel One, 24 October 2002.

32. *Newsru*, 15 December 2002. http://www.newsru.com/russia/15dec2002/terrorism.html
33. Leonid Parfenov, interview with the author, October 2013.
34. Parfenov's speech, 25 November 2010. http://www.1tv.ru/sprojects_edition/si5817/fi6319
35. Ernst's comment was made in *Namedni 20 let. Posidelki*, a documentary about the twentieth anniversary of *Namedni*.
36. Yuri Saprykin, interview with Konstantin Ernst and Anatoly Maksimov, *Vozdukh Afisha*, 19 December 2004. http://vozduh.afisha.ru/archive/dhevnoj_dozor/
37. *Seans*, 15 December 2006. http://seance.ru/blog/sobesednik-konstantin-ernst/
38. Quoted in Ostrovsky, 'Broadcast Views', p. 22.
39. Ibid.
40. C. J. Chivers, 'For Russians, Wounds Linger in School Siege', *New York Times*, 26 August 2005.
41. Quoted in Arkady Ostrovsky, 'Broadcast Views', p. 22.
42. Ibid.
43. Ibid.
44. Konstantin Ernst, interview with the author, December 2014.
45. 'A Scripted War', *The Economist*, 14 August 2008, p. 22.
46. Konstantin Ernst, interview with the author, December 2014.
47. Konstantin Ernst, speech at the *GQ* awards ceremony, 20 September 2014.
48. 'Chelovek goda 2014: Konstantin Ernst', *GQ*, October 2014. www.gq.ru/moty/2014/87508_chelovek_goda_2014_konstantin_ernst.php

EPILOGUE

1. Yuri Levada, '"Chelovek sovetskii": chetvertaia volna', *Polit.ru*, 24 December 2003. http://polit.ru/article/2003/12/24/vciomsov/
2. Maxim Shevchenko, 'My ne Evropa? I slava bogu!' *Moskovskii komsomolets*, 10 February 2011, p. 3.
3. Putin's speech was made at the Valdai International Discussion Club. http://valdaiclub.com/politics/62880.html
4. *Vesti Nedeli s Dmitriem Kiselevym*, Rossiya Channel, 8 December 2013.
5. 'Kak delat' televidenie', Uchebny proekt, film 8, BBC Training and Development, DFID and Internews, 1999.
6. http://en.kremlin.ru/events/president/news/by-date.18.03.2014
7. Alexander Nevzorov, 'Bezumtsev net v Kremle – oni pragmatiki', *Snob*, 24 March 2014. http://snob.ru/profile/20736/blog/74068#comment_709311
8. Alexander Nevzorov, 'Zheleznye lapti Kremlia', *Snob*, 21 April 2014. http://snob.ru/selected/entry/75143
9. Nemtsov's post on Facebook of 3 May 2014. https://www.facebook.com/boris.nemtsov/posts/622917747777829?fref=nf
10. Vladimir Yakovlev's post on Facebook of 18 March 2015. https://www.facebook.com/vladimir.yakovlev.359/posts/738741086242476

Select Bibliography

Albats, Yevgenia, *Mina zamedlennogo deistviia (Politicheskii portret KGB)* (Moscow: RUSSLIT, 1992)

——, *KGB: State Within a State. The Secret Police and its Hold on Russia's Past, Present and Future,* (London: I. B. Tauris, 1995)

Almqvist, Kurt and Alexander Linklater (eds), *On Russia. Perspectives from the Engelsberg seminar 2008* (Stockholm: Axel and Margaret Ax:son Johnson Foundation, 2009)

Amalrik, Andrei, *Will the Soviet Union Survive until 1984?* (New York: Harper & Row, 1981)

Aron, Leon, *Yeltsin: A Revolutionary Life* (New York: St Martin's Press, 2000)

——, *Roads to the Temple: Truth, Memory, Ideas, and Ideals in the Making of the Russian Revolution, 1987–1991* (New Haven and London: Yale University Press, 2012)

Aven, Peter and Alfred Kokh, *Revolutsiia Gaidara. Istoriia reform 90-kh iz pervykh ruk* (Moscow: Alpina Publisher, 2013)

Bakatin, Vadim, *Doroga v proshedshem vremeni* (Moscow: Dom, 1999)

Baker, Peter and Susan Glasser, *Kremlin Rising* (New York: Scribner, 2005)

Billington, James, *The Icon and the Axe: An Interpretative History of Russian Culture* (New York: Vintage Books, 1970)

Bobkov, Filipp, *KGB i vlast'. 45 let v organakh gosudarstvennoy bezopasnosti* (Moscow: Veteran MP, 1995)

Brodsky, Joseph, *Less Than One* (London: Viking, 1986)

Brown, Archie, *The Gorbachev Factor* (Oxford University Press, 1996)

Bovin, Alexander, *XX vek kak zhizn* (Moscow: Zakharov, 2003)

Bunin, Ivan, *Cursed Days: A Diary of Revolution*, trans. by Gaiton Marullo (London: Phoenix Press, 2000)

Chernyaev, Alexander, *Sovmestnyi iskhod. Dnevnik dvukh epokh. 1972–1991 gody* (Moscow: Rossiiskaia politicheskaia entsiklopediia, 2010)

Chernyaev, Alexander, A. Veber, and V. Medvedev (eds), *V Politburo TsK KPSS: 1985–1991* (Moscow: Alpina Bizness Books, 2006)

Clark, Bruce, *An Empire's New Clothes: The End of Russia's Liberal Dream* (London: Vintage, 1995)

Colton, Timothy J., *Yeltsin: A Life* (New York: Basic Books, 2008)

Conquest, Robert, *The Great Terror: A Reassessment* (London: Pimlico, 1990)

Copetas, A. Craig, *Bear Hunting with the Politburo. American Adventures in Russian*

Capitalism (Lanham, MD: Madison Books, 2001)

Cohen, Stephen F., (ed.), *An End to Silence: Uncensored Opinion in the Soviet Union from Roy Medvedev's Underground Magazine Political Diary* (New York: W. W. Norton and Company, 1982)

Cohen, Stephen and Katrina vanden Heuvel, *Voices of Glasnost: Interviews with Gorbachev's Reformers* (New York: W. W. Norton and Company, 1989)

Freeland, Chrystia, *Sale of the Century: Russia's Wild Ride from Communism to Capitalism* (New York: Crown Books, 2000)

Gaddy, Clifford G., *The Price of the Past: Russia's Struggle with the Legacy of a Militarized Economy* (Washington: Brookings Institution Press, 1996)

——, and Barry Ickes, *Russia's Virtual Economy* (Washington: Brookings Institution Press, 2002)

Gaidar, Yegor, *Days of Defeat and Victory*, trans. by Jane Ann Miller (University of Washington Press, 1996)

——, *Collapse of an Empire: Lessons for Modern Russia*, trans. by Antonia W. Bouis (Washington: Brookings Institution Press, 2007)

——, *Gibel' imperii: uroki dlia sovremennoi Rossii* (Moscow: Rosspen, 2007)

——, *Vlast' i sobstvennost': Smuty i instituty. Gossudarstvo i evolutsiia* (St Petersburg: Norma, 2009)

Gall, Carlotta, and Thomas de Waal, *Chechnya: A Small Victorious War* (London: Pan Books, 1998)

Gessen, Masha, *The Man Without a Face: The Unlikely Rise of Vladimir Putin* (New York: Riverhead Books, 2012)

Gevorkyan, Natalia, Natalia Timakova, and Andrei Kolesnikov, *Ot pervogo litsa: razgovory s Vladimirom Putinom* (Moscow: Vagrius, 2000)

——, *First Person: An Astonishingly Frank Self-Portrait by Russia's President Vladimir Putin*, trans. by Catherine A. Fitzpatrick (New York: PublicAffairs, 2000)

Grossman, Vasily, *Life and Fate*, trans. by Robert Chandler (New York: Random House, 2011).

Grachev, Andrei, *Gorbachev* (Moscow: Vagrius, 2001)

——, *Kremlevskaia Khronika* (Moscow: Eksmo, 1994)

Gorbachev, Mikhail, *Memoirs* (New York: Doubleday, 1995)

——, *Zhizn i reform*, 2 vols (Moscow: Novosti, 1995)

Gorbachev, Mikhail and Zdeněk Mlynář, *Conversations with Gorbachev – On Perestroika, the Prague Spring, and the Crossroads of Socialism* (Columbia University Press, 2003)

Hill, Fiona, and Clifford Gaddy, *The Siberian Curse: How Communist Planners Left Russia Out in the Cold* (Washington: Brookings Institution Press, 2003)

——, *Mr Putin: Operative in the Kremlin*, (Washington: Brookings Institution Press, 2013)

Hoffman, David, *The Oligarchs: Wealth and Power in the New Russia* (New York: Public Affairs, 2003)

Ivanova, Natalia, *Nostal'iashchee* (Moscow: Raduga, 2002)

Jack, Andrew, *Inside Putin's Russia* (Oxford University Press, 2004)

Khodorkovsky, Mikhail and Leonid Nevzlin, *Chelovek s rublem* (Moscow: Menatep-Inform, 1992).

Klebnikov, Paul, *Godfather of the Kremlin: Boris Berezovsky and the Looting of Russia* (New York: Harcourt, 2000)

Kokh, Alfred, *The Selling of the Soviet Empire* (New York: SPI Books, 1998)

Kolesnikov, Andrei, *Ia Putina videl!* (Moscow: Eksmo, 2005)

Korzhakov, Alexander, *Boris Yeltsin: ot rassveta do zakata* (Moscow: Inerbuk, 1997)

Kustyllo, Veronika, *Zapiski iz belogo doma* (Moscow: Kommersant, 1993)

Kuvshinova, Maria, *Balabanov* (St Petersburg: Seans, 2013

Latsis, Otto, *Tshchatel'no splanirovannoe samoubiistvo* (Moscow: Moskovskaia shkola politicheskikh issledovanii, 2001)

Ledeneva, Alena, *How Russia Really Works* (Ithaca, NY: Cornell University Press, 2006)

Levada, Yuri, *Ot mnenii k ponimaniiu* (Moscow: Moskovskaya shkola politicheskikh issledovanii, 2000)

Lieven, Anatol, *Chechnya: Tombstone of Russian Power* (New Haven and London: Yale University Press, 1998)

Lipman, Maria and Nikolai Petrov (eds), *Russia 2025: Scenarios for the Russian Future* (London: Palgrave Macmillan, 2013)

Lloyd, John, *Rebirth of a Nation: An Anatomy of Russia* (London: Michael Joseph, 1998)

Lucas, Edward, *The New Cold War* (New York: Palgrave Macmillan, 2008)

Matthews, Owen, *Stalin's Children: Three Generations of Love and War* (London: Bloomsbury, 2008)

McFaul, Michael, *Russia's Unfinished Revolution: Political Change from Gorbachev to Putin* (Ithaca, NY: Cornell University Press, 2001)

Medvedev, Roy, *Andropov* (Moscow: Molodaya gvardiya, 2006)

Mickiewicz, Ellen, *Changing Channels: Television and the Struggle of Power in Russia* (Durham, NC: Duke University Press, 1999)

Mitrokhin, Nikolai, *Russkaia partiia: Dvizhenie Russkikh natsionalistov v SSSR 1953–1985* (Moscow: Novoe literaturnoe obozrenie, 2003)

Nemtsov, Boris, *Ispoved' buntaria* (Moscow: Partizan, 2007)

Orwell, George, *Nineteen Eighty-Four* (London: Secker and Warburg, 1949)

Ostrovsky, Arkady, 'Ariel Combat. How the Truth got Lost in the Battle for Post-Soviet TV', *Financial Times Weekend Magazine*, 9 October 2004, pp. 16–22

Parfenov, Leonid, *Namedni. Nasha era 1946–1960* (Moscow: KoLibri, 2014)

——, *Namedni. Nasha era 1961–1970* (Moscow: KoLibri, 2010)

——, *Namedni. Nasha era 1971–1980* (Moscow: KoLibri, 2010)

——, *Namedni. Nasha era 1981–1990* (Moscow: KoLibri, 2010)

——, *Namedni. Nasha era 1991–2000* (Moscow: KoLibri, 2010)

——, *Namedni. Nasha era 2001–2005* (Moscow: KoLibri, 2012)

——, *Namedni. Nasha era 2006–2010* (Moscow: KoLibri, 2013)

Pikhoia, R. G., S. V. Zhuravlev and A. K. Sokolov, *Istoriia sovremennoi Rossii: Desiatiletie liberal'nykh reform: 1991–1999* (Moscow: Novyi khronograf, 2011)

Pipes, Richard, *Russia under the Old Regime* (New York: Charles Scribner's Sons, 1974)

Politkovskaya Anna, *A Dirty War* (London: The Harvill Press, 2001)

Pomerantsev, Peter, 'Putin's Rasputin', *London Review of Books*, Vol. 33, No. 20, 20 October, 2011

——, *Nothing Is True and Everything Is Possible* (London: Faber & Faber, 2014)

Prokhorova, Irina (ed.), *1990. Russians Remember a Turning Point* (London: Maclehose Press/Quercus, 2013)

Remnick, David, *Lenin's Tomb: The Last Days of the Soviet Empire* (New York: Random House, 1993)

——, *Resurrection: The Struggle for a New Russia* (New York: Random House, 1997)

Revzin, Grigory, *Russkaia arkhitektura rubezha XX–XXI vekov* (Moscow: Novoe izdatel'stvo, 2013)

Roxburgh, Angus, *The Strongman* (New York, I. B. Tauris, 2012)
Rozanov, Vasiliy, *Apocalipsis nashego vremeni*, (Moscow: Zakharov, 2001)
Sakharov, Andrei, *Vospominaniia*, 3 vols, (Moscow: Vremia, 2006)
——, *Memoirs*, trans. by R. Lourie (London: Hutchinson, 1990)
Sappak, Vladimir, *Televidenie i my. Chetyre besedy* (Moscow: Iskusstvo, 1963)
——, *Bloknoty 1956 goda* (Moscow: Moskovskii Khurdozhestvenny teatr, 2011)
Shenderovich Viktor, *Zdes' bylo NTV i drugie istorii*, (Moscow: Zakharov, 2004)
Shevtsova, Lilia, *Putin's Russia* (Washington: Carnegie Endowment for International Peace, 2005)
Shvarts, Evgeniy, *Drakon* (Leningrad: Sovetskii pisatel', 1972)
Sinyavsky, Andrei, *Soviet Civilization. A Cultural History* (New York: Arcade publishing, 1990)
Stites, Richard, *Russian Popular Culture: Entertainment and society since 1900* (Cambridge University Press, 1992)
Smeliansky, Anatoly, *Mezhdometiya vremeni*, (Moscow: Iskusstvo, 2002)
Sokolov, Maxim, *Poeticheskie vozzreniia rossiian na istoriiu*, 2 vols (Moscow: Russkaia panorama, 1999)
Solzhenitsyn, Alexander, *The Oak and the Calf*, trans. by Harry Willets (London: Collins/ Harvill Press, 1980)
Stoppard, Tom, *The Coast of Utopia* (New York: Grove Press, 2007)
Talbot, Strobe, *The Russia Hand* (New York: Random House, 2002)
Taubman, William, *Khrushchev: The Man and His Era* (London: Simon & Schuster, 2003)
Tomilina, N. (ed.), *Nikita Sergeevich Khrushchev, Dva tsveta vremeni: Dokumenty iz lichnogo fonda N.S. Khrushcheva*, 2 vols (Moscow: Mezhdunarodny fond 'Demokratia', 2009)
Tregubova, Yelena, *Baiki kremlevskogo diggera* (Moscow: Ad Marginem, 2003)
Tvardovski, Alexander, *Tyorkin and the Stove Makers* (London: Carcanet Press, 1974)
——, *Novomirski dnevnik*, 1961–1966 (Moscow: PROZAiK, 2009)
Venturi, Franco, *Roots of Revolution: A History of the Populist and Socialist Movements in Nineteenth Century Russia* (New York: Grosset & Dunlap, The Universal Library, 1966)
Volkov A., Pugacheva M., Iarmoliuk S., *Pressa v obshchestve, 1959–2000* (Moskovkaia shkola politicheskikh issledovanii, 2000)
Wilson, Andrew, *Virtual Politics: Faking Democracy in the Post-Soviet World* (New Haven and London: Yale University Press, 2005)
Wegren, Stephen K., and Dale R. Herspring (eds), *After Putin's Russia: Past Imperfect, Future Uncertain* (Lanham, MD: Rowman & Littlefield, 2010)
Yakovlev, Alexander, *Omut pamyati*, 2 vols (Moscow: Vargius, 2001)
——, *Sumerki*, (Moscow: Materik, 2005)
Yakovlev, Yegor, *Ia idu s toboi* (Moscow: Molodaya gvardiya, 1965)
Yanov, Alexander, *Posle Yeltsina. Veimarskava Rossiia* (Moscow: Moskovskaia gorodskaia tipographiia Pushkina, 1995)
Yeltsin, Boris, *Prezidentskii marafon* (Moscow: Ogonyok, 1994)
——, *Zapiski prezidenta* (Moscow: Rosspen, 2008)
——, *Ispoved' na zadannuiu temu* (Moscow: Rosspen, 2008)
——, *Midnight Diaries*, trans. by Catherine A. Fitzpatrick (New York: PublicAffairs, 2000)
——, *The Struggle for Russia*, trans. by Catherine A. Fitzpatrick (New York: Times Books, 1994)
Zorin, Andrei, *Kormia dvuglavogo orla* (Moscow: Novoe literaturnoe obozrenie, 2001)

——, *By Fables Alone: Literature and State Ideology in Late Eighteenth and Early Nineteenth-Century Russian Literature*, trans. by Marcus C. Levitt (Boston: Academic Studies Press, 2014)

——, *Gde sidit fazan: ocherki poslednikh let* (Moscow: Novoe literaturnoe obozrenie, 2003)

——, *Are We Having Fun Yet?* Available at: http://web.stanford.edu/group/Russia20/volumepdf/zorin.pdf

Zygar', Mikhail, and Valeriy Paniushkin, *Gazprom: Novoe russkoe oruzhie* (Moscow: Zakharov, 2008)

Index

A Day in the Life of the President (TV programme) 160
Abramovich, Roman 257–8, 258, 301–2, 307
Abuladze, Tengiz 65–6
Achalov, Vladislav 162
Adamovich, Adam, 112
Afghanistan, Soviet invasion of 49–50, 182–3
Afisha (Playbill) (magazine) 287–8, 290, 334
agriculture, Soviet investment 90
Akhedzhakova, Liya 170
Akhmatova, Anna 59, 70
Aksenenko, Nikolai 258
Albats, Yevgenia 102
Alexei II, patriarch 290
Alksnis, Viktor 111
All Russia Party 257–8
Amalrik, Andrei, *Will the Soviet Union Survive Until 1984?* 52–3
Andreeva, Nina 76–8, 84, 94, 190, 340
Andropov, Yuri 35, 56, 246, 248, 290–1
Anpilov, Viktor 157–8, 164–5, 165–6, 167–8, 190, 340
anti-Americanism 252, 254, 322–3, 337, 347
anti-Semitism 44, 46, 78
anti-Utopian novels 101–2
anti-Yeltsin rebellion, 1993 164–73
Arafat, Yasser 249
Archangel 23
archival revolution, 1980s 59–60
assassination 1–2
authoritarianism 5
Aven, Peter 260–1, 285–6
Averintsev, Sergei 96, 127–8

Babel, Isaak 22
Bagrov, Danila 328–30
Bakatin, Vadim 110
Balabanov, Alexei 330
Balkan crisis, 1998 251–4
Baltic states, declare sovereignty 97, 106
'bankers' war, the 224–30
Banditskii Peterburg (Gangsters' Petersburg) (TV programme) 288–9
Barayev, Movsar 311
Barkashov, Alexander 163, 172
Barsukov, Mikhail 194, 195
Basayev, Shamil 201–2, 230–1, 276–82
Batkin, Leonid 203
Bazhov, Pavel 89
BBC 319
  Russian service 72
Berezovsky, Boris
  and Nevzorov 173–4
  and Yeltsin 188, 207
  image 206–7
  and Gusinsky 207
  and presidential election, 1996 214–15
  and oligarchs political power 217–18
  Svyazinvest auction 223, 224
  and the bankers' war 225
  Yeltsin fires 226
  and Chechnya 233

and Yeltsin's successor 241, 263
flees Russia 255–6
banishment 257–8
relationship with Putin 259, 272–3
and Dorenko 265–6
return to Russia 267–8
breakdown of relationship with Putin 300–2
and Ernst 315
Beria, Lavrentiy 27, 52, 78
Berlusconi, Silvio 7
Besedovsky, Grigory 22
Beslan school hostage crisis 318–20
billionaires 86
black market 85
Black Sea Fleet 152–3, 341
Bobkov, Filipp 67, 189, 261
Bolshevik Revolution, the 6, 54–5
books
banned 17–20
archival revolution, 1980s 59–60
Borodai, Alexander 341–5
Bovin, Alexander 15, 19, 29, 34, 35, 40–1, 42
Bragin, Vyacheslav 158, 166, 186
Braithwaite, Sir Rodric 107–8, 119
Brat (Brother) (film) 278–9
Brat 2 (film) 328–30
Brezhnev, Leonid 15, 19
background 34–5
and the Prague Spring, 1967–8 39–41
reaction to 'Against Anti-Historicism' 49
death of 50, 56
New Year's Eve speech, 1970 50
stagnation under 50–5
Brodsky, Joseph 19, 51
Buddenovsk crisis 201–2, 230–1
budget deficit 240
Bukharin, Nikolai 54–5, 76, 78, 79
Bukovsky, Vladimir 51
Bulgakov, Mikhail 298
Bunin, Ivan 21
bureaucracy 40
bureaucrat-entrepreneurs 331
Burtin, Yuri 60

Canada 49–50, 63
Capitalism, emergence of 141–50
car ownership 53
Castro, Fidel 157
censorship 43, 69, 106, 135, 186
Central Committee 32, 35, 39, 40, 44, 80, 90, 91–2, 124–5
Central Television 192–3, 258
Channel One 181, 207, 224, 226, 233, 242, 255, 260, 268, 301, 310, 315, 317, 319, 320, 326, 343–4
Chechnya
Putin's policy 1
first Chechen war 194–5, 195–8, 201–2, 213, 230–3, 297
Yeltsin visits 213
1996 peace accord 230
journalist kidnappings 230–3
second Chechen war 276–81, 297, 308
human rights abuses 280–1
popular resentment of 336
Chernenko, Konstantin 56, 58
Chernichenko, Yuri 37
Chernobyl nuclear station disaster 66–9
Chernomyrdin, Viktor 86–7, 159, 170, 200, 201–2, 202, 203, 216, 241, 249
Chernyaev, Anatoly 111, 191
China 27
Tiananmen Square massacre 92
Ch.K (Cheka) 21–2
Chubais, Anatoly 146–7
and presidential election, 1996 207–9, 209, 214–15, 217
appointed deputy prime minister 222
political agenda 222, 223–4
and Svyazinvest auction 222–4
and the bankers' war 225, 226
book scandal 226
resignation 226

on Putin 273
and second Chechen war 281
Chudakova, Marietta 137, 169–70, 203–4
Clark, Bruce 166–7
class consciousness 142
Clinton, Bill 200
CNN 12, 171, 302, 319
Cohen, Stephen 76, 83
Cold War, the 3
collectivization 31, 37, 47, 54, 62, 87
Columbia University 48
Comintern 50
Committee for Emergency (GKChP) 119–24
Communist Party
elite 28
Alexander Yakovlev's attack on 45–6
loss of control 102
compromise 42
conformism 64
Congress of People's Deputies 92–6, 154–5
consumerism 239, 332–3
co-operatives 84–5, 133–4
Copetas, A. Craig 143
corruption 193, 335
counter-propaganda 72–3
counter-revolution 5
coup attempt, 1991 119–24
aftermath 124–8
Crimea
annexation of 1, 7, 327, 339–42
polite green men 7, 327
transfer to Ukrainian Soviet Republic 152
Russian claim to 152–3, 238n
criminality 186, 288–9
crony capitalism 85
Cuba 157
Czech Republic 304
Czechoslovakia 103
the Prague Spring, 1967–8 38–41, 60–1
Soviet invasion of 40–2, 43, 61
State Security Service (STB) 105

debt default, 1998 243
debt pyramid 241
defiance, early 1990s 151
Den' (*Day*) (newspaper) 153, 159
Deng Xiaoping 27
de-Stalinization 75
Deti XX s'ezda' (*Children of the 20th Congress, The*) (TV documentary) 235–6
developed socialism 50
dissidents 15, 17, 41–2
Dittmer, Thomas 143–4
Dni (*Days*) (TV programme) 233
Dobrodeev, Oleg 183–6, 189–90, 196, 197, 231, 232, 253, 254, 281–2, 307, 320–1, 338
Doctors' Plot, the 77
Dolgoruky, Yuri 267
Dorenko, Sergei 224, 226, 228, 255, 264, 265–72, 280, 295, 300, 301
Dostoevsky, F. 93, 114
Dresden 103–4
Dubcěk, Alexander 38–41, 60, 61
Dubin, Boris 74, 268
Dukhobors 49–50
Dyachenko, Tatyana 209, 215, 241, 257, 258, 260–1
Dzerzhinsky, Felix 125

Eastern Europe, withdrawal of Soviet troops from 101
Echo Moskvy (radio station) 186, 226, 299, 319
economic crisis, 1998 240–4
economic recovery, 1999 243–4
education 17–20
elections, parliamentary
1993 174–5
1999 257–8, 286
2000 274–5
2003 330–1
2011 333–4
elections, presidential

1996 205–19
2000 284
émigrés 49–50
Erenburg, Ilya 30
Ernst, Konstantin 236–7, 313–14, 314–18, 320–1, 323–5, 327, 343
Estonia 97, 113
ethnic cleansing 253–4
European Court of Human Rights 296
European football championship, 2008 321
Eurovision Song Contest 323
Exhibition of People's Achievements (VDNKh) 325

Fakt (co-operative) 133–4, 143
fascism 46–7, 78, 152, 340
Fatherland Party 257–8
Filatov, Sergei 163
film industry 315–17, 329–30
financial crisis, 2009 333
Financial Times 217
flight MH 17 345
food shortages 82–3, 83–4, 141
Forbes Magazine 86
Foros 119
freedom of speech 39, 69, 101, 203, 304, 308
Fridman, Mikhail 222
Friedman, Milton 89
Fulbright scholars 48

Gaidar, Arkady 89
Gaidar, Yegor
background 88–91, 182
'The Foundation Pit' 90
and the storming of the White House 124
on collapse of Soviet Union 126, 141
reforms 151
Rutskoi attacks 154–5
replaced as prime minister 159
return to the government 161
defence of Ostankino 168–70, 171, 179–80
and populism 174
loss of influence 194
and Buddenovsk crisis 202
elections, 1996 205, 210, 217
on Kiriyenko 242
on bureaucrats 295
on change 347
Gazprom 86–7, 222, 243, 303, 304
generational shift 129–33
Georgia 152
Tbilisi massacre, 1989 92–3
Georgian war, 2008 321–3
Germany 151
Gevorkyan, Natalia 102–5
Girkin, Igor 342
Glasnost 13
opening-up of the media 64, 69, 69–73
and Chernobyl catastrophe cover-up 68–9
role 69
Stalinist attack 76–8
Glavlit 135
Golubkov, Lenya 149–50, 174, 175
Gorbachev, Mikhail 3–4
dissolution of Soviet Union 11–14
relationship with Alexander Yakovlev 13, 63
recognizes need for reform 57
and *Uncle Vanya* 57
appointed general secretary of the Communist Party 58
Leningrad speech, 1985 58–9
new thinking 59
and the Prague Spring, 1967–8 60–1
launches Perestroika 62–3
and Chernobyl catastrophe cover-up 68–9
understanding of Glasnost 69
and the Andreeva letter 77
Yeltsin writes to 79

October Revolution seventieth anniversary speech 79–80
opposition to 79–83
and Yeltsin 80, 106–7
on the market 84
loosens political control 92
and the Tbilisi massacre, 1989 93
Congress of People's Deputies, 1989 95
New Year's greeting, 1990 98
refusal to resort to force 105–6
and Yeltsin's secession threat 109–11
and the crackdown in Vilnius 115
considers media control 117
Alexander Yakovlev warns of coup attempt 118, 119
meeting with Yeltsin, 23 July 1991 118
coup attempt against, 1991 119–24
suffered a victory 126
leaving party 132
resignation 192
Putin and 291
Govorukhin, Stanislav 100
GQ (magazine) 325
Grachev, Pavel 170, 171
Great Break, the 24, 54
Gromyko, Andrei 80
Grossman, Vasily 47, 59
Grozny 196, 197, 280
Gudkov, Lev 74
GUM 26
Gusinsky, Vladimir 179, 186, 232
background 186–7
rise of 187–8
security services 188–9
media interests 189, 218, 222
television channel 189–90
Malashenko on 190
NTV shutdown threat 199–200
and Berezovsky 207
and presidential election, 1996 219
and Svyazinvest auction 221–2, 223, 224
satellite channel venture 222, 243
and the bankers' war 224–5, 226
prepares floatation 240
floatation scrapped 243
Gazprom loans 243, 304
and Yeltsin's succession 260, 262–3
and second Chechen war 281
Putin attacks 293, 294–7
arrest 294–5
forced to sell NTV 296
leaves Russia 296
relationship with Putin 297–8
refuses to sell NTV shares 302

Hamlet (Shakespeare) 29–30
Havel, Václev 105, 304
Hearst William Randolph 7–8
Hemingway, Ernest 37
higher education 52–3
history
and Perestroika 74–9
replaced by mythology 239
Hoffman, David 187, 301
home-ownership 53
Homo soveticus 94–5
housing 30–1, 34, 53
human rights 2, 280–1
Hurd, Douglas 107–8

ideological constraints, removal of 13
ideology 14, 15, 19, 78
IKEA 287
Illarionov, Andrei 287
individual consciousness, post-Stalinist thaw 30–41
individualism, early 1990s 143
inflation 141
information war 343–7
instability, 1997 233–4
intellectual space, post-Stalinist thaw 30–41
Interfax 112
Internet, the 335, 341
Iron Curtain, the, permeability 35–6

Itogi (magazine) 214
Itogi (*Conclusions*) (TV programme) 179–80, 181, 185–6, 218, 253–4, 262, 272, 273, 275, 280–1
Izvestia 55

Jews 44, 46, 187
Jordan, Boris 303, 309–10, 312

Kabakov, Alexander 83, 101–2, 121, 127
Kadyrov, Ramzan 1, 336
Kalugin, Oleg 104–5
Kaplan, Richard 12
Karaulov, Andrei 130–1
Karyakin, Yuri 175
Karpinsky, Len, 'Words are Also Deeds' 42–3
Kennan, George 48, 97
Keynes, J. M. 89
KGB 18, 39, 44, 47, 55, 72, 182–3
  Moskovskie novosti articles 102–5
  demoralized 105–6
  and Yeltsin 106–7
  and coup attempt, 1991 124
  fall of 124–5
  Putin joins 247
  Putin becomes head of 247
  mystique 248
  role 261–2
Khasbulatov, Ruslan 154–5, 159, 160, 167, 171–2
Khodorkovsky, Mikhail 85, 145, 225, 312, 313, 330, 331
Khrushchev, Nikita 15, 19–20, 24, 25, 27
  secret speech 26–7
  motivation 27
  coup attempt against, 1957 28
  fall of 28, 34
  urban projects 30–1
  post-Stalinist thaw 30–41, 325–6
  and *One Day in the Life of Ivan Denisovich* 32–3
  Alexander Yakovlev on 33
  failure to deliver economic and political reforms 34
  transfer of Crimea to Ukraine 152
Kiev 67
  Maidan protests 2, 326–7, 338
Kilibaev, Bakhyt 150
King, Larry 302
Kiriyenko, Sergei 241–2, 243
Kiselev, Dmitry 3
Kiselev, Evgeny 181–3, 184, 185–6, 189–90, 195, 209, 211, 214, 215, 218, 228, 232, 253–4, 263, 265, 272, 273, 275, 280–1, 302, 305, 338
Klyuchevsky, Vasily, *A History of Russia* 74
Kokh, Alfred 224, 225, 303
Kommersant (newspaper) 132–41, 142, 143–4, 146, 147–9, 164, 173, 234, 248, 251
Kommersant (pre-revolutionary newspaper) 135
Kommunist (magazine) 19, 35, 89, 90
Komsomol 61, 85
Kornai, János, *Economics of Shortage* 89
Korotich, Vitaly 69, 78
Korzhakov, Alexander 170, 194–5, 198, 205, 207, 209, 214–15
Kosovo crisis 253–4
Kravchenko, Leonid 111, 119
Kremlin, the, Soviet flag lowered 12
Krupskaya, Nadezhda 18
Kudrin, Alexei 287
Kukly (*Puppets*) (TV programme) 197–8, 200–1, 202–3, 292–3
kulaks, exile of 31
Kursk disaster 298–9, 301, 302
Kutsyllo, Veronika 163, 164, 165

La Tribune de l'Expansion 143–4
Latsis, Otto 15, 19, 33–4, 42, 50, 54–7, 74–5, 89, 126
Latvia 97
Lebed, Alexander 214, 234
legitimacy 15

Lenin, Vladimir 6, 17, 54, 55, 76, 87–8, 315
Leningrad 58–9, 98
Lesin, Mikhail 296
Levada, Yuri 95, 173, 275, 332
Liberal Democratic Party 174–5
liberal thought, advances of 30–41
libraries, closed sections 18
Ligachev, Yegor 65, 77
Listyev, Vladislav 175, 313
literary journals, circulation 59–60
Literaturnaya gazeta (*Literary Gazette*) 45–6, 127–8
Lithuania 93, 97, 106, 112–16
living space 30–1
loans-for-shares scheme 208–9, 217, 224
Luzhkov, Yuri 187–8, 188–9, 238–9, 257–8, 263, 268, 269–70, 275
Lyubimov, Alexander 72–3, 173–4

Maclean, Donald 104
Malashenko, Igor
  on Gorbachev 91
  on role of television 156
  and White House siege, 1993 179
  names NTV 180
  on Dobrodeev 184
  on Gusinsky 190
  background 190–4
  and Yegor Yakovlev, 192–3
  and first Chechen war coverage 195–6
  and *Kukly* (*Puppets*) 197–8
  and NTV closure threat 199–200
  and freedom of speech 204–5
  presidential election , 1996 209–10, 213, 214–15, 215–16, 218
  Yeltsin asks to be chief of staff 218–19
  opinion of oligarchs 219–20
  and the bankers' war 224–5
  on lack of responsibility 229–30
  and first Chechen war 231–3
  suggested as prime minister 241
  and Putin as successor to Yeltsin 260–2
  and second Chechen war 276, 281
  and attack on NTV 302
Malgin, Andrei 130, 131–2
Malkina, Tatyana 122–3
market, the 64–5, 84, 89
market reforms, support for 147n
Marx, Karl 17, 63
Marxist internationalism 44
Masyuk, Elena 197, 230–3, 279
Matador (TV programme) 314–15
Mavrina, Tatyana 37
Mavrodi, Sergei 149–50
media, the
  role 6–7, 67
  control of 6–8
  Western 12–13
  role in Soviet Union 31
  and the Prague Spring, 1967–8 39–40
  need to open up 64, 69–73
  Chernobyl catastrophe cover-up 66–9
  and Yeltsin's secession threat 110–11
  Gorbachev considers imposing control 117
  and coup attempt, 1991 121–3
  presidential election coverage, 1996 212–14
  impact of bankers' war on 229–30
  Yeltsin's attitude towards 250, 254–5
  Balkan crisis coverage 253–4
  power 260
  and Yeltsin's succession 260–4
  expectations of Putin 285
  Kursk disaster coverage 298–9
Media Most 189, 261, 264, 293, 294, 304
Medvedev, Dmitry 323, 333
Medvedev, Sergei 123
Memorial (human rights group) 75
Menatep Bank 145
middle class
  unity 53–4
  growth 332–3
  aspirations 335
military and industrial complex 52–3

miners strike, Kuzbas, 1998 242
Mishka 'the Jap' 22
Mitkova, Tatyana 113, 302–3
Mlynář, Zdeněk 61
MMM (pyramid scheme) 149–50
Moldova 152
Molodaya Gvardiya (Young Guards) (journal) 44, 45
Molotov, Vyacheslav 27, 28
Molotov–Ribbentrop pact 97
Moment istiny (Moment of Truth) (TV programme) 130, 131
Moscow 25–6
  Pushkin Square 70
  White House 120–1, 123–4
  early 1990s 141–2
  White House siege, 1993 162–3, 164, 165, 172
  anti-Yeltsin rebellion, 1993 164–73
  850th anniversary of foundation 238–9
  Cathedral of Christ the Saviour reconstruction 238–40
  terrorist attacks, 1999 276–7
  theatre siege, 2002 310–12
  anti-Putin protests, 2011 333–4
  creative class 334–5
Moscow Film-Makers Club 113
Moscow Party Organization 82
Moscow State Historical Archival Institute 20
Moscow State University 89
Moskovskie novosti (The Moscow News) 14, 67, 69–71, 75, 75–6, 77, 82–3, 86, 91, 96, 97, 98, 102, 109, 110–11, 113, 116, 117, 126, 127, 132, 135, 138, 158

Namedni (Recently) (TV programme) 236, 308–9, 312–13, 314
Narochitskaya, Natalia 152
Nash sovremennik (Our Contemporary) 152, 153
national anthem, restoration of 289–90
national ideology, search for 234–5
national poets 45
National Unity party 163
nationalism, Russian 5, 45–6, 152, 153, 155, 252, 335, 347
NATO, Yugoslavia bombing campaign 251–4
Nautilus Pompilius 252
Navalny, Alexei 335–6, 337
Ne dai Bog (God Forbid) (newspaper) 211
Nemtsov, Boris 226, 227–9, 234, 243, 291–2, 308, 345–6
  murder 1–2, 8, 346
neo-Nazis 246n
Nezavisimoe rassledovanie (Independent Investigation) (TV programme) 293
Nevsky, Alexander 46
Nevzorov, Alexander 99–100, 114–15, 119, 161, 161–2, 162–3, 167, 168, 173, 173–4, 233, 340, 344
New Economic Policy 54, 61, 78–9, 84, 88
New Russians 148–9
new thinking 59
New York Times 26, 237–8
News Press Agency (APN) 70, 103
NKVD 25–6, 27
Nochnoi Dozor (Night Watch) (film) 315–17
nomenclatura, the 17, 24, 88
Norkin, Andrei 308
North Korea 6
nostalgia, for the Soviet past 235–40
Novikov (district military commissar) 48
Novocherkassk uprising, 1962 67, 84
Novy Mir (New World) (journal) 31, 32, 44, 44–5, 60, 97
NTV
  launch 179–86
  status 193–4
  first Chechen war coverage 195–8, 213, 230–3, 297
  Kukly (Puppets) show 197–8, 200–1, 202–3, 292–3
  raid, 1994 198–9
  shutdown threat 199–200
  audience share 201

Banditskii Peterburg (Gangsters' Petersburg) (TV programme) 288–9
Buddenovsk crisis coverage 202
presidential election coverage, 1996 213, 215
Gazprom holdings 222
bankers' war coverage 226
Nemtsov coverage 228
power 228
impact of bankers' war on 229
nostalgia for Soviet past 235, 236
Balkan crisis coverage 253–4
and Yeltsin's succession 260, 262–3
second Chechen war coverage 280–1, 297, 308
Putin and 291–7
Gusinsky forced to sell 296
Kursk disaster coverage 298
Putin's conflict with 302–8
Gazprom coup 303
defence of 306
under Kremlin's licence 308–13
Moscow theatre siege coverage, 2002 310–12
Putin's inauguration coverage, 2004 312–13
targets liberals 345–6
nuclear physicists 52–3
nuclear war, possibility of 346–7
nuclear weapons 2–3
Nusinova, Elena 142

Obshchaya gazeta (Common Newspaper) 122, 296, 306
Obshchestevnnoe Rossiiskoe Televidenie, ORT (Russian Public Broadcaster) 301
October Revolution, seventieth anniversary 79–80
Odessa 21–2, 342
Ogonyok (Little Flame) (magazine) 44, 49, 69, 78, 133
oil industry 85
prices 287, 332
Oktiabr (October) (journal) 44
Old Russians 148
oligarchs 188
use of state capital 186
security services 188–9
and presidential election, 1996 206–9, 217–18
and the loans-for-shares scheme 208–9
and television 217–18
Malashenko's opinion of 219–20
war amongst 220
origin of term 227
impact of bankers' war on 229–30
tax evasion 240
Olson, Alexander 264, 273, 278
openness 64
optimism 149, 150–1
organized crime 288–9
Orwell, George, *Nineteen Eighty-Four* 6, 191
Ostankino television centre attack, 1993 165–7
Ostankino television centre siege, 1992 157–8

Pamyat (Memory) (nationalist organization) 75
Parfenov, Leonid 182, 235–6, 237–8, 245, 246–7, 305, 308–9, 312–14, 314, 335
Parkhomenko, Sergei 162, 163, 163–4, 172
Parlamentskii chas (Parliamentary Hour) (TV programme) 160–1
Pasternak, Boris 19, 59, 60
Patrushev, Nikolai 312
Pavlov, Ivan 6
Pavlovsky, Gleb 134, 143, 257, 274, 275, 285
Perestroika 13, 14, 16–17, 19–20, 42, 69
slogans 60
spiritual roots of 60
and the Prague Spring, 1967–8 60–1
idea of history 61–2
Gorbachev launches 62–3

press 69–71
radio under 72–3
television under 73, 77
and history 74–9
opposition to 79–83
shift of economic power 86
achievements 100–1, 102
suffered a victory 126
perks 87, 88
pessimism, 1990 100–1
Petrograd 6
Petrovskaya, Irina 247, 308
Philby, Kim 72
Pinochet, Augusto 285–6
Platonov, Andrei 90
Pokaianie (*Repentance*) (film) 65–6
Pole chudes (*Field of Miracles*) (TV game show) 175
police 110
Politburo 80, 95, 110
political satire 197–8
Politkovskaya, Anna 319
popular culture
wave of *noir* 98–100
nostalgia for Soviet past 235–8
Western 237–8
populism 174
Postfaktum news agency 134, 143
Potanin, Vladimir 208, 217, 222–3, 224
Pozdniak, Elena 123
Prague 50
Prague Spring, 1967–8 38–41, 42, 60–1
Pravda (*Truth*) 31, 106, 107, 115, 147–8
price controls 83–5, 141
Primakov, Evgeny 184, 248–52, 257–8, 259, 263, 268, 269, 270–2, 275
Pripyat 67
private initiative, early 1990s 143
private ownership 33–4, 64–5
private property, elimination of 87
private space 30–1
privatization 86–7, 146–7, 227, 257–8
Svyazinvest auction 221–4, 228, 230
Putin and 273
privatization cheques 146–7
Problemy mira i sotsializma (*Problems of Peace and Socialism*) (journal) 50
Prokhanov, Alexander 153
propaganda 48, 115, 347
protests, Red Square, August, 1968 42
publishing, Soviet control of 18–19
Pugo, Boris 111, 118, 125
purges 24, 27, 29
Pussy Riot 336–7
Putin, Vladimir
Chechnya policy 1, 278
blame 5
use of the media 7
crony capitalism 85
and Timchenko 85
restoration ideology 100
Gevorkyan interview 103–4
KGB career 103–4
political cover 104
propaganda 115
becomes head of KGB 247
first television appearance 247
joins KGB 247
relationship with Yeltsin 258–9
selection as Yeltsin's successor 260–2, 263–4, 272–5
Yeltsin appoints prime minister 263–4
popularity 272, 273–4, 332, 334, 336, 345
and privatization 273
appearance 274
and second Chechen war 276, 280
and the Ryazan' incident 278
image 279–80, 317, 323, 334
becomes president 283–4
manifesto
millennium message 284–5
expectations of 285
and Stalin 286
first years of rule 287–91
stabilization policy 288–9

view of Russia 289
restoration of the Soviet national anthem 289–90
and the Soviet past 289–91
and Gorbachev 291
mission 291
and NTV 291–7
obsession with television 292
attacks Gusinsky 293, 294–7
relationship with Gusinsky 297–8
and *Kursk* disaster 298–9, 301, 302
breakdown of relationship with Berezovsky 300–2
conflict with NTV 302–8
Yegor Yakovlev on 306
on freedom of speech 308
and Moscow theatre siege, 2002 311–12
inauguration, 2004 312–13
and the Georgian war, 2008 322
Sochi Winter Olympics 323
legitimacy 331–2
appeal 332
becomes prime minister 333
anti-Putin protests, 2011 333–4, 335–7
anti-Americanism 337
defence of system of governance 337
annexation of Crimea 339–42
Ukraine policy 342

radio 72–3
Radio Moscow 72, 183
reality, creation of 7–8
Red Square protests, August, 1968 42
red–brown coalition 151–4, 155, 340
Refco 143–4
reformation 16–17
rehabilitations 78
religion, communist attacks on 17
Remnick, David 76–7, 117, 130–1
restoration ideology 100
Revzin, Grigory 325–6
Rodina (Motherland) Party 330–1
Rogov, Kirill 217, 290
Rogozin, Dmitry 330–1
Rossiyskaya gazeta (newspaper) 198
rouble 315
depreciation 146
Rozanov, Vasily 124
Ruml, Jan 104
Russia, bankruptcy 141
Russia Channel 160–1, 168–70, 320, 338
Russia Project advertising campaign 236
Russian Army, Dzerzhinsky Division 161, 165–6
Russian Democratic Choice 217
Russian Federation 108
Russia's Choice 174
Rutskoi, Alexander 154–5, 162, 171–2
Ryazan' incident, the 277–8, 293
Ryazanov, Eldar 160
Ryzhkov, Nikolai 86–7, 110

Saddam Hussein 249
St Petersburg 247, 259
Sakharov, Andrei 2–3, 25, 39, 70, 73, 94, 95–7
samizdat 37, 51, 70, 134
satire 197–8
Savostyanov, Evgeny 195–6, 199
scientists 52–3
Sebastopol 7, 153, 238n
Second World War 3, 14, 19, 46, 48
Security Council 194, 217
security services, oligarchs 188–9
Segodnya (Today) newspaper 162
self-preservation 42
Semichastny, Vladimir 34
Semnadtsat' mgnovenii vesny (Seventeen Moments of Spring) (TV series) 245–7
Semyonov, Yulian 246
Serbia 252
Shadkhan, Igor 247
Shafarevich, Igor 153
Shatrov, Mikhail 76, 130
Shelepin, Alexander 34
Shenderovich, Viktor 197–8, 293

shestidesiatniki, the 20, 36–7, 63, 129–30
Shevardnadze, Eduard 65, 112
Shevchenko, Maxim 337
Shmelev, Nikolai 109
Shoigu, Sergei 275
Sholokhov, Mikhail 49
shortages 89, 98
show trials 24, 82
shuttle traders 141–2
Shvarts, Evgeny 95
Simonov, Alexei 172
Sinyavsky, Andrei 17, 51
Sivkov, Nikolai 62
600 sekund (*600 Seconds*) (TV programme) 99–100, 161, 161–2, 172
Skuratov, Yuri 257
small-time trade 84
Smeliansky, Anatoly 59, 171
Smolensky, Alexander 145–6
Snow, C. P. 32
Sobchak, Anatoly 104, 259
Sobchak, Ksenia 324–5
Sochi 298
Sochi Winter Olympics 323–6, 327
socialism 37–8
- with a human face 38–9, 41, 60, 78, 100, 116, 129
- and morality 144

Sofronov, Anatoly 44, 48–9, 69
Sokolov, Maxim 138–9, 140, 151, 164, 228, 297
Solovyov, Sergei 74
Solzhenitsyn, Alexander 6, 32, 55
- *One Day in the Life of Ivan Denisovich* 32–3
- expulsion 51
- *Gulag Archipelago* 51, 60, 97
- 'Live Not by Lies' 51–2

Sorokina, Svetlana 303
Soros, George 224, 230
Soskovets, Oleg 205–6
South Ossetia 322
sovereign democracy 331
Sovetskaya Rossiya (newspaper) 76–7, 118–19, 152
Soviet empire, collapse of 152–4
Soviet iconography 55
Soviet instincts, revival of 238–40
Soviet Trade Representation 24
Soviet Union
- collapse of 3–4, 6, 15–17, 87, 124–8, 130, 140
- dissolution of 11–14
- ideology 14, 15, 19
- violence 14–15, 27–8
- reformation 16–17
- aristocracy 30
- post-Stalinist thaw 30–41, 325–6
- paternalistic state 31
- role of the media in 31
- private ownership rules 33–4
- travel restrictions 36
- official press image 37–8
- siege mentality 37–8
- bureaucracy 40
- invasion of Afghanistan 49–50, 182–3
- loss of legitimacy 91–7
- crackdown in Vilnius 112–16
- information sources under 133
- nostalgia for 235–40

Sovok 100
Spanish Civil War 37
stagnation 50–5
Stalin, Josef 3, 14, 19, 24, 54, 298
- death of 25, 88
- denunciation of 26–7, 29
- cult of personality 29
- rehabilitation 43–4
- fascism 46–7
- historical re-examination 75
- and the NEP 87–8
- Putin and 286

Starye pesni o glavnom (*Old Songs about Important Things*) (TV programme) 237, 315
state capital, oligarchs use of 188

state enterprises, loosening of control over 85
state ownership, ideology of 88
Stepashin, Sergei 258, 263
Stierlitz, Max Otto von 245–7, 248
Stolichny Bank 145–6
Stolitsa (Capital City) (magazine) 131–2
Strelyany, Anatoly 61–2
styob 138, 175, 182
suicides, post-coup 125–6
Supreme Soviet 106–7, 111
Surkov, Vladislav 330–1, 341
survival 33
Suslov, Mikhail 43, 51, 65
Suzdal' 37
Svyazinvest auction 221–4, 228, 230

Tallinn 113
Tak zhit' nel'zia (You Can't Live Like That) (film) 100
Tarasov, Artem 134
TASS 70, 119
Tatum, Paul, murder of 270
Taubman, William 27
Tbilisi, massacre, 1989 92–3
television
  importance of 7–8, 114, 165
  role 67, 156, 166, 317, 320–1
  under Perestroika 73, 77
  Congress of People's Deputies coverage, 1989 93–4
  Alexander Yakovlev on 94
  nationalists and 155–8
  Yeltsin and 158–9, 159–60
  game shows 175, 242
  Latin American soap operas 175
  launch of NTV 179–86
  Soviet 180–1
  audience 181
  Gusinsky and 189–90
  corruption 193
  first Chechen war coverage 195–8, 230–3
  Buddenovsk crisis coverage 202
  presidential election coverage, 1996 210, 212–14, 215
  and oligarchs 217–18
  power 228, 343
  nostalgia for Soviet past 235–8
  second Chechen war coverage 280–1, 308
  Putin's obsession with 292
  Kursk disaster coverage 298–9, 301
  Moscow theatre siege coverage, 2002 310–12
  news coverage 317–18
  Beslan school hostage crisis coverage 318–20
  Georgian war coverage 321–3
  Ukraine war coverage 338, 343–4, 345
  annexation of Crimea coverage 339–40
  information war 343–7
ten-year sentences 18
Terror, the 18, 25
terrorism
  the Ryazan' incident 277–8
  Chechen 201–2, 276–8, 310–12, 318–20
  Moscow theatre siege, 2002 310–12
  Beslan school hostage crisis 318–20
thaw, post-Stalinist 30–41, 325–6
theatre siege, 2002, Moscow 310–12
Third International, the 50
Tiananmen Square massacre 92
Tikhonov, Vyacheslav 246
Timashuk, Lidia 77
Timchenko, Gennady 85
Timofeevsky, Alexander 130, 140–1, 297
transition, 1991 129–39
travel, Soviet restrictions 36
Tretyakov, Vitaly 131
Trifonov, Yuri 23, 24
Truman, David 48
Tsentsiper, Ilya 288
TSN 307
Turner, Ted 294

Tvardovsky, Alexander 31–3, 44, 44–6, 45, 48–9, 60

Ukhod (Departure) (TV documentary) 11–14
Ukraine
- war against 1–2, 327, 338, 339–45
- television coverage 7–8
- transfer of Crimea to 152, 238n
- revolution 326–7
- Russian propaganda 343–4
- information war 343–5

Union of Right Forces 286
United Russia Party 331, 336
United States of America
- Alexander Yakovlev's education in 48
- Fulbright scholars 48
- Yugoslavia bombing campaign 251–4
- as a utopia 252
- reset proposal 323

Unity Party 274–5

values 331
Venediktov, Alexei 299
Vidyaevo 299
Vilnius 112–16
vlast 256–7
Voice of America 72
Vologda 23
Voloshin, Alexander 258, 260
Vremya (TV news programme) 123, 155–6, 255, 266–7, 315, 317–18
Vyakhirev, Rem 222, 243, 304
Vzglyad (Viewpoint) (TV programme) 72–3, 77, 99, 112, 169, 173–4

Wall Street Journal 147
White House, Moscow 120–1, 123–4
- siege, 1993 162–3, 164, 165, 172

words
- communist control of 17–18
- ability to transcend closed borders 19
- as weapons 43

Yakovlev, Alexander
- on importance of the media 6
- relationship with Gorbachev 13, 63
- role 13–14
- support of Perestroika 16, 17
- evolution to liberal freethinker 17
- and the fall of Khrushchev 28
- on Khruschev 33
- and the invasion of Czechoslovakia 41
- on the rehabilitation of Stalin 43–4
- opposition to nationalists 45–6
- birth 47
- family history 47–8
- resentment of Stalinism 47–9
- at Columbia University 48
- military service 48
- as ambassador to Canada 49–50, 63
- on Dukhobors 49–50
- review of system 63
- and the free market 64–5
- memo, December 1985 64–5
- and private ownership 64–5
- release of *Pokaianie (Repentance)* 65–6
- understanding of Glasnost 69
- stops jamming of foreign radio stations 72
- and the Andreeva letter 77, 77–8
- and Yeltsin 80–1
- on television 94, 165
- on pessimism 101
- support for Gorbachev 108
- and *Moskovskie novosti (The Moscow News)* 109
- Kryuchkov smears 111
- and Yeltsin's secession threat 111
- warns Gorbachev of coup attempt 118, 119
- quits Party 119
- prevents attack on KGB building 125
- appointed chairman of Ostankino 175–6
- beliefs 193
- on freedom of speech 203

on Primakov 250
and restoration of the Soviet national anthem 289
Yakovlev, Vladimir 85, 116–17, 122
editorship of *Kommersant* 132–8, 140–1, 143–4
traits 133
anti-journalism 135
on Soviet period 137
on class consciousness 142
on early 1990s 143
on language 144
borrowing 146
and presidential election, 1996 211
Yakovlev, Vladimir Ivanovich 21–4
Yakovlev, Yegor 11–14, 121, 122–3
funeral 14
relationship with Gorbachev 14
status 14
background 19, 20–1
family history 21–4
father 21–4
grandparents 22
death of father 23
Ia idu s toboi (I Am Walking Alongside You) 23, 132
mother 24
support for Stalin 24, 29
joins Communist Party 25
first journalistic job 26
and Khrushchev's secret speech 26–7
on *Novy Mir* 31
post-Stalinist thaw 31
as editor of *Zhurnalist* 36–9
and the invasion of Czechoslovakia 42
Prague exile 50, 55
and Lenin's image 55
editorship of *Moskovskie novosti (The Moscow News)* 69–71, 102, 109
and the Andreeva letter 77
and Perestroika 83
and the Tbilisi massacre, 1989 93
KGB articles 102
attitude to Yeltsin 107
support for Gorbachev 108
and Yeltsin's secession threat 110–11
and the crackdown in Vilnius 113
quits party 116
sixtieth birthday 116–17
Malgin debate 131–2
on generational shift 132
last issue of *Moskovskie novosti* 132
as head of post-Soviet television 155–6, 158
and Ostankino television centre siege, 1992 158
Yeltsin fires 158, 186
Malashenko and 192–3
rescue of NTV 200
defence of NTV 306
on Putin 306
Yanayev, Gennady 120, 122–3
Yanov, Alexander 155
Yanukovych, Viktor 326
Yaroslavl' 47
Yavlinsky, Grigory 281
Yefremov, Oleg 57
Yeltsin, Boris 12, 13, 28
and Perstroika 79–82
and Gorbachev 80
popularity 82, 121, 160, 169, 213, 254, 273–6
campaign against privileges 88
elected president of Russia 106–7
drinking 107, 194–5, 211
Perestroika reformers attitude to 107
foreign governments attitude to 107–8
quits party 108
secession threat 109–11
and the crackdown in Vilnius 113
meeting with Gorbachev, 23 July 1991 118
and coup attempt, 1991 119, 120–1, 122–3
advisors 129, 194
inauguration as president 140

privatization policy 146–7
parliamentary power struggle 154–65
fires Yegor Yakovlev 158, 186
and Ostankino television centre siege, 1992 158
and television 158–9, 159–60
impeachment vote 159–60
special rule decree 159–60
Odin den' iz zhizni prezidenta (A Day in the Life of the President) (TV programme) 160
dissolves parliament 161–2
appearance 168, 274
and rebellion, 1993 170–1
appoints Alexander Yakovlev chairman of Ostankino 175–6
and first Chechen war 194–5, 230, 231–2, 232–3
and freedom of speech 203–4
as guarantor of freedom 204–5
health 205, 215–16, 254
election campaign, 1996 205–6, 209–16
oligarchs support for 206–9, 217–18
and Berezovsky 207
visit to Chechnya 213
presidential inauguration, 1996 216–17
asks Malashenko to be chief of staff 218–19
and the bankers' war 225–6
and Nemtsov 227, 228–9
search for a national ideology 234–5
sacks Chernomyrdin 241
successor debate 241, 248, 258–9, 260–4, 268–75
appoints Kiriyenko 241–2
on miners strike, Kuzbas, 1998 242
appoints Primakov prime minister 248–9
attitude to media 250, 254–5
on Primakov 251
sacks Primakov 256
family financial scandals 257
legacy 257
relationship with Putin 258–9
appoints Putin prime minister 263–4
resignation 283–4
view of Russia 289
Yugoslavia, NATO bombing campaign 251–4
Yukos oil company 313
Yumashev, Valentin 209, 209–10, 241, 257, 258, 260–1

Za obraztsovuiu torgovliu (For the Exemplary Trade) (newspaper) 26
zastoi (stagnation) 50–5
Zhirinovsky, Vladimir 174–5, 194
Zhukov, Georgy 28
Zhurnalist (Journalist) (magazine) 36–9
Zinoviev, Alexander 153–4
Zolotaia likhoradka (Gold Rush) (TV game show) 242
Zorin, Andrei 52, 54, 74, 239
Zverev, Sergei 186
Zyuganov, Gennady 151–2, 205, 206, 210, 214

A Note about the Author

Arkady Ostrovsky is a Russian-born, British journalist who has spent fifteen years reporting from Moscow, first for the *Financial Times* and then as a bureau chief for *The Economist*. He studied Russian theatre history in Moscow and holds a PhD in English Literature from Cambridge University. His translation of Tom Stoppard's trilogy, *The Coast of Utopia*, has been published and staged in Russia.